PEOPLE of FAITH

PEOPLE of FAITH

Religious Conviction in American

Journalism and Higher Education

John Schmalzbauer

Cornell University Press · *Ithaca and London*

Chapter 3 appeared in a slightly different form in John Schmalzbauer, "Between Professional and Religious Worlds: Catholics and Evangelicals in American Journalism," *Sociology of Religion* 60(4): 363–386. Copyright © 1999 Association for the Sociology of Religion, Inc. All rights reserved.

First published 2003 by Cornell University Press

Printed in the United States of America

Library of Congress Cataloging-in-Publication Data

Schmalzbauer, John Arnold, 1968–
   People of faith : religious conviction in American journalism and higher education / John Schmalzbauer.
       p.   cm.
Includes bibliographical references and index.
   ISBN 0-8014-3886-1 (alk. paper)
   1. Sociology, Christian—United States.   2. Journalists—Religious life—United States.   3. College teachers—Religious life—United States.   4. Social scientists—Religious life—United States.   I. Title.

   BR517 .S32 2002
   200'.88'097—dc21   2002005771

Cornell University Press strives to use environmentally responsible suppliers and materials to the fullest extent possible in the publishing of its books. Such materials include vegetable-based, low-VOC inks and acid-free papers that are recycled, totally chlorine-free, or partly composed of nonwood fibers. For further information, visit our website at www.cornellpress.cornell.edu.

Cloth printing   10   9   8   7   6   5   4   3   2   1

For Evelyn Viken, 1913–2001,
and for Susan

Contents

List of Illustrations   ix

List of Figures   xi

Preface   xiii

1   Secular Callings   1

2   From the Margins to the Mainstream   18

3   Faith in Journalism   44

4   Faith in the Academy   73

5   Journalism and the Religious Imagination   110

6   Religious Ways of Knowing   146

7   Openness and Obstacles   189

    Appendix: The Sample   207

    Notes   209

    Index   261

Illustrations

Commonweal Cover   *57*

Fred Barnes   *65*

Andrew Greeley   *88*

George Marsden   *95*

Kenneth Woodward   *129*

Figures

1. Journalists and social scientists interviewed for the study, with affiliations at the time of the interviews   *4*

2. Percentage of each religious group with college degree by age cohort (General Social Surveys 1972–96)   *21*

3. Percentage of each religious group in professional–managerial occupations by age cohort (General Social Surveys 1972–96)   *22*

4. Catholic and evangelical subcultural institutions   *24*

5. The Catholic and Protestant imaginations as reflected in five recurring story lines   *144*

Preface

This study focuses on the place of religious faith in the fields of journalism and higher education. Drawing on interviews with forty Roman Catholics and evangelical Protestants in both professions, it argues that the news media and the professoriate are more open to religious perspectives than has been acknowledged.

The final draft of this book was completed in the weeks following 11 September 2001. As I watched the public response to the attacks in Washington, D.C., and New York, I was struck by the prominence of religious speech. From President George W. Bush to the Reverend Billy Graham and the eulogies for New York City's firefighters, Americans drew on religious language to make sense of great tragedy. So thick were the religious references that some atheist groups decried the country's "post-attack focus on God," fearing a religious takeover of American public life.[1]

Despite such fears, a careful examination of the religious reaction reveals anything but a united effort to seize control of the public square. Instead, the religious response to 11 September—whether Protestant, Catholic, Jewish, Muslim, Hindu, or Buddhist—mirrored the pluralism of American religious life. The continual refrain of "God Bless America" notwithstanding, America's religious communities did not speak with one voice.

The journalists and academics interviewed for this project were among the public religious voices that responded to the terrorist attacks. Rather than confining their religious convictions to private life, they brought the resources of the Catholic and evangelical traditions into the pages of America's leading newspapers and opinion magazines and into college and university classrooms. In "Unshakable Rockaway," the *Washington Post* columnist E. J. Dionne wrote movingly about a New York City neighborhood hit hard by the attack on the World Trade Center and the crash of an American Airlines jet.[2] Home to his inlaws, Belle Harbor, Queens, is a close-knit Irish and Italian community bound together by "ties of clan and ethnicity and faith." According to Dionne, "People in Belle Harbor don't much debate a word like 'communitarian.' They don't have to. That's just what these people are. I know from family experience that when a neighbor gets sick, whole blocks mobilize instantly. Food just shows up. . . . Nobody ever asks questions. Nobody thinks about being paid back." Later in the column, Dionne described the efforts of Monsignor Martin Geraghty to make sense of the neighborhood's suffering. In this intensely personal tribute to an intensely Catholic place, Dionne focused on the role of faith, family, and community in healing the wounds of 11 September.

Like their counterparts in the churches, the journalists and social scientists I spoke with expressed themselves in ways that are consistent with America's religious diversity. On the right, the syndicated columnist Cal Thomas (a former associate of Jerry Falwell's) questioned President Bush's statement that Islam is a "religion of peace," arguing that fundamentalist Muslims believe "the Koran commands them to fight Jews and Christians." Turning his attention to American Christians, Thomas noted that "many clergy in this country once were fellow travelers with communism," castigating those who would "blame America first."[3] On the left, Colman McCarthy urged Americans to "reject vengeance," adding that a "nonviolent response to 11 September is in the tradition of Gandhi, Martin Luther King Jr., Dorothy Day, Jeannette Rankin, and groups like the Fellowship of Reconciliation and Pax Christi," reflecting his own convictions as a Catholic pacifist. In a similar way, Father Andrew Greeley criticized America's "holy war of vengeance," adding that "it would be much wiser of Bush to remind the bloodthirsty element in our population that vengeance still belongs to God" and that "God is not likely to approve of a country [the United States] that tries to usurp his role."[4] Holding down the religious center, Dionne, Peter Steinfels, and the Yale political scientist Bruce Russett expressed cautious support for America's war against terrorism, arguing that, although "civilians will die as a result of our military strikes . . . we must not descend to indiscriminate destruction."[5] By calling for a war that does not intentionally target civilians, they appealed to one of the most important principles of Catholic just-war theory: the need to discriminate between combatants and non-combatants. Together, the study's respondents have contributed to a public square increasingly hospitable to religious faith.

Although it was completed in 2001, this project originated ten years earlier, in a graduate seminar at Princeton University. Intrigued by claims that religion had been excluded from fields such as journalism and academia, I set out to examine the political and social attitudes of evangelical Protestants who worked in the college-educated professions. My findings convinced me that the advocates of secularization theory had seriously underestimated the resilience of religion in professional life. Persuaded by Robert Wuthnow to widen my focus to U.S. Catholics, I embarked on a much larger study of the place of religion in the professions of journalism and the academic professoriate.

Like most academic projects, this study has deeper roots than a graduate seminar paper. It is also an outgrowth of my struggle to make sense of the relationship between Christian faith and the academic profession. Raised an evangelical, educated in Ivy League Princeton University's graduate program, and employed by a Catholic liberal-arts college, I have lived on the boundary between professional and religious worlds. As the great-grandson of a German Catholic immigrant (Otto Schmalzbauer) and the grandson of a Norwegian American fundamentalist (my maternal grandmother, Evelyn Viken), I have experienced firsthand the journey of both subcultures from the margins to the center of American life. As a Protestant with an affinity for Catholicism's communitarian and sacramental imagination, I have felt a kinship with the Catholics and evangelicals in my sample.

This book was written with the help of a supportive network of mentors, colleagues, friends, and family. First, the graduate-student community at Princeton University provided much encouragement. At various stages of the project, Courtney Bender, Julian Dierkes, Tim Dowd, John Evans, Jeff Hass, Michael Moody, Tracy Scott, Brad Verter, Maureen Waller, Gray Wheeler, and Brad Wilcox offered helpful comments. The Religion and Culture Workshop at Princeton's Center for the Study of American Religion (now the Center for the Study of Religion) served as a forum for presenting chapters in progress. The visiting scholars Patrick Allitt, Nancy Ammerman, Michael Baxter, Daniel Olson, and Kathy Rudy gave helpful feedback during their time at the center. During my years at Princeton, Professor John Wilson and, especially, Professor Michele Lamont provided invaluable scholarly advice and support. From the very beginning, Lamont challenged me to frame this project in a way that would appeal to a wide academic audience. Her comments helped make this study a much better piece of work.

Portions of the book were presented in talks at Baylor University, the Boisi Center for Religion and American Public Life at Boston College, and the Catholic Studies faculty discussion group at Holy Cross. Thanks to Gene Burns, John Dart, William Durbin, Cynthia Eller, Stewart Hoover, James Mathisen, John Mulder, Rick Murphy, Mark Noll, David O'Brien, Mark Regnerus, Susan Rodgers, Mathew Schmalz, Christian Smith, James Turner, Beau Weston, Rhys Williams, and Alan Wolfe for helpful comments on parts of the study. Sheri Englund, Frances Benson, and Karen M. Laun of Cornell University Press provided expert guidance at every stage of the publication process. Thanks to Tom Landy, Kathleen Mahoney, the anonymous reviewers, and Robert Wuthnow for commenting on the entire manuscript. No one did more to encourage this project than Robert Wuthnow. Through his perceptive comments, insightful scholarship, and normative commitments he has been both a role model and a mentor.

The research for and writing of this study were supported by grants and fellowships from the Louisville Institute, the Center for the Study of American Religion, the Society for the Scientific Study of Religion, and Princeton University. I am particularly grateful for the support I received as a postdoctoral fellow at the Center for the Study of Religion and American Culture at Indiana University/Purdue University–Indianapolis (IUPUI). My time at IUPUI was made more pleasant by Conrad Cherry, Tom Davis, Betty Deberg, William Durbin, Bill Jackson, Kathleen Mahoney, Amanda Porterfield, Tony Sherrill, and Andrew Walsh. A junior research leave from the College of the Holy Cross, together with the encouragement of my colleagues in sociology and anthropology, allowed me to complete the manuscript. I owe a debt of gratitude to Lilly Endowment for providing me with a semester's leave to work on an evaluation of Lilly's ten-year Religion and Higher Education Initiative. Though not directly connected to this book, the evaluation work added greatly to my knowledge of religion and intellectual life. Margaret Post provided much appreciated secretarial support, and Holy Cross students Kaitlyn Lyons and Nesse Saunders helped with many mundane tasks during the final stages of the project. Finally, Peggy Spurling and All Type Medical Transcription Service did a masterly job of transcribing the interviews.

The Catholic and evangelical journalists and scholars who agreed to be interviewed for this project deserve a special note of appreciation. In the midst of filing stories, meeting deadlines, and fulfilling the mundane duties of academic life, they took the time to talk about their lives and (in many cases) took this graduate student to lunch. Special thanks to Fred Barnes, the *Christian Century, Commonweal,* Andrew Greeley, Jack Harkema, Mario Petitti, June Rosner Public Relations, and the Holy Cross College Archives for the use of photographs and illustrations. Thanks also to those respondents who provided feedback on my interpretations of their interviews.

Last, but certainly not least, a special group of people encouraged me during the writing of this book. My undergraduate mentor at Wheaton College, Lyman Kellstedt, has continued to serve as a mentor and friend. It is fitting that Alan Wolfe's *Atlantic Monthly* cover story "The Opening of the Evangelical Mind" begins with a scene from Kellstedt's classroom, for it was there that I began my intellectual journey.[6] My parents, Arnold and Norma Schmalzbauer, have constantly affirmed me in my professional life, as has my sister Julie, who is embarking on an academic career of her own. On more than one occasion, John Henry Schmalzbauer has told me to "come home, daddy," reminding me of the importance of life outside work. Finally, Susan Schmalzbauer has encouraged me with her ready wit, kind words, tactful advice, and boundless affection. From the inception of this project, she has been an unfailing source of friendship and support. Without her, I would not have made it.

Although my grandmother Evelyn Viken did not live to see the completion of this project, she has had a profound impact on my life's work. As a young woman in Minneapolis in the midst of the Great Depression, she left the mild-mannered culture of Norwegian Lutheranism for the religious intensity of Protestant fundamentalism, entering a world of Gospel tabernacles, radio preachers, and revivals. I remember her commenting favorably in the 1970s on the "born-again" status of presidential candidates Jimmy Carter and Gerald Ford. In the 1980s, she sent checks to Jerry Falwell and Pat Robertson. In a religious subculture often portrayed as sexist and patriarchal, she was the spiritual matriarch of our family. We often disagreed, but her religious and political commitments are responsible for my own interest in evangelicalism's public role. Had she remained a Lutheran, this book probably would never have been written.

PEOPLE of FAITH

1 Secular Callings

While working as a Vatican correspondent for the *New York Times*, E. J. Dionne covered a visit by Pope John Paul II to the African country Cameroon. While reporting the Pope's arrival in a remote village in foul weather, Dionne witnessed a series of events that astonished and amused him:

> The Pope was visiting up-country Cameroon, and the press plane got there early. . . . It was pouring rain and had been for six days, and this gentleman from the local information office, who was a college-educated Catholic, said, "Don't worry. It won't rain on the Pope," and I said, "How do you know?" and he said, "The rain doctors understand these things." So I wrote all this down, and it's still pouring rain, and then the Pope's plane lands. The rain stops. The Pope starts saying mass, and the sun comes [out]. Then the Pope gets back on his plane at the end of all this, and the pouring rain comes down. My new friend from the Cameroon information office, with a huge smile on his face, points triumphantly to the heavens and says, "I told you." And the story I wrote about African spirituality began something like, "It's not clear Who had done the work, but Someone was clearly on the job," and I recounted the story.

When I first called Dionne for this study, he told the story of the rain doctors and the papal visit, expressing particular glee when recounting the supernatural punchline that made up the lead paragraph of his story for the *Times*. When I interviewed him at a Washington, D.C., restaurant, he repeated the story, adding that he had often told it to journalism students. One year later, at a public forum on religion and the media sponsored by *Commonweal* magazine, which included fellow journalists Cokie

Roberts and Timothy Russert, Dionne told the story once more, calling it "my favorite story in the entire time I was covering the Vatican."[1]

What was it about the story of the Pope's trip to Africa that led Dionne to tell it again and again? Was it just a good story with a humorous ending, or was there more to it? In his book on the culture of foreign correspondents, Mark Pedelty argues that journalists tell stories as a way to construct and reconstruct their public identities.[2] Through the ritual of journalistic storytelling, reporters act out their roles as professionals, engaging in what Erving Goffman called the "presentation of self in everyday life."[3] When a story captures what it means to be a professional journalist, it gets told and retold.

As a practicing Catholic in American journalism, Dionne works at the intersection of professional and religious worlds. As a member of what he calls the quintessential enlightenment profession, Dionne views the world through the lens of journalistic empiricism, confining his observations to verifiable "facts." As a man of faith, he is open to the world of the supernatural, trusting in a God who created all things, seen and unseen. In the tale of the Pope and the rain doctors, these two worlds collide, allowing Dionne to reflect on the relationship between journalism and religious belief.

Peter Berger locates humor in the incongruities of human experience. Like religion and magic, the comic is often experienced as a disruption of everyday life, providing a glimpse of "an otherwise undisclosed dimension of reality."[4] In the case of Dionne's story, we laugh because of the juxtaposition of empirical facts and supraempirical forces, objective reporting and animist weather forecasting, stenographic accuracy ("I write all this down") and theological speculation ("Someone was clearly on the job"), the *New York Times* and African spirituality. Through its bizarre combinations, the Cameroon story calls attention to the uneasy relationship between journalistic empiricism and realities that transcend empirical description.

It is precisely this tension that Dionne highlights when he shares the story with journalism students:

> I always tell journalism students, your assumption going into this story would be that this was pure fluke and accident; that it couldn't possibly have anything to do with what this gentleman thought was true. But how do you know that? Journalism is supposed to be an empirical craft, and we are supposed to operate on the basis of those facts that we know. On the basis of the facts that

we know about that particular story, I think it is not intellectually honest to rule out by fiat that there may have been something to the realm that this gentleman from the Information Ministry was talking about. . . . I got a great kick out of trying to see how you could try to explain, in terms comprehensible to a largely secular audience, what a good proportion of the people of the world believe, in different ways, in the existence of a non-material, non-secular realm.

Remaining open to multiple interpretations of reality, Dionne neither endorses nor rejects the information officer's account of the Pope's visit. Conscious of both facts that we know and the existence of a non-material, non-secular realm, he recognizes the limits of empirical observation. Positioning himself between professional and religious worlds, he refuses to rule out what a good many people believe.

Far from an isolated incident, Dionne's story points to a larger tension between professional and religious ways of knowing in American society. This tension is especially acute for professionals who are religious. Socialized by their colleagues to separate facts from values, the empirical from the unobservable, and work from religion, they face a difficult set of questions. What place does religious belief hold in professional life? What role can personal religious commitments play in my work? What difference, if any, might those commitments make? How can I talk about religion without compromising my professional reputation?

This book explores such questions through an examination of the careers of forty Roman Catholics and evangelical Protestants[5] who work in the national news media and the academic social sciences (the disciplines of history, sociology, and political science).[6] Those interviewed for the project include the journalists Fred Barnes, E. J. Dionne, Colman McCarthy, Mary McGrory, Richard Ostling, Cokie Roberts, Peter Steinfels, Cal Thomas, Robin Toner, and Kenneth Woodward, and the scholars John DiIulio, Jay Dolan, Elizabeth Fox-Genovese, Andrew Greeley, George Marsden, Mark Noll, Gary Orfield, and Bruce Russett (see Figure 1).

These journalists and social scientists are of sociological interest for the same reasons that we laugh at Dionne's story. Like a *New York Times* reporter who chooses to write about African spirituality, they must negotiate among competing definitions of reality and truth. As people of faith, they believe in the reality of the supernatural. As journalists and social scientists, they work in professions committed to empiricism and the principle of methodological atheism.[7] Like the Cameroonian information

Figure 1. Journalists and Social Scientists Interviewed for the Study, with Affiliations at the Time of the Interviews

	Journalists	
Catholic		Evangelical
Dan Balz, *Washington Post*		David Aikman, *Time*
E. J. Dionne, *Washington Post*		Fred Barnes, *New Republic*
Brian Healy, *Eye to Eye with Connie Chung*		Don Holt, *Fortune*
Colman McCarthy, *Washington Post*		Marianne Kyriakos, *Washington Post*
Mary McGrory, *Washington Post*		Wesley Pippert, formerly of United Press
Cokie Roberts, ABC News and National		International
Public Radio		Richard Ostling, Associated Press
Peter Steinfels, *New York Times*		Russ Pulliam of the *Indianapolis News*
Robin Toner, *New York Times*		Jeffery Sheler, *U.S. News and World Report*
Kenneth Woodward, *Newsweek*		Cal Thomas, Los Angeles Times Syndicate
Don Wycliff, *Chicago Tribune*		

	Social Scientists	
Catholic		Evangelical
John DiIulio, political science, Princeton University		Kenneth Ferraro, sociology, Purdue University
Jay Dolan, history, University of Notre Dame		Robert Frykenberg, history, University of Wisconsin
Elizabeth Fox-Genovese, history, Emory University		John Green, political science, University of Akron
Philip Gleason, history, University of Notre Dame		Nathan Hatch, history, University of Notre Dame
Andrew Greeley, sociology, University of Arizona/National Opinion Research Center		George Marsden, history, University of Notre Dame
Maureen Hallinan, sociology, University of Notre Dame		Michael Nelson, political science, Rhodes College
Michael Hout, sociology, University of California, Berkeley		Mark Noll, history, Wheaton College
Gary Orfield, political science, Harvard University		Margaret Poloma, sociology, University of Akron
Dudley Poston, sociology, Texas A&M University		George Thomas, sociology, Arizona State University
Bruce Russett, political science, Yale University		John Van Engen, history, University of Notre Dame

officer, they call attention to realities that transcend empirical description. Like Dionne, they confine their observations to "facts that we know." Living in the tension between professional and religious worlds, they work to reconcile faith and knowledge.

The Quintessential Enlightenment Professions

This study focuses on the place of personal religious faith in the national news media and the academic social sciences. As quintessential enlightenment professions, journalism and social science have long been associated with the secularization of American life. Periodic surveys of the academic professorate and the national news media reveal much lower levels of religious affiliation than among the general public.[8] According to a 1989 study by the Carnegie Foundation for the Advancement of Teaching, 49 percent of sociologists, 39 percent of historians, and 36 percent of political scientists list "none" as their religious affiliation.[9] This compares with 8 percent of the American public.[10] Along the same lines, the controversial 1980 survey of the "media elite" by S. Robert Lichter, Stanley Rothman, and Linda Lichter found that 50 percent of New York and Washington journalists have no religious affiliation (this figure dropped to 22 percent when the survey was readministered in 1995).[11]

As part of the "new class"—that cluster of occupations concerned with the production of knowledge and symbols—these people have been portrayed as the most secular segment of the American workforce.[12] According to Steven Brint, the "professional stratum contains a disproportionate number [of those] outside of the more conservative moral traditions: not only better-educated people, but younger people, less religious people, and residents of cities."[13] In an analysis of national data from the General Social Surveys, Brint found that professionals were liberal on issues of morality and culture (though not on economics), embracing what he called the new libertarianism.[14] Such anti-traditionalism often extends to matters of faith. A recent study found that 37 percent of highly educated Americans hold "intensely antagonistic feelings" toward conservative Christians, and another 19 percent view them negatively.[15] In an era of desecularization, the college-educated professions, especially journalism and academia, are the great exception, described by Peter Berger as the "principal 'carrier' of progressive, Enlightened beliefs and values."[16]

More significant than any overt secularism is the tendency among
many professions to make rigid distinctions between professional and religious forms of knowledge. In "Science as a Vocation," Max Weber wrote
that the tension between the "value-spheres of 'science' and the sphere
of 'the holy' is unbridgeable" and called for the exclusion of religious perspectives from the lecture hall.[17] The tension between science and the
holy is also a major theme in the sociology of the professions. Wedded to
an empiricist mindset, the modern professions have tended to narrow the
scope of legitimate inquiry to the observable world.[18] Participating in
what Alvin Gouldner called the culture of critical discourse, the modern
professions reject truth claims "grounded in traditional societal authority," privileging "self-grounded rationality" over supernatural revelation,
and "organized skepticism" over deference to the past.[19] Discrediting "ordinary knowledge" and "competitive paradigms" as unscientific, they defend their professional jurisdictions against potential challengers, such as
homeopaths, creationists, rain doctors, and theologians.[20]

The epistemological divide between professional and religious ways of
knowing is especially wide in journalism and the social sciences.[21] Historically, both occupations have appealed to the rhetoric of objectivity in
establishing their professional credibility, drawing a firm boundary
between facts and values. "As journalism moved toward professionalization," writes Richard Flory, "such scientific values as empiricism ('fact'
gathering and reporting), rationality, and rigor in method, were emphasized as being core elements of the journalism profession."[22] In the
process, non-empirical approaches to knowledge, including supernatural
revelation and religious tradition, were discredited as unprofessional.[23]
Operating out of a "just the facts, ma'am" epistemology, the news media
have tended to "reduce religious and moral claims to private and often
idiosyncratic hobbies."[24]

For most of the twentieth century, the social sciences, including history, have been equally committed to an empiricist approach to the making of knowledge.[25] Emphasizing scholarly objectivity over ethical engagement, they have contributed to the marginalization of morality in the
academy.[26] Choosing to think small, they have largely abandoned questions of ultimate meaning, preferring to focus on the specialized pursuit
of empirically verifiable knowledge.[27] Committing themselves to methodological atheism and naturalistic reductionism, they have, in the words of
Jon Roberts and James Turner, pruned their "discourse of references to
God and other spiritual forces," excluding religious phenomena from historical and sociological analysis.[28]

The tension between religion and social science has been especially intense because of the disciplinary imperialism of the latter. "Social science," notes James Gilbert, has ventured "into almost every place where religion once held sway: into politics, psychology, and sociology, for example."[29] Using the rhetoric of reductionism to expand their professional jurisdictions, social scientists have reduced religious realities to social and psychological explanations. Viewing the sacred through the lenses of their disciplines, rather than their disciplines through the lens of the sacred, they have preferred to "keep religion exclusively an object of study and not an intellectual partner."[30]

The Secularization of Journalism and Social Science

Religion's marginal presence in journalism and social science is remarkable, given the central role of American Protestantism in the development of both fields. In journalism, from Puritan broadsheets to the denominational newspapers of the early nineteenth century, divine providence was frequently invoked. As Mark Silk writes, "Earthquakes were viewed as occasions for sinners to tremble and seek reconciliation with God, [while] a recovery from illness was considered evidence of God's mercy."[31] With the birth of the penny press and the growth of mass-circulation daily newspapers, such providentialism gave way to literary realism and an emphasis on empirical facts.[32] Nevertheless, as late as the 1880s, newspapers such as the *New York Times* "showed a notable tendency toward an explicitly pro-religion, and more specifically, pro-Protestant Christianity, editorial content," while the small-town, evangelical backgrounds of the muckrakers gave American journalism a distinctly moralistic tone.[33]

In higher education, an alliance for progress between so-called secular academics and Social Gospel reformers dominated the early years of American social science.[34] While sociology and political-science departments offered courses in social ethics, the inaugural issue of the *American Journal of Sociology* included an article on Christian sociology.[35] Like their colleagues in sociology and political science, many historians saw their discipline as an instrument of social transformation. Viewing social science as extension of—or, in some cases, a replacement for—Protestant morality, scholars devoted themselves to the improvement of American society.[36]

Filled with a sense of moral purpose, journalists and social scientists espoused an ideology of social reform.[37] Committed to the fusion of

morality and trained intelligence, they saw no conflict between professional objectivity and ethical engagement. Drawing on both civic and
religious vocabularies, they devoted themselves to what Harold Perkin has
called the professional social ideal.[38] Combining "civic-minded *moral*
appeals and circumscribed *technical* appeals," they saw themselves as professionals in the service of the common good.[39]

The connections between professionalism and Protestant religion
that were so central to the early history of journalism and social science
were gradually severed, the consequence of a decades-long process of
"de-Christianization."[40] As Protestant colleges and universities loosened
their ties to sponsoring denominations, the academic disciplines proclaimed their autonomy from religious thought.[41] Convinced that religion and morality "contaminated scientific research by confusing subjective values with objective facts," social scientists distanced themselves
from religious ways of knowing.[42] A similar dynamic was at work in the
discipline of history, according to Peter Novick, as the ideology of objectivity moved to the "very center of the professional historical venture."[43]
By the 1920s, secular positivists had redefined objectivity to mean the
exclusion of moral values, expelling the "do-gooders" from sociology and
political science.[44] Always somewhat fragile, the alliance between Social
Gospelers and social scientists collapsed, with the former retreating to
fields such as theology and social work. The "retreat of religionists" from
social science was accompanied by a "decline of interest in the study of
religion."[45] Although the sociology of religion experienced a rebirth in
the 1950s and '60s, most social scientists continued to regard Christianity as a "rather quaint legacy from the oral tradition of a largely agrarian
society"—that is, "ultimately of little importance to the main intellectual
and social currents of society."[46]

With the growing professionalization of American journalism, a similar process of de-moralization took place, as reporters sought to emulate
the neutral detachment of the natural sciences. Through professional
associations, journalism schools, and trade publications, reporters and
editors emphasized the importance of objectivity, drawing a sharp boundary between personal values and publicly verifiable facts. Although traces
of the Protestant establishment remained (such as the Presbyterian Henry
Luce's control of *Time* magazine), Richard Flory notes that journalists
"ultimately privileged scientific authority over religious authority in
reporting and editorial content." During the same period, both the space
devoted to religion reporting and the positive presentation of traditional
religion declined.[47] By the 1950s, religion had become the least presti-

gious beat in the newspaper, relegated to the Saturday morning "church page," a situation that did not change until the 1980s.

Thus, between 1870 and 1950, religion, once central to professional life, was pushed to the margins.[48] In the language of secularization theory, the relationship between religion and both professions was gradually reshaped by the dual processes of institutional differentiation and privatization. Through institutional differentiation, journalists and social scientists were emancipated from the authority of religious institutions (denominations, churches, religious newspapers), operating according to the autonomous procedures of their own professions and disciplines. Through privatization, religion was increasingly excluded from the public worlds of the newsroom and the academy, confined to the realm of private life.[49] Journalists and social scientists could be religious as long as they kept their beliefs to themselves.

Religious Deprivatization and Professional Life

In the wake of such secularization, what place does religion hold in professional life today? Are journalism and social science completely secular, or is there room for religious faith in the professions? Must the sacred be restricted to private life, or can journalists and social scientists take their religious beliefs into the workplace?

In the classic formulation of secularization theory, the decline of religion was an irreversible, unidirectional process, culminating in the permanent demise of the sacred. In recent years, the classic formulation has come under fire as more and more scholars acknowledge the possibility of desecularization.[50] In the 1980s and 1990s, religion burst onto the political scene as religious groups from across the ideological spectrum challenged the exclusion of the sacred from the public square. While the U.S. Catholic bishops sounded the themes of justice and peace in the realm of public policy, Christian conservatives mobilized on the issues of abortion and "family values."

In *Public Religions in the Modern World,* Jose Casanova chronicles this resurgence of public faith, arguing that we are "witnessing the 'deprivatization' of religion in the modern world." According to Casanova, "religious traditions throughout the world are refusing to accept the marginal and privatized role which theories of modernity as well as theories of secularization had reserved for them." Questioning the autonomy of state and market from religious and ethical concerns, people of faith have

worked for the "re-normativization" of the public sphere. While acknowledging that institutional differentiation, including the separation of church
and state, is a more or less permanent feature of modernity—at least, in
the West—Casanova argues that privatization is a historical option that
can be reversed through the deprivatization of modern religion.[51] Central
to such deprivatization is the rejection of a rigid boundary between public and private life.

The heightened visibility of religion in American politics suggests the
potential for religious deprivatization in other areas of public life. In
recent years, a growing number of observers have called attention to a
revival of religion in the professions of journalism and higher education.[52] Although this religious resurgence has begun to receive scholarly
attention, little is known about the role of religious faith in the careers of
individual professionals.

In this study, I argue that an important subset of journalists and social
scientists resists individual-level privatization, engaging in the deprivatization of religion.[53] Drawing on interviews with Catholics and evangelicals
in both professions, I document the profound influence of religious commitments on their work. Challenging the claims of secularization theory,
I argue that the new-class professions are more open to individual acts of
religious self-expression than has been recognized.

Catholics and Evangelicals in the Professions

Although I acknowledge the contributions of other faiths to the deprivatization of religion, especially those of liberal Protestantism and Judaism,
this study focuses on the experiences of Catholic and evangelical Protestant professionals. Moving from the margins to the mainstream, Catholics
and evangelicals have taken their places alongside mainline Protestants
as the most visible religious voices in American public life.[54] Casanova's
Public Religions in the Modern World holds up Catholicism and evangelicalism as the prime sources of religious deprivatization in late-twentieth-
century America. Likewise, as Robert Bellah and colleagues, the authors
of *Habits of the Heart,* note, "Just when the mainline Protestant hold on
American culture seemed decisively weakened, the Roman Catholic
church . . . entered a much more active phase of national participation."
Finally, a recent study by Mark Regnerus and Christian Smith finds that
evangelical Protestants are the most publicly oriented religious group in
American society.[55]

   Most scholars have focused on the activities of Catholics and evangelicals in American politics. An analogous, albeit less visible, phenomenon can be found in the professions of higher education and American
journalism.[56] Andrew Greeley celebrates the rise of a "Catholic intellectual and cultural elite in the United States," noting that "in many cases
their work reflects Catholic vision." Citing data from the General Social
Surveys, Greeley argues that there has never "been a larger or more
devout elite."[57] Along the same lines, Douglas Sloan describes the arrival
of a "new generation of evangelical scholars," adding that mainline
Protestants' abandonment of engagement with the university coincided
with an "upsurge of conservative evangelical Protestantism."[58] Heralding
the growing influence of figures such as Maureen Dowd, Chris Matthews,
and Cokie Roberts, the *National Journal* points to the emergence of an
Irish Catholic "tribe" in Washington journalism with its own distinctive
take on American politics. Providing harder evidence of the same phenomenon, a recent study reports that the percentage of national journalists who identify themselves as Roman Catholics rose from 12 percent
in 1980 to 19 percent in 1995.[59] During the same period, evangelicals
served as the top religion reporters at *U.S. News and World Report, Time,*
and ABC News, and the evangelical pundit Cal Thomas became the most
widely syndicated political columnist in America.[60]
   Catholic and evangelical professionals provide an interesting sociological case study because of their historical marginality in the new class.
For much of this century, Catholics and evangelicals were severely underrepresented at elite news publications such as the *New York Times* and in
the halls of academia, reflecting their working-class origins in rural, small-
town and urban, immigrant enclaves. As relative newcomers to their
fields, Catholics and evangelicals come from religious communities that
historically have defined themselves in opposition to the secular ethos of
the modern professions. Believing in the unity of the good and the true,
the Catholic and evangelical traditions have long criticized the separation
of facts from values. As witnesses to the reality of the transcendent, they
have resisted the reduction of the supernatural to this-worldly explanations. Trusting in the authority of the Bible and church teaching, they
have rejected the new class's emphasis on skepticism and self-grounded
rationality.[61]
   In light of these enduring tensions, many scholars have emphasized
the incompatibility of professional and religious identities, highlighting
the secularizing consequences of professionalization. Among American
Catholics, this kind of accommodation has been likened to a process of

ethnic assimilation, whereby the children of white ethnics abandon their primordial religious identities in favor of the secular cosmopolitanism of the cultural elite.[62] In *The Rise of the Unmeltable Ethnics*, Michael Novak describes the homogenizing pressures of upward mobility:

> In order to move up in the world of journalism or television, especially on a national level, it is important to be able to see the whole national picture, and to escape merely regional, ethnic, or denominational views. Persons who enter the professional elites of journalism and broadcasting, or the corporate and academic worlds, tend to think of themselves as nonparochial. But one becomes a professional only through long submission to training, discipline, and carefully criticized experience. One enters, that is, a new and not less disciplined culture. . . . To become a professional is ordinarily to acquiesce in separation by no little gap from the people among whom one was born.[63]

James Davison Hunter paints an equally pessimistic portrait of professionalization among conservative Protestants, emphasizing the "accommodation, even acculturation" of college-educated evangelicals to the secular new class. In the cultural interchange between religion and the new class, religion is "by far the weaker partner," he says. As people of faith in secular professions, new-class evangelicals must guard constantly against the "cognitive contamination" of the evangelical worldview.[64]

By highlighting the dangers of assimilation and cultural accommodation, the Americanization–secularization hypothesis calls attention to the very real pressures that Catholic and evangelical professionals face.[65] Socialized into occupational cultures that exclude religious ways of knowing, they are encouraged to separate faith and work into separate compartments. By "unreservedly embracing the norms and values" of their professions, they risk losing the very cultural values that make them distinctive. In American Catholicism, such pressures led to the dismantling of a whole network of religious professional and academic associations in the 1960s, says Philip Gleason, as "Catholic scholars in a variety of disciplines [discarded] the belief that their faith dictated an approach different from that of non-Catholic workers in the same fields."[66] Among American evangelicals today, a similar dynamic may be at work, as many Christian scholars wonder whether they "share a set of assumptions that make their writing and teaching different from that of their non-believing colleagues."[67] In both cases, the assimilationist perspective helps make sense of the situation of religious professionals.

Although the Americanization–secularization thesis captures important truths, it ultimately fails to do justice to the complexity of Catholics'
and evangelicals' engagement with the professions. In emphasizing the
accommodation of Catholics and evangelicals to the secular new class, it
ignores the potential for religious resistance to secularization. In highlighting the dangers of assimilation, it underestimates the ability of religious groups to hold on to their cultural distinctiveness. In focusing on
the cognitive contamination of religious thought, it overlooks the possibility that Catholics and evangelicals may fruitfully combine religious
and professional ways of knowing.

Perspectives that recognize individuals' capacity to forge connections
between professional and religious identities, without collapsing one into
the other, are more helpful for understanding new-class Catholics and
evangelicals. In recent years, scholars across the disciplines have focused
on the blending, fusing, and mixing of social identities, criticizing the
false dichotomy between "'assimilation' (which denies the reality of difference)," according to Stephen Warner, and "'multiculturalism' (which
denies the reality of inclusion)."[68] Applying this critique to the experience
of American Catholics, David O'Brien sees the relationship between
Catholicism and American higher education as a process of interaction
in which the "church and each of its members ... must necessarily be
bilingual and bicultural"; appropriating a metaphor from W.E.B. Dubois,
he notes that, "for people of serious religious faith in this American land,
'two-ness, two unreconciled strivings' may always mark their vocation."[69]
Along the same lines, Christian Smith emphasizes American evangelicals'
ability to create a clear distinction from and significant engagement with
the wider society, arguing that the encounter with modern pluralism has
actually strengthened evangelicals' identity.[70] Making much the same
point, Paul Bramadat describes evangelical undergraduates at a secular
university who combine tendencies of compromise and resistance, articulating both "clear boundaries and possible commonalities" between the
sacred and secular.[71]

The Study and the Sample

My research on religion and the professions has taken me in a similar direction. In an analysis of national survey data, I found that evangelical professionals are significantly more conservative than their non-evangelical

counterparts, suggesting that professionalization does not inevitably lead to the loss of cultural distinctiveness. Although they are somewhat more liberal than their blue-collar co-religionists, evangelical professionals have retained much of their social conservatism. I conceptualize evangelicalism as an oppositional subculture that is beginning to penetrate the new class from within and argue that this penetration has taken place without the total abandonment of evangelical moral and political values.[72]

This study arose from an interest in the religious staying power of Catholic and evangelical professionals. After demonstrating the cultural distinctiveness of new-class evangelicals, I began to doubt the adequacy of the cultural-accommodation model of professional mobility. Inspired by several recent studies on religion and economic life, especially Robert Wuthnow's *God and Mammon in America,* I set out to examine the relationship between faith and work in the purportedly secular new class.[73] Expanding the scope of my research beyond evangelical Protestants, I turned my attention to the experiences of Catholics and evangelicals in journalism and social science.

Despite a growing literature on religion and the professions, we still know very little about how religiously committed professionals talk about faith and work. Broad studies of the American professions have only touched on the religious dimensions of professional identity, focusing on more general concerns.[74] Narrower studies of religion and the professions have been confined to historical accounts of secularization, small-scale content analyses, and theoretical arguments about the secularity of the new class.[75] Finally, systematic studies of religion and economic life— qualitative and quantitative—have focused on the American workforce as a whole rather than on the narrower occupational category of the professions.[76]

To address this gap, I analyze the careers of prominent Catholics and evangelical Protestants who work in national journalism and in the academic social sciences (see Figure 1). I obtained the sample, which is divided between journalists and social scientists and between Catholics and evangelicals, through snowball sampling. I then used CD-ROM indices such as the Social Science Citation Index to identify the top-published and top-cited Catholics and evangelicals in sociology, history, and political science. Reflecting a similar focus on elites, the sample of journalists was confined to those who have worked in New York and Washington at influential publications such as *Time, Newsweek,* the *New York Times,* and the *Washington Post.* This elite-oriented sampling strategy represents an intentional effort to capture the heightened tensions between professional and religious identities at the upper levels of both fields, where studies show that journalists and social scientists are more secular. (For more information about the sample, see the Appendix.)

This study relies on two primary sources of data: 1) semi-structured, qualitative interviews averaging seventy-five minutes with twenty journalists and twenty social scientists, conducted between 1994 and 1996; and 2) a sample of the interviewees' news stories and academic publications.

During the first part of the interview, I asked respondents general questions about their work in journalism and social science. In the second half of the interviews, I focused more directly on the relationship between faith and work. The topics covered included the place of moral and political convictions in professional life, attitudes toward objectivity, perceptions of co-workers, and the connections between religious commitments and writing. Respondents were allowed to go off the record, but the bulk of each interview was conducted on the record. The methodology of non-anonymous interviews provided a useful test of the extent to which Catholics and evangelicals were willing to talk about the connections between faith and work in a public setting.

I also analyzed a cross-section of my respondents' news stories and academic publications. Fifty news stories were selected from the body of each journalist's work available on Lexis–Nexis and examined for their religious and normative content. To follow up on this analysis, word searches were done using certain key terms (such as "culture wars," "community," "dialogue," and "justice") in an effort to identify recurring themes. For the academic social scientists, I analyzed major books (those published by university and religious presses) and articles (in major secular and religious journals) before and after the interviews, with an eye toward discovering the influence of religion on their work.

The Plan of the Book

Catholic and evangelical professionals clearly take their religious beliefs to work. In their public talk about work, analyzed in chapters 3 and 4, my respondents use a variety of bridging languages to relate the religious and professional worlds. These languages are multivocal, incorporating meanings from both secular and religious sources. Some of these languages exploit submerged connections between Christianity and professional ideologies—for example, the connections between journalistic notions of "truth" and the biblical themes of justice and peace.[77] Others draw on discourses that question the exclusion of values from professional life—postmodernism, multiculturalism, and civic journalism, to name a few. Together they demonstrate the potential for translating religious concerns into professional categories, and the reverse.

My respondents have been equally adept at bringing religion into their writing, a subject analyzed in chapters 5 and 6. Working at the intersection of two public-storytelling communities, they have articulated a fit between religious and professional narratives. Grafting the stories of their religious communities onto the dominant story lines of journalism and social science, they have brought their religious commitments into the pages of the *New York Times* and the *American Sociological Review*. Drawing on the resources of the Catholic and Protestant imaginations, they have produced news stories and academic monographs that bear the marks of their religious traditions.

Bridging professional and religious worlds, Catholics and evangelicals articulate multiple connections between faith and work. Resisting the temptation to conceal their religious identities, they engage in the deprivatization of religion. To be sure, bringing religion into the workplace has not always been easy. Many of my respondents qualified displays of religious faith with reminders of their professional credibility, drawing a line between advocacy and objectivity. Still others downplayed the particularity of their religious commitments. Finally, a small number of the people I contacted refused to be interviewed for the project, fearful of jeopardizing their professional reputations. While documenting the public presence of religion, this book uncovers persistent tensions between professional and religious worlds.

Chapter 7, "Openness and Obstacles," acknowledges these tensions and discusses both the opportunities and the constraints governing religious self-expression in professional life. Noting the profound influence of religious faith on the careers of my respondents, it argues that there is a surprising openness toward religion in the media and higher education. Recognizing the lingering tensions between professional and religious identities, it points out that the public expression of religion in the new class is often fragmented, piecemeal, and hard to detect. Avoiding a one-sided emphasis on accommodation or resistance, it portrays Catholics and evangelicals as cultural hybrids whose "odd combinations" of sacred and secular blur the boundaries between professional and religious discourse.[78]

In recent years, both secularists and Christians have questioned the compatibility of religious and professional identities. While religious scholars such as George Marsden have protested against the exclusion of Christian faith from professional life, secular thinkers such as Richard Rorty have described religion as a "conversation stopper," arguing that religious perspectives have no place in public discourse.[79] By showing that is possible for Christian journalists and academics to bring religious perspectives into fruitful conversation with the stories, frameworks, and debates of their professions, this study addresses the concerns of both Marsden and Rorty.

Before considering the careers of Catholics and evangelicals in the professions, it is instructive to consider how they got there. The next chapter chronicles the rise of Catholics and evangelicals from the working class to the new-class professions, including journalism and social science. It is to these stories of social mobility that we will now turn.

2   From the Margins
     to the Mainstream

Then: When Daniel Callahan entered Harvard University as a graduate student in 1956, there were no Catholics on the philosophy faculty and only "two or three among the students."[1] The so-called Harvard fundamentalists felt even more out of place at the Harvard Divinity School of the 1940s. "For a fundamentalist, pentecostal, or sectarian evangelical of another sort," says Joel Carpenter, "enrolling in Harvard was like walking into the belly of the beast."[2]

Now: In 1998, Father Bryan Hehir took over as head of the Harvard Divinity School, where Catholics make up 20 percent of the student body and 17 percent of the faculty.[3] More than 1,000 graduate students are now on the e-mail list of the evangelical InterVarsity Christian Fellowship, and the divinity school has a visiting professorship in evangelical studies.[4] According to Mark Noll, Harvard University now employs more "self-consciously Christian scholars whose academic work reflects in meaningful ways their religious convictions than ever in its existence."[5]

Then: Throughout the 1940s and 1950s, the *New York Times* was suspected of having anti-Catholic biases and "clearly made little if any effort to attract a Catholic readership below the most elite levels."[6] Although they were largely absent from the ranks of reporters and columnists, Catholics dominated the copy-editing staff, toiling at their "tedious and unheralded craft" in a part of the newsroom known as the "Catholic bullpen."[7]

Now: Today the Pulitzer Prize–winning Maureen Dowd writes a column for the *New York Times*. A graduate of Washington's Immaculata High School and the Catholic University of America, Dowd succeeded Anna Quindlen, another Irish Catholic, on the *Times*'s op-ed page. Other

18

Catholic journalists at the Gray Lady include Elaine Sciolino, Peter Steinfels, and Robin Toner.

Then: In the 1920s, H. L. Mencken dubbed fundamentalists the "gaping primates of the upland valleys," and the *New Republic* faulted Catholics for embracing a culture of "absolutism . . . obedience, uniformity, and intellectual subservience." In *Anti-Intellectualism in American Life,* Richard Hofstadter singled out Catholics and evangelicals as particularly hostile to the life of the mind, using them as prima facie evidence of the intellectual stagnation of American religion.[8]

Now: In the October 2000 issue of the *Atlantic Monthly,* Alan Wolfe chronicled the "opening" of the evangelical mind, arguing that "conservative Christians [have] created a life of the mind broader and more imaginative than anything previously found in their tradition."[9] Along the same lines, the *New York Times* praised the University of Notre Dame for combining "serious scholarship with a deeply religious environment," noting its burgeoning endowment, now at $3 billion, and nationally recognized faculty.[10]

Catholics and evangelicals have enjoyed a dramatic increase in cultural and intellectual prestige. Since the 1960s, a growing number of Catholics and evangelicals have joined the ranks of the national news media and the academic professoriate. Taking their places in the new-class occupations, they have moved from the margins to the mainstream of professional life.

Given their longtime status as outsiders, how did Catholics and evangelicals make it into the knowledge elite? What has changed in American society and in the Catholic and evangelical communities? This chapter traces the rise of Catholics and evangelicals in the college-educated professions. It argues that Catholics and evangelicals passed through three overlapping stages on their way to professional influence: upward mobility; subcultural institution building; and deghettoization.[11]

Very few blue-collar religious groups have managed to exert a powerful influence on the cultural and intellectual world. Upward mobility into the professional middle class (stage one) was crucial to ensuring the wider impact of Catholicism and evangelicalism on American public life. In addition to putting Catholics and evangelicals in positions of influence, this mobility provided the resources necessary to build distinctively religious professional and academic subcultures (stage two), including colleges and universities, journals and magazines, and professional and academic associations. Constructed from 1920 to 1960, these subcultural institutions insulated Catholics and evangelicals from the acids of modernity that overtook mainstream American intellectual culture during the first half of the twentieth century. In an era in which many mainline Protestant institutions—particularly colleges and universities—followed the path of secularization, Catholics and evangelicals emerged with their institutions largely intact.

At the same time, subcultural isolation exacted a heavy price from both groups. Hemmed in by religious separatism and antimodernism, Catholics and evangelicals found themselves outside the mainstream of American intellectual and professional life. Criticized and reviled for their anti-intellectualism, authoritarianism, and sectarianism, both groups experienced waves of self-criticism. This self-criticism in turn led to a loosening of group boundaries and a gradual process of de-ghettoization (stage three), experienced by Catholics in the 1960s and by evangelicals in the 1970s and 1980s (with important antecedents in the 1940s and 1950s).

With de-ghettoization has come heightened engagement in American public life, as well as a greater Catholic and evangelical presence in higher education and journalism. Although some religious distinctiveness has been lost, particularly among Catholics, Catholics and evangelicals have continued to maintain an impressive array of magazines, journals, professional associations, and colleges and universities, including Notre Dame, Georgetown, Boston College, Baylor, Pepperdine, and Wheaton.

Drawing on Christian Smith's theory of religious subcultural strength, this chapter argues that Catholics and evangelicals have influenced professional life by combining support for a distinctive set of beliefs and institutions, made possible by subcultural institution building, with public engagement, made possible by de-ghettoization.[12] The remainder of the chapter traces the movement of Catholics and evangelicals through the stages of upward mobility, subcultural institution building, and de-ghettoization, then turns to an assessment of their place in the knowledge professions today.

Stage One: The Professionalization of Catholics and Evangelicals

For much of the twentieth century, Catholics and evangelical Protestants were overwhelmingly concentrated in the American working class in urban, immigrant or rural, small-town enclaves.[13] In his classic essay

Figure 2. Percentage of each religious group with college degree by age cohort (General Social Surveys 1972–96)

	Decade Respondent Reached College Age						
	1920–29	1930–39	1940–49	1950–59	1960–69	1970–79	1980–89
Evangelical	4.6%	6.7%	8.6%	11.4%	16.6%	18.2%	19.2%
Catholic	5.5%	7.9%	11.4%	17.8%	24.9%	26.3%	31.8%
Mainline Protestant	13.6%	13.1%	20.1%	26.5%	32.1%	33.9%	40.9%
Jewish	18.5%	27.4%	39.8%	53.0%	71.1%	69.3%	73.9%
Nonreligious	18.3%	20.0%	32.0%	29.3%	40.7%	30.7%	23.0%
African American Protestant	3.6%	6.3%	5.3%	8.8%	14.1%	11.6%	14.0%
TOTAL	8.7%	10.3%	13.9%	18.7%	26.0%	25.3%	26.6%

"American Catholics and the Intellectual Life," Monsignor John Tracy Ellis wrote that the poverty, hardship, and even illiteracy of immigrant Catholics made it "impossible . . . for our ancestors to produce anything approaching a thriving intellectual life." More recently, Robert Wuthnow noted the historic confinement of American evangelicals to the "disadvantaged ranks of the stratification system," describing the appeal of evangelicalism among "the remnants of the dustbowl, recent immigrants from Germany and Scandinavia, Appalachian coal miners, blacks, displaced migrants from the South, [and] day laborers in the smoke-belching factory cities of the Northeast."[14]

Despite the humble status of most Catholics and evangelicals, dramatic changes in higher education and the professions would eventually make it possible for both groups to join the middle class. In countless books and articles, Andrew Greeley has enthusiastically narrated the story of the Catholic ascent to the college-educated professions. Although Catholics as a whole were below the national average in college attendance before 1950, Irish Catholics and German Catholics enjoyed an early burst of educational mobility in the opening decades of the twentieth century. Irish Catholics who reached college age in the 1920s were just as likely as Protestant Americans to attend college, according to Greeley. By the 1970s and 1980s, all of the white ethnic Catholic groups had caught up with the national average for occupational and educational attainment, and Irish Catholics had become the "richest and best educated white Gentile group in America."[15]

My analysis of the General Social Survey (1972–96 cumulative file) paints much the same picture. Figure 2 shows the percentage of respondents with college degrees in each age cohort within the religious groups.

Figure 3. Percentage of each religious group in professional–managerial occupations by age cohort (General Social Surveys 1972–96)

	Decade Respondent Reached College Age					
	1920–29	1930–39	1940–49	1950–59	1960–69	1970–79
Evangelical	16%	15.4%	16.9%	20.4%	21.9%	23.6%
Catholic	16.1%	15.2%	18%	24.6%	29.4%	25.4%
Mainline Protestant	26.1%	25.0%	28.5%	32.0%	36.2%	39.6%
Jewish	22.2%	31.1%	45.8%	48.8%	68.2%	72.7%
Nonreligious	27.6%	24.4%	38.9%	31.7%	41.0%	33.0%
African American Protestant	5.6%	11.1%	9.7%	13.8%	17.4%	11.6%
TOTAL	19.0%	19.1%	21.3%	25.2%	29.5%	27.6%

Paralleling the enormous expansion of higher-education opportunities for all Americans, the percentage of Catholics with college degrees increased from 5.5 percent for those reaching college age in the decade 1920–29, to 17.8 percent of those reaching college age in the 1950–59 age cohort, to 31.8 percent of the 1980–89 cohort.[16] The story of Catholic upward mobility in the professional and managerial occupations is much the same (see Figure 3).

The surge of American educational mobility that helped propel Catholics into the college-educated professional class had a delayed effect on evangelicals. Whereas 7.9 percent of the 1930–39 cohort of Catholics graduated from college, evangelicals did not attain that level of educational achievement until the 1940–49 cohort (Figure 2). According to Wuthnow, the federal government's decision to invest in higher education in the post–World War II era propelled an unprecedented number of evangelicals into the ranks of the college-educated population.[17] The percentage of respondents in evangelical denominations reporting college degrees grew from 6.7 percent for those reaching college age in the decade 1930–39 to 8.6 percent for the 1940–49 cohort, 11.4 percent for the 1950–59 cohort, and 19.2 percent for the 1980–89 cohort (Figure 2).[18] Likewise, the proportion of respondents in evangelical denominations working in the professional and managerial occupations rose steadily over the course of the postwar era, reaching 23.6 percent for evangelicals in the 1970–79 age cohort (Figure 3).

Although members of evangelical denominations are still underrepresented in the college-educated professions, the evangelical professional middle class is now substantial. Moreover, if evangelicalism is measured according to religious self-identification, as it is in Smith's recent study, evangelicals have caught up with other Americans in educational and occupational attainment. Smith points out that "self-identified evangelicals have more years of education than fundamentalists, liberals, Roman Catholics, and those who are nonreligious; and only slightly fewer years than mainline Protestants."[19]

Stage Two: Building the Catholic and Evangelical Subcultures

Sociologists have usually depicted upward mobility as a secularizing force, arguing that movement into the college-educated professions leads to the loss of religious belief and accommodation to secular modernity.[20] This study challenges the scholarly consensus on religion and class by arguing that upward mobility provided Catholics and evangelicals with the resources they needed to create distinctively religious professional and academic subcultures. Membership in the professional middle class supplied Catholics and evangelicals with the economic and human capital necessary for a sustained period of subcultural institution building. In many ways, these subcultures functioned as religious social movements determined to transform the new-class occupations from within.[21]

Despite tremendous upward mobility, Catholics and evangelicals did not simply assimilate into the mainstream of the American professional middle class. Rather, the initial rise of Catholics and evangelicals into the college-educated professions occurred at a time that both religious groups defined themselves against the mainstream of American culture. Under the influence of antimodernist ideologies, both Catholics and evangelicals attempted to isolate themselves from the liberal Protestant and, later, secular ethos of mainstream American higher education. They did so primarily by constructing alternative academic and professional subcultures.

These subcultures were made possible both by the existence of a critical mass of college-educated Catholics and evangelicals and the strong symbolic boundaries each group constructed between itself and the larger culture. Without continuous upward mobility, Catholics and evangelicals would have lacked the economic resources and college-educated professionals necessary to sustain colleges and universities, magazines and journals, and scholarly and professional societies (see Figure 4). Without strong boundaries between themselves and American society, Catholics and evangelicals probably would have experienced the same tide of secularization that swept over mainstream academia and the professions.[22]

Figure 4. Catholic and Evangelical Subcultural Institutions

Magazines/Journals	
Catholic	Evangelical
America (1909)	*Christianity Today* (1956)
Catholic Historical Review (1915)	*Fides et Historia* (1968)
Commonweal (1924)	*Christian Scholar's Review* (1971)
Review of Politics (1939)	*Books and Culture* (1995)
American Catholic Sociological Review (1940)	

Academic and Professional Associations	
Catholic	Evangelical
American Catholic Historical Association (1919)	American Scientific Affiliation (1941)
Catholic Anthropological Conference (1926)	Evangelical Theological Society (1949)
Catholic Sociological Society (1938)	Conference on Christianity and Literature (1956)
Catholic Economic Association (1941)	Christian Association for Psychological Studies (1956)
Catholic Theological Society of America (1946)	Christian Legal Society (1961)
Catholic Psychological Association (1947)	Conference on Faith and History (1967)
Catholic Renascence Society (1949)	Christian Sociological Society (1972)
	Society of Christian Philosophers (1978)

Publishing Houses/Religious Imprints	
Catholic	Evangelical
Sheed & Ward–New York City (1933)	Eerdmans (1911)
Doubleday Image (1954)	Zondervan (1931)

Memories of a Catholic Ghetto

In "Memories of a Catholic Boyhood," Garry Wills begins an insightful account of 1950s ghetto Catholicism with the simple declaration: "We grew up different." According to Wills, the church was "stranded in America, out of place," enveloping its adherents in a "total weave of Catholic life."[23] Although it is partly attributable to social class and ethnicity, this profound sense of cultural difference was rooted in the conviction that modern American culture posed a threat to the faith of immigrant Catholics along with a general belief in the superiority of Catholic ideas.

This sense of cultural alienation also shaped Catholic attitudes toward American higher education and the professional and managerial occupations. While the pioneers of the American research universities embraced a liberal Protestant religion of scientific progress and the social gospel, American Catholics continued to emphasize a classical curriculum heavy on Latin and philosophy. The opening of Johns Hopkins University in 1876 marked the birth of the modern American research university. Unable to embrace mainstream American higher education, Catholic leaders chose to participate in the academic revolution in their own way, founding the Catholic University of America in 1889. Although Catholic University began its life with a relatively liberal rector and faculty, they were eventually purged in the wake of successive papal condemnations of "modernism" and "Americanism." Even as academic freedom was becoming a sacred value in the mainstream academy, Margaret Reher writes, an "inquisitorial spirit" overtook American Catholic higher education. In a period that saw the rise of Darwinian evolution, biblical criticism, social-scientific positivism, and Freudian psychology, Catholics, in the words of Philip Gleason, chose to challenge modernity.[24]

At the same time, the strong boundaries between Catholicism and the outside world helped keep alive a religious vision of higher education during an era in which liberal Protestant institutions were secularizing. While the mainstream professions emphasized the rhetoric of specialization, objectivity, and the separation of facts from values, American Catholics envisioned a value-laden approach to professional life. According to George Marsden, American Catholics were "among the few major groups in America to dissent substantially from assumptions of the virtuous neutrality of liberal American culture," questioning the claim that empirical observation was the source of all "universally valid" knowledge.[25] In particular, says David Salvaterra, Catholics defined themselves against the "naturalistic, mechanistic view of man and of modern life," rejecting the notion that reality could be reduced to matter in motion.[26]

Enrollment at Catholic colleges and universities began to swell in the first three decades of the twentieth century, buoyed by the upward mobility of Irish and German Catholics. In 1899, only 5,500 college students attended Catholic institutions; by 1926, this figure had grown to 18,986. Further, the number of professional and graduate students increased from 1,000 in 1899 to 27,359 in 1926. By 1926, Creighton, DePaul, Detroit, Duquesne, Fordham, Georgetown, Loyola-Chicago, Marquette, Notre Dame, and St. Louis universities all had more than 1,000 professional or graduate students, and three of them—Fordham, Loyola, and Marquette—had enrollments of more than 3,000. By 1930, more than 105,000 students were enrolled in Catholic colleges and universities.[27] This expansion of Catholic higher education was no doubt aided by the vitality of Catholic high schools, which had enrolled more than 180,000 students by 1931.[28]

The period 1920–60 was characterized by what David O'Brien calls "subcultural higher education."[29] Rejecting European philosophy after Kant, the Vatican actively promoted the revival of Thomism as an antidote to the skepticism of modern thought.[30] Catholic colleges and universities were central to this effort; a host of Catholic scholarly and professional societies also played a key role in institutionalizing a Catholic, and neo-Thomist, perspective on the various disciplines. The American Catholic Historical Association, founded in 1919, served as the prototypical Catholic disciplinary association. In sharp contrast to the positivistic, evolutionary models of historiography common among early-twentieth-century historians, Catholic historians envisioned history as "the realization of a great divine plan, a vast supernatural process, more God's than man's," criticizing the "inadequacy . . . of that positivism which rejects all metaphysics, of that materialism that denies all spiritual reality, and of that rationalism which will endure no mystery."[31] Encouraged by the example of the Catholic historians, a wide range of Catholic academic and professional organizations soon appeared, including the American Catholic Philosophical Association (1926), Catholic Anthropological Conference (1926), Catholic Sociological Society (1938), Catholic Economic Association (1941), and Catholic Psychological Association (1947).[32]

In the words of Will Herberg, "every interest, activity, and function of the Catholic faithful [was] provided with some Catholic institution," including Catholic "associations of doctors, lawyers, teachers, students, and philosophers," Catholic hospitals, and Catholic colleges and universities (see Figure 4).[33] While magazines such as *Commonweal* and *America* helped nurture Catholic intellectual life, movements and organizations such as Catholic Action, the Association of Catholic Trade Unionists, the Catholic Worker, and the National Catholic Welfare Conference brought a distinctively Catholic voice to social and economic questions.[34]

A minority of American scholars expressed admiration for the neo-Thomist Catholic revival, seeing in Catholic higher education an alternative to the specialized, fragmented curriculum of the modern research university. Moreover, the links between the Catholic ghetto and such European luminaries as Christopher Dawson, Jacques Maritain, and Etienne Gilson helped legitimate the neoscholastic revival in America. Yet "ghetto Catholicism" had serious shortcomings. Its intellectual stagnation was widely noted by Catholics and non-Catholics alike. For all the talk of ushering in an era of Catholic social science, only 48 percent of the membership of the Catholic Sociological Society reported contributing a scholarly article to a non-Catholic publication or publishing a book in 1947–52.[35] Even someone as favorably disposed to the Catholic tradition as the University of Chicago's president Robert Maynard Hutchins believed that Catholic colleges and universities had "imitated the worst features of secular education and ignored most of the good ones."[36]

Outside the Catholic ghetto, Catholics were beginning to have an impact on American popular culture. In postwar Hollywood, filmmakers such as John Ford and Frank Capra brought an ethnic Catholic sensibility to the silver screen. In the late 1950s, Bishop Fulton J. Sheen's television program "Life Is Worth Living" had higher ratings than Milton Berle.[37] During the same period, Catholic journalists such as Ed Sullivan, Dorothy Kilgallen, and Jimmy Cannon dominated the pages of big-city tabloid newspapers, bringing a populist, working-class sensibility to their writing.[38] Yet, as noted earlier, Catholic journalists were largely absent from the *New York Times, New Republic,* and *The Nation.* While *The Nation* serialized Paul Blanshard's inflammatory *American Freedom and Catholic Power,* the *New Republic* regularly contrasted the "authoritarian" culture of Catholicism with American democratic values. Although they had captured the attention of readers from Brooklyn to South Boston, Catholic journalists had a long way to go before they would penetrate the media elite.[39]

"Revive Us Again": Building an Evangelical Subculture

Since the humiliation of the Scopes trial in 1925, fundamentalists have been depicted as "stigmatized outsiders" in the "theories, story lines, plots, and images" of America's journalists, writers, and filmmakers.[40] Exhausted by the fundamentalist–modernist battles of the 1920s, the "fighting fundamentalists" turned inward during the 1930s, withdrawing from the mainline Protestant denominations, which had been won by modernist liberal Protestants, and from American public life. In what Noll describes as "the intellectual disaster of fundamentalism," conservative Protestants separated themselves from higher education, the arts, politics, cultural affairs, and the mainstream denominations. For decades after the Scopes trial, the larger evangelical impact on the American academic and professional world was barely noticeable.[41]

Nevertheless, the subcultural networks forged by fundamentalist leaders in the 1930s, through Bible conferences, radio evangelists, Bible institutes, and small Christian colleges, provided the organizational base necessary for evangelical academic and professional mobilization in the post–World War II era. By the early 1940s, evangelicals had begun to form national transdenominational coalitions that helped pave the way for the institutionalization of an alternative evangelical academic and professional subculture.[42] In 1942, more than one hundred fifty delegates from thirty-four denominations gathered in St. Louis for the first meeting of what would become the National Association of Evangelicals (NAE), envisioning a national organization that would "provide a clearinghouse for evangelical radio broadcasting, evangelical missions, evangelism, Christian education, separation between church and state, and other interests common to evangelicals."[43] Reflecting a new emphasis on transforming American culture, the NAE's leaders called for the "rescue of western civilization [through a] revival of evangelical Christianity."[44]

The NAE's leaders repudiated the fundamentalist attitude of cultural separatism, calling for a renewed evangelical engagement with modern intellectual and professional life. Yet despite this repudiation of separatism, evangelicals continued to pursue an organizational strategy of separate institutions, building a conservative Protestant subculture. Rejecting the modernism of mainline Protestant and public higher education, evangelicals flocked to a network of Christian colleges and seminaries, including Wheaton College, founded in 1863, and Fuller Seminary, founded in 1947. Such institutions experienced tremendous growth during the 1940s and 1950s, buoyed by the upward mobility of conservative Protestants. The number of students grew from 224 in 1936, to 575 in 1948, to 1,126 in 1958 at the Free Methodist Seattle Pacific College; from 820 in 1936, to 1,539 in 1948, to 2,056 in 1958 at the nondenominational Wheaton; and from 357 in 1936, to 1,245 in 1948, to 1,908 in 1958 at the Dutch Calvinist Calvin College.[45] On secular college and university campuses, the first major evangelical campus ministry group, InterVarsity Christian Fellowship, established in 1939, drew more than 15,000 evangelical college students to its 1948 missions conference.[46] Organizations that joined the InterVarsity Christian Fellowship included the Navigators (1949), Campus Crusade for Christ (1951), and the International Students Fellowship (1953).[47]

The dramatic increase in the number of evangelical college students after World War II provided a critical mass of college-educated professionals necessary for the formation of numerous evangelical academic and professional associations (see Figure 4). These associations included the American Scientific Affiliation (1941), the Evangelical Theological Society (1949), the Conference on Christianity and Literature and the Christian Association for Psychological Studies (1956), the Christian Legal Society (1961), the Conference on Faith and History (1967), the Christian Sociological Society (1972), and the Society of Christian Philosophers (1978).[48] These organizations rejected the ideology of value-free objectivity and were formed to "explore the implications of faith for scholarship and provide a venue for evangelical scholars to interact."[49]

The increasing wealth of the evangelical subculture resulted, according to Michael Hamilton, in a "flurry of nonprofit institution building" in the post–World War II era.[50] The result of this institution building was an evangelical network that was strikingly similar to the one forged by Roman Catholics during the interwar years.[51] Like the institutions of the Catholic ghetto, this subculture helped evangelicals cope with their status as a "cognitive minority" within the larger academic and professional world.[52] And like their Catholic counterparts, evangelical intellectuals defined themselves against a culture they felt was "hurtling over the Great Falls of secularism." Rejecting the liberalism of mainline Protestant and public higher education, Carl F. H. Henry called on evangelicals to "challenge and storm the high places of culture and learning." Although evangelicals did not have a unifying ideology that was comparable to neoscholasticism, they were committed to bringing a Christian "world-life view" into academic life.[53]

Outside academia, the evangelical-culture industries of religious publishing and broadcasting flourished throughout the postwar era, showing particularly strong growth during the 1970s and 1980s. Beginning largely with the founding of *Christianity Today* in 1956, which was funded by the Sunoco oil magnate J. Howard Pew, the evangelical-magazine sector had mushroomed to more than three hundred publications by 1990.[54] In the 1970s, six evangelical books sold more than 2 million copies each, and sales in the Christian publishing industry grew from $108 million in 1967 to $685 million in 1986.[55] By the 1980s, evangelicals controlled more than five hundred radio stations and at least one cable-television network, the Christian Broadcasting Network, demonstrating their commitment to building an alternative set of institutions for symbol production.[56]

Like Catholics, evangelicals often found—and in some cases, still find—themselves ensconced in a network of ghetto institutions that isolated them from mainstream American society. Like the Catholic ghetto, the evangelical subculture helped keep alive a religious approach to higher education and mass communication. At the same time, the isolation of the evangelical subculture prevented its members from fully engaging the academic and cultural mainstream.

Until the 1970s and 1980s, evangelicals were not major players in higher education and the media. With the exception of McCandlish Phillips at the *New York Times,* who is immortalized in Gay Talese's book *The Kingdom and the Power,* and Wesley Pippert at United Press International, evangelicals were hard to find in the national press corps. In 1966, George Cornell, an Episcopalian with evangelical leanings and the religion columnist for the Associated Press, wrote that Christianity's evangelical wing "pays scant heed to the mass media." Similarly, evangelicals were almost entirely absent from major research universities. Timothy Smith of Johns Hopkins became the first evangelical historian in the United States to "make it in the secular research university," according to Grant Wacker. And when Alvin Plantinga left graduate school in 1957, there were "few Christian philosophers in the United States, and even fewer Christian philosophers willing to identify themselves as such."[57] Although the evangelical empire of Christian colleges and universities, campus ministries, publishers, and broadcasters was truly vast, it reached an overwhelmingly evangelical audience.[58] Like the Catholic ghetto of the 1940s and 1950s, the evangelical subculture was preaching mostly to the choir.

Stage Three: De-ghettoization

As Catholics and evangelicals climbed the socioeconomic ladder into the professional middle class, they inevitably had greater contact with the larger society. Greater contact between a religious subculture and the outside world frequently results in the redefinition of group boundaries. Exposure to the pluralistic world of the larger society makes it difficult to preserve a firm sense of "us" and "them." The boundaries are renegotiated as religious subcultures appropriate some elements of the dominant culture while rejecting others.[59]

In recent decades, American Catholicism and evangelicalism have experienced such a redefinition of group boundaries (Catholicism more so than evangelicalism). Members of both religious traditions have increasingly found themselves working or attending school in secular professional and academic environments. More than ever, Catholics and evangelicals have opened themselves up to the intellectual currents of the modern academy, initiating a dialogue with evolutionary biology, feminism, the great world religions, and those engaged in the critical investigation of their own traditions. In a similar way, Catholic—and, in some cases, evangelical—colleges and universities have opened their faculties to people outside their religious communities.

Taken together, these changes could be called a process of de-ghettoization. On the individual level, de-ghettoization has led college-educated Catholic and evangelicals to adopt views that are more in sync with American culture, leading some critics to lament the assimilation of both groups to the values of the mainstream professions. On the group level, de-ghettoization has sometimes resulted in an identity crisis for religious institutions, leading church-related colleges and universities to reevaluate their religious missions and religious professional associations to question their reason for being.[60] Despite these problems, de-ghettoization has also helped contribute to the greater visibility of Catholics and evangelicals in American public life. Rather than speaking only to their own subcultures, members of both groups have learned to translate their convictions into terms that are comprehensible to those outside their religious communities.

Breaking Out of the Catholic Ghetto

As Catholics rose from working-class, urban enclaves into the ranks of the professional middle class, they encountered strong prejudice.[61] Although many Catholics challenged such stereotypes, the negative images of American Catholics propagated by U.S. scholars in the 1940s and 1950s helped spawn a period of Catholic self-criticism. This was epitomized in Monsignor John Tracy Ellis's 1955 essay "American Catholics and the Intellectual Life." Citing Denis Brogan's comment that, "in no Western society is the intellectual prestige of Catholicism lower than in [the United States]," Ellis and other Catholic self-critics attributed the lack of Catholic intellectuals to the ghetto mentality of American Catholics.[62]

Between 1962 and 1965, the world's Roman Catholic bishops gathered in Rome for the Second Vatican Council. Meeting under two popes (John XXIII and Paul VI), they crafted a series of sixteen documents that articulated a new understanding of Catholicism. The changes of Vatican

II further complicated the identity of American Catholics. John XXIII's call for *aggiornamento*, or bringing the church up to date, signaled a new willingness among Roman Catholicism to engage the modern world on its own terms. The acceptance of modern notions of religious freedom, the redefinition of the church as the "people of God," the shift to a vernacular liturgy, and the endorsement of interreligious dialogue were all revolutionary changes. In the words of the Protestant theologian Langdon Gilkey, Catholicism was forced to absorb the "vast modern development from the Enlightenment to the present in the short period between 1963 and 1973."[63]

In the aftermath of Vatican II and the upheavals of the 1960s, notes Gleason, the American Catholic academic world experienced a severe "identity crisis." Catholic scholars abandoned the neo-Thomist attempt to integrate faith and knowledge, along with the idea that there was a specifically Catholic approach to their disciplines. The American Catholic Sociological Society became the Association for the Sociology of Religion, and the name of its journal was changed from the *American Catholic Sociological Review* to *Sociological Analysis*.[64]

Nowhere were the changes more dramatic than in Catholic colleges and universities. The switch to lay boards of trustees, the decrease in religion and philosophy requirements, and the sharp increase in non-Catholic faculty changed Catholic higher education forever. Scholars such as James T. Burtchaell and Gleason have argued that, in the wake of such seismic shifts, American Catholic higher education is undergoing a process of secularization that, if left unchecked, could result in the disengagement of Catholic colleges and universities from their religious roots. (Pope John Paul II also raised these concerns in *Ex Corde Ecclesiae*, the Apostolic Constitution on Catholic Universities).[65] Eugene McCarraher has raised equally serious concerns about de-ghettoization, blaming the upward mobility of American Catholics for fostering what he calls "Starbucks Catholicism"—a therapeutic, managerial, and consumerist vision of the faith that is indistinguishable from corporate capitalism.[66]

Assimilation and secularization pose very real dangers. At the same time, however, many scholars have ignored an equally important dimension of de-ghettoization: It has given American Catholics unprecedented visibility in the academy and the professions. As Bruce Russett has pointed out, his generation was "really the first generation of Catholic intellectuals in the secular world." Along the same lines, Greeley argues that the upward mobility of American Catholics has resulted in the creation of a

Catholic "intellectual and cultural elite" in the United States. General Social Survey data show that 2 percent of American Catholics—about the same proportion as in the general population—fall into the occupational category of "scholars, writers, performers, and artists." Greeley estimates that "almost 1 million Catholics . . . can make some claim to be part of the intellectual and cultural creative elites." Greeley has also found that the Catholic cultural and intellectual elite is more devout than the American Catholic population as a whole, with 56 percent attending mass at least two or three times a month.[67]

The emergence of an American Catholic academic and cultural elite has coincided with the coming of age of American Catholic higher education. Once known more for its prowess on the gridiron, the University of Notre Dame has moved into the ranks of the top-twenty American research universities. (It is ranked nineteenth by *U.S. News and World Report*.) Notre Dame has amassed an endowment of more than $3 billion, surpassing Brown, Duke, Johns Hopkins, Purdue, and Vanderbilt in wealth. Similarly, Georgetown, ranked twenty-third among national universities; Boston College, ranked thirty-ninth in the same category; and Holy Cross, ranked thirtieth among national liberal-arts colleges, have enjoyed dramatic increases in institutional prestige since the 1970s.[68]

Finally, de-ghettoization has led to a growing sophistication in American Catholic public discourse. The past thirty years have seen the advent of a "Catholic modernity," in the words of Charles Taylor, that has largely come to terms with the legacy of the Enlightenment. By accepting liberal democracy, the separation of church and state, the relative autonomy of scientific inquiry, and the contributions of feminism, Catholic intellectuals have signaled a new willingness to participate in contemporary intellectual discourse.[69]

Evangelical *Aggiornamento*

Vatican II marked a clear turning point in American Catholicism. No single event triggered the de-ghettoization of American evangelicalism. The initial burst came in the 1940s and 1950s with the founding of the National Association of Evangelicals and the emergence of a new generation of graduate-trained evangelicals. Young evangelical theologians such as Carl F. H. Henry and Edward J. Carnell used the terms "neo-evangelical," "new evangelical," or simply "evangelical" to differentiate themselves from their more conservative, "fundamentalist" brethren. They rejected fundamentalism's negative cultural outlook, encouraging Christian participation in the this-worldly spheres of politics, intellectual life, and the arts.[70] While fundamentalists enforced a rigid lifestyle code that prohibited such activities as smoking and going to the movies, neo-evangelicals called for a Protestant orthodoxy engaged in "remaking the modern mind."[71]

Yet, as noted earlier, the anti-separatist rhetoric of postwar evangelicalism was often combined with a contradictory emphasis on the building of separate evangelical institutions. At the same time, quiet changes were taking place within the evangelical subculture that would pave the way for future de-ghettoization. Greater contact with Dutch Calvinist and British evangelicals did much to rejuvenate postwar American evangelical intellectual life.[72] Moreover, during the 1960s and early 1970s, evangelical intellectuals became more involved in the world of politics and social issues. The influence of the social movements of the 1960s helped produce something that had been unheard of in American evangelicalism: an "evangelical left." In magazines such as the *Post-American* (later *Sojourners*) and *New Freedom* (later *The Other Side*), evangelicals grappled with the relationship between Christianity and politics, and organizations such as the Daughters of Sarah articulated an explicitly evangelical version of feminism.[73]

The 1976 election of the Southern Baptist Jimmy Carter as president of the United States further contributed to the de-ghettoization of evangelicals in American society. Carter's open discussion of his religious faith, together with the dramatic religious conversion of the Watergate felon Charles Colson, made "born-again Christian" a household term. Both *Time* and *Newsweek* put stories about the growing influence of evangelicalism on their covers, and George Gallup, Jr., an evangelical Episcopalian, dubbed 1976 the year of the evangelical. By the 1980 presidential election, Christian conservatives had become major players in American politics, although many evangelical intellectuals had little sympathy for the politics of the religious right.[74]

Along with the increasing visibility of evangelicals in the public square, the 1970s and 1980s saw a progressive weakening of the symbolic boundaries that separated evangelical academic institutions from the outside world.[75] Theologians at evangelical seminaries and colleges entered into dialogue with mainline Protestant scholars, expressing a new affinity for neo-orthodox thinkers such as Karl Barth and Dietrich Bonhoeffer. Evangelical campuses relaxed rules against dancing, rock music, and movie attendance (while retaining prohibitions against alcohol and tobacco use).

Campus ministry groups such as InterVarsity and Campus Crusade experimented with contemporary folk-rock music and addressed political and social issues in their publications. Evangelical authors articulated a more positive attitude toward human sexuality and the body. Evangelical scientists cautiously entertained the possibility of a reconciliation between evolutionary biology and Christian theism. Evangelical literature scholars explored postmodernism. Sounding much like John Tracy Ellis, evangelical academics—notably, Noll in *The Scandal of the Evangelical Mind*—criticized their co-religionists for perpetuating fundamentalist anti-intellectualism, forming what Wolfe calls a "network of modernizers."[76]

In light of these changes, scholars such as James Davidson Hunter and Richard Quebedeaux have argued that college-educated evangelicals are accommodating to the culture of secular modernity. In particular, Hunter has written that new-class evangelical leaders have entered into "an almost complete and uncritical alliance with left-liberal political values and ideology."[77] Rather than interpreting the changes in American evangelicalism as evidence of secularization, it may be more illuminating to view these changes as signs that evangelicals have rejected the isolation of twentieth-century fundamentalism in favor of a more engaged Protestant orthodoxy. Christian Smith argues that the evangelical movement has opened a "space between fundamentalism and liberalism in the field of religious collective identity, [creating] an agenda distinct from fundamentalism's around which a variety of Protestants [can rally]."[78]

Evangelicals have become much more visible in the cultural and academic elite (although less so than American Catholics). A growing number of evangelicals have obtained tenure-track positions at Duke, Harvard, Princeton, UCLA, the University of Wisconsin, and Yale. In a recent article, James Turner argued that an evangelical intellectual revival has established a "visible evangelical presence in literary scholarship, psychology, history, philosophy, and other fields."[79]

And like Catholic colleges and universities (although again less so), many evangelical institutions of higher learning have seen significant increases in their resources and prestige in the past twenty years. The Baptist-affiliated Baylor University currently has an endowment of $645 million; Wheaton College's endowment has soared to $300 million; and five evangelical institutions have accumulated endowments that exceed $200 million.[80] Pepperdine is ranked forty-ninth among national research universities by *U.S. News and World Report*. What is more, Baylor and Wheaton each boasted more than fifty national merit scholars in the

class of 1999, and the latter is now regarded as more selective than
Carleton, Vassar, and Oberlin colleges. Together, the 101 member institutions of the Council of Christian Colleges and Universities enroll
183,000 students, a figure that increased 24 percent between 1990 and
1996 (a period in which enrollment in secular institutions rose by only
4–5 percent).[81] To be sure, many evangelical colleges continue to struggle with meager resources. At the same time, however, the quality of evangelical higher education has greatly improved.

Catholics and Evangelicals in the Knowledge Professions Today: Engaged Yet Distinctive

In his study of American evangelicals, Smith identifies the tension
between engagement and distinctiveness as a key factor in the shaping of
strong religious communities.[82] I argue that tension between engagement and distinctiveness is also a key ingredient in fostering vigorous religious participation in American public life. As has been shown, Catholics
and evangelicals are no longer isolated from the academic and professional mainstream. After Vatican II, as Turner notes, Catholics "stepped
out of a kind of intellectual ghetto and became full and equal participants
in the broader intellectual life of the United States."[83] Along the same
lines, William Shea argues that the "neo-evangelical journey from a fundamentalist sectarian pose to a constructive and critical engagement of
culture parallels that of Catholics in the twentieth century."[84] Through
the process of de-ghettoization, both groups have entered the pluralistic
dialogue of American public life.

At the same time, Catholics and evangelicals have not completely
assimilated to mainstream American culture. Smith's study, which drew
on in-depth interviews and a national survey, found that evangelicals
continue to see strong boundaries between themselves and the outside
world, regardless of social class. Despite their exposure to American pluralism (indeed, because of it), evangelicals are "clearly able to establish
strong religious identities and commitments."[85] My analysis of General
Social Survey data found that new-class evangelicals in the professional
and managerial occupations differ significantly from their secular counterparts on a host of social and political attitudes.

Consistent with the analogical sensibility of the Catholic tradition,
Catholics have moved closer to mainstream American culture than have
their evangelical brothers and sisters.[86] As early as 1969, Gleason was able

to write that "assimilation had brought the Catholic population to the point where it differed only marginally from American society at large."[87] Nevertheless, there is strong evidence that American Catholics have held on to at least some distinctive beliefs. Despite declining support for the church hierarchy, American Catholics continue to see the sacraments, social justice, helping the poor, and community as central to being Catholic, according to a 1999 Gallup poll. This is true regardless of educational attainment. Likewise, Greeley's research shows that most Catholics continue to view the world through the lens of a "Catholic imagination" that is both communitarian and sacramental. Analyzing data from the International Social Survey Program, the General Social Surveys, and the World Values Survey, Greeley found statistically significant differences between Catholics and Protestants on political, economic, and social issues.[88]

In addition to possessing distinctive religious and social attitudes, Catholics and evangelicals have maintained distinctively religious institutions, continuing to support colleges and universities, professional associations, and magazines and journals that differ appreciably from their secular counterparts. Despite fears of secularization, Nathan Hatch notes, universities such as Notre Dame and Boston College remain among the "few environments where people with deep roots in both worlds [religious and intellectual] comprise a community," providing what Wolfe calls "a different kind of education from that offered in the dominant research universities." On a much smaller scale, evangelical colleges such as Wheaton and Calvin continue to nurture an intellectual life premised on the integration of faith and learning.[89] Similarly, professional associations such as the Conference on Faith and History, the Society of Christian Philosophers, Gegrapha (an international organization of Christian journalists), and the American Catholic Philosophical Association help sustain religious approaches to professional life. The membership of some Christian professional associations is large enough to constitute a significant proportion of the total number of scholars in a given discipline (from 2 to 12 percent).[90] Finally, publications such as *Commonweal, National Catholic Reporter, Christianity Today, Christian Scholar's Review, America,* and *Books and Culture* have nurtured Catholic and evangelical communities of discourse. In most cases, the circulation of these publications exceeds that of comparable mainline Protestant publications.[91]

Although they have opened their religious subcultures to the outside world, Catholics and evangelicals have maintained what Marsden calls the

"institutional infrastructures" necessary for sustaining Christian intellectual life.[92] The result is a productive tension between religious distinctiveness and cultural engagement. Without distinctive beliefs and institutions, Catholics and evangelicals would have nothing to contribute.
Without a critical engagement with modernity, they would not be taken
seriously by their colleagues. Because Catholics and evangelicals have
maintained this balance, they have emerged as influential advocates of
religious perspectives in two fields at the heart of the knowledge professions: academia and the national news media.

Catholic and Evangelical Academics: Custodians of Public Religion

For much of the postwar era, mainline Protestants such as Reinhold Niebuhr and Paul Tillich served as the chief custodians of public religious discourse in the academy. Through Protestant divinity schools, the field of
religious studies, and a host of faculty and student organizations, they promoted the integration of faith and knowledge. Today, the picture is quite
different. Although they are still an important part of the conversation,
mainline Protestants no longer exercise hegemony over academic religious discourse. In the decades since the 1960s, Catholics and evangelicals have taken their place alongside liberal Protestants as prominent
advocates of religious viewpoints in American higher education.[93]

In American philosophy, evangelicals such as Nicholas Wolterstorff
and Alvin Plantinga, along with the Catholics Alasdair MacIntyre and
Charles Taylor, have helped lead a "renaissance of religious belief."[94] In
a field once dominated by strict empiricism, they have contributed to the
"development of a positive Christian philosophy" and the growth of the
philosophy of religion and of a well-articulated critique of Enlightenment rationality. Since its founding by evangelicals in 1978, the Society of
Christian Philosophers has grown to more than a thousand members.[95]

A similar Catholic and evangelical surge has taken place in the interdisciplinary field of American religion. A 1993 survey of five hundred
American religion scholars from a range of disciplines found that 32 percent identified themselves as evangelical Protestants, and 26 percent identified themselves as Catholics. In a field once dominated by scholars at
mainline Protestant divinity schools, self-identified liberal Protestants
constituted only 18 percent of the sample. ("Other" Protestants made up
9 percent.) By blurring the lines between their "personal faith commitments as Christians and their salaried careers as professional historians,"

according to Harry Stout and Robert Taylor, Jr., evangelical scholars have brought a "Christian particularism" into their writing.[96] In the same period, a recovery of historical consciousness among Catholics has produced a renaissance in American Catholic historiography.[97]

In political science, evangelical scholars such as John Green, James Guth, Lyman Kellstedt, and Corwin Smidt, along with the Catholics Clarke Cochran, Booth Fowler, and Ted Jelen, have played a key role in establishing the subfield of "religion and politics." For decades, writes Jelen, most American political scientists dismissed the possibility that religion "could be politically consequential." However, he notes that the volume of scholarship devoted to religion and politics has increased dramatically since the early 1980s, producing journal articles, books, a religion-and-politics section of the American Political Science Association, and courses on religion and politics. Not surprisingly, many of these scholars are also heavily involved in the activities of the Christians in Political Science group, an organization with more than one hundred dues-paying members.[98]

Once strangers to Washington think tanks, Catholics and evangelicals are now important voices in debates over religion and public policy. With the downsizing of the welfare state, public-policy experts are increasingly exploring the relevance of religion to social problems such as crime, poverty, and urban decay. More than any other groups, Catholics and evangelicals have advocated faith-based organizations as a solution to the problems of urban America. Nine of the thirteen articles in a recent issue of the *Brookings Review* titled, "What's God Got to Do with the American Experiment?" were written by Catholics or evangelicals, including John DiIulio, E. J. Dionne, Glenn Loury, and Ronald Sider. Catholics such as Dionne, Mary Ann Glendon, David Hollenbach, and Charles Taylor, together with the Jewish scholars Amitai Etzioni, Alan Ehrenhalt, and Philip Selznick, have also played an important role in the communitarian movement, making what Robert Bellah calls a "specifically Catholic contribution to a revitalized commitment to the common good."[99]

Although religious studies and theology have remained an area of mainline Protestant (or post-Protestant) dominance, Catholics and evangelicals have made inroads into these fields. The rise of liberation theology, the flowering of Catholic social ethics, and the increasing prominence of Catholic biblical studies have all contributed to the growing visibility of Catholic scholars.[100] Catholics made up a little less than one-third of a ranked list of top religious-studies scholars in a recent survey of officers, editors, editorial boards, and prize-winners of the principal religious studies journals and associations. The same study found that evangelicals have dramatically increased their share of Protestant seminary and divinity-school lectureships, rising from 13 percent in 1965–74 to 33 percent in the late 1990s. When neotraditional and neoconservative mainline scholars are added to that figure, the share of conservative Protestants is even greater. The share of enrollment in the twenty largest American seminaries belonging to evangelical institutions increased from 57 percent in 1969 to 79 percent in 1997, which means that a vast majority of seminarians in the United States are attending evangelical schools. Finally, a number of mainline Protestant divinity schools—notably, those at Yale and Duke—have hired prominent evangelicals, and Harvard University has established a visiting professorship in evangelical studies.[101]

Catholics and evangelicals, along with a number of mainline Protestant scholars, have also been key players in the 1990s effort to revitalize religion and higher education. Central to this movement is the claim that American colleges and universities have been the victims of a gradual process of secularization. Although the secularization thesis originated in sociology—most notably, in the works of Peter Berger—its application to the field of higher education is comparatively recent. Beginning with the publication of Burtchaell's "The Decline and Fall of the Christian College" in 1991 and continuing with George Marsden's *The Soul of the American University* in 1994, the cultural construction of the "secular academy" as a social problem was accomplished in large measure by the efforts of Catholic and evangelical scholars. Of the dozen or so major studies on religion and higher education published over the past ten years, eight were written by Catholics or evangelicals, including Burtchaell and Marsden.[102]

Wolfe has called Marsden the leader of the "movement to reintroduce faith into American intellectual life."[103] Indeed, a glance at the roster of the thirty-member Lilly National Seminar on Religion and Higher Education, perhaps the most distinguished gathering of scholars in the area of religion and the academy, reveals a heavy Catholic and evangelical presence—about half of the participants. The seminar was led by a Catholic, James Turner, and an evangelical, Nicholas Wolterstorff, and held at the University of Notre Dame, the nation's leading Catholic university, symbolizing the central role of Catholics and evangelicals as custodians of public religion in American higher education. Evangelical scholars have figured even more prominently in programs funded through the religion division of the Pew Charitable Trusts, receiving more than $14 million since the early 1990s.[104] Together, the financial support of Pew, Lilly, and Templeton has enabled Catholics and evangelicals, along with mainline Protestants, to heighten the visibility of religion in the academy. The Indianapolis-based Lilly Endowment has been a leading supporter of religion scholarship in the United States, and the John Templeton Foundation has poured millions of dollars into areas such as religion and science and character education.

Catholics and Evangelicals in the Media Elite: Move Over Mencken

In the 1920s, Catholics and evangelicals were frequently caricatured by national journalists. Walter Lippmann, for example, wrote that the Catholic church was "hostile to democracy and to every force that tended to make people self-sufficient," and H. L. Mencken lampooned the "yokels," "peasants," "hillbillies," "Babbits," "morons," and "mountaineers" who rallied behind William Jennings Bryan at the Scopes trial in Dayton, Tennessee.[105] Because Catholics and evangelicals were largely absent from publications such as the *New York Times, New Yorker,* and *New Republic,* they were unable to control the depiction of their religious traditions in the national media elite.

Catholics and evangelicals are no longer excluded from the media elite. The annual ranking of the top-fifty journalists by *Washingtonian* magazine routinely includes practicing Catholics such as E. J. Dionne, Maureen Dowd, Paul Gigot, Mary McGrory, Cokie Roberts, and Timothy Russert, along with the evangelical Fred Barnes. As noted earlier, a recent study found that the proportion of Catholics in the media elite rose from 12 percent in 1980 to 19 percent in 1995. During the same period, the percentage of Protestants in national journalism surged from 20 percent to 36 percent (unfortunately, the study did not distinguish evangelicals from mainline Protestants).[106] Given the new presence of evangelicals at ABC News, the *New Republic, Time, USA Today, U.S. News and World Report,* and the *Washington Post,* along with the recent formation of Gegrapha, at least a portion of this increase is probably due to the entry of evangelical Protestants into national journalism.[107]

At the national level, Catholics and evangelicals have had an important influence on the op-ed pages of America's leading newspapers and on the television talk-show circuit. In the past twenty years, at least five Catholic journalists—E. J. Dionne, Michael Kelly, Colman McCarthy, Mary McGrory, and Mark Shields—have written regular opinion columns for the *Washington Post,* bringing references to Catholic social teaching,

Boston Irish Catholicism, the anti-abortion movement, communitarian-ism, the Bible, and religion and politics into their columns. On the right, Fred Barnes and Cal Thomas have brought the perspectives of religious conservatives to the pages of the *New Republic*, the *Weekly Standard*, and the papers that belong to the Los Angeles Times Syndicate.[108] Thomas is now the most widely syndicated political columnist in the United States, appearing in more than five hundred newspapers—more than George Will, Robert Novak, and Ellen Goodman.[109] Whereas it is difficult to name a mainline Protestant opinion writer or broadcast personality who is well known for being a liberal Protestant (Bill Moyers comes the clos-est), Catholics and evangelicals have been visible representatives of their religious traditions.

As members of the media elite, Catholic and evangelical journalists are also strategically placed to influence how the press depicts their reli-gious communities. For most of the 1980s and 1990s, the top religion reporters at *Newsweek*, the *New York Times, Time, U.S. News and World Report*, and (in the 1990s) ABC News and National Public Radio were practicing Catholics and evangelicals. (Important exceptions to this pattern were Gustav Niebuhr and Ari Goldman of the *New York Times*.) During his two decades at *Time*, Richard Ostling wrote more cover stories than any other journalist at the magazine, including several on evangelicals. *Newsweek*'s Kenneth Woodward has brought an insider's perspective to the coverage of American Catholics, as exemplified by his 1971 cover story "Has the Church Lost Its Soul?" A study by a progressive media-watchdog group found that religion is "one of the favorite cover stories of *Time, Newsweek*, and *U.S. News and World Report*" and complains that "religious topics are handled with kid gloves to avoid offending the believers who are likely to buy such issues as the newsstands."[110] One reason for the kid-gloves treat-ment may be the presence of Catholic and evangelical religion reporters at the big-three weekly newsmagazines. Having moved from the outside into the elite of American journalism, both groups now possess the capac-ity to shape media constructions of themselves.

Conclusion

Catholics and evangelicals have come a long way. Once dismissed by intel-lectual and journalistic elites as ignorant hillbillies and superstitious peas-ants, they have taken their places in Ivy League universities and Washington newsrooms. In the space of a few decades, they have moved from the margins to the mainstream in the media and higher education. In the process, Catholics and evangelicals have loosened the boundaries that separate their religious subcultures from the outside world. Catholics have come to terms with modern notions of religious freedom and the developments of post–Enlightenment thought, and evangelicals have entered into dialogue with political liberalism, evolutionary biology, and postmodernism. By critically engaging the challenges of modernity and postmodernity, Catholics and evangelicals have won new respect for their religious communities.

Some scholars fear that de-ghettoization has gone too far. They worry about the secularization of Catholic and, in some cases, evangelical higher education and the accommodation of both religious subcultures to secular culture. There is an element of truth in their critiques. In an age of increasing religious pluralism, Catholics and evangelicals will have to find new ways to sustain their religious identities. Yet pessimism about the future should not overshadow the gains of the past.

Contrary to the conventional wisdom, movement into the knowledge professions has not led to the attenuation of religious belief. Rather, it has led to a growing prominence of Catholic and evangelical voices in American public life. Precisely because of upward mobility, Catholics and evangelicals were able to build colleges and universities, publishing houses, professional associations, and magazines and scholarly journals. As a result of de-ghettoization, Catholics and evangelicals are visible in American higher education and the national news media. In fields such as American religion, political science, and philosophy they have become influential advocates of religious points of view, taking their places alongside the once dominant mainline Protestant establishment. As members of the media elite, Catholics and evangelicals have brought their co-religionists into the news in a way that was unthinkable in the heyday of Mencken and Lippmann. By combining religious distinctiveness with public engagement, Catholics and evangelicals have made important contributions to American public life.

3 Faith in Journalism

The White House reporter Wes Pippert had just written an op-ed piece for the *New York Times* criticizing his colleagues for ignoring what he called the "moral dimension of the news." The piece reflected Pippert's religious convictions as an evangelical Christian, calling for a more ethically engaged approach to daily journalism. The day the article was to appear—20 January 1978—a huge snowstorm hit Washington, D.C., making the delivery of the *New York Times* impossible. At the time, Pippert thought, "How lucky." He was glad that his colleagues in the Washington press corps would not be able to read the article. "I knew this was coming out, and I was embarrassed," he recalled. "I didn't want my colleagues to see it, because I just don't wear my heart on my sleeve." That morning, Pippert and a host of White House correspondents flew with President Jimmy Carter to Atlanta on *Air Force 1* and the accompanying press plane. To Pippert's dismay, a stack of *New York Times*es lay on the tarmac, waiting for the presidential entourage. His colleagues would be able to read his piece after all. "It seemed to me that the first thing they did is to turn to that page and start shaking their heads," Pippert said. Yet, as it turned out, their reaction was "uniformly positive."

This story illustrates some of the tensions experienced by religious people in the modern professions. On the one hand, Pippert's op-ed piece for the *Times* reflected a personal desire to relate his religious convictions to the practice of everyday journalism. On the other hand, his anxiety betrayed a fundamental uncertainty about the place of religious values in professional life. Because journalism often draws a boundary between the private values of the reporter and the public world of professional journalism, Pippert's display of religious commitment risked transgressing an invisible line between journalistic objectivity and moral conviction. In a field that places great importance on the distinctions between facts and values, news and opinion, and public and private life, Pippert's article represented a potentially stigmatizing show of personal religious conviction. In his case, the fear of rejection turned out to be ill-founded. Yet a basic tension between professional and religious identities continues to shape the lives of religious people in American journalism.

As noted in chapter 1, the modern professions, including journalism, have been dominated by an ideology that emphasizes detachment, empiricism, and the separation of facts from values.[1] To maintain public credibility, professionals are expected to keep their private political and moral convictions to themselves. Among American journalists, professionalism has long been equated with the goal of objectivity. Consistent with this goal, Herbert Gans's ethnography of the newsrooms of CBS, NBC, *Time,* and *Newsweek* found that reporters practice "value exclusion," attempting to eliminate "preference statements about nation and society" from their copy.[2] This focus on professional detachment has led journalists with unconventional identities—such as gays and lesbians, socialists, and followers of the religious right—to keep quiet about their personal convictions.[3]

Given the longstanding emphasis on objectivity in American journalism, it is not difficult to see why Pippert felt awkward discussing his religious beliefs in the presence of professional colleagues. By confessing his embarrassment about wearing his heart on his sleeve, he acknowledged the difficulties of bringing religious identity into a profession committed to value exclusion.[4]

In the face of such obstacles, how did the twenty Catholic and evangelical journalists interviewed for this project talk about the relationship between faith and work? Some scholars argue that individuals tend to conceal their religious identities in American journalism, saying that silence about religion is the price of professional success. Consistent with such arguments, some of the reporters interviewed for this project complained about the secularism of the national news media. Fred Barnes called religion a "taboo subject," for example, and E. J. Dionne noted that there is an intolerance of religion in Washington journalism. Cal Thomas said, "In this town, you pay a social price for being up-front about your faith. People don't invite you to parties."[5]

In light of these complaints, one might expect Catholic and evangelical journalists to downplay the influence of religion on their work. Not surprisingly, a small proportion of the journalists contacted for this study separated religion and profession, confining their religious convictions to the private worlds of home, family, and church. At the same time, most articulated strong connections between faith and work, seeing their religious identities as intimately bound up with their journalistic careers. Building bridges between professional and religious worlds, they have found ways to translate their convictions into the language of their secular colleagues.

Catholic and evangelical journalists connect faith and work in a professional culture that prizes objectivity and detachment. First, recent developments in American journalism have made it easier to speak about religion in the American newsroom. According to a recent study, national media coverage of religion doubled during the 1990s, and the proportion of major media journalists who regularly attend religious services increased from 14 percent in 1980 to 30 percent in 1995.[6] More will be said about these developments in the concluding chapter.

Second, Catholic and evangelical reporters have benefited from a growing disillusionment with the ideology of objectivity among American journalists. There are growing indications that objectivity, once central to American definitions of journalistic professionalism, has lost much of its grip on the newsroom. The rise of advocacy journalism, investigative journalism, alternative newspapers (such as the *Village Voice*), the "new journalism," and, most recently, civic journalism, has led to a gradual transformation in the way journalists perceive their roles.[7] Surveys of professional journalists show that reporters increasingly see themselves as participants in the events that they cover rather than as mere observers.[8] Although objectivity is still an important ideal for many reporters, the term does not appear in the most recent version of the Society of Professional Journalists' Code of Ethics.[9] By appealing to trends in American journalism that run counter to the dominant ideal of objectivity, Catholic and evangelical journalists have increasingly been able to bring their own perspectives into the news.[10]

Despite their willingness to bring religion into professional life, Catholics and evangelicals have not completely abandoned a commitment to professional detachment. In the interviews, most of them expressed qualified support for the ideals of objectivity, balance, and detachment. Surprisingly, my respondents were most likely to invoke the rhetoric of objectivity immediately after displays of religious conviction. Part of the task of this chapter is to explain the paradoxical ways in which Catholics and evangelicals talk about objectivity.

This chapter describes three types of strategies Catholic and evangelical journalists have used to negotiate the boundary between professional and religious identities:

- Privatization and bracketing to separate their professional and religious identities.
- Bridging, relying on new openness to religion and on the critique of journalistic objectivity to justify the influence of religious perspectives on their work.
- Using the rhetoric of objectivity to separate and bridge professional and religious identities.

Separating Faith and Work

Catholic and evangelical journalists have used two styles of boundary management implicitly and explicitly to separate their professional and religious lives. Some have totally privatized their religious identities, categorically refusing to talk about the connections between faith and work or to identify publicly as Catholics and evangelicals. Others have bracketed religious language off from their professional lives, confining it to areas that appear to have little to do with the content of their work, such as individual moral character, spirituality, and personal relationships.

Privatization: "Who Told You I Was an Evangelical?"

In *Stigma: Notes on the Management of Spoiled Identity,* Erving Goffman describes how individuals engage in "passing" by concealing potentially stigmatizing facts about themselves. In an analogous way, secularization theorists describe how religious people privatize religious convictions in the non-public spheres of home, family, and church.[11] Three Catholic and evangelical reporters—roughly 10 percent of those contacted—refused to participate in this study and consequently can be seen as engaging in passing or privatization. Most of those who declined said they were afraid of harming their professional credibility. One reporter expressed surprise and dismay when I told her that another journalist had identified her as a fellow evangelical. She seemed upset that someone had revealed her religious identity. She explained her preference for keeping faith and work in separate compartments and said she feared opening a women's magazine someday and seeing her faith "projected" onto her journalistic work. Another reporter asked to remain anonymous because, she said, she fears that colleagues will find out that a family member works in the pro-life movement. She cited Linda Greenhouse, the *New York Times* Supreme Court reporter, who was reprimanded for taking part in a pro-choice march in Washington, D.C., and added that her publication had circulated several memos cautioning reporters against participation in political demonstrations and movements.

Because two reporters did not consent to be interviewed, it is difficult to explain their decisions to conceal their religious identities. Yet it should be noted that all three of those who engaged in passing were women. Given the continuing marginal position of women at the elite level of American journalism, and the double marginality of Catholic and evangelical women, this is not surprising.[12] In addition, two of the three women mentioned social issues such as abortion and sexuality. It may be especially difficult for religious women to reveal traditional positions on culture-wars issues, given the progressive views of many New York and Washington journalists.[13]

Bracketing Religious Language: Don Holt and Mary McGrory

An enduring tradition in Western Christianity emphasizes the sacredness of a job well done, regardless of its religious content. In the words of Martin Luther, "the Christian shoemaker does his Christian duty not by putting little crosses on the shoes, but by making good shoes, because God is interested in good craftsmanship."[14] A modern incarnation of this tradition can be found in the careers of those journalists who have distanced themselves from overtly Christian approaches to journalism. For such journalists, making "good shoes" has often been enough. Bracketing "God talk" from talk about work, they have rejected the notion that their beliefs give them an explicitly religious perspective on the news. At the same time, they have acknowledged the subtle ways that religious commitments enter into their work.

Don Holt, editor of *Fortune* magazine's international edition when I conducted the interviews, has worked in New York journalism for nearly thirty years.[15] In his former capacity as a correspondent for *Newsweek,* he covered a range of stories, including the Civil Rights Movement and presidential campaigns. I spoke with him in his office overlooking midtown Manhattan.

During the first part of the interview, in which I asked generic, open-ended questions about work, Holt did not mention his evangelical background, except to say that he had attended Wheaton, an evangelical liberal-arts college. When asked to describe the satisfaction he gets from his work, Holt said, "The satisfaction is the pure reporting aspect of getting the story and getting it right. You're also exposed to a lot of fascinating stuff at a front-row level. . . . Involving yourself with action and with events and trying to present them under deadline pressure to your audience. That's just a lot of fun." In this answer, he confined himself to citing values such as competence and excitement. In evaluating his colleagues, Holt focused on technical expertise and competence, the qualities that make up the core of contemporary American professional identity.[16] He argued the media are strong because they have "a collection of very good people," are "highly competitive," have "good pay," "attract the best," and are "very well trained."

When I asked Holt about the relationship between faith and work, he reframed the question. "I think it's faith and life," he said. "I think, I guess part of me says, I don't really see why there should be anything special about a journalist who has a particular faith any more than there should be [about] a businessman or a doctor or a lawyer."

Holt sees no special relationship between his religious identity and his work, apart from the obligation all Christians have to live out their faith in everyday life. In this view, there is no such thing as Christian journalism or Christian medicine or Christian law. In response to evangelicals who criticize the press for being secular, Holt said, "How could it be otherwise? As I understand the meaning of that term, [the press is] absolutely secular, as are the courts and the legislatures. They need to be free of any kinds of partisan, religious, or parochial concerns. It needs to be able to cover [Louis] Farrakhan as well as Billy Graham, so I don't quite understand that criticism." Here Holt draws a firm boundary between professional journalism and private religious convictions, emphasizing the journalistic values of fairness and non-partisanship.

Holt talked openly about his faith at work. In fact, when a colleague told others "she'd become born again," he said, they told her, "'Oh, you've got to go talk to Don Holt,' so I guess it's well known." Likewise, in an article for the *Wheaton Alumni* magazine, Holt wrote, "Some of the stories I have covered have had a strong moral content. In those a Christian perspective presumably led to a heightened sensitivity and, I hope, a better story." At the same time, Holt noted that, "in many others, solid journalistic ethics and practices (get the facts straight, spell the names right, cover all sides) carried me through quite well."[17]

Four other Catholic and evangelical journalists have employed a cultural style similar to Holt's, bracketing religious language from talk about work. For example, Mary McGrory, a *Washington Post* columnist, said that she loves her job because she likes "talking to people about what they do [and] going to places where other people can't go." When asked how her faith relates to her work, she replied concisely, "It doesn't come in a formal way." Although she confessed, "I would like to think I have Christian values," McGrory did not specify the links between her religious identity and the content of her columns. When asked about her columns on the Catholic bishops' support for arms control, for example, McGrory admitted that she was "very encouraged when they supported the nuclear freeze," calling the bishops "a force for good, enlightened, and forward-looking and compassionate." Yet she did not elaborate on the connections between her religious beliefs and arms control.

What did the Catholic and evangelical journalists who engaged in bracketing have in common? First, some did not feel comfortable with public displays of religious conviction. McGrory described with revulsion the mixture of religious and political language used by the Boston Irish Catholic politicians of her youth. "I came from a culture where the politicians went to the altar rail and received communion, and it was just disgusting, so I am offended by a show of religion," she said. "I don't think anybody looks up to me because I'm a Catholic. I don't think you should try and blackmail people into thinking you're special because you go to church." Consistent with McGrory's account, David J. O'Brien notes that Irish Catholic politicians often used religion to further the self-interest of the ethnic group.[18]

Second, most of the journalists who engage in bracketing have articulated what Stephen Hart calls the language of religious voluntarism, emphasizing the personal over the professional aspects of faith and morality. An important tradition within Christianity emphasizes a personal relationship with God, individual moral character, and acts of service as the heart of the Christian life. Hart argues that such voluntarism tends to confine religious faith to personal life.[19]

Multivocal Bridging Languages: Connecting Journalism and Religion

The vast majority of Catholic and evangelical journalists interviewed for this project did not privatize or bracket their religious identity. Rather, they translated their religious convictions into professional jargon, and vice versa, forging what I call multivocal bridging languages. Such combinations of professional and religious vocabularies are multivocal (literally, containing multiple voices) because they incorporate multiple meanings—professional and religious—that can elicit more than one interpretation.[20] From one angle, these vocabularies may appear religious; from another, they may not. They are called bridging languages because they allow Catholics and evangelicals to bridge the gap between professional and religious identities through modes of public discourse drawn from both American journalism and their religious communities. By drawing on frameworks, metaphors, language, and rhetoric from both religious and professional worlds, the journalists have connected faith and work.

How have Catholic and evangelical journalists articulated a fit between the cultural scripts of their religious communities and the vocabulary of professional journalism? In most cases, they have justified their use of religiously, morally, or emotionally charged language by appealing to submerged journalistic traditions that counter the dominant "ideal of objectivity."[21] These traditions include such well-institutionalized genres as advocacy and investigative journalism, as well as the longstanding tradition that views journalists as public intellectuals and social critics.[22] Still other respondents have taken their religious commitments into the workplace as part of a populist critique of the secular press. Criticizing the antireligious biases of the media elite, they have argued that the presence of Christian journalists enhances the ability of news organizations to cover middle America.

Catholics and evangelicals have used four bridging languages to fuse the vocabularies of journalism and religion: 1) the language of justice and peace; 2) the language of intellectual refinement; 3) the language of Catholic feminism; and 4) the language of populist anti-elitism.

Justice and Peace: Wesley Pippert and Colman McCarthy

By the 1960s, notes Michael Schudson, many young journalists had grown frustrated with the value-free posture of their profession, faulting mainstream journalism for masking the political assumptions of the news with the language of objectivity. Meanwhile, young, college-educated journalists brought the concerns of campus social movements into the newsroom. In this climate, new journalistic genres emphasized the role of

the reporter as an advocate for social change. By the 1980s, elements of
the new ethically attuned journalism had been absorbed by the journalistic mainstream.[23]

During this period, parts of the evangelical Protestant and Roman
Catholic communities moved to engage issues raised by the social movements of the 1960s. Many Catholics became involved in the civil-rights
and antiwar struggles through religious channels such as the Catholic
Worker movement.[24] Progressive evangelicals also began to call for
greater Christian political engagement, appropriating biblical themes
such as social justice, peace, and community.[25] By the 1980s, the focus on
justice and peace had become part of the Catholic mainstream, while the
evangelical left continued to draw the support of many evangelical professionals, despite the rise of the religious right.[26]

Four of the Catholic and evangelical journalists in the survey have
combined the journalistic critique of American society with religious
themes of social justice and peace. The evangelical Wesley Pippert, a
reporter for United Press International (UPI) from 1955 to 1988, has epitomized this effort to articulate a fit between journalism and the language
of justice and peace. I interviewed Pippert in his office at the University
of Missouri's Washington journalism program, where he serves as director. Personal notes from Watergate Judge John Sirica and former President Jimmy Carter hung on the wall, visible reminders of the years Pippert spent covering Watergate, the Carter White House, Congress, and
the Arab–Israeli conflict.

Throughout the interview, Pippert focused on what he calls the
"moral dimension of public issues." In the 1970s, he gradually came to the
conclusion that "the pursuit of truth would automatically lead a reporter
to check out the dimensions of justice and peace in whatever the assign-
ment was." When I asked him how he came to see his writing this way,
Pippert immediately invoked his religious identity: "While I'm a Christian,
I didn't know what that meant for sure in terms of my job for a long, long
time, and Christians believe that faith should impact on every aspect of
your life, and I wasn't certain how it impacted on my job." Pippert said he
began to examine how the Bible addressed the concept of truth, which
he sees as the central focus of a journalist's work:

> The Old Testament is rich in these discussions. I found that in almost every
> case that truth is discussed, that justice is discussed, and peace at the same
> time and uprightness. So it seemed to me that there was an organic relation-

ship among truth, peace, and justice and uprightness. And if that's the case, and the job of the journalist is to pursue truth, that's how I came to the conclusion that the pursuit of truth in any story would lead the reporter into issues of justice and peace.

In addition to framing his work in the biblical vocabulary of progressive evangelicalism, Pippert was able to articulate his focus on justice and peace in the language of professional journalism:

> What I'm pleading for is [that] we need to get to the heart of the story. [T]hat will push us into the dimensions of justice and peace. And if you want to say that in a news way, you could say, "Get the lead right." That's what I'm saying: "Get the lead." There's nothing controversial about that. . . . I think that what I drape my reasoning around may be alien to some people—the idea that this really has its origin in scripture, and the way I flesh it out saying this will compel you to deal with issues of justice and peace. Not everyone may be willing to buy that, but who can disagree with saying that the reporter ought to get to the heart of the story?

In restating his idea "in a news way," Pippert translates the biblical themes of justice and peace into journalistic verbiage without eliminating their normative focus. The journalist's notion of the core of the story and the need to "get the lead right" serve as multivocal phrases that Pippert can overlay with biblical meanings.

Pippert also said that the mass media "must take note of wrong and oppressive conditions in our society and write stories for the express purpose of bringing about justice and peace." Thus, he situated himself in a submerged tradition in journalism that dates back to the muckrakers.[27] Richard Hofstadter and Bruce Evensen point out that the reformist impulse of progressive-era journalism can be traced back to the small-town, evangelical roots of many of its journalists. Indeed, muckraking reporters frequently used the language of social justice to frame crusades against the political machines and giant business monopolies of their time.[28] In the 1960s, journalists revived this tradition, focusing on racial injustice, the Vietnam war, and the plight of America's poor.[29] Pippert fondly recalled this era of ethically engaged reporting. "In recent history, when the media unleashed the truth, it resulted in the eradication of injustice and wrong," he said. "The coverage of the blacks in the 1960s helped arouse the dulled conscience of the American people and led to the passage of a body of law providing rights for all men and women, regardless of color."[30]

Several other journalists, including Colman McCarthy, a *Washington Post* columnist at the time of the interviews, have used the language of peace and justice to bridge professional and religious worlds.[31] When asked to describe his most meaningful stories, McCarthy immediately launched into normative themes: "Well, I like to write about people who are on the margins, who are voiceless, who have been locked out of the power system, and do what I can to align myself with their hopes for reform, or to ease their suffering somehow. I think that's a legitimate use of your journalistic skills. Otherwise you're just an entertainer. Other columnists are very entertaining writers, but I don't know what they do as far as social reform goes."

He criticized other journalists for being "very weak on understanding the theories of non-violent social change. . . . [T]here is not really an understanding of pacifism in American journalism." McCarthy described his columns as "a faith-based way of writing," and asked, "How many people have written about St. James on the op-ed page, or Amos or Isaiah on the op-ed page?"

What are the social sources of the language of justice and peace? All of the journalists who have used this bridging language have social ties to parts of the evangelical and Catholic communities that emphasize social activism. Pippert, for example, came out of the progressive wing of evangelicalism, a network with a strong base in evangelical colleges and parachurch groups. Pippert earned a master's degree in biblical literature from Wheaton College while working for UPI in the late 1960s, when evangelical scholars began to turn their attention to biblical themes of social justice. Over the years, he has given hundreds speeches at evangelical colleges and parachurch groups on diverse topics that include Christianity, politics, and journalistic ethics. McCarthy came out of a network within American Catholicism that strongly emphasizes social justice. After graduating from Spring Hill College, a small, Jesuit liberal-arts school, in the early 1960s, McCarthy entered a Trappist monastery for five years. In the monastery, he said, he "learned a little about religion, and not just Christianity. . . . I studied Hebrew. . . . I studied Hinduism, I studied Buddhism." Through his involvement with the Trappists, McCarthy also developed ties to the Catholic Worker movement and its charismatic founder, Dorothy Day. "I knew Dorothy Day," he said. "She came to the monastery in 1962. Gave a wonderful talk. . . . Dorothy was wonderful.

When I came out of the monastery, I visited her a lot in New York City, and she said, 'Go use your skills for journalism. You can do as much for the church and human beings, as you'll ever do anywhere else.' " Both the Trappists and the Catholic Worker movement were important nodes of the 1960s' Catholic counterculture, which stressed devotion to the poor, pacifism, and social justice.[32]

Instead of translating religious language into secular terminology, this radical wing of Catholicism focused on defining "issues and responses in Christian terms."[33] Through exposure to the progressive wings of the evangelical and Catholic subcultures, Pippert and McCarthy gained access to the bridging language of justice and peace. Because of the shift in journalism towards greater social concern, they have been able to articulate a fit between these normative religious themes and their professional milieus.

The Language of Intellectual Refinement: Peter Steinfels and E. J. Dionne

In an era in which scholars lament the death of the public intellectual, one category of intellectuals has enjoyed something of a renaissance: Catholic and evangelical writers have served as bridges between the worlds of religion and public intellectual discourse.[34] Nowhere has this bridging role been more apparent than in the career of Peter Steinfels. While writing the biweekly "Beliefs" column for the *New York Times*, Steinfels has held academic posts at two Catholic universities, Georgetown and Notre Dame; written occasionally for the Catholic press, especially *Commonweal;* participated in spirited discussions of the future of Catholic higher education; and helped lead discussions of the role of religion in the media. Although he is careful to differentiate his role as a Catholic intellectual from his role as a reporter, Steinfels clearly has brought a liberal Catholic sensibility to his job as a journalist.

Steinfels, along with E. J. Dionne of the *Washington Post,* has used the language of particularizing refinement to bridge journalism and American Catholicism. Steven Brint, who uses the term "particularizing refinement," calls this the dominant rhetorical approach of intellectual publications such as the *Atlantic Monthly, New Republic, New York Times,* and *New York Review of Books*. Instead of emphasizing explicit ideological claims, intellectual refinement focuses on bringing out the nuances and ambiguities of a debate, debunking established interpretations, and dissecting the logic of arguments. Rather than making moral arguments it gives the appearance of intellectual cultural capital by showing great facility in analyzing the underlying categories of the debate.[35]

As in the world of New York intellectuals, liberal Catholic intellectual circles have stressed the importance of nuanced arguments, ambiguity, and finely grained distinctions, rejecting polarized conceptions of the political order. Since the 1950s, liberal Catholic intellectuals have attempted to distance themselves from both authoritarian forms of Catholicism and aggressively secular versions of liberalism.[36] Because liberal Catholicism holds a complicated position on the political spectrum, it is ideally situated to serve as a bridge between left and right, religious and secular. In the interviews, Steinfels and Dionne used the rhetoric of nuance and ambiguity to challenge oversimplified accounts of religion and politics.

I interviewed Steinfels in the downtown Manhattan offices of *Commonweal*, the liberal Catholic weekly he edited before taking his current job at the *New York Times*.[37] Before he went to the *Times*, he was often quoted in the press as a "liberal Catholic" spokesman. Although he is no longer on staff, his ties to *Commonweal* have remained strong: the magazine is currently edited by his wife, Margaret O'Brien Steinfels. In addition to editing and writing a column for *Commonweal*, Steinfels worked at the Hastings Center, a medical-ethics clearinghouse, and wrote often for publications such as *Dissent* and the *New York Times Book Review*. Steinfels joined the *Times* rich in the cultural capital of public intellectual discourse. In the interview, he said he probably was hired because the paper saw him as someone who could "write and interpret religion in terms of the larger world of politics and secular events." Steinfels speculated that his self-identified liberal background was also an advantage. He pointed out that A. M. Rosenthal and Arthur Gelb, editors of the *Times* when Steinfels was hired, appeared to want someone in the tradition of John Cogley, a famous editor of *Commonweal* who went on to cover religion for the *Times*.

When asked about his journalistic heroes, Steinfels cited the "historical and moral insight" of those he called engaged journalists, naming non-Catholic intellectuals such as Hannah Arendt, Albert Camus, and George Orwell, and Catholics such as G. K. Chesterton and John Cogley. Throughout the interview, Steinfels used Brint's rhetoric of particularizing refinement, focusing on the underlying categories of public debates

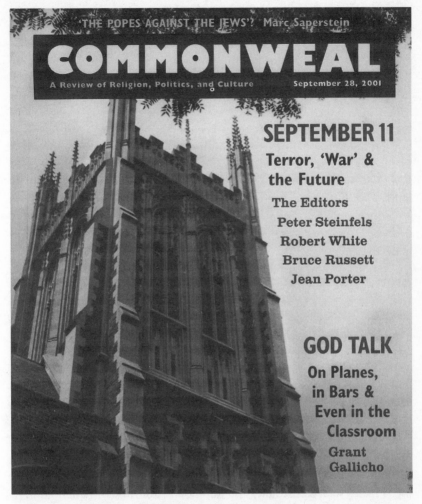

'THE POPES AGAINST THE JEWS'? Marc Saperstein

COMMONWEAL
A Review of Religion, Politics, and Culture   September 28, 2001

SEPTEMBER 11
Terror, 'War' &
the Future

The Editors
Peter Steinfels
Robert White
Bruce Russett
Jean Porter

GOD TALK
On Planes,
in Bars &
Even in the
Classroom
Grant
Gallicho

Commonweal magazine has long been a center for liberal Catholic intellectual life in the United States. In this issue, Peter Steinfels of the *New York Times* and the political scientist Bruce Russett reflect on the 11 September 2001 tragedy. Cover design by Christopher Young; cover art by George Spelvin. (© 2001 Commonweal Foundation; reprinted with permission. For subscriptions, call toll-free: 1-888-495-6755.)

rather than taking a stand himself. His major strength as a journalist, he said, was his ability to "inform readers of a development in the world of religion . . . with some degree of nuance and complexity, [in a] part of our society which is underreported . . . and fit into oversimplified and blatantly inaccurate categories."

Steinfels has often used the rhetoric of particularizing refinement to criticize media coverage of religion. At a forum on religion and the media sponsored by *Commonweal,* he faulted journalists for applying the "winners and losers" framework of politics and sports to the world of religion. Instead, he said, reporters need to "spell out the nuances and qualifications attached to almost any religious statement."[38] And in an essay published in Harvard University's *Nieman Reports,* he criticized the use of "pre-existing plot lines," which too often "ultimately descend from the tension between religious faith and the 18th-Century Enlightenment."[39] Finally, he has called attention to his own attempts to move beyond reified liberal–conservative frameworks: "I . . . wanted to give voice and visibility to those people and positions that get squeezed out when conflicts are reported only in terms of two sides—conservatives and liberals; orthodox and dissenters—rather than the spectrum of perspectives that normally exists."[40]

Significantly, when Steinfels was the editor of *Commonweal,* he often used language that is identical to the kind he uses today. For example, in an appeal to the magazine's supporters, he wrote that "a journal which maintains its convictions while respecting complexity and ambiguity has a special role to play amidst today's polarizations."[41] In fact, this rhetoric of nuance has characterized much of liberal Catholic discourse in the postwar era, as when one *Commonweal* contributor in the early 1950s lamented that "Catholic attitudes have been all black or white, without distinguishing the neutral grays."[42] This metaphorical focus on neutral grays, as opposed to polarized blacks and whites, reflects liberal Catholicism's ambiguous position on the religious and political spectrum. Although *Commonweal* has often embraced liberal positions on economic and foreign-policy issues, it has tended toward cultural conservatism on social issues such as sexuality, the family, and abortion.[43] When Steinfels said that he seeks to bring voice and visibility to the spectrum of perspectives between right and left, he was using the same kind of rhetoric.[44]

Three other Catholic journalists interviewed for this project, including Dionne, have used the language of intellectual refinement. When I asked him who has influenced his political views, Dionne located himself at the intersection of a heterogenous blend of secular and religious intellectual movements, journals, and thinkers:

> Well, I read a lot. As a lover of opinions, I either currently subscribe to, or have at some point in my life, almost every conceivable journal of opinion—

obviously not every one. Being Catholic has influenced everything I see and I think. It's influenced me in a certain communitarian direction, which is where the church's social teachings lead, and it also made me anticommunist and critical of that style of the left.... A second would be the democratic socialists around *Dissent:* Michael Harrington, Irving Howe, Michael Walzer, whom I took a couple courses from in college. That view of the world had a lot of influence, still has a lot of influence, on me. And oddly, the libertarians had a lot of influence on me for a while because I found I admired the consistency of their views and their exultation of human freedom.... Reading Reinhold Niebuhr, and especially *Children of Light, Children of Darkness,* was a very important experience to me.... The Catholic Worker [movement] and the Catholic pacifists during the Vietnam war had a lot of influence on me.

In this answer, Dionne expresses his affection for liberal Catholic social teaching, communitarianism, democratic socialism, libertarianism, Niebuhrian realism, and the Catholic Worker movement. In addition, he links himself to the intellectuals surrounding *Dissent,* including his former teacher at Harvard, Michael Walzer. This bricolage of religious and secular influences from across the political spectrum has allowed him to project a multifaceted public self that can resonate with a wide range of religious and secular publics. Like Steinfels, Dionne has rejected an ideologically polarized stance toward the political debate and sees liberal Catholicism as a potential bridge between the left and the right. At a forum on Catholics and American culture in Washington, he argued that Catholic social thought is "unusually well placed to overcome what has become a fruitless debate in our country between contemporary liberals and contemporary conservatives."[45]

How have journalists such as Steinfels and Dionne articulated a fit between liberal Catholicism and an intellectual approach to journalism? Most Catholic journalists who have employed the language of intellectual refinement have had multiple points of access to religious and secular intellectual networks. Several grew up in families that emphasized the importance of political and religious intellectual involvement. Steinfels was raised in a household that subscribed to *Commonweal,* the *Catholic Worker,* and other religious intellectual journals, with a father who worked as a religious artist. "My father's daily effort as an artist to glorify God's house and reinforce the church's prayer made it clear that my religion was neither a Sunday affair nor a 'spiritual' thing," he said. "It was instead a matter of one's everyday job. It was a matter of all that one did with

whatever skills and materials were at hand: the words of a prayer and
one's ability to mean them, paint and one's ability to spread it, and school-
books and one's ability to study them."[46]

"If I had any life plan," Steinfels said, "it was simply to combine intellectual work with engaged public commentary as a writer." Similarly,
Dionne said that he grew up in a family that got four Sunday newspapers,
a "very politically heterogenous family where we always argued about
politics, and so I ended up with affection for a lot of points of view I disagreed with."

In addition, most of these Catholic journalists were exposed to high-
cultural-capital religious thought through higher education. Steinfels
forged important ties to other young Catholic intellectuals as an undergraduate at Loyola University in Chicago and solidified his academic cre-
dentials by earning a doctorate in European intellectual history at Columbia University in New York. Dionne's undergraduate education at Harvard
University exposed him to academic luminaries such as Harvey Cox, Nathan Glazer, and Michael Walzer. Cox introduced Dionne to the thought
of Reinhold Niebuhr, America's foremost public theologian, and Glazer
and Walzer familiarized him with the legacy of the New York intellectuals.[47]

Most important, all of the Catholic journalists who have used the rhetoric of refinement have maintained loose ties to the network of liberal
Catholic intellectuals surrounding *Commonweal* magazine. As Steinfels
recalled in an interview with *Newsweek*, "When I was a student, there was
a whole series of conveyor belts for someone like me. . . . I fell in with
Catholic intellectuals, and was conveyed by that network to New York to
work at *Commonweal*."[48] Similarly, Dionne has been an occasional contributor to the magazine since the 1970s and called himself a "*Commonweal* Catholic" in the interview. (His *Washington Post* column is regularly
reprinted in *Commonweal*.) The *Commonweal* circle extended to other
Catholic journalists in this study, including Don Wycliff of the *Chicago
Tribune*, Kenneth Woodward of *Newsweek*, and Cokie Roberts of ABC
News/National Public Radio. Charles Kadushin argues that small magazines such as *Commonweal* perform an institutional gatekeeping role by
certifying the intellectual reputations of those who write for them.[49]
Indeed, the liberal Catholic network surrounding *Commonweal* is partic-
ularly suited to cultivating an intellectual style that bridges the world of
Catholicism and the wider intellectual community.

Since the 1950s, liberal Catholics have emphasized the theme of breaking out of the so-called Catholic ghetto and participating in the larger dia-

logue of American intellectual life. David O'Brien argues that liberal Catholics historically have emphasized a pluralistic "balancing act" among multiple publics—ecclesiastical, political, and intellectual and cultural.[50] In the interview, Steinfels described how his career trajectory as a liberal Catholic in secular settings prepared him to speak to multiple publics:

> I went to an Ivy League graduate school. I worked in the area of medical and scientific ethics for part of a decade. I wrote a book on politics that wasn't in any specific way religious. . . . One has to exist in a milieu where the assumptions that are common for conversation, the terms and categories, tend to be those that are not religious, and . . . even when you are explicitly religious, you have to present them in ways that also translate those beliefs or views or experiences into something analogous, in general terms, that people from nonreligious as well as other religious traditions might be able to connect with.

This ability to "translate" religious language into more general terms has allowed liberal Catholic journalists to convert religious identity into a form of cultural capital at newspapers such as the *New York Times* and the *Washington Post*. By translating liberal Catholicism's concern for ambiguity, nuance, and the "neutral grays" into the language of particularizing refinement, they have bridged the worlds of religious and secular journalism.

The Language of Catholic Feminism: Cokie Roberts

The pictures in Cokie Roberts's office speak volumes about her special place in American public life. A signed photograph of the young Corinne Boggs (her maiden name) standing next to Lyndon and Lady Bird Johnson graces the wall next to the door.[51] Known for her high-profile role as a celebrity journalist, Roberts is also a daughter in a powerful Louisiana political family. Her father, Hale Boggs, served sixteen terms as a congressman from New Orleans, rising to the rank of House majority leader before his death in a plane crash in 1972. Her mother, Lindy Boggs, served as U.S. ambassador to the Vatican after a long career in the House of Representatives, where she took over her husband's seat. Her late sister, Barbara Boggs Sigmund, was well on her way to becoming a prominent political figure.

Consistent with her Louisiana Catholic roots, Roberts is a self-described "serious Catholic" who attends church "pretty much every Sunday," a fact that has become increasingly well known to her viewers. Less well known is Roberts's considerable familiarity with Catholic intellectual life. Unlike many on-air personalities, she is able to describe the influence of serious religious thinkers on her intellectual development. Educated by Sacred Heart nuns at Stone Ridge, a Catholic girls' school in suburban Washington, D.C., Roberts recalls reading everything from Augustine and Aquinas to John Courtney Murray, John Tracy Ellis, and Teilhard de Chardin.

Roberts came of age in the years immediately before the Second Vatican Council, and, she says, she grew up with a "very strong sense that *we* were the church. It was not a sense that there were a bunch of guys in Rome who handed down truth. . . . [T]ruth was something you seek, not something that you had been handed. . . . Once you had your First Communion, you were on your own, with the help of the nuns, to explore." Roberts added, "That really was the tradition in which women like me were raised by Sacred Heart nuns." She "did not have one of these childhoods of knuckle-rapping nuns. Quite to the contrary. These were elegant ladies who were highly educated and very sophisticated."

At first glance, Roberts's intellectual influences seem to identify her as yet another representative of liberal Catholicism in American journalism. Her participation in a recent *Commonweal* forum on religion and the media shows that she is a part of the same intellectual network inhabited by Steinfels and Dionne. She even wrote a blurb for Dionne's book *Why Americans Hate Politics*.[52] Yet Roberts is much more outspoken than either Steinfels or Dionne in her support of the ideals of feminism and the modern women's movement. As a 1964 graduate of Wellesley College, Roberts witnessed and participated in what she called "this great social movement of the century."[53] Along with her close friends Linda Wertheimer and Nina Totenberg, Roberts helped bring women's voices into the news at National Public Radio (NPR) during a period that saw great advances for women across the journalistic profession.[54] At NPR, gender integration sometimes attracted criticism. "One horrified colleague called our little corner the 'Fallopian Jungle,' " Roberts said. "We had suffered discrimination and harassment at a time when that just was simply the way it was, and now we were in positions of some influence in our organization."[55]

Part of the rhetoric of feminism in American journalism is that women bring a distinct perspective to the newsroom. In her reflections on gender and the press, Roberts clearly articulates this claim, saying that women "brought a different sensibility to political reporting."[56] In subtle ways,

Roberts has also brought the sensibility of a moderate Catholic feminism to her work as a broadcast journalist.

Although the television and radio-news formats have limited her ability to express her private opinions (she also writes a column), Roberts has occasionally revealed her thoughts on gender and the church. This was certainly the case on an April 1996 episode of *This Week with David Brinkley* in which Roberts, along with Brinkley, Sam Donaldson, and George Will, interviewed Boston's Cardinal Bernard Law and U.S. Secretary of Health and Human Services Donna Shalala about their views on abortion. Roberts confronted the cardinal with the statistics showing that Catholics are more likely to have abortions than Protestants and asked him whether he should "be looking [to his] own flock and seeing what the problem is there rather than making political statements about this."[57]

Significantly, Roberts waited until she was interviewing Shalala to identify herself as a practicing Catholic, reminding Shalala, "You and I have met at many a mass." Although she asked Shalala an especially difficult question about partial-birth abortions, subtle indications were present that Roberts had more in common with the secretary than with the cardinal. In particular, Roberts's use of the pronouns "you" and "I" seemed to place her and Shalala on the same level, even as her failure to identify herself as a member of the cardinal's "flock" seemed to distance her from the hierarchy.[58]

Roberts's views became apparent toward the end of the program, when David Brinkley asked his colleagues who should decide whether a woman may have an abortion. He addressed the query directly to Roberts, who, sounding more like Shalala than Cardinal Law, noted the pro-choice sentiments of many American women. "Most of us would support . . . the idea that women can make moral decisions for themselves," she said.[59] Although it was unclear whether Roberts was speaking for herself or for all American women, her use of the phrase "most of us would support" seemed to show that she was on the side of reproductive choice.

Roberts has been criticized by progressive media critics for failing to bring an "aggressive feminist analysis of Washington power" to her work as a journalist.[60] Yet in other settings she has articulated positions that are at odds both with the teachings of the Catholic hierarchy and with the women's movement. In the syndicated column she writes with her husband, Steve Roberts, she has criticized both pro-choice and anti-abortion activists for ignoring the wisdom of the "sensible center."[61] And although both Robertses have expressed strong disagreement with Pope John Paul II on the role of women in the church, they have also called him a "bright beacon of moral authority."[62]

In *Defecting in Place: Women Claiming Responsibility for Their Own Spiritual Lives,* Miriam Therese Winter and her co-authors use the phrase "reformative feminists" to describe women who want "some changes in the present structure [of the church] but who prefer to keep the prevailing denominational and congregational structures intact." They contrast reformative feminists with "transformative feminists," who "promote systemic change throughout the church in leadership, liturgy, and theology."[63] Given Roberts's ambivalence about abortion, as well as the relatively few instances in which she has publicly criticized official church teaching, it makes sense to call her a reformative rather than a transformative Catholic feminist. That said, it is clear that Roberts brings a perspective to her job that is almost entirely absent among the male Catholic respondents interviewed for this study. By combining a mildly feminist critique of American journalism, most recently in her book *We are Our Mothers' Daughters,* with a reformative version of Catholic feminism, Roberts has used the language of the women's movement to bridge the worlds of journalism and religion.

The Language of Populist Anti-Elitism: Fred Barnes

One morning in October 1984, Fred Barnes found himself on the telephone with Chuck Conconi, the *Washington Post*'s gossip columnist. The night before, Barnes had served as a panelist in the presidential debate between Walter Mondale and Ronald Reagan, asking each candidate whether he considered himself a born-again Christian.[64] Confronting Barnes with his own question, Conconi said, "I understand that you're a born-again Christian. Is that true?" Barnes did not know how to answer and, he said, he panicked: "The fact was that I did consider myself a born-again Christian, but being in journalism, I knew what most journalists thought that meant. You know that you were a follower of Jerry Falwell and maybe even Bob Jones and that you were a narrow, bigoted person, and that you were a fundamentalist. And that's not what I was, so I said, 'Well, can I call you back? I'm working on something,' which I wasn't."

Later that day, he called Conconi back and gave a "long-winded, highly nuanced explanation of what kind of a born-again Christian I was, and it was preposterous," he said. The lead sentence of the story in the

A veteran print and broadcast journalist, the evangelical Fred Barnes
was a co-founder of the neoconservative *Weekly Standard*. (Courtesy
Fred Barnes and *Weekly Standard*.)

Washington Post's style section read: "Fred Barnes, the *Baltimore Sun*
reporter who raised the 'born again' question at last Sunday's Reagan–
Mondale debate in Louisville, said yesterday that he probably could be
considered a 'born-again' Christian, but added, 'it is not something I go
around calling myself.' "[65]

Barnes publicly identified himself as an evangelical at a time that very
few New York and Washington journalists would have considered themselves "born-again" Christians. Eight years earlier, NBC's John Chancellor
followed a discussion of Jimmy Carter's religious beliefs with the comment, "By the way, we've checked this out. Being 'born again' is not a
bizarre, mountaintop experience. It's something common to many millions of Americans—particularly if you're Baptist."[66] As noted earlier, a
survey of the media elite conducted in 1979 and 1980 found that only 8
percent of New York and Washington journalists attended church or syn-
agogue at least once a week.[67] By calling attention to the religious backgrounds of the candidates, Barnes was focusing on a part of American culture that his colleagues knew little about.

Although the situation has improved somewhat since the mid-1980s, many Catholic and evangelical journalists continue to feel like religious minorities. (Evangelicals are in fact a minority in New York and Washington journalism.) Drawing on a long tradition of populist anti-elitism, along with the neoconservative movement's critique of the new class, they have criticized the secularism of the press. Contrasting the religiosity of the country with the religious tone-deafness of their colleagues, they have charged that the news media are incapable of representing the views of middle America.[68]

In his interview for this study, Barnes noted that the press is "not even aware of how strongly religious a country the United States is." He said that "reporters are incredibly out of touch with the rest of the population outside the beltway." In Washington, "you have now basically in journalism an upper-middle-class educated elite that dominates national journalism in a way it didn't used to and that is not in line with the thinking of the rest of the country on political [grounds], on religious grounds, on values grounds, on practically anything. The fact is, Washington has become more like New York and less like the rest of the country over the last several decades." While politicians "have to go back to their districts," he added, most journalists "spend their time here in Washington." This insularity "gives you a warped view of America and the world."

Barnes has been equally critical of the national media in speeches and articles, noting the "peculiar bias in mainstream journalism against traditional religions."[69] In one column, he wrote that he has a political problem with American movies, because "in most thrillers, it's some conspiratorial right-wing group or religious sect or business mogul who's to blame for whatever bad occurs."[70] In another, he criticized the *Washington Post* for describing Christian conservatives involved in national politics as "largely poor, uneducated, and easy to command."[71]

Barnes also said that he has not felt stigmatized or victimized because of his religious beliefs. The veteran political reporter and commentator is recognized as one of the top journalists in Washington.[72] At the same time, his faith has set him apart from many of his peers. When I asked him whether he felt different from his colleagues, he said:

I'm the most conservative person here. . . . Very few of them are actively religious, particularly committed Christians, very few here in particular but elsewhere in journalism, as well. . . . I'm married, have four kids, and live in the suburbs. Most people here are single, younger, and live in Washington. We

have remarkably different lifestyles. I spend my weekends going to my kids'
athletic events and church and Bible study groups and things like that, and
they're doing other things, things that single people, single secular people, do
in an urban environment.

At the time of the interview, Barnes was senior editor and White
House correspondent for the *New Republic,* where he was highly regarded
for his reporting on the Bush and Clinton administrations. He was also a
regular panelist on *The McLaughlin Group.* In 1995, Barnes left the *New
Republic* to found the neoconservative *Weekly Standard,* along with John
Podhoretz and William Kristol, where he is now executive editor.[73]More
recently, he has served as co-host of the Fox News Channel's *Beltway Boys,*
a chief correspondent for PBS's *National Desk,* and a commentator for
CBS This Morning.

Fox News and the *Weekly Standard* are owned by the conservative
media executive Rupert Murdoch. Both see themselves as alternatives to
the liberal media. The neoconservative movement that gave birth to the
Weekly Standard has long been critical of the media elite. In the 1970s,
Irving Kristol, William Kristol's father, wrote an article criticizing the
"adversary culture" of the academic and cultural elite, articulating a neoconservative critique of the new-class occupations.[74] The critique was
later picked up by religious conservatives, who blamed journalists and
academics for the "perceived social and cultural decline in America."[75]

The stated mission of the Fox News Channel is to present the news in
a "fair and balanced" manner, suggesting that the mainstream media has
fallen short in this regard. Although Fox has been called the "most biased
name in news" by liberal media critics, Marshall Sella writes that the men
and women at the network "see themselves and market themselves as cor-
rectors of an old injustice: namely the hegemony of liberal bias in television news." By promoting a "populist aesthetic," Sella notes, Fox has attracted a large and loyal audience in the "'red' states—the Bush-leaning
segment of the country sandwiched between the coasts."[76] Through journalists such as Barnes, Bill O'Reilly, and Cal Thomas, Fox has served as an
outlet for the views of conservative Catholics, evangelicals, and other critics of bicoastal liberalism, although the network recently hired the liberal
Geraldo Rivera.[77]

In recent years, Barnes has called on evangelicals to "go into the
mainstream media," arguing that this is the "only way the negativity, cyn-
icism and cruelty of the present media will change."[78] In appearances

before groups such as the Association of Christian Collegiate Media and Gegrapha, he has urged his co-religionists to "shine a Christian light into the newsroom."[79] Barnes made a similar point in a column for the *Weekly Standard*, noting that the secular media needs Christian journalists who can "bring the Christian worldview to bear on journalism, [and save] secular journalism from its self-destructive, amoral tendencies."[80]

At first glance, this emphasis on Christian perspectives seems to be in tension with the journalistic ideology of objectivity. Indeed, Barnes has been criticized from the left for being a "populist of the right."[81] Yet by portraying Christian journalists as an antidote to secular bias, Barnes has suggested that a newsroom with more evangelicals would be less, not more, biased. Invoking the principle that American journalism should "reflect the society it observes and interprets," this argument echoes the claims of others—such as women, minorities, and gays—that diversity enhances fairness.[82] By blending the journalistic emphasis on covering all sides with a populist critique of media bias, evangelicals such as Barnes and Cal Thomas have articulated a forceful argument for the inclusion of religious voices. Whether this argument ultimately will prevail may depend on the viewing preferences of the audience. Judging by the ratings of Fox News, there is a good chance that it will.

The Rhetoric of Objectivity

Sociologists argue that professionals use objectivity rhetoric to separate themselves symbolically from other social worlds, reinforcing their professional authority and autonomy. Surprisingly, the journalists interviewed for this study have used objectivity rhetoric—or, in some cases, rhetoric about truth—to both separate and bridge the professional and religious worlds.[83]

Objectivity Rhetoric as a Fence

When asked to define their attitudes toward professional notions of objectivity, more than half of the journalists in the study drew a boundary between their private views and their professional writing. Paradoxically, objectivity rhetoric was most passionately mobilized immediately following displays of religious or moral conviction. In fact, many of the journalists who used bridging language to unite their professional and religious worlds also used objectivity language to reassert their professional detachment.

Steinfels drew firm boundaries to separate his professional and religious life following his use of the bridging language of intellectual refinement. After describing the moral engagement of such intellectual heroes as Hannah Arendt and John Cogley, both of whom inspired him as a writer, Steinfels noted that "there is a difference between what they were doing and what the first responsibility of a reporter is." When asked how his job as a religion correspondent for the *New York Times* compared to morally engaged journalism, Steinfels made a sharp distinction between the evaluative journalism that he produced at *Commonweal* and his reporting for the *Times*.[84] "In leaving *Commonweal* and going to the *Times* there really was a certain break with that.... My first responsibility, which I was quite happy to insist on, was to try and just report stories.... The first objective was to tell people what was happening without making any kind of strong evaluation of whether this development was good or bad. And that's a certain amount of sacrifice. It certainly cramps your prose style a little bit."

Some of the interviewees did not talk about objectivity until they were asked about it. For those respondents, objectivity served as a convenient script for describing the professional role of the journalist. But for some journalists, the rhetoric of objectivity did more: It helped restore the line between professional and religious worlds after the line had become blurred. By qualifying displays of moral or religious engagement with the use of objectivity language, these journalists called attention to the boundary between news reporting and more normative genres of writing. (This boundary is especially important for journalists who have worked in other genres.) Gaye Tuchman argues objectivity language is a credibility-enhancing "strategic ritual" that journalists use to counter potential threats to their professionalism.[85] For some journalists, the potential threat lies in appearing to be a political activist; for others, such as Steinfels, it lies in appearing to be a morally engaged intellectual. For these journalists, the rhetoric of objectivity restored the symbolic boundary between news and opinion, facts and values, and the professional and religious worlds.

Objectivity Rhetoric as a Bridge

Significantly, the language of objectivity and truth was not always used to separate professional and religious worlds. Many Catholic and evangelical journalists also used the rhetoric of objectivity to bridge these worlds. They harmonized the empiricist focus of journalistic objectivity with the normative emphasis of religious language by talking about truth. The term "truth" has a rich and heterogenous array of meanings that resonate in both the religious and the professional worlds. The Catholic and evangelical subcultures have intellectual and folk traditions that emphasize epistemological realism, as well as the supernatural and moral dimensions of truth.[86] In the journalistic profession, truth tends to be equated with the accurate reporting of empirical facts and the balanced representation of all sides in a debate. Although the religious and journalistic definitions of truth are not entirely compatible, the Catholic and evangelical journalists usually downplayed the potential conflicts in meaning.

For example, a number of Catholic journalists forged a bridging language of "truth," combining journalism's liberal and utilitarian emphasis on the marketplace of ideas with a liberal Catholic defense of pluralism, dialogue, and empirical inquiry.[87] They merged journalistic and liberal Catholic conceptions of public discourse and argued that public debate cannot be based on appeals to religious authority alone. Rather, it must be grounded in reason, dialogue, and empirical evidence. When I asked him how his faith related to his journalism, Steinfels saw the relationship in his "motivation to tell the truth." But what did he mean by truth? In a speech at Notre Dame, Steinfels put truth in the context of a liberal Catholic conception of the social order:

> Liberal Catholicism accepted the notion that different spheres of activity enjoy a relative autonomy. . . . Thus, liberal Catholics defended the value of independent scholarship and scientific investigation, the need of artistic creativity to be free of censorship and moralizing condemnations, the importance of the empirical and prudential judgments in the political order, and the wisdom of guarding that order against clericalism. . . . Overall, it displayed an exceptional confidence in the power of truth . . . to be ultimately vindicated through the processes of free inquiry and discussion.[88]

Liberal Catholicism as outlined here furnishes Steinfels with a religious ideology that emphasizes the relative, not absolute, autonomy of different spheres of activity; the importance of empirical and prudential judgments; and the power of truth, justifying the journalistic distinction (though not the total separation) of professional and religious domains.

Only a few of the interviewees were willing explicitly to reject main-stream journalism's emphasis on the distinction between fact and value. One of them, the evangelical Wesley Pippert, criticized what he called "mere objectivity" and "mere accuracy," quoting Jacques Ellul, who condemns the "modern practice of using facts as the criterion of truth."[89] According to Pippert, "People these days want value-free curricula, and they want value-free reporters, and I think that's nonsense. . . . [Y]ou can't be value-free." Although the notion of truth still served to connect Pippert's religious and professional identities, he argued that truth has a moral dimension, and he perceived an "organic relationship between truth, peace, and justice." Just as Steinfels used liberal Catholic social thought to affirm the relative autonomy of empirical inquiry from religious tradition, Pippert used the rhetoric of progressive evangelicalism to call for their integration.

Conclusion

What is the place of personal religious identity in American journalism? How have Catholics and evangelicals negotiated the boundary between their professional and religious worlds? This chapter has described my respondents' use of privatization and bracketing, multivocal bridging languages, and the rhetoric of objectivity to manage the tension between professionalism and religious commitment in New York and Washington journalism.

Each of these strategies reveals something important about the relationship between religion and American public life. Privatization and bracketing call attention to the potentially stigmatizing nature of public religious identities in the modern professions. The few respondents who concealed their religious identities totally or partly from their professional colleagues said they did so to avoid damaging their credibility as objective journalists. For these journalists, the boundary between public and private precluded the display of religious convictions in professional life, especially on controversial topics such as abortion and gay rights.

By contrast, the far larger proportion of respondents who used multivocal bridging languages such as Catholic feminism, intellectual refinement, justice and peace, and populist anti-elitism attempted to translate their religious convictions into terms that are comprehensible to the wider journalistic profession. When Pippert likened the pursuit of justice and peace to getting to the "heart of the story," he was engaging in multivocality, translating between religious terms and professional language. By drawing on journalism's submerged normative traditions, these respondents were able to articulate a fit between professional and religious vocabularies, and by bridging the spheres of religion and the media, they provided strong evidence that there is room for religious self-expression in American journalism.

Finally, the tendency of many respondents to qualify their displays of religious conviction with countervailing appeals to the rhetoric of objectivity showed that there are limits to the expression of normative religious language in the news media. Although journalists may translate their religious convictions into professional terms, they must take care to maintain a distinction between their professional and religious identities. The rhetoric of objectivity helped to restore the boundary between the professional and religious worlds after it became blurred.

The relationship between the public and the private in American society is complex. In *Christianity and Civil Society,* Robert Wuthnow argues that religious people must learn to translate the languages of their religious communities into the broader vocabulary of American civil society to gain a wider hearing.[90] My respondents clearly demonstrated such bilingual sophistication, repeatedly translating their religious convictions into professional terms and the other way around. By bridging the spheres of journalism and religion while continuing to insist on their separation these journalists illustrated the porous nature of the boundary between the public world of the professions and the world of their religious communities.

4 Faith in the Academy

In *The Culture of Disbelief*, Stephen Carter, a law professor at Yale University, argues that religious faith has been reduced to the status of a hobby in the worlds of law, politics, and higher education. "One good way to end a conversation—or to start an argument," he writes, "is to tell a group of well-educated professionals that you hold a political position (preferably a controversial one, such as being against abortion or pornography) because it is required by your understanding of God's will." Carter says that religion has been trivialized to such a point that belief in supernatural intervention has become the dividing line between "that which is suspect and that which is not."[1]

I have discussed the charge that American journalism is hostile to religion; in the view of many observers, the situation in the academic social sciences is not much better. Quantitative surveys of faculty routinely show that social scientists are less religious than natural scientists and the American public at large.[2] Moreover, a Weberian emphasis on professional detachment, objectivity, and the separation of moral values from academic research was a central feature of the disciplines of sociology, history, and political science through much of the twentieth century.[3]

In the mid-1960s Alvin Gouldner observed that "all the powers of sociology . . . have entered into a tacit alliance to bind us to the dogma that 'Thou shall not commit a value judgment,' especially as sociologists.'" This ideology proclaimed "the separation and not the mutual connectedness of facts and values."[4] Peter Novick similarly argues that the "noble dream" of scholarly objectivity has been "one of the central sacred terms of professional historians, like 'health' for physicians, or 'valor' for the profession of arms." Thus, "the objective historian's role is that of a neutral, or disinterested, judge [and must] never degenerate into that of advocate, or, even worse, propagandist."[5] Finally, James Farr notes that American political science has stressed the importance of factual or empirical inquiry, following the assumption that only the observable is "admissible as fact into behavioral research," and drawing a firm boundary between "fact and value, between 'is' and 'ought.'"[6]

Consistent with this fact–value separation, Farr says, normative topics such as "freedom, justice, or authority" often have fallen outside the boundaries of legitimate professional discourse.[7] Historically, the emphasis on value-neutral objectivity and positivism led to the rhetorical devaluation of religious perspectives in the fields of history, sociology, and political science. By emphasizing the need to confine professional discourse to empirical facts, rather than philosophical, ethical, and religious convictions, social scientists discredited truth claims that rely on appeals to the moral, the supernatural, and the metaphysical.[8] By privileging "is" over "ought," facts over values, and the empirical over the normative, the social-science disciplines erected a wall between professional and religious domains. Implicit in many of the social-scientific arguments for value neutrality and professional objectivity was the positivist conviction that the academic world had moved beyond the "dark ages of theological, metaphysical, and philosophical speculation, only to emerge in the triumph of the positive sciences."[9] Because social scientists—especially sociologists and anthropologists—historically have regarded religion as a human social projection, the public expression of traditional religious beliefs continues to be seen as intellectually retrograde. Even postmodernists are "committed to exclusively naturalist premises for understanding human belief and behavior," according to George Marsden, viewing supernatural beings and metaphysical realities as social and cultural constructions and nothing more.[10]

Not surprisingly, a number of the Catholic and evangelical social scientists I interviewed for this study complained about the pressures to conceal religious faith. In *The Outrageous Idea of Christian Scholarship* (1997), Marsden described a process of acculturation that "teaches those entering the profession that concerns about faith are an intrusion that will meet with deep resentment from at least a minority of their colleagues and superiors." This acculturation process "trains scholars to keep quiet about their faith as the price of full acceptance" in the academic community.[11] Similarly, in *An Ugly Little Secret: Anti-Catholicism in North America,* Andrew Greeley complains that young Catholic scholars—especially "ethnic" Catholic scholars—find themselves barred from access to the elites of American intellectual life, "unless and until they repudiate their ethnic Catholic backgrounds."[12]

Given such obstacles, how did the Catholic and evangelical scholars I interviewed talk about the relationship between religious and academic life? From what has been shown so far, one might expect Catholic and evangelical academicians to confine their talk about their religious faith to what Erving Goffman called the "backstage" region of social life, far from the eyes and ears of professional colleagues.[13] Yet a majority of the Catholic and evangelical sociologists, historians, and political scientists interviewed for this project, including Marsden and Greeley, articulated strong connections between faith and work (see the Appendix). Like their counterparts in journalism, most of the social scientists found ways to bridge academic and religious discourse. To be sure, a few of the scholars I interviewed proclaimed their support for the value-neutral model of social-scientific inquiry. Yet even those respondents admitted that their religious backgrounds had influenced their work.

Catholic and evangelical academics have bridged the worlds of religion and scholarship in part by taking advantage of broad changes in higher education over the last three decades, which have helped to create a climate that is more conducive to the expression of religious viewpoints in professional life. Across the academy, says James Turner, "multiculturalism and post-modernism . . . have encouraged more explicit attention to the perspectival character of knowledge and to the influence of values on academic discourse."[14] In nearly every discipline, write Joel Carpenter and Kenneth Shipps, scholars have acknowledged that "pretheoretical commitments and philosophical assumptions about the nature of reality shape their thought and research."[15] Appropriating these critiques of value-free scholarship, Catholics and evangelicals have demanded a place at the table.

At the same time, my respondents have not abandoned the rhetoric of objectivity. On the contrary, some of the most eloquent spokespeople for the relevance of religious categories to academic research have used the rhetoric of objectivity to distance themselves from their own beliefs. Like their counterparts in journalism, Catholic and evangelical scholars have used objectivity rhetoric to reassert the boundary between professional and religious worlds after this boundary has blurred.

In this chapter I apply the analytical framework developed in chapter 3, describing how Catholic and evangelical scholars have used privatization and bracketing, multivocal bridging languages, and the rhetoric of objectivity to negotiate the boundary between professional and religious worlds. In addition, I analyze the ways in which respondents have switched back and forth among these strategies, describing how Catholics and evangelical scholars have positioned themselves between the extremes of positivism and postmodernism.

Distinguishing Between Religious and Professional Worlds

A small minority of the Catholic and evangelical social scientists contacted for this project attempted to distinguish between their professional and religious identities through privatization and bracketing. Those engaged in privatization erected a sharp boundary between their religious and professional selves, refusing to agree to an interview. Those engaged in bracketing were willing to be interviewed but articulated a clear distinction between their personal religious values and the practice of social research (although many did articulate subtle connections between faith and work).

Privatization: "Scared to Death to Come Out of the Closet"

A number of the Catholic and evangelical social scientists I contacted refused to be interviewed for this project. Instead of speaking openly about their religious convictions, they chose to conceal them. Although most dealt extensively with religious themes in their academic research, they were unwilling to talk about the connections between personal convictions and academic scholarship in the context of a non-anonymous interview. The reasons for the reticence varied from scholar to scholar. One Catholic scholar said that he had had a bad experience with a personal interview: A journalist had interviewed him at length about his intellectual biography, only to misrepresent his views in print. Another said he had not thought about the relationship between faith and scholarship. "Put me down as non-reflective," he said before hanging up the telephone. Finally, a well-known scholar was unwilling to go on the record as a member of a particular religious tradition for fear that being identified as religious would make it impossible to address secular audiences.

In each of these cases, the potential interviewees engaged in the privatization of religious identity. Rather than publicly displaying their religious identities in the interview, they opted to confine them to what Goffman calls the backstage region of social life.[16]

Bracketing Religion and Social Science: Maureen Hallinan

Three respondents engaged in bracketing, distancing themselves from overtly "Catholic" or "Christian" approaches to social science. At the same time, most were able to articulate some kind of connection between faith and work when asked to do so, and many did so quite eloquently.

Maureen Hallinan of the University Notre Dame was more than willing to talk about her religious convictions, yet she articulated a clear distinction between personal values and social research. As a past president of the American Sociological Association (ASA), Hallinan has occupied a position that only a few self-identified Catholic social scientists (and even fewer Catholic women) have attained in the American academic world—the chief executive office of a disciplinewide professional organization. At the same time, she has been known not as a "Catholic sociologist," as Andrew Greeley has, but as a sociologist who happens to be Catholic.

Hallinan was born in the New York City borough of Queens to Irish immigrant parents. Her father worked as a subway motorman. In the late 1950s, Hallinan attended Marymount College, earning a bachelor's degree in mathematics. From 1961 to 1968 she taught high-school mathematics as a nun in a Catholic school, subsequently earning her master's degree in mathematics from the University of Notre Dame. In the early 1970s, Hallinan earned her doctorate in education and sociology from the University of Chicago. During this period, she left her religious order.

Over the past twenty years, Hallinan's quantitative studies of school tracking, interracial friendship patterns, and skillful network analyses have made her a leader in the sociology of education field. A prolific scholar, she has written more than ninety articles for academic sociology journals and is cited in more than 170 articles by other sociologists.[17] For many years, Hallinan taught at the University of Wisconsin–Madison before taking an endowed chair in sociology at the University of Notre Dame in the late 1980s. Near the end of the interview, she said that Notre Dame had recruited her in part because of her Catholic background.

Bracketing and Value-Neutrality

During the first part of the interview, Hallinan spoke at length about her sociological research without directly mentioning her Catholic identity. Although she acknowledged the public-policy implications of her research on schools, she did not articulate a religious or moral vision of education. Instead, Hallinan focused on the technical contributions of her work to the public debate on tracking in the schools. She criticized the "murky thinking" of the tracking debate and explained that her work has attempted to "pinpoint the issues, identify questions," and "show how tracking is simply an organizational technique that has strengths and weaknesses, that can be modified."

James Jasper calls this kind of argumentation "instrumental rhetoric": While "moralist rhetoric" invokes questions of right and wrong or good and evil, instrumental rhetoric "attempts to delineate possible and impossible goals and activities. In Weberian terms, the moralist style sees certain policies as wrong in and of themselves (the ethic of ultimate ends), while the instrumental style traces all the ramifications and weighs all the consequences of each policy (the ethic of responsibility)."[18] By using instrumentalist language, Hallinan conveyed her status as an expert with "clear professional training that provides esoteric tools for understanding a certain realm of reality."[19]

Moreover, Hallinan has embraced a qualified version of social-science value-neutrality, joining a long tradition of religiously sympathetic scholars, including Max Weber and Peter Berger, who have nevertheless emphasized the separation of religious values from empirical research. "I've believed in value-free sociology for a long time," she said, "partly, I think, because I was coming from such a strong Catholic background, and values were so prominent that it was reaction against that. But today I still veer toward de-emphasizing my own personal values in doing research. . . . I try and do that."

Later in the interview Hallinan criticized those who have called for the teaching of "Christian" or "Catholic" perspectives across the curriculum at Notre Dame, drawing a sharp distinction between proselytizing and intellectual inquiry:

> Notre Dame is on a great thrust toward defining its mission as a Catholic university, so [the administration is] spending a lot of time and energy talking to faculty. . . . But this dialogue makes many of us uncomfortable because to me it seems anti-intellectual. When you're talking about the Catholic character, I think they almost want us to focus on things like mission. They wouldn't use the word proselytizing, but I do think that's part of it. "How do we teach chemistry from a Christian perspective, from a Catholic perspective?" That kind of thing. Whereas I believe . . . teaching chemistry and teaching it well is holy.

Over the past decade, Catholic universities such as Notre Dame have been involved in an ongoing debate over the nature of Catholic identity.[20]

By arguing that "teaching chemistry and teaching it well is holy," Hallinan can distance herself from those who have called for a stronger emphasis on explicitly Catholic perspectives in the curriculum.

Finally, Hallinan has not been perceived primarily as a Catholic sociologist in her role as president of the American Sociological Association. Her religious affiliation as a Catholic is not directly mentioned in the extensive professional biography that appeared in the ASA newsletter *Footnotes*. The biography, written by a friend and colleague, starts with a playful reference to Hallinan's Irish ethnicity: "Those who do not believe that the Irish have a special way have never met Maureen Hallinan. With a sparkle in her eye, she easily disarms even the most skeptical skeptic with her deep commitment to her work, boundless energy, and engaging sense of humor."[21] The profile goes on to highlight Hallinan's commitment to social change, professional accomplishments, status as a social researcher of "the highest quality," and identity as a "professional woman who has successfully balanced the demands of family and career," describing her marriage and her "two energetic teenagers."[22] Despite such personal details, the closest the article gets to revealing Hallinan's Catholic identity is its account of her education at Marymount College and the University of Notre Dame.

Catholic Identity and Sociology: Value-Commitment Backstage

Although she had bracketed Catholicism from the empirical dimensions of her research, Hallinan has not completely separated faith and work. Indeed, she articulated several points of contact between her Catholic identity and her sociological craft when prompted by more specifically religious questions. Consistent with Weberian value-neutrality, these connections between faith and work were centered primarily on her religiously derived motives rather than on the content of her social-science research.

In a particularly significant example of value commitment, Hallinan said that the empirical search for knowledge was consistent with her own conception of God's nature as intellect: "Well, on one level, my research, my work, is perfectly consistent with my values because I feel very, very strongly that part of God's nature—and I do believe in God—is intellect, is thought, and anything that I can do, any time I think or am part of that intellectual process, I'm engaged in God-like behavior." In addition, she has viewed her work as contributing to the progression toward a better state, as described by the Jesuit scientist and theologian Teilhard de Chardin. "On a conceptual level, at least," she said, "I want to think that my work is part of Teillhard de Chardin's whole omega point and that everything that we do that's good is moving the world a little closer to an ultimately better state. And if I didn't believe in that, I think I would find little meaning in anything, including my work."[23]

Finally, Hallinan said that the period she spent living in community as a nun was a "very enriching experience, because it gives you a sense of the power of a group that you might not have unless you have actually lived it. So that was very useful . . . in my thinking of groups as a sociologist."

Ambivalence and Religious Identity in Professional Life

In her career as a sociologist, Hallinan has both bracketed and connected religion and professional life. On the one hand, she has tentatively adopted the value-neutral stance of mainstream sociology. On the other, she has articulated numerous connections between her Catholic identity and her sociological career. This ambivalent combination can be understood better by examining her religious self-understanding.

In the interview, Hallinan described the strict Catholicism of her childhood and her subsequent rejection of the church's claim to absolute truth. "I grew up in a strict Irish Catholic home," she said. "My parents were born and raised in Ireland, so they brought all that Irish conservatism to our family, and it was only when I became an adult that I realized how rigid that system was and how little respect it had for individual thought." Despite her deep disillusionment, Hallinan said, she has continued to identify as a believer, expressing affection for the liturgical and symbolic life of Catholicism while distancing herself from much of its doctrine and morality:

> I believe in God. I believe that this God is a God of love; I believe that it's a personal God who I can relate to and who in some way, shape, or form is involved in my future and after death, and that's pretty much it. . . . But that says everything. What I think of the church? I was born and raised a Catholic and never officially left it, though I'm sure they've excommunicated me for a number of things—at least, they would if they had a chance. I love certain aspects of the Catholic church. I love its sacramental life, its symbol system. I love its rituals. I still say the Divine Office on occasion, and I appreciate and take advantage of the way I was taught to pray and meditate in the church. I don't relate to its morals, in many ways. I find it highly sexist. I find it anti-intellectual in many ways. I find some of its doctrines ludicrous, and I find some of its codes for behavior unacceptable.

Hallinan identifies herself as a "liberal Catholic" who has "not taken the step of rejecting the church totally." She rarely participates in her local congregation, except on "major feast days," because she finds "parish life so male, so hierarchical, so clerical, so sexist that it causes me great distress," a sentiment shared by many educated Catholic women in American society.[24]

For Hallinan, Catholicism has been both a badge of communal and religious belonging and a negative symbol of dogmatism and rigidity. Because of religion's double-sided meaning in her life, combining value-neutrality and value-commitment has made sense. This attitude of ambivalence has helped Hallinan to feel a continuing connection to her religious background while allowing her to reject the parts of the Catholic tradition that are incompatible with her rigorously empirical vision of the academic life.

Multivocal Bridging Languages: Connecting Religion and the Academy

The vast majority of Catholic and evangelical social scientists interviewed for this project did not engage in the privatization or bracketing of religious identity. Like their counterparts in journalism, most of my respondents were able to translate between religious convictions and professional jargon, forming various bridging languages.[25]

The bridging languages that my academic respondents used fall into two major categories. The first category draws on pragmatic public-policy-oriented rhetorics, connecting the social-justice tradition in Christian thought with the vocabulary of the social sciences. By public-policy-oriented rhetorics, I mean rhetorics that have originated in the applied branch of the social sciences found in public-policy schools and Washington think tanks. Policy-oriented rhetorics draw on a tradition of the social scientist as a public intellectual and social critic that goes back to the origins of the American social-science disciplines.[26] Interestingly, the users of this type of bridging language (about one-fifth of the sample) were exclusively Catholic.[27]

The second category draws on epistemological rhetorics from the social sciences to justify the introduction of religious perspectives into academic life. By epistemological rhetorics, I mean rhetorics that focus on ways of knowing. In particular, Catholic and evangelical social scientists frequently have used the rhetorics of post-positivism, postmodernism, multiculturalism, and (paradoxically) empiricism to argue for the inclusion of religious perspectives and topics in the social sciences.[28] Like feminist, minority-group, and postmodernist scholars, many Catholics and evangelicals have rejected the positivist ideal of value-free objectivity, echoing the perspectivist claim that "how you see is a function of who you are—that is, where you stand."[29] The case studies of Andrew Greeley, George Marsden, and Margaret Poloma provide examples of the range of epistemological challenges to positivism and professional objectivity I found in my sample. While Greeley has combined mainstream appeals to quantitative survey data with the value-laden language of Catholic "story theology," Marsden has articulated a head-on critique of the hegemony of Enlightenment objectivity in American higher education. Finally, in her research on Pentecostalism, Poloma has pushed the boundaries of positivist social science to their limits, drawing on her personal religious experiences (getting slain in the spirit) as a form of ethnographic research.

Social-Science Pragmatism and the Catholic Social Ethic: John DiIulio

John DiIulio, a political scientist and former White House official, enjoys a high profile as Washington policy expert and public intellectual on issues such as crime, prison reform, inner-city neighborhoods, and at-risk youth. Described by the *Los Angeles Times* as one of Washington's "in-vogue" scholars, he has collaborated with diverse groups of thinkers, ranging from the conservative pundit William Bennett to the unabashedly Afrocentric Pentecostal clergyman Eugene Rivers of Boston.[30] The author of more than a dozen books, DiIulio currently heads the Center for Research on Religion and Urban Civil Society at the University of Pennsylvania and maintains ties to the Manhattan Institute and the Brookings Institution.

During the early months of George W. Bush's administration, DiIulio, as director of the White House Office of Faith-Based and Community Initiatives, "walked the line between his personal Roman Catholic beliefs and his professional role" as a government official. Although he was frustrated by the difficulty of achieving consensus, DiIulio was praised for his ability to balance faith with facts, stressing "results, not religion."[31] As a social scientist he has maintained a similar balance between professionalism and religious commitment, combining social-science pragmatism with the Catholic social ethic.

DiIulio's closest mentor as a graduate student at Harvard University was James Q. Wilson, a political scientist (and lapsed Catholic) who is widely perceived as a "conservative thinker."[32] More recently, DiIulio has forged ties with what he calls leading figures on the Protestant religious left, such as Ronald Sider of Evangelicals for Social Action (ESA) and Jim Wallis of Call to Renewal, and leading figures on the Protestant religious right, such as Chuck Colson and Gary Bauer of the Family Research Council.[33] The *Boston Globe* has called DiIulio "hard to label."[34] While DiIulio's reputation as a get-tough-on-crime advocate has earned him the praise of conservatives (and the ire of liberals), his involvement in Boston and Philadelphia African American churches has led the *American Prospect,* a progressive public-policy journal, to label him a "sheep in wolf's clothing."[35]

Rather than segregating his religious convictions from his work, DiIulio described himself as a "born-again Catholic" who sees the "face of Jesus Christ" in the faces of poor, inner-city kids and feels "morally obliged to do something about it." In DiIulio's opinion, "there is no beauty in social-science research unless it translates into some news you can use." By demanding that social science produce news that can be used, he categorically rejects the notion that the social sciences can be justified solely on the basis of knowledge for the sake of knowledge. Although he says he is "happy to support people who read and teach Sanskrit, English, history for history's sake, [and] music," and to fund research in quantum mechanics and the pure sciences, DiIulio holds social science to a more pragmatic, street-level test of usefulness:

> This is not fine arts, and this is not string theory. This is not quantum mechanics. This is pretty simple. Are you close to the problem, or are you far from it? Do you have something useful to say, that makes a difference and that can translate, or don't you? What I cannot abide is the implicit sense, "This is a self-justifying activity." You know, "We study it because we study it because we study it." That I cannot abide. . . . I don't care if you're agnostic, you're an atheist. Fine, fine. You're a member of the Ethical Culture Society, good. You're a secular humanist, lovely. What's your view of what we ought to do to help these kids at 22nd and Lehigh in North Philadelphia? How is what you're doing with your grant money, your research, your students, your teaching, your book writing, your lecturing, your consulting—how, if at all, is it going to translate?

By embracing a pragmatic view of the social sciences, DiIulio has located himself within a long and venerable tradition of the social scientist as public intellectual, as well as a more recent tradition of the social scientist as public-policy expert.[36] In the interview, DiIulio defended his applied approach to political science by appealing to the early history of the American social science disciplines: "The social sciences are a hundred years old, essentially, in this country at least . . . and they made a claim at the beginning. The claim was, we have news you can use. That was the claim . . . on which all these associations are based. And they have failed to deliver by and large on their promises."

Social Science of the Streets

Although DiIulio has justified his pragmatic, results-oriented view of the social sciences using academic arguments, his passion for research that translates into "news you can use" ultimately has its roots in something much deeper: his own experience of the streets of Italian American South Philadelphia. The son of a Philadelphia deputy sheriff and the product of inner-city Catholic schools, DiIulio professes to have intimate knowledge of the pragmatic realities faced by Italian Americans, African Americans, and others who inhabit America's urban neighborhoods. Just as the working-class Italian American Catholics profiled in Robert Orsi's book *The Madonna of 115th Street* embraced a "theology of the streets" rooted in the neighborhoods of New York City and the pragmatism of southern Italy, so DiIulio has demanded that social science speak to the everyday life experiences of blacks and white ethnics in urban America.[37] Growing up in what he called "rough-edged, white-ethnic, working-class neighborhoods" in the 1960s and 1970s and continuing to live in such neighborhoods has given him a "different perspective from that of most white intellectuals."[38]

Perhaps the strongest influence on DiIulio's recent career trajectory has been the Reverend Eugene Rivers, a forty-eight-year-old, Harvard-educated African American clergyman whose success in mentoring former gang members in Boston's poverty-stricken Dorchester section recently made the cover of *Newsweek*.[39] When I arrived to interview DiIulio at Princeton University, he was on the telephone with Rivers, to whom he talks nearly every morning. "He and I are best buddies of sorts," DiIulio said, adding that his "work on juvenile justice, criminal justice, and youth and community development has brought [him] together with a coalition of black inner-city ministers, most of whom are Pentecostalists."

DiIulio's close professional and personal involvement with African American Pentecostal clergy has had more than a little to do with his own reawakening as a practicing Catholic. During his years as an undergraduate at the University of Pennsylvania and a graduate student at Harvard, DiIulio seldom attended mass. Although he started going back to church several years ago on a "regular, every Sunday basis," it was not until he became involved with Rivers that he began to see his work as a religious calling. A *New Yorker* profile published in 1997 describes DiIulio's religious transformation: "On Palm Sunday, 1996, when he was sitting in church with his wife and their three children, he suddenly decided that his life had to change. He had spent his career defining problems . . . but these ministers seemed to be living the solutions. 'They were committed to doing it twenty-four, seven, three sixty-five, and I decided that if I didn't do that too—if I didn't spend my life helping them—then damn *me*.' "[40]

In his work with Rivers and other inner-city clergyman, DiIulio has attempted to bring his research acumen as a social scientist and his connections as a Washington insider to the task of strengthening the social fabric of African American communities. "My comparative advantage is not that I am able to walk among the poor better than them," DiIulio said in the interview; rather, it is his "ability to read more boring academic shit than anyone else on the planet" and to "mobilize financial and political resources across the political spectrum, from Bill Bennett to Bill Moyers."[41]

DiIulio and Rivers's long-term goal is to find a way to replicate the success of church-based programs in Philadelphia and Boston on a national level, "to see whether in fact we can take it national, whether we can franchise it, whether we can create a national network of churches, create some kind of training institute or structures to teach people, to teach ourselves, what works and what doesn't." In pursuit of this goal, DiIulio wants to develop of body of research on the role of the "faith factor" in preventing crime, drug abuse, and other social ills. In his eyes, "faith is the 'forgotten factor' and religion remains the great 'omitted variable.' "[42] As a "good social scientist," DiIulio hopes to use the tools of quantitative social science to establish the efficacy of religious faith. "Purely as a good social scientist," he has said, "you need to look at the efficacy of religious commitment, attachment to religious institutions, and so on, as a factor in explaining variants in juvenile crime rates. You simply cannot explain variants in juvenile crime rates without some reference to the religion variable, or the so-called faith factor."[43]

The Catholic Social Ethic: Family, Neighborhood, and Church

Although several of the social scientists interviewed for this project have attempted to bring elements of Catholic social teaching into their research, none has come as close as DiIulio in embodying the central tenets of what Greeley has called the "Catholic social ethic." In an important chapter in *The American Catholic: A Social Portrait,* Greeley describes the centrality of family, neighborhood, and church in the Catholic worldview. Local, familial, and religious ties provide Catholics with an "unselfconscious Catholic view of human nature and society," he writes, so that "the police sergeant, the politician, the union leader, [and the parish priest are] all equipped with a set of templates for organizing, interpreting, and responding to behavior which have been carried along in the Catholic tradition."[44] DiIulio inherited the "set of templates" he has used to organize the world from his deputy-sheriff father, from the Immaculate Heart of Mary nuns who taught in his parish school, and from the Catholic neighborhoods of South Philadelphia.

Consistent with the Catholic social ethic's emphasis on the "informal, the particular, the local, the familial," DiIulio has advocated a "block by block, street by street, kid by kid" strategy for dealing with the problems of youth at risk. Although he has strongly criticized Republican cuts in welfare, he does not believe that there is any one solution to urban ills that can be administered "through public policy, let alone through Washington." Rather, neighborhood institutions—and churches, in particular—are the key to providing inner-city youth with the networks of support they need to survive. In DiIulio's view, "kids who grow up with parents, teachers, coaches, clergy, or other adults in their lives who love and care for them, guide and nurture them, even under conditions of relative material deprivation . . . are likely to do better."

DiIulio's emphasis on the public-policy implications of the black church can be attributed partly to his friendship with Rivers, but it is also a product of the Catholic social ethic. It is probably no accident that DiIulio's intellectual partnerships often have been with Catholics (lapsed and practicing) who emphasize the importance of local religious institutions in addressing social problems.[45] Significantly, DiIulio saw his new focus on religion and public policy as an outgrowth of his Catholic background: "There's nothing I'm doing now that isn't an outgrowth of what was drummed and drilled into my head by my family and the . . . nuns in Philadelphia: 'With every right, there is a corresponding duty.' "[46]

In articles and interviews DiIuilio has proclaimed his support for the "Catholic social doctrine of subsidiarity," bringing the vocabulary of Catholic social teaching into the national policy debate.[47] Quoting the Roman Catholic catechism, DiIulio has stressed the importance of "local institutions" (family, neighborhood, and church) and "larger communities" in promoting the "common good."[48] In the end, it is difficult to assess whether DiIulio's linkage of religion and "social science of the streets" has its origins in the Catholic social ethic or the pragmatic success of the black church. What is clear is that religious and professional identities are deeply intertwined in his career.

Empiricism and Interpretive Social Science: Andrew Greeley

Throughout his career as a sociologist, popular writer, and priest, Andrew Greeley has articulated a fit between the world of academic social science and that of American Catholicism, using both the quantitative language of empiricism and the post-positivist language of interpretive social science. At first glance, these two styles of academic self-presentation—hardnosed empiricism and interpretation—may seem at odds. Yet Greeley has combined them in ways that cross multiple academic and disciplinary boundaries.

The language of empiricism has identified Greeley as a quantitative social scientist at home in the world of the National Opinion Research Center, while his use of storytelling and myth has connected him to contemporary Catholic theologians such as John Shea and David Tracy and to interpretive social scientists such as Clifford Geertz. Finally, his prodigious output of social-science monographs, articles, novels, and newspaper columns has allowed Greeley to communicate with a large academic and non-academic public.[49]

Understanding Suburban, Middle-Class Catholics

The son of a middle-class Irish Catholic family, Greeley was himself a product of the social changes he would later chronicle as a sociologist. In many ways, Greeley's journey from his boyhood Irish Catholic neighborhood to the University of Chicago paralleled the larger American Catholic passage from the immigrant ghetto to the professionalized suburbs that he has celebrated in his social science and fiction. In the 1940s

A native of the Windy City, Father Andrew Greeley often writes about the connections among religion, ethnicity, and place among Chicago's Irish Catholics. (Courtesy Mario Petitti.)

and 1950s, Greeley's family lived in the Chicago neighborhood of Austin, where they belonged to St. Angela's parish. His father was a middle-class businessman and manager who had "struggled up the economic and social ladder in the first three decades of this century," only to have much of his fortune wiped out in the Great Depression.[50] Greeley was the first in his immediate family to receive any kind of higher education. After attending St. Mary of the Lake Seminary in Mundelein, Illinois, he was assigned to the upper-middle-class Christ the King parish in the Chicago suburb of Beverly Hills.

In an effort to understand the upper-middle-class, college-educated Catholics who populated his new parish, the young Greeley turned to the writings of contemporary sociologists such as C. Wright Mills, David Riesman, and William F. Whyte. A group of clergy friends in the Chicago archdiocese persuaded Greeley that he "needed the discipline and the methodology of professional sociological education . . . to be a commentator, an interpreter, and a resource for the diocese and the church."[51] With the blessing of Cardinal Albert Meyer, Archbishop of Chicago, Greeley entered the University of Chicago's graduate program in sociology in 1960, finishing two years later, in 1962.

The Uses of Empirical Social Science: Proving Catholics Can "Make It"

When Greeley entered graduate school in the early 1960s, most Catholic sociologists still suffered low prestige and "status anxiety" in relation to the U.S. sociological profession.[52] Young Catholic sociologists were attempting to become part of the discipline's empirical mainstream during an era in which the American academy stereotyped Catholics as anti-intellectual, authoritarian, and dogmatic. From the 1920s to the 1960s, notes John McGreevy, Catholics were portrayed by mainstream social scientists as being averse to empiricism, experimentation, and the scientific method, and Catholicism was seen as incompatible with the liberal values of disinterestedness, tolerance, and pluralism.[53] A distinguished demographer at the University of Chicago rejected an early effort to hire the young Greeley as an assistant professor, explaining, "I would no more permit that man [Greeley] in our department than I would a card-carrying Communist, and for the same reason."[54]

Although an earlier generation of Catholic sociologists had called for a highly normative "supernatural sociology" that integrated theology, neo-Thomist Catholic philosophy, and ethics with the discipline of sociology, young Catholic social scientists repudiated this vision as unscientific.[55] In the context of the early 1960s, Greeley's embracing of empirical sociology can be interpreted as a decision to join the mainstream. Indeed, the quantitative, empirical branch of sociology was by far the most important emphasis of his professional training at the National Opinion Research Center and in graduate school at the University of Chicago.[56] According to a biographer, the young Greeley was "an empirical sociologist . . . possessed of a certain style, with a new role in the Catholic intellectual community; and much of what he would produce would bulge with tables of percentages, coefficients of association, statements of probability, appendices—all the appurtenances of survey research 'facts.' "[57]

Time after time, the language and findings of empirical social science have given Greeley a way to critique theoretical perspectives that are hostile or indifferent to religion. Although he acknowledged that Marxism "sometimes produces useful findings" in the interview, he also said that most Marxist scholarship is "so heavily prejudiced" by the author's perspectives that he does not find it "very satisfactory." In one of his most recent sociological works, *Religion as Poetry*, Greeley writes that he was "struck by how 'unscientific'" Marx's "attack on religion as the opiate of the people" is "by the standards of contemporary social science. . . . [The] arguments are aprioristic and deductive."[58] In the interview, Greeley confessed that he was "depressed by the dogmatism" of contemporary sociology, recalling that when he moved from the church to the university, he expected to "move into a world where there was more freedom of discussion, more freedom to explore." In characterizing the academy as closed-minded and unscientific and arguing that academic social scientists are the true dogmatists, Greeley turns the stereotype of Catholicism as dogmatic and anti-intellectual on its head.[59]

Empirical social science has also served as a tool to debunk what Greeley calls myths about Catholics in American society. In response to postwar claims about Catholic anti-intellectualism, the young Greeley marshaled survey data showing that Catholics could penetrate the highest ranks of the research university. In particular, Greeley's dissertation argued that young Catholics were more likely to attend graduate school than young Protestants, challenging the academic stereotype of U.S. Catholics as authoritarian anti-intellectuals. In countless interviews and writings, Greeley has recounted the reaction of his mentor James Davis, then the director of NORC, to this finding: "Looks like Notre Dame beats Southern Methodist this year!" In the interview, Greeley said that he "got a taste of debunking in that, and I've enjoyed doing it ever since."[60] When his fellow sociologists failed to accept his findings, Greeley learned to "never expect cocktail-party liberals [and] anti-Catholicism to yield easily to empirical evidence."[61]

The Language of Interpretive Social Science: Sociological Storytelling

Since his career began, Greeley has been criticized by both professional colleagues and Catholic intellectuals for his devotion to the research model of empirical sociology. In his autobiography, he recalls that one professor called him a "naive empiricist" at a forum sponsored by *Commonweal* magazine.[62] Yet despite his commitment to empirical social science, Greeley has not advocated a value-neutral approach to sociology. He has criticized the sociology of religion of the early 1960s, calling it "the blindest kind of empiricism, which NORC ... left behind ten years ago." While reading the post-positivist philosophy of Michael Polanyi in graduate school, Greeley said, he "learned that human knowledge did not follow the paradigm of the 'scientific method'"; rather, sociologists "followed instincts, hunches, intuitions, much like a detective solving a mystery story." Social-scientific methodologies provided only "techniques for experiments which would prove what we already knew to be true—perhaps refining our intuitions in the process."[63] In the interview, Greeley argued that "nobody is objective, nobody is detached, everybody has emotions, and if they're not strong emotions, then they're not fully human."

Although Greeley has used the language of empiricism to criticize the myth and dogmatism of anti-Catholicism, much of his sociology has focused on developing an interpretive and culturalist theory of the religious imagination that puts "myth," in the non-pejorative sense of the word, at the center. In the process, Greeley's work has come close to becoming a form of sociological theology (or theological sociology), blurring the boundaries between religion and social science.

Over the past twenty years, Greeley has embraced a narrative conception of religion and social research that synthesizes elements of contemporary Catholic "story theology" with the interpretive turn in the humanities and social sciences. He has summarized his narrative approach to religion by arguing that "religion (to paraphrase Clifford Geertz and John Shea) is the set of answers a person has available to the fundamental questions of the meaning of life and love, answers which are normally encoded in pictures, images and stories (symbols) and purport uniquely to give purpose and meaning to human existence."[64] In other words, religion is a story more than a set of doctrinal formulations, moral rules, or traditional dogmas—although it is also doctrine, ethics, and morality.

Greeley turned gradually toward a narrative definition of religion through exposure to scholars in a number of fields from the mid-1960s to the mid-1970s. While he was a young instructor at the University of Chicago, Greeley became friendly with Clifford Geertz, who was then beginning to develop his hermeneutical and interpretive approach to cultural anthropology.[65] In the mid-1970s, Greeley has said, he "began to comprehend, slowly at first, from my study of religion and ethnicity that religion was storytelling before it was much else."[66] Under the influence of thinkers such as Geertz (particularly his "Religion as a Cultural System"), the Catholic theologians David Tracy of the University of Chicago, John Shea of Chicago's Loyola University, and Paul Ricoeur of the University of Chicago; and the comparative religionist Mircea Eliade at the University of Chicago, Greeley began to see the importance of narrative approaches to religion. "The emphasis on the narrative dimensions of religion can be found in many different disciplines, one of the most fascinating convergences of scholarship that I have ever witnessed— hermeneutics, exegesis, anthropology, literary criticism, cognitive psychology. All now tend to agree that a person's religion is that set of stories (narrative symbols) which s/he uses to provide directive interpretation for himself and others."[67]

Tracy and Shea encouraged Greeley to combine social theory and a story-based approach to theology. These multidisciplinary insights enabled him to "synthesize theology and the social sciences into a new style of religious reflection, a new method of theological thought."[68] He "pulled together the theology that Tracy and Shea and John Navone were doing with empirical sociology," and says that it "changed my life."[69]

Moreover, in the mid-1970s Andrew Greeley the sociologist became Andrew Greeley the bestselling novelist, beginning with the publication of *The Cardinal Sins*.[70] In the interview, he noted the "peculiar effect on my sociology of beginning to write in fiction" and recalled that Kenneth Prewitt, a former director of NORC, said, after reading his second novel that he would "never again read any of my monographs because it was all in the novels and much more palatable." Greeley does not see a sharp boundary between his fiction and his sociology. "I don't see sociological analysis and storytelling as being different activities," he said. "[W]riting an article or a report and writing a novel [are] exercises in storytelling. They may be a little different in the tools you use, but they're essentially the acts of the same dimension of the personality."

Greeley acknowledged that his novels and his research are based on the Irish American Catholic experience. "They influence one another," he said. "I mean, I write stories about the kinds of people I study sociologically, particularly the Irish, who have been here for four generations, are now very American, very successful, but also distinctive from other Americans. I write stories about those kinds of people, fourth- or fifth-generation American Catholics, but I also do research on them. . . . So Prewitt was right. He doesn't have to read any of the monographs, because it's all going to turn up there."

Greeley has even come to see survey-data analysis as a form of poetic expression. Using the "interactive data analysis techniques developed by my friend Norman Nie in the Statistical Package for the Social Sciences . . . was like writing poetry," he has said. "[Y]ou could become locked in an affective relationship with the data and follow hunches and intuitions with ease."[71] According to Greeley, fiction and social research "are both offspring of the narrative impulse by which we humans strive to make sense of the world around us. [The] distinction between theory and data with which social scientists are obsessed is a post-hoc reflection, and a very inaccurate one, on what actually happens in the analytic enterprise."[72]

Greeley's diverse descriptions of the social-scientific enterprise blend empiricist and narrative approaches in a combination that appears to defy easy categorization. In the mid-1960s, Greeley wrote hopefully about his role as a bridge between the worlds of academia and the Catholic church in the essay "Anything but Marginal."[73] The crossing of bridges between church and university, theology and social science, fiction and empirical research, and priesthood and profession has been ubiquitous in Greeley's reflections on his work. In the end, Greeley's wide range of academic styles has allowed him to speak across disciplines, across religious traditions, and across the divide between professional and religious worlds.

Postmodernism in the Service of Evangelical Christianity: George Marsden

George Marsden is perhaps the preeminent historian of evangelicalism and fundamentalism in America. His book *Fundamentalism and American Culture* (1980) became the standard history of American Protestant fundamentalism in the fields of history and religious studies, solidifying Marsden's reputation as a first-rate professional historian.[74] As Leonard Sweet has written, "Marsden has become to fundamentalism what Kochel is to Mozart—the name everyone knows and no one can do without." In Sweet's estimation, Marsden and his fellow evangelical Mark Noll are "key players" in the "new evangelical historiography," a "batch of entrepreneurial historians, who collaborate in projects, critique each other's manuscripts, co-author and co-edit some of the discipline's most unrolling, rollicking discussions, and foray into popular historical writing."[75] The Religion Index, 1949–96, contained 279 references to Marsden's work. Moreover, a large-scale survey of historians and social scientists in

American religion identified Marsden as one of the four most influential scholars in the field of American religious history, alongside Martin Marty, Jon Butler, and Nathan Hatch.[76]

Outside the study of fundamentalism, Marsden has carved out a highly visible place as an advocate of religious points of view in the American university, beginning with the publication of *The Soul of the American University: From Protestant Establishment to Established Nonbelief* (1994). This pathbreaking history of the secularization of American higher education argues that religious beliefs have been unfairly marginalized in the American academy. The book received favorable attention in the *New York Times Book Review* and a host of academic and religious publications.[77] In November 1993, Marsden issued an even more direct call for the inclusion of religious perspectives in higher education in his plenary address to the American Academy of Religion, later taking his crusade for religion in the academy to the *Wall Street Journal* and the *New York Times*.[78] "If there is a movement to reintroduce faith into American intellectual life," says Alan Wolfe, "George Marsden is its leader."[79]

The Importance of Being Marginal

Like many evangelical scholars, Marsden tells his life story in a way that calls attention to the marginality of conservative Protestantism in American life.[80] In constructing an autobiography of marginality, Marsden follows the pattern of feminists, minorities, and other academic outsiders. These autobiographies of marginality provide the speaker with a claim to authenticity and with a warrant to challenge the exclusion of one's group from the public debate.

In the interview, Marsden recounted how his upper-middle-class Presbyterian family moved from the center of the Protestant establishment to the margins of religious respectability. His father, a University of Pennsylvania graduate, was a student at the Princeton Theological Seminary, where he studied under the fundamentalist biblical scholar J. Gresham Machen. During the height of the fundamentalist–modernist controversies of the 1920s, Machen left Princeton in disgrace to found the more theologically conservative Westminster Theological Seminary in Philadelphia. Marsden's father followed his mentor, leaving Princeton to attend the fundamentalist Westminster, a decided step down in academic prestige.

THE Christian Century

July 2-9, 1997
$2.00

Faith and the university

George Marsden fights the 'establishment of nonbelief'

by Glenn Tinder

Walter Brueggemann: Learning from the exiles

David Heim: McVeigh and the death penalty

Aida B. Spencer: Gender confusion and the NIV Bible

Jonathan Frerichs: Starving off-camera in North Korea

Historian George Marsden is one of the leading advocates of religion in American higher education. He is shown here on the cover of *Christian Century,* mainline Protestantism's leading journal of opinion. Illustration by Jack R. Harkema. (Reprinted by permission from *Christian Century,* 2–9 July 1997. Subscriptions: $49.00/year from P.O. Box 378, Mt. Morris, Ill. 61054.)

After graduating from the seminary, Marsden's father became the pastor of a Presbyterian church in Middletown, Pennsylvania. But his tenure there was not long. Further tensions between theological conservatives and theological liberals in the Presbyterian church led to the formation of a breakaway denomination that became known as the Orthodox Presbyterian church (OPC). In 1936, Marsden's father left his mainline Presbyterian congregation to found a new congregation affiliated with the OPC. According to Marsden, that was "not an acceptable thing to do in a small town as far as the social elite, such as they were, thought." Although his mother and grandmother had come from a relatively well-to-do family, Marsden said, the decision to leave the Protestant mainline thrust the family into a situation of status inconsistency between the town's upper-middle-class elite and the decidedly unfashionable world of fundamentalism.

From very early on, Marsden said, "I was in a situation of being in this very marginalized sort of religious group [and] was . . . aware of that tension going on all the time." This sense of marginality was further accentuated during Marsden's undergraduate years at Haverford College, where, he said, he "went through a real crisis of faith, intellectually, [experiencing a] divided mind—half believed, and half didn't believe." Only after a year at Westminster Theological Seminary was Marsden able to "find an intellectual way of putting [faith and intellectual life] back together again."

Alan Wolfe has questioned whether evangelical scholars such as Marsden are entitled to the marginal status they have so eagerly cultivated. "Claims of victimization are tiresome enough, even when advanced by real victims," Wolfe argued in a review of Marsden's *Soul of the American University.* "[T]here is something truly ill-fitting when they are advanced by white male Christians." Yet according to Robert Wuthnow, evangelicalism's stigmatized past has provided evangelical scholars with a critical perspective on American society akin to Georg Simmel's "stranger" or Robert Park's "marginal man." Despite Marsden's upper-middle-class background, his family's decline in social status, along with a personal crisis of belief, gave him what Wuthnow calls a "creativity that comes with marginality."[81]

Challenging the Hegemony of Scientific Objectivity

After graduate study at Yale under Sydney Ahlstrom and Edmund Morgan, Marsden taught in the history department at Calvin College in

Michigan, a bastion of Dutch Calvinist piety and learning affiliated with the Christian Reformed Church, a small immigrant denomination. At Calvin, Marsden pursued an semiautobiographical research agenda that focused on evangelicalism, fundamentalism, and American religion. In *Fundamentalism and American Culture* (1981), Marsden sought to debunk the anti-intellectual image of fundamentalism made popular by scholars such as Richard Hofstadter. Because of his family's background in Ivy League fundamentalism, Marsden had firsthand experience with a form of conservative Protestantism that contradicted the stereotype.

Marsden's public advocacy of religion in the American university did not begin until the early 1990s, emerging out of his research for *The Soul of the American University*.[82] Although the book was intended as a serious work of academic history, Marsden acknowledged that it had an agenda. In the book's "Concluding Unscientific Postscript," Marsden argues that "only purely naturalistic viewpoints are allowed a serious academic hearing," resulting in the "near exclusion of religious perspectives from the academic life of American universities."[83] In the interview, he characterized the book as a "version of deconstructing the university—seeing how it was constructed and then, when you expose how it was constructed, [asking whether] it could be constructed some other way than it is." (It is important to note Marsden's use of postmodern jargon here.)

Attacking the notion of value-free objectivity has been central to Marsden's critique of the secular university.[84] Pointing to fields such as women's studies and African American studies, Marsden has argued there is no reason that religious scholars should be prevented from bringing their normative convictions into their work. Just as no one would think of proposing that "no feminist should teach the history of women—or no African-American should teach African-American history," he has written, so, too, should evangelicals and fundamentalists be free to write and teach about their own religious traditions from a faith perspective.[85]

Along with multi-culturalist rhetoric, Marsden has invoked the critique of positivism advanced by thinkers such as Thomas Kuhn (*The Structure of Scientific Revolutions* [1962]), arguing that religious scholars should be allowed to bring their pre-empirical assumptions about God, the universe, and human nature into their academic scholarship:

> [M]any prominent scholars have agreed that science typically operates within frameworks of assumptions that are not themselves established on scientific grounds. . . . It is now commonplace among contemporary scholars, including

many moderate liberal scholars, to acknowledge that, while empirical investigation should be valued in its place, pretheoretical influences such as social
location substantially shape interpretations in the humanities and social science.... One might think, therefore, that it would be relatively easy to gain
agreement that, since strongly held religious views are often part of one's
social location, religious perspectives should be accepted as playing potentially
legitimate roles in academic interpretation.[86]

Because few scholars now believe in "neutral objective science," according to Marsden, post-positivism and postmodernism have undercut any
justification for excluding religious claims from academic discourse.[87]

Bridging Christian Theism and Postmodernism

Many non-evangelical scholars have questioned whether Marsden's use of
postmodernist rhetoric is consistent with his beliefs as an orthodox Christian. Wolfe argues that "as a believer ... Marsden cannot really be a postmodernist ... since the truth of God's existence would in no way be
altered if a community of interpreters concluded otherwise."[88] Stanley
Fish, a literary theorist at Duke University, is even more blunt in his criticism of Marsden's rhetorical inconsistencies. He calls Marsden's appeal
to postmodernism a "self-defeating argument because it amounts to saying that when it comes to proof, religious perspectives are no worse off
than any other."[89]

How has Marsden managed the apparent conflict between postmodern relativism and Christian theism in the face of such criticism? Harry
Stout, a historian at Yale, argues that evangelical historians such as Marsden may be more accurately classified as "pre-modern, that is, as scholars
who reject both modernism's faith in reason and post-modernism's
nihilism."[90] Marsden's inherent distrust of Enlightenment objectivity and
value-neutrality is far from an opportunistic appropriation of postmodern
rhetoric, however; it can be traced back to his days as a student at Westminster Theological Seminary. While he was there, Marsden studied
under Cornelius Van Til, a Dutch Reformed scholar who introduced generations of conservative Presbyterian seminarians to the writings of Abraham Kuyper, the turn-of-the-century Dutch Calvinist theologian and
philosopher. Kuyper's approach was particularly helpful because it challenged the Enlightenment conceit that truly scientific knowledge must
put aside all religious presuppositions.

Marsden's writings on Christian historiography in the 1970s and 1980s borrowed heavily from the thought of Van Til and Kuyper, as well as from secular thinkers such as Carl Becker. Marsden went so far as to argue that "the very facts of history differ for the Christian and the non-Christian historian."[91] Although statements that closely resemble this claim can be found in the works of many postmodernist scholars, Marsden's critique of scientific objectivity ultimately can be traced back to a religious intellectual tradition that predates postmodernism. Indeed, Marsden has commented on the affinities between the "Dutch Protestant thought of a century ago" and the writings of Kuhn.[92] In the end, Marsden's premodern religious convictions have enabled him to find common cause with secular critics of positivism because of a shared antipathy toward modernity and the Enlightenment project.[93]

Charismatic Religious Experience and "Christian Sociology": Margaret Poloma

During thirty years as a sociologist, Margaret Poloma has written widely in the fields of family sociology and the sociology of religion. She has also held offices in the Society for the Scientific Study of Religion, the Association for the Sociology of Religion, and the Christian Sociological Society.[94] Two of her books on the sociology of religion, *The Charismatic Movement: Is There a New Pentecost?* and *The Assemblies of God at the Crossroads: Charisma and Institutional Dilemmas,* have centered on the spirituality and institutional context of the charismatic Pentecostal movement in American Christianity.[95]

Since she returned to Christianity in the late 1970s, Poloma has openly acknowledged the connections between her religious identity as a charismatic evangelical Christian and her sociological exploration of the Pentecostal and charismatic movements. By using her religious experiences as a method for studying Pentecostalism, Poloma has gone much farther than Marsden and Greeley in integrating personal faith into her research.

From Catholicism to Agnosticism to Charismatic Christianity

In the interview, Poloma recounted her spiritual journey from belief to unbelief to renewed belief, describing her sociological and religious odyssey from Catholicism to agnosticism to charismatic Christian faith. Raised as a Roman Catholic, Poloma began to question the teachings of the church during her college years. "Pre-Vatican II Catholicism was a very tight-knit, ethnocentric, and autocratic system," she said. "The church fed me the answers to the questions that I was not asking while neglecting to address topics (especially the changing role of women, the emerging antiwar movement, poverty and racism) that were key sociological concerns."

During graduate school at Case Western Reserve University in Ohio Poloma found "many more significant questions being addressed," as well as faculty members who spoke openly about abandoning their religious convictions. "I can still remember reading Durkheim, *The Elementary Forms of the Religious Life,* and coming upon the line: 'The old gods were dying or already dead, and the new ones were yet to be born,'" she said. "I thought: 'That's a good description of the state of religion in modern society.'" Poloma began to see religion as socially constructed after studying the theories of Durkheim and Marx. "Recognizing that religion is a social construct, as is the rest of culture, moved me closer to the stance of an agnostic," she said. "Within eighteen months after beginning graduate school, I had reasoned my way through the classical sociological writings on religion to embrace the agnostic posture of its authors."

In 1974, as a new assistant professor at the University of Akron, Poloma was asked by a local Episcopal rector to conduct a sociological evaluation of his parish. "I told him I was an agnostic, but he claimed it didn't matter," she said. "I then agreed to do the study." Although their personal styles clashed, "this man constantly challenged me with his faith." After nearly a year of working with the rector, Poloma said, she asked herself, "Why does this man make me so angry when he tries to share his religious experiences and convictions? So I began to question what it was that I was running from. Why was it that I was so threatened by someone else's sincere religious faith?"

This newfound awareness led Poloma to talk to a Catholic priest at Akron's Newman Center, the Catholic campus ministry at the university. He welcomed her to worship with the community, demonstrating an openness that she had not experienced in her Catholic upbringing. The noncombative nature of the encounter led Poloma to accept his invitation—and to increased soulsearching. She recognized that, although she had reasoned her way out of Catholicism, reason proved to be ineffective in resolving her religious quest:

I thought of Kierkegaard—that notion of a "leap of faith"—and knew that I couldn't make the leap on my own. It was only grace that could bring me into contact with the ultimate, if indeed there was any ultimate to be brought into contact with. What I did next was to say a version of the agnostic's prayer. "God, if you exist, do something." Immediately I found myself filled with the sense of the holy and knowing that God existed deep down in my spirit. How did I know it was a sense of the holy? It was a very familiar sense from my childhood—the kind of feeling I would sometimes have after receiving Holy Communion, making a visit to church, or reflecting on the lives of Jesus, Mary, or my favorite saints. It was an experience I had not had in years. For me it was a sense of the Divine Presence—a kind of union with God.

Despite this dramatic turning point in her spiritual journey, Poloma was afraid to return uncritically to the religious beliefs and practices of her childhood:

I didn't want to get into a Christian rut again. . . . The sociologist in me knew that I had been socialized into Christianity as part of my culture. If I lived in India, most probably, I would be a Hindu; if in the Far East, most likely a Buddhist. . . . I did not want to be duped in that way. I needed another religious experience before I could reembrace Christianity. So I spent much of Lent following my initial conversion experience wondering what I did believe about Jesus.

The evening before Easter Sunday, Poloma's faith crisis reached a crescendo as she found herself walking out of a Roman Catholic Holy Saturday service: "I didn't know what I believed about Jesus' resurrection, and I could take only so much of the celebrative Easter ritual before I said to myself, 'I've got to get out of here.'" Although she was a very sound sleeper who rarely awoke during the night, Poloma said, she woke up around 2 A.M. and could not fall back asleep. She began to read the New Testament accounts of the resurrection. "When I finished reading John's account," she said, "I just knew deep in my spirit that Jesus was alive and he was Lord. That feeling has never left me." The next day, at Easter Sunday mass, Poloma approached her priest."I hugged him and said, 'I don't accept the Catholic church, but I do know Jesus is risen and that he is Lord.' Although he did not reply, the puzzled look on his face seemed to say, 'Where on earth did that come from?'"

Combining Charismatic Religious Experience
and Sociological Research

After she returned to Christianity, Poloma had no desire to continue
teaching or researching the sociology of religion. She even considered
changing careers. Having once used the sociological study of religion to
reason her way to agnosticism, she said, she feared that she might "jeop-
ardize this newly found gift of faith." At the same time, however, she
sensed that she was being called to remain in sociology and that "somehow God wanted to guide my career." Under the influence of George
Hillery, founder and coordinator of the Christian Sociological Society
who had become a close personal friend, and her own sense of divine calling, Poloma agreed to write about the charismatic Pentecostal movement
as part of a series of books on social movements. At the same time,
Poloma said, she made it clear that she would "have to approach the work
as a believer [and allow] readers to know where I was coming from and
that I was a charismatic Christian."

Poloma described in the interview how the book's ethnographic-
research methodology intersected with her experiences of God's supernatural presence:

> There are things that I had to experience personally before I could write
> about them. In anthropological terms, I "went native," taking a stance that
> allowed me to be open to whatever God wanted me to do. I went about col-
> lecting my information, participating in different services, and trying to get
> a sense of the differences between the Pentecostals, their newer charismatic
> cousins, and rapidly growing independent sectors of the movement with an
> open spirit. There were a number of things that I saw while gathering data
> that were not part of my Catholic charismatic community. Being slain in the
> spirit was one such experience.[96]

Poloma said that she allowed herself to be slain in the spirit in the
course of her research only after she sensed that God was telling her to
do so:

> The first time I observed it I became unnerved and walked out of the serv-
> ice. I saw people falling to the floor, including some of my good friends, and
> I didn't find myself in a place where I could figure it out. Perhaps I was fear-
> ful about exactly what it was that I had gotten myself into by yielding to

other Pentecostal charismatic experiences. Sometime later, the same evangelist who had conducted the service was coming through town. I sensed God say to me: "You are going to the service, and this time you are going up for prayer. You are not going to walk out the door without it." Once I had the experience of being slain in the spirit, it was a lot less mysterious. I could write about it within a sociological frame with more certainty and precision than I could have done before.

Poloma justified the autobiographical dimensions of her work in the interview by appealing to the ethnographic concept of "membership roles" and her position as a "complete member." She also cited Patricia and Peter Adler's *Membership Roles in Field Research* (1987). Poloma elaborated:

My role as an insider has not only given me a better understanding of the particular Pentecostal charismatic religious experiences about which I write, but it has also alerted me to the important role experience plays in the social construction of religious reality. Sociologists have acknowledged the experiential dimension of religion but have been remiss in using it in their research. More specifically, it has shown me the importance of distinguishing between spirituality and religiosity long before it became fashionable to write about the distinction. Recognizing the centrality of religious experience for Pentecostal and charismatic Christians is what set me on the path of researching different types of personal prayer and the relationship that prayer experiences have to health and well-being.[97]

Poloma has described her work as a kind of "dialectical dance" between her religious faith experiences and her sociological training.[98] She believes that the synthesis coming out of this process has led to insights into topics (such as prayer and the effects of spirituality on health) that go beyond the Pentecostal and charismatic world. Thus, Poloma has used the language of post-positivist sociological theory to justify an explicitly religious approach to her work as a Christian sociologist.

The Rhetoric of Objectivity: Separating and Bridging

Given the tendency of Catholic and evangelical scholars to criticize the positivist vision of value-neutral social science, one might expect to find little support for professional notions of objectivity and scholarly detachment

among my respondents. This is not the case. Although many of my interviewees have rejected the ideal of value-free scholarship, most have also
resorted to the rhetoric of objectivity at various times in their careers—
and in the interviews. They have used the rhetoric of objectivity both to
separate and to bridge the religious and professional worlds.

Objectivity as a Fence

Most of my interviewees distanced themselves from the more normative
roles of theologian, ethicist, or religious advocate. Respondents repeatedly
proclaimed, "I'm not a theologian" and "I don't proselytize in my work."
Paradoxically, these statements were often uttered by the same scholars
who had earlier described the importance of bringing religious perspectives into social research. Indeed, the scholars who were the most articulate about the influence of theological categories on their research often
were also the most likely to emphasize their commitment to objectivity. As
noted earlier, Gaye Tuchman describes objectivity as a credibility-enhancing rhetorical strategy that can be mobilized in situations in which professional claims to expertise or detachment come under attack.[99] Again,
for many of my respondents, objectivity rhetoric provided a way to restore
the boundary between professional and religious identities.

In *Confessions of a Parish Priest,* Greeley repeatedly defends himself
against those who have accused him of producing biased social science.
Although he calls attention to his interdisciplinary interest in the relationship of sociology and theology, he notes that he is an empirical sociologist before he is anything else. Although he describes his quest to
"synthesize theology and the social sciences into . . . a new method of theological thought,"[100] he also provides (in a different context) the dis-
claimer, "I am not a moral theologian":

> Periodically, I am accused of attacking the church's doctrine on birth control.
> However, I have never publicly attacked it. . . . I am not a moral theologian;
> I am not competent to make a public judgment on the teaching. I am a soci-
> ologist, capable of reporting the simple fact that whatever people ought to be
> doing, they do not in fact accept the teaching. Once more I find myself in the
> peculiar position where many Catholics are incapable of distinguishing
> between fact and value. The sociologist who reports the fact does not neces-
> sarily endorse it, he merely says it is true.[101]

The familiar distinction between fact and value is a hallmark of the rhetoric of objectivity.

Several other scholars have used similar language to describe the separation of private religious convictions from public scholarship. In *The Outrageous Idea of Christian Scholarship,* Marsden follows an impassioned call for the inclusion of religious perspectives in academic discourse with a strong statement of support for the "value of the liberal pragmatic academy." In response to an argument made by his critics that the introduction of religious viewpoints into mainstream academia would "undermine some of the hard-won achievements of the liberal academy," Marsden argues that Christian belief is compatible with support for "scientifically sound investigation."[102]

Objectivity as a Bridge

While many Catholic and evangelical scholars have used objectivity rhetoric to separate their professional and religious identities, others have seen objectivity, or some version of epistemological realism, as central to the vocation of being a "Catholic" or "Christian" scholar. Some of these scholars have sharply criticized "secular" social scientists for failing to live up to the ideals of objective scholarship, turning objectivity into a weapon in the fight against postmodernism, poststructuralism, and, in a few cases, multiculturalism. Still others have focused on developing a theological and philosophical rationale for their belief that "some such knowledge cuts across all theories and paradigms," arguing that there are Christian reasons for believing that some types of knowledge are relatively objective.[103] In both cases, my respondents have used objectivity rhetoric to bridge their professional and religious identities.

Since she converted to Catholicism in the 1990s, Elizabeth Fox-Genovese has epitomized the combative style of religious support for objectivity, arguing that postmodernists, feminists, and multiculturalists have abandoned scholarly rigor in favor of ideological advocacy. "A new emphasis on multiculturalism, normally taken to include women and homosexuals as well as national and ethnic groups," she has written, "merged with these tendencies to promote the view that most canons of historical scholarship, notably objectivity and the identification of facts, should be dismissed as inherently suspect if not intentionally oppressive."[104]

In Fox-Genovese's opinion, the loss of scholarly detachment has been accompanied by strong antireligious biases.[105] Fox-Genovese is so disillusioned with the "rising tide of post-modernism" that she has joined two hundred other historians, including her husband and fellow Catholic convert, Eugene Genovese, in forming a new professional organization, the Historical Society, designed to serve as an alternative to the American Historical Association and the Organization of American Historians.[106]

Other respondents were less likely to attach support for objective scholarship to opposition to secularism. In "Common Sense and the Spiritual Vision of History," Marsden offers an explicitly Christian rationale for his belief that "when we look at the past . . . what we find will in large measure correspond to what other historians find." In Marsden's view, human beings' capacity to discover reliable data about the past "provides all people of good sense with a solid reality basis for testing some aspects of their theories. . . . From a Christian perspective, we may explain this phenomenon simply by observing that God in his grace seems to have created human minds with some abilities to experience and know something of the real world, including the past."[107]

Many Catholic and evangelical scholars have articulated a similar theological justification for their belief in the relatively objective character of social-scientific knowledge. When asked whether belief in God would bias his research, for example, DiIulio has replied, "Not unless God chooses to repeal the laws of statistical analysis or change regression coefficients."[108]

In perhaps the most explicitly theological rationale for social-scientific objectivity, Greeley has reached into the writings of Thomas Aquinas to justify the autonomy of sociology from theology. By failing to recognize the distinction between theology and social science, he has said, Catholic scholars of the 1950s "ignored St. Thomas on the distinction between the disciplines." While theology focuses on the supernatural dimensions of God's grace, sociology uses natural reason and empirical observation to examine the "natural concomitants of grace" in the social world. "Since the Catholic tradition has always contended that grace and nature are intimately linked, there is no reason to deny that the natural concomitants of grace can be studied."[109]

For Greeley and many other respondents, a modest version of objectivity can be justified on explicitly religious grounds. Instead of seeing detached scholarship in sharp conflict with Christian faith, my respondents offered religious arguments for abiding by what David Tracy has called the "liberal" epistemology of a "pluralist and democratic society" (an epistemology that emphasizes appeals to "public, shared reason").[110] A longstanding tradition of common-sense realism, as exemplified by Marsden's "Common Sense and the Spiritual Vision of History," has given evangelical scholars a language with which to articulate their support for the importance of rigorous empirical research.[111] Among Catholics, the natural-law tradition's confidence in the power of human reason, as illustrated by Greeley's appeal to the works of Aquinas, and the openness of Catholic thought to the social sciences in the wake of Vatican II have served a similar function. Together, the Catholic and evangelical communities have given my respondents religious arguments that support the standards of investigation embraced by their disciplines.

Conclusion

The stories of the scholars profiled in this chapter reveal their use of privatization and bracketing, multivocal bridging languages, and the rhetoric of objectivity. Taken as a whole, they cast doubt on Stephen Carter's depiction of the total marginalization of religion in public life. As overtly religious scholars, they have occupied positions at some of America's most prestigious research universities. Together, Catholics and evangelicals have brought some of the best elements of their religious traditions, such as the theology of David Tracy, Catholic social thought, and the philosophy and theology of Abraham Kuyper, into dialogue with leading voices of today's intellectual life (Thomas Kuhn, Clifford Geertz, Peter Berger), showing the potential for reconciliation between the academic social sciences and the world of religion.

Despite such efforts to reconcile religion and social science, my respondents' discourse has not always been free of tension or conflict. On the contrary, this study shows that Catholics and evangelicals talk about faith and scholarship in ways that are shot through with rhetorical inconsistency and seeming contradictions. The respondents' tendency to follow displays of religious conviction with appeals to the rhetoric of objectivity is especially telling of such conflictedness. The very fact that Greeley can describe his forays into the realm of theology and distance himself from the role of the theologian in the space of a single book shows the shifting character of the boundary between professional and religious identities. Likewise, Marsden's oscillation between the rhetoric of post-positivism (even postmodernism) and the rhetoric of objectivity raises questions about the internal consistency of his position.

How can these seeming contradictions in my respondents' rhetoric be explained? One possible explanation is that Catholic and evangelical scholars are engaged in a precarious balancing act between two distinct rhetorical objectives. They are trying to demonstrate their capacity to play by what Marsden called the "rules of the academic game," which are often construed to include a commitment to professional detachment. At the same time, they are attempting to justify the use of religious perspectives in their academic disciplines.

Of these two rhetorical objectives, demonstrating a capacity to play by the rules is by far the more crucial. DiIulio and Marsden have built their reputations not on public advocacy of religious viewpoints but on scholarship that is perceived to conform to the highest standards of their disciplines. Only after they had established a track record of professional competence did DiIulio and Marsden engage in the more speculative vocation of religiously informed social criticism. Their careers show that a reputation for scholarly rigor is a necessary, but not a sufficient, condition for being taken seriously as a religious public intellectual in the contemporary academy.[112]

Scholars who aspire to be social critics must persuade their readers that they are capable of doing credible empirical research. "Criticism can hardly be effective if it gets reality wrong," Wolfe points out. "[T]he critic must develop respect for what his methods find or he will have no credibility. One can get away with a sermon—once. But the critic who keeps finding the same reality in book after book—and, lo and behold, a reality which just happens to conform with the critic's own political position—will have lost all claims not only to scientific objectivity but to criticism."[113] The need to establish a professional reputation may explain why many of my respondents waited until their careers were well under way to embark on a explicitly religious scholarly agenda.

Although the "balancing-act" explanation seems to make sense of the interviews, a second explanation is available for why my respondents seemed to oscillate between strong critiques of positivism and equally strong defenses of professional detachment: A middle-of-the-road epistemology conforms best with their religious beliefs. As members of religious communities that make strong truth claims about the nature of ultimate reality, my respondents were uncomfortable with the radical subjectivism and relativism of postmodernist thought. Unlike many postmodernists, they have refused to accept the notion that reality is nothing more than a social construction. At the same time, they showed little sympathy for the positivist ideal of a value-free social science, believing that religious and moral values cannot be separated from academic research. In the words of Mark Noll, they have attempted to steer a course "between scientistic positivism and relativistic historicism," recognizing both the importance of empirical inquiry and the role of religious and philosophical presuppositions in shaping that inquiry.[114]

In this respect, the Catholic and evangelical scholars interviewed for this project did not sound all that different from their secular colleagues, embracing what Peter Novick has called a "middle-of-the-road grounding for the historical [and social-scientific] venture."[115] In the discipline of history, scholars such as Thomas Haskell have attempted to redefine scholarly objectivity in a way that makes room for strong political and moral commitments.[116] In sociology and political science, scholars such as Robert Bellah, Richard Bernstein, and Alan Wolfe have made a similar case for the compatibility of moral inquiry and empirical research.[117] By rejecting the extremes of positivism and postmodernism, the evangelical and Catholic scholars in this study have located themselves in the mainstream of contemporary debates over what Novick calls the "objectivity question."

Because an increasing number of their secular colleagues reject the notion of a value-free social science (or value-neutral history), Catholic and evangelical scholars have been able to legitimate the use of religious perspectives in their work. At the same time, their commitment to a modest version of objectivity has allowed them to gain the trust and confidence of those who do not share their religious views. This middle-of-the-road position has made it possible for my respondents to combine scholarship grounded in religious tradition with respect for the integrity of their academic disciplines. Through skillful use of a variety of bridging languages and the rhetoric of objectivity, these Catholics and evangelical scholars have found ways to articulate a fit between the worlds of academic social science and religious belief.

5 Journalism and the Religious Imagination

At the height of the scandal involving President Bill Clinton and Monica Lewinsky, William Powers wrote in *National Journal* that a "Roman Legion" of Irish Catholics had arisen in the Washington press corps who were especially critical of Clinton's behavior. Noting the scorn expressed for Clinton by Cokie Roberts, Mary McGrory, Tim Russert, and Chris Matthews, Powers asked whether it was a mere coincidence that so many of them had "come out of the same church?" Later in the article, he argued that their views reflected that church's moral history and that "the desire for complete honesty is of course very Catholic."[1]

Was Powers right? Did the "moral history" of Catholicism shape the journalism of Roberts, Russert, and Matthews in a way that led them to be harder on Clinton? To what extent are stories by Catholic and evangelical journalists influenced by their religious traditions?

One of the most striking things about the journalistic profession is its claim to tell stories without morals. In the textbook version of reporting, journalists come to a story tabula rasa: Political, moral, and religious convictions are checked at the newsroom door. In light of American journalism's public disavowal of moral questions, what place does religious faith play in the crafting of stories? Given the historic commitment of American journalists to the ideology of objectivity, there would seem to be little room for a religious or moral imagination. Journalists simply report on the world; they are not supposed to judge it.[2] Yet few scholars take the textbook version of the profession at face value anymore.

In *The Content of the Form,* Hayden White writes that narrative "is not merely a neutral discursive form"; instead, it reflects choices about the representation of reality that have "distinct ideological and even specifically political" consequences.[3] Along the same lines, Michael Schudson argues that journalism's conventional story forms "reinforce certain assumptions about the political world" while narrowing "the range of what kinds of truths can be told."[4] By including some newsmakers, plot lines, and explanatory frameworks and excluding others, journalistic narratives dramatize an implicit vision of which aspects of reality are politically and morally significant. Investigative journalists defend "traditional virtue by telling stories of terrible vice."[5] Foreign correspondents condemn torture by calling attention to the suffering of victims. "Insofar as journalists are defenders of a set of values," writes Herbert Gans, "they are more than technicians who transmit information from sources to audiences."[6]

The Catholic and Evangelical Imaginations

Given the value-laden character of journalistic narratives, what role do religious values play in stories by Catholic and evangelical journalists? Just as media analysts have rediscovered the importance of narrative, scholars from across the disciplines have increasingly stressed the role of stories in transmitting religious identities. From Bible stories to the lives of the saints and civil religious stories of "Christian America," such narratives furnish believers with cultural resources to make sense of the world and to "talk about the good society."[7] Catholic and evangelical journalists work at the intersection of two public storytelling communities: the profession of American journalism and their religious traditions. Along with the cultural conventions of the journalistic profession, the Catholic and evangelical traditions help fill the "cultural tool kits" of the respondents, providing the building blocks (stories, symbols, and metaphors) from which their news stories and columns are constructed.[8]

In *The Catholic Myth*, Andrew Greeley writes that Catholics and Protestants tell "different stories of God" and argues that the differences between the two heritages "are but manifestations ... of more fundamentally differing sets of symbols."[9] Concurring with Greeley, Robert Bellah says that there are deep differences between the "Protestant cultural code" and its Catholic counterpart.[10] Along the same lines, scholars have called attention to the presence of a Catholic sensibility in the works of, among others, John Ford, Andy Warhol, Flannery O'Connor, and Martin Scorsese.[11]

Given the internal pluralism of American Catholicism and American evangelicalism, it is dangerous to make any firm generalizations about the components of the Catholic and evangelical Protestant imaginations. Nevertheless, I will call attention to three sets of opposing qualities that capture some of the differences between the two traditions that scholars have identified.

(1) Catholic Sacramentalism and Evangelical Biblicism. In the opening paragraphs of *The Catholic Imagination,* Greeley provides an evocative description of the sacramental orientation of American Catholics:

> Catholics live in an enchanted world, a world of statues and holy water, stained glass and votive candles, saints and religious medals, rosary beads and holy pictures. But these Catholic paraphernalia are mere hints of a deeper and more pervasive religious sensibility which inclines Catholics to see the Holy lurking in creation. As Catholics we find our houses and our world haunted by a sense that the objects, events, and persons of daily life are revelations of grace. . . . The workings of this imagination are most obvious in the Church's seven sacraments, but the seven are both a result and a reinforcement of a much broader Catholic view of reality.[12]

This focus on the physicality of religious symbols and rituals contrasts sharply with evangelicalism's reverence for what Peter Thuesen calls the "leather-bound shrine in every home."[13] Evangelicals stress the inerrancy, infallibility, inspiration, and truth claims of the scriptures and have pointed to the Bible as a central point of contact between human beings and God.[14] Although these differences are by no means absolute, evangelicals have tended to see words (and the Word of God) as more sacred than things.[15]

(2) Analogical Catholics and Dialectical Evangelicals. The Catholic confidence in the capacity of rituals and symbols to mediate the sacred is related to an even more profound difference between the two religious traditions. In *The Analogical Imagination,* David Tracy argues that the Protestant and Catholic traditions incorporate different models of the relationship of God to the world and of Christianity to human culture. While the Protestant tradition tends to see the world as full of sin, the Catholic tradition sees the world as "charged with the grandeur of God."[16] Because of this culture-affirming orientation, Catholics are more likely to

view human society, the body, and the material world analogically (or as analogies for the divine), looking for "similarities in difference" between "God, self, other selves, and the world." By contrast, the Protestant tradition emphasizes the differences between creation and creator, nature and grace, and sacred and profane.[17] The qualities of this dialectical imagination are especially apparent in evangelicalism. More than any other branch of American Protestantism, evangelicals emphasize the boundaries between Christ and culture, sacred and secular, and church and world.[18]

(3) Catholic Communitarianism and Evangelical Individualism. Italian American films, "from *Mean Streets* through *Moonstruck, Sleepers,* and *Johnny Brasco,*" observes Greeley, are "about an intense family life, intricate extended family relations, and a close-knit neighborhood community."[19] Social scientists from Weber and Durkheim to Greeley and Bellah have long contrasted the communitarian orientation of the Catholic tradition with Protestant individualism. While the "Protestant cultural code" places enormous stress on personal faith, Catholicism sees the individual as embedded in a network of relationships and groups.[20] In sharp contrast to Catholic communitarianism, evangelicals have been "largely incapable of seeing how supraindividual social structures, collective processes, and institutional systems" shape human beings.[21] Along the same lines, recent surveys indicate that the vast majority of American Catholics consider "social justice" a central part of being Catholic.[22] By contrast, evangelicalism has emphasized personal morality and individual responsibility, embracing a "moral-reform agenda" of family values and opposition to abortion.[23]

This sketch of the Catholic and evangelical imaginations should not obscure the internal pluralism of both religious communities. Christian Smith warns against "treating conservative Protestants as a monolithic social group," noting that evangelicals "can be found spread across the political and ideological map . . . taking positions as diverse as pro-American conservatism, traditional liberalism, peace-and-justice activism, and theonomic reconstructionism."[24] Similarly, David O'Brien argues that, "after two centuries of organized existence in the United States, the American church has not evolved a coherent understanding of its public role and responsibilities."[25] From the pacifism of the Catholic Worker movement to the conservatism of William F. Buckley, American Catholics have integrated their religious views with a host of conflicting ideologies.

The Religious Imagination in American Journalism

Assessing the influence of religion on the journalists interviewed for this project was a difficult task. Besides the limitations of working with a small sample of ten Catholics and ten evangelicals, each journalist had written hundreds (and in some cases, thousands) of news stories and columns over the course of his or her career. Instead of analyzing every story written by every journalist, I chose to begin with a sample of fifty stories per journalist. These stories were culled evenly from across the careers of each person in the sample using the LEXIS-NEXIS Academic Universe database. I then searched for additional stories using key terms such as "culture wars," "community," and "justice" as broad themes emerged.

Eventually, I recognized recurring patterns in the respondents' stories. For example, it became evident that the evangelical journalists Cal Thomas, Fred Barnes, and Russ Pulliam had an affinity for the "culture wars" account of American politics, emphasizing the boundaries between conservative Christians and secular liberals. Similarly, the Catholic journalists E. J. Dionne, Kenneth Woodward, and Don Wycliff continually returned to the themes of community and individualism. As I worked through a sampling of stories by each journalist, I found it helpful to keep in mind an insight that is now commonplace among media scholars: Journalists tell the same stories over and over, plugging new facts into "pre-existing plotlines."[26] Mark Silk writes about this tendency in *Unsecular Media,* identifying seven recurring story lines that he calls the "topoi" of religion news.[27]

Borrowing Silk's approach, I have identified five recurring story lines that seem to reflect the influence of the Catholic and evangelical Protestant imaginations in my respondents' stories. Although these five story lines do not begin to exhaust the multitude of religious themes found in their writings, they do illustrate the influence of Catholicism and evangelicalism on their work:

(1) Culture wars: This story line of polarized conflict between religious conservatives and secular liberals embodies the dialectical, individualistic, and morality oriented outlook of the Protestant imagination.

(2) Cultural consensus: Reflecting an analogical emphasis on similarities in difference,[28] this story line stresses dialogue and points of agreement between liberals and conservatives, Catholics and non-Catholics, and religious and secular.

(3) Communitarian: This story line reflects Catholicism's focus on family, neighborhood, church, and the mediating institutions of civil society, along with an emphasis on the sacramentality of religious community and connectedness.

(4) Peace and justice: Reflecting the influence of the Catholic and evangelical left, this story line emphasizes the evils of social injustice and of violence.

(5) Testing the scriptures: This story line reflects evangelicalism's single-minded focus on the historical truth claims of the Bible, calling attention to scholarship that validates the accuracy of the scriptures.

To a large extent, these story lines embody the Catholic and Protestant imaginations as described by Tracy, Greeley, and others. While Catholics have told stories that are analogical and communal (the cultural-consensus, communitarian, and peace-and-justice story lines), evangelicals have emphasized individual morality and the truth claims of the Bible (the culture-wars and testing-the-scriptures story lines). At the same time, not all Catholic and evangelical journalists have told stories that conform to the textbook version of the Catholic and Protestant imaginations. Despite evangelicalism's tendency to downplay issues of social justice, at least one of the evangelical journalists has employed the peace-and-justice story line. Along the same lines, some Catholic journalists (though none in the sample) have made use of the culture-wars story line. These deviations from the standard accounts of the Catholic and Protestant imaginations are a reminder of the internal pluralism of both traditions.

Besides reflecting the religious backgrounds of their creators, the stories of my respondents have been shaped by the values and organizational divisions of professional journalism. In *Deciding What's News*, Gans describes eight "enduring values" that characterize the American news media: "ethnocentrism, altruistic democracy, responsible capitalism, small-town pastoralism, individualism, moderatism, social order, and national leadership." Many of these values are also shared by Catholic and evangelical journalists and have been integrated into the five story lines listed earlier. For example, there are deep affinities between political "moderatism" and the story of cultural consensus.[29] Nevertheless, some of the enduring values (individualism, responsible capitalism, and moderatism) are in tension with some of the story lines (communitarianism, peace and justice, and culture wars). Because of these tensions, Catholic and evangelical journalists have had to work to make their stories fit into the cultural context of American journalism.

Along with the enduring values outlined by Gans, the organization of news gathering into bureaus, beats, and topical specializations—what Gaye Tuchman calls the "news net"—has influenced stories by Catholic and evangelical journalists. Because journalists' reporting is limited to a relatively narrow range of organizations, sources, and topics, news is allowed to "occur at some locations but not at others": Even opinion columnists are constrained by the need to write about national issues.[30] The challenge for Catholic and evangelical reporters has been to find ways to tell the stories they want to tell (culture wars, communitarianism, peace and justice) in their particular spot in the news net (the White House, the United Nations, national politics).

The Catholic and evangelical journalists in this study have told stories at the intersection of professional and religious worlds. The stories they have written are both like and unlike those of their professional colleagues. Like African American journalists, gay journalists, female journalists, and other journalists who juggle multiple identities, they have engaged in a process of cultural bricolage, grafting the stories of their religious communities onto those of American journalism.[31] How Catholics and evangelicals have brought their religious commitments into American journalism through the five story lines of culture wars, cultural consensus, communitarianism, peace and justice, and testing the scriptures is the subject of the rest of this chapter. I will also look at how they have articulated a fit between the five story lines and the values and topical specializations of American journalism, creating hybrid story forms that reflect the influence of both social worlds.

The Culture-Wars Story Line: Cal Thomas

Christian Smith argues that "evangelicals operate with a very strong sense of boundaries that distinguish [them] from non-Christians and from nonevangelical Christians."[32] Nowhere is this more the case than in the rhetoric of Christian conservatives in American politics. In *Culture Wars: The Struggle to Define America* (1992), James Hunter describes conservative Protestants' (and other religious conservatives') affinity for the dualistic picture of the world contained in culture-wars rhetoric.[33] On issues such as abortion, the family, school prayer, and the media, the leaders of the new Christian right have drawn sharp boundaries between themselves and their political opponents. In contrast to the analogical imagination's focus on similarities in difference, this kind of rhetoric envisions a clear distinction between Christianity and the world. By choosing a language of difference rather than similarity, negation rather than affirmation, and conflict rather than consensus, the culture-wars story line is nearly a pure expression of the dialectical imagination.

Although several studies have shown that most American evangelicals do not view the world through a culture-wars lens, the story line has been used by several of the evangelical journalists interviewed for this project, including Fred Barnes and Russ Pulliam. By far the most frequent use of this story line is found in the writings of Cal Thomas of the Los Angeles Times syndicate. Although Thomas has moderated his rhetoric in recent years, he continues to be an outspoken advocate for religious conservatism. Thomas's column appears in more than five hundred newspapers, making it the most widely syndicated political column in the United States—surpassing George Will, Robert Novak, and Ellen Goodman in the number of newspapers reached.[34]

In 1987, Thomas published a collection of his columns under the title *Occupied Territory,* employing a metaphor from the culture wars.[35] Thomas's "raging red necktie [on the cover] tells the story," a review in the *Fundamentalist Journal* noted, that he "is angry that the conservative worldview [is] virtually absent [from] the public arena."[36] Although Thomas uses the term "culture wars" only occasionally, a culture-wars map of the world is implicit in much of his writing. In column after column, Thomas describes a struggle between two polarized camps battling for the soul of the nation. On one side are "conservatives," "social and religious conservatives," "Christians," the "Christian Right," and the "champions of traditional morality."[37] On the other are the "liberal secularists," the "pagan left," the "'heroes' and 'heroines' of the '60s," the "'60s flower children," "feminists," "television journalists," "big media," the "entertainment industry," the "tenured radicals," the "bigots" (against Christian conservatives), and the "protected classes."[38] The binary oppositions that run through Thomas's columns map out a clearly defined battle between two sides:

Conservatives	*Liberals*
Christians	Secularists
The Greatest Generation	Baby Boomers
Pre-1960s/1980s	1960s
Ordinary Women	Feminists
Ordinary Americans	Media Elites/Academics

"Defining the enemy" is a key feature of culture wars rhetoric, as James Hunter points out.[39] This list makes clear that Thomas's journalism divides the world into two warring factions.

Thomas regularly cites public-opinion surveys to show that a majority of Americans agree with the positions of religious conservatives. He has portrayed religious conservatives as the guardians of middle American values and the "Judeo-Christian tradition" and depicted liberals and the mass media as the agents of the nation's moral destruction.[40] In one column, Thomas blamed the "imposed immorality [of the] pagan left" for divorce, teen pregnancy, abortion, single-parent families, and murder.[41] In another, he accused "liberal secularists" of having "spiritually strip-mined" America.[42] In yet another, he used Hollywood celebrities and the media to symbolize the general moral decay of American society, holding up actor Hugh Grant's encounter with a prostitute as a sign of a general "sexual impurity in entertainment and real life." For Thomas, both Grant's sex scandal and a *Newsweek* article on bisexuality served as "evidence of social decay," a "new strain of depravity," and a sign that "jumbo jets full of societal viruses are stacked up over our nation."[43] The metaphors of impurity, sickness, and decay are repeatedly used to draw boundaries against liberals, secular humanists, and the entertainment industry.

Thomas also invests time with moral significance. In his writings, the 1960s in general—and the 1962 Supreme Court ruling against prayer in the schools in particular—are the symbolic starting point of America's spiritual and moral decline. "The liberals said no [to school prayer,] and no it has been for 32 years," Thomas wrote in a 1994 column. "[O]ur prayerlessness has promoted our growing secularism, and, many argue, the decay of our society into violence, lawlessness, and moral poverty."[44] As the children of the 1960s, baby boomers are singled out as especially culpable for the de-moralizing of American culture. Thomas has compared them unfavorably to the virtuous men and women of the World War II generation as the "intellectual and moral dwarfs . . . who can't see beyond their own comfort and for whom sacrifice was sitting still long enough to listen to a lecture from their parents about why they should love their country."[45] Thomas has also contrasted the piety of the Pilgrims with the secularism of "those who proclaimed God dead in the '60s," noting that it is "fitting that at Thanksgiving time, a national holiday that celebrates prayerful thanks, there would be a controversy about prayer in public schools."[46] Along the same lines, he has held up the faith of the "Founding Fathers" as an antidote to the reign of secular humanism.[47]

Why does Thomas draw such sharp boundaries between religious conservatives and secular liberals? What are the sources of his dialectical imagination? Michael Lienesch provides a clue in *Redeeming America: Piety and Politics in the New Christian Right* (1993) when he says that religious conservatives have tended to describe the polity in "dualistic terms, as a place of good and evil, right and wrong, allies and enemies."[48] Such dualistic rhetoric has deep roots in American evangelicalism, but it also serves a strategic purpose by mobilizing supporters against a common enemy through fund-raising letters, speeches, and political-campaign slogans. Before he began writing a column for the Los Angeles Times Syndicate, Thomas worked for Jerry Falwell's Moral Majority.

In addition to echoing the rhetoric of the new Christian right, many of Thomas's columns have been influenced by the storytelling conventions of American journalism. Hunter has noted journalists' "predisposition to dichotomize" and argued that "the narrative structure of most journalism depends in large part upon the interplay of antagonists and protagonists, heroes and villains, victims and victimizers, and so on." By contrasting the views of Christian conservatives and liberal secularists, Thomas fits his stories into journalism's "grid of rhetorical extremes."[49]

Thomas's stories also echo a number of Gans's enduring values in American journalism, including social order, individualism, and nationalism. By focusing on the so-called moral decay of American society, decline of the family, and "breakdown of culture," Thomas traffics in what Gans calls "social-disorder news." Such stories often romanticize the past while expressing a "fear of contemporary disintegration."[50]

The enduring journalistic value of individualism is also on display as Thomas returns again and again to the themes of "morality," "individual character," and "virtue."[51] His columns locate the problems of American society in the nuclear family or in individual lives, ignoring the larger social context of neighborhoods, churches, and civil society (something to which Catholic communitarians such as Kenneth Woodward and E. J. Dionne pay more attention). He has viewed government as part of the problem in columns that call for "smaller government, less dependence on the state and a reformation in moral and social values."[52] This single-minded focus on personal character to the exclusion of larger social institutions reflects evangelicalism's individualistic "moral-reform agenda."[53]

Consistent with evangelicalism's emphasis on the authority of the Bible, Thomas occasionally appeals to the biblical text. He quoted extensively from Psalm 139 in a column on abortion: "You created my inmost being; you knit me together in my mother's womb. . . . I am fearfully and wonderfully made."[54] Yet the civil-religious myths of American society—the story of Thanksgiving, the heroism of the Greatest Generation—figure far more prominently in his columns than the stories of the Bible. Thomas is a nationally syndicated political columnist. Because of his position in the news net, he has located his stories of moral decline within a narrative of the American nation rather than the story of the Christian church, reflecting journalism's emphasis on the "nation as a unit" and "national leadership."[55] Instead of relying on Christian terminology to make his arguments, which he does only occasionally, Thomas has appealed to "absolutes," "virtue," "objective standards," and "morality."[56] As the *Fundamentalist Journal* reviewer wrote, Thomas is "careful to let reason, statistics, and authorities—on both ends of the pole—present his case."[57]

A Truce in the Culture Wars? Critiquing the Religious Right from the Inside

Although the culture-wars story line can be found throughout Thomas's corpus, it does not dominate his work. Indeed, Thomas has used a small number of his columns to tell stories about agreement between conservatives and liberals, extolling the virtues of what Gans calls political moderatism.[58] Thomas wrote that "adoption can be a middle ground on which pro-life and pro-choice people ought to be able to meet" in a column celebrating Hillary Clinton's support for adoption as an alternative to abortion.[59] In another column, he urged religious conservatives to moderate their goals, warning that "the great danger is that they will overreach, alienate those who don't always share their agenda and win nothing."[60] In still another column, he reported on the reconciliation between Jerry Falwell and the gay evangelical Mel White, praising both men for "speaking and acting biblically."[61]

Along the same lines, Thomas's *Blinded by Might: Can the Religious Right Save America?* (1999, co-written with Ed Dobson, a former Moral Majority staff member) articulates a Christian critique of the new Christian right. In the book, Thomas and Dobson take conservative Christians to task for selling their souls. Rejecting the polarized rhetoric of direct-mail campaigns and political speeches, they argue that conservative Christians "must not . . . demonize those with whom we disagree."[62] And stressing Christian love over partisan rancor, they urge religious conservatives to reach out to their political opponents:

We stand in wholehearted agreement with conservative leaders who decry the condition of this country. We just think it's time to admit that because we are using the wrong weapons, we are losing the battle. Instead of modeling the message of Jesus, we model the message of political parties and interest groups.... Jesus said to love our enemies (he loved his enemies), to pray for those who persecute us (as he did on the cross) because in doing so we will heap coals of fire on their heads.[63]

Thomas and Dobson include several stories about friendly exchanges between conservatives and liberals, including an account of Thomas's friendship with Senator Edward Kennedy, as well as an interview with the television producer Norman Lear. In a remarkable exercise in self-criticism, they go so far as to "confess some of our own 'sins,'" rejecting the harshness of their former rhetoric.[64]

In repudiating the sins of the religious right, Thomas and Dobson have gained the admiration of many moderate and liberal Christians. The *Christian Century,* for example, praised *Blinded by Might* for recognizing the "limits of politics," and Richard Mouw called it a "bold and honest" book.[65] By contrast, the reaction of some religious conservatives has been scathing. In a review in *Christianity Today,* James Dobson, founder of Focus on the Family (and no relation to Ed Dobson), blasted *Blinded by Might*'s "isolationism" and criticized those who would "declare the culture war lost."[66]

Have Thomas and Dobson given up on the culture wars? The introduction of *Blinded by Might* suggests otherwise: "We are emphatically not calling for retreat or surrender by conservative Christians, or by anyone else on the 'right.'"[67] Although the authors reject the demonization of political opponents, a dualistic understanding of American society is implicit in much of their analysis. "We are called upon by Jesus to love our enemies, whether they be homosexuals, abortionists, Democrats, or liberals," Thomas writes in Chapter 3, suggesting that such groups remain enemies.[68] While attempting to be conciliatory they use words such as "secularists," "secular establishment," and "secular left" to describe their political opponents.[69] And although they reject the "impotent weapons of political activism," they portray America as a battleground, using military metaphors such as "surrender," "retreat," "enemies," and "weapons."[70] Urging evangelicals to "focus on the family, not on politics," they advocate a change in tactics rather than wholesale surrender.[71]

Consistent with the dialectical outlook of the Protestant imagination, Thomas and Dobson stress the tensions between Christ and culture, church and world, and evangelicalism and America. Although they soften the rhetoric of the religious right, they do not eliminate the boundaries between Christian conservatives and the outside world. Far from minimizing evangelical distinctives, they highlight the contrast between true Christianity and the immorality of contemporary society. Thus, despite its criticism of the religious right, *Blinded by Might* reflects the ongoing influence of the culture-wars framework on evangelical political thought.

The Cultural-Consensus Story Line: Peter Steinfels and E. J. Dionne

The Catholic journalists Peter Steinfels and E. J. Dionne have rejected the culture-wars narrative in favor of the cultural-consensus story line, reflecting a very different religious sensibility. Instead of focusing on the right and the left, both men have written about the center. And instead of pitting one era of American history against another (the 1960s versus the 1950s, the Pilgrims versus the baby boomers), they have focused on the ambiguities in each generation's experience. In place of martial metaphors ("occupied territory" and "culture wars"[72]), they have used terms such as "consensus,"[73] "agreement," "dialogue," and "complicated."[74]

Demonstrating a keen awareness of the story forms of American journalism, Steinfels and Dionne have criticized the "pre-existing plotlines" and frameworks of culture-wars reporting, arguing for narratives that do justice to the complexities of American life. Steinfels has written that he has tried to "give voice and visibility to those people and positions that get squeezed out when conflicts involving religion are reported only in terms of two sides—conservatives and liberals; orthodox and dissenters—rather than the spectrum of perspectives that normally exists."[75] Similarly, Dionne has lamented the fact that the 1960s have been the subject of rival conservative and liberal "parodies" (such as Cal Thomas' stories of declension), arguing that "each misses the other's truth and each fails to grasp how painfully complicated the 1960s were."[76]

Steinfels writes the "Beliefs" religion column for the *New York Times*. (When the interview was conducted, he was also the *Times*'s senior religion correspondent). Dionne writes a political-opinion column for the *Washington Post*. Despite differences in their beats and genres, both have exemplified the analogical imagination as described by Tracy and Greeley. Tracy defines analogy as "a language of ordered relationships articulating similarity-in-difference."[77] It focuses on the ways in which phenomena are like rather than unlike each other.[78] By encouraging the building of bridges rather than the building of walls, analogical thinking allows people of faith to engage in dialogue with those from outside their traditions.

In describing the political and religious landscape of American society, Steinfels and Dionne have told stories of similarities in difference, highlighting points of agreement between conservatives and liberals, left and right, and secular and religious. Conversation, dialogue, and a meeting of the minds figure prominently in both men's work. Reflecting his location in the news net—the religion beat—Steinfels has often used academic, religious, and political meetings and conferences as the scenic backdrop for stories about dialogue and agreement. In one column, he wrote about a United Nations meeting in Copenhagen at which the "Vatican converged with feminist lobbies," and "the forces of faith agreed, with each other and their secular counterparts." Criticizing the journalistic motif of conflict, Steinfels asked, "Was this a classic example of 'no conflict, no news?' "[79] Likewise, in a news story about the United Methodist's General Conference meetings, he reported on the "conference's determination to steer a cautious middle course on homosexuality." The article quoted a Methodist bishop as saying that he had come to the General Conference fearing that he would witness "a dramatic exhibition of polarization, [but] up to now . . . I haven't seen it."[80] Finally, Steinfels wrote that the election of an Eastern Orthodox priest to the presidency of the National Council of Churches represented a "'growing pluralism' and recognition of an Eastern Orthodox tradition that could mend the breach between liberal and conservative Christians."[81]

Dionne occupies a very different position in the news net: national politics. Yet he has incorporated similar motifs into his analyses, using public-opinion data to ground a consensus interpretation of American culture. In a column focusing on the extremism of the Anita Hill–Clarence Thomas hearings, Dionne argued that the United States "as a whole is not as neatly polarized as are the Washington-based interest groups. . . . [T]he polls showed pluralities or majorities of women supporting Thomas and a significant majority of men backing Hill, [showing] us that the world out there is far more complicated than men versus women, left versus right."[82] Rather than portraying sharp partisan divisions between liberals and conservatives, Dionne has focused on the ambivalence many Americans feel within themselves about many of the social changes of the past two decades. Citing a Times-Mirror survey on gender roles, Dionne wrote that, although "68 percent of those surveyed said that 'too many children are being raised in day-care centers,'" a similar percentage "rejected the idea that 'women should return to their traditional role in society.'" From these findings, Dionne concluded that "conventional political labels like conservative and liberal, even Democratic and Republican, are of little use [in] describing the American electorate."[83]

Dionne articulated the same themes in *Why Americans Hate Politics* (1991). In the book, he argues that the "false polarization" between liberals and conservatives was caused by the "cultural civil war that broke out in the 1960s."[84] Dionne also says that "America's cultural values are a rich and not necessarily contradictory mix of liberal instincts and conservative values"—a sharp contrast to the polarized discourse of the elites.[85] Even on abortion, he argued, evidence from polls shows that Americans "resist yes/no answers," and on other social questions, the "public's ambivalence suggests how deep is its thirst for compromise on the issues raised by the cultural civil war that began in the 1960s."[86] Rejecting "either/or" politics based on ideological preconceptions, Dionne called in the book for a "'both/and' politics based on ideas that broadly unite us."[87] In doing so, he exemplified the analogical imagination's emphasis on similarity in difference (both/and) and common ground over ideological polarity (either/or).

Steinfels and Dionne have condemned the use of inflammatory language in the public square and called for a return to what they see as civility and reasoned public discourse. Dionne sharply criticized both liberals' and conservatives' willingness to "flout all the rules in order to win" in a column about the Clarence Thomas–Anita Hill debate. "It is precisely when the issues at stake involve such explosive matters as race and sexuality that the country has a right to expect politicians, and especially the White House, to do more than just play around with social dynamite for cheap political points."[88] Steinfels has praised Andrew Sullivan, editor of the *New Republic,* for the unusual civility of a speech that he gave at Notre Dame titled, "The Gay Catholic Paradox." "What was noteworthy about [the] speech was the manner in which [Sullivan] presented the case," Steinfels wrote. Sullivan avoided "cheap shots [such as using AIDS] as an emotional club for winning agreement." The Notre Dame students were "impressed . . . with the way in which [Sullivan] argued his case within the framework of church teaching, and with the tone of the argument."[89]

Finally, both Dionne and Steinfels have highlighted the similarities in difference between Catholicism and American culture. In his final months as a Vatican correspondent for the *New York Times,* Dionne wrote an article titled, "America and the Catholic Church," that opened with a vignette: "Long before it was popular to do so, a Roman Catholic clergyman from the United States favored celebrating mass in English instead of Latin, the election of the leadership of the American church by its own priests instead of its appointment by Rome, and a strong role for the laity. The man in question was not a latter-day Catholic dissident, but John Carroll, the first Catholic bishop of the United States, elected by his fellow clergymen in 1789."[90] By drawing on the "new Americanism" in Catholic historiography, Dionne and Steinfels have emphasized the democratic strain within American Catholicism.[91] Along the same lines, many of their news stories have challenged the binary story line of the church versus the modern world. Instead of characterizing Pope John Paul II as a staunch traditionalist at war with modernity, Dionne has written: "[T]o assert that he is 'anti-modern' is too simple, since the 66-year-old Pope is himself a man of paradoxes and contradictions, the latter being one of his favorite words."[92] Likewise, Steinfels has criticized stories that descend from "the tension between religious faith and the 18th-Century Enlightenment" and called for a more nuanced account of religion and modernity.[93]

To what extent can Dionne's and Steinfels's analogical style be attributed to their liberal Catholic religious backgrounds? In an autobiographical essay published in 1965, Steinfels described the influence of two styles of Catholicism on his intellectual development:

> The Politician is my father's child: he read *Theology and Sanity* in high school (I think Cogley and *The Commonweal* were his, too) and admires the realistic things Eugene McCarthy has said about the nature of compromise; he understands strategy, waiting, the double effect, and sees five sides to every question. The Prophet is the son of my mother: his was Dorothy Day and the *Catholic Worker* and *The Woman Who Was Poor* and he wonders if the world is not beyond strategy and at what point calculation is the death of the soul. Every Christian, I think, carries these two figures within his soul and senses the tension between them.

Sometime between the 1960s and the 1980s, this tension was resolved in favor of the Politician. One of Steinfels's early intellectual heroes was John Cogley, editor of *Commonweal.* In the 1940s, Cogley separated himself from the Catholic Worker movement, criticizing the movement for its total pacifism.[94] Echoing the trajectory and views of his hero, Steinfels has emphasized the motif of compromise while identifying "five sides to every question." His stories bear a much greater resemblance to the analogical rhetoric of Cogley and *Commonweal* than they do to the pages of the *Catholic Worker.*

Dionne, too, has called attention to the Catholic roots of his politics. In a passionate *Washington Post* column following Pope John Paul II's visit to Denver in 1993, Dionne urged the press to focus on liberal Catholicism's contribution to American public life. "My heroes in American Catholicism," he wrote, "are the progressives, people like Archbishop Rembert Weakland, Father Bryan Hehir and Peggy Steinfels, the editor of *Commonweal.*"[95]

Dionne's and Steinfels's careers must be seen in the context of the ongoing interaction between American liberal culture and Catholic intellectual life. As Catholics, they are the intellectual heirs of Cogley and McCarthy. As liberal intellectuals, they reflect the influence of non-Catholics such as Reinhold Niebuhr; Arthur Schlesinger, Jr.; and Daniel Bell.[96] Scholars of rhetoric have long pointed out the affinities between certain metaphors and ideological traditions such as liberalism, conservatism, and Marxism. By praising consensus, paradox, and complexity, Steinfels and Dionne have appropriated the vocabulary of postwar American liberalism. As Godfrey Hodgson points out, "irony, paradox, complexity, and other safely non-political abstractions" became the metaphors of choice for liberal consensus thinkers such as Bell, Richard Hofstadter, Niebuhr, and Schlesinger.[97] They are also congruent with American journalism's emphasis on moderatism.[98]

American Catholicism has not always enjoyed such a harmonious relationship with the liberal tradition. As recently as the 1940s and 1950s, prominent American liberals depicted Catholicism as a dangerous threat to American democratic values.[99] Perceived by liberal elites as hierarchical, authoritarian, and intolerant, American Catholics were criticized for violating what Jeffrey Alexander calls the "discourse of civil society."[100] Postwar *Commonweal* Catholicism of the sort exemplified by Cogley was a response to the liberal denunciation of Catholic culture found in books such as *American Freedom and Catholic Power* (1949).[101] By focusing on "neutral grays" rather than black and white, liberal Catholicism helped integrate Catholics into the world of liberal public intellectual discourse.[102]

In recent years, Steinfels and Dionne have brought a similar approach to religion and politics into American journalism. This combination of religious and democratic values is apparent in Dionne's comments at a

1994 forum on the religious right. Civil society, Dionne argued, "is the place where most of these arguments should take place.... [The] purpose of democratic politics is not to provide chances to pronounce anathemas or to cast fellow citizens into darkness."[103] By drawing firm boundaries against incivility, intolerance, and pronouncing "anathemas," while emphasizing the importance of vigorous public debate, Dionne and Steinfels have demonstrated the capacity of American Catholics to play by the rules of democratic civil society.

The Communitarian Story Line:
E. J. Dionne, Kenneth Woodward, and Don Wycliff

In recent years, a growing number of thinkers have soured on American individualism, arguing that the Lone Ranger ethos of American society has been taken too far. Organizing themselves under the banner of "communitarianism," they have called for a renewed commitment to the common good, emphasizing solidarity over solitariness, responsibilities over rights, and community over individualism.[104] Of particular concern to communitarians is the strengthening of civil society—the sector of society made up of families, voluntary associations, churches, and neighborhoods that stands apart from the state and the market.[105]

Although communitarianism is not a religious movement per se, many of its leaders have been shaped by religious traditions of one kind or another. Bellah, the author of *Habits of the Heart: Individualism and Commitment in American Life* (1996), is an Episcopalian; Ann Swidler, his coauthor, and the Harvard sociologist Daniel Bell are observant Jews, and Jean Bethke Elshtain is a Lutheran. Even many of the secular thinkers identified with communitarianism, such as Adam Seligman, Philip Selznick, Michael Walzer, and Alan Wolfe, come out of an intellectual world that has been strongly influenced by American Jewish culture.[106]

Thomas Landy points out that Catholics and Jews have been far more central to the development of communitarianism than liberal Protestants.[107] Landy views liberal individualism as a largely "Protestant project" and argues that the "religio-cultural template" of Catholicism has a much greater affinity for communitarian habits of mind.[108] The list of Catholic scholars associated with communitarianism is impressive: John DiIulio, Mary Ann Glendon, David Hollenbach, Alasdair MacIntyre, William Sullivan, Charles Taylor, and James Q. Wilson. In the world of American journalism, Catholics have also been active in advancing a communitarian vision. Sometimes this has been overt, as in Kenneth Woodward's glowing review of *Habits of the Heart* for *Newsweek*.[109] At other times, it has been implicit, reflected in the subtle choices journalists make in writing about American society.

The most prominent Catholic communitarian in U.S. journalism is Dionne. He is somewhat unusual in the world of Washington journalism in that he serves as a senior fellow at the Brookings Institution while continuing to write for the *Washington Post*. Together with John DiIulio, Dionne has helped put faith-based institutions, religion, and "God talk" back on the agenda of American liberalism, articulating a vision that has been called "communitarian," "neo-progressive," and "neo-liberal."[110] At Brookings, Dionne and DiIulio coordinated a project on congregations and social justice titled, "Sacred Places, Civic Purposes." Its goal was to forge a "new dialogue [that is] less ideologically polarized" than past discussions of religion and politics.[111]

Unlike many thinkers in the communitarian movement, Dionne is hopeful about the future of U.S. society. "The United States is experiencing a quiet civic revival," he said. This theme is reflected in his *Post* columns and in the titles of two of his books, *Community Works: The Revival of Civil Society in American Society* and *What's God Got to Do with the American Experiment?* (co-edited with DiIulio).[112] Taking his cues from Catholic social teaching, the turn-of-the-century progressive movement, and social scientists such as Wolfe, Dionne has advanced a vision of communitarianism that combines concern for social equality with a "tolerant traditionalism" on matters of faith and family.[113] Central to this vision is concern for the "rich networks built around families and neighborhoods, churches and civic groups, professional societies and sports clubs."[114]

Although he is not as well known as Dionne, the veteran *Newsweek* religion writer Kenneth Woodward has been an important advocate of communitarianism, bringing the voices of Jean Bethke Elshtain, Alasdair MacIntyre, Martha Nussbaum, Charles Taylor, and James Q. Wilson into the pages of one of America's leading magazines.[115] In 1978, he praised Christopher Lasch's work on the culture of narcissism, contending that the "most immediate benefit of the ongoing debate may well be that new theories of narcissism will reattach importance to the role of parents and support those who are struggling to give their children an internal set of values as well as a sense of moral and social responsibility."[116] Similarly, Woodward's 1985 review of *Habits of the Heart* gave a boost to the com-

A graduate of the University of Notre Dame, *Newsweek*'s Kenneth Woodward has maintained close ties to the world of Catholic higher education. He is shown delivering the commencement address at the College of the Holy Cross. (Courtesy Holy Cross College Archives.)

munitarian movement, calling the book the "richest and most readable study of American society since David Riesman's '50s classic *The Lonely Crowd*." Praising Bellah and his co-authors for providing "a fresh lexicon of terms like 'communities of memory and hope,'" Woodward wrote, "*Habits* offers a grammar of moral clarity, substance, and promise."[117]

It is this communitarian grammar that Woodward has employed in many stories for *Newsweek*. In 1994, he reviewed the debate over William

Bennett's *Book of Virtues*, simultaneously outlining his own communitarian vision. Invoking Aristotle, as well as MacIntyre and Taylor, Woodward
wrote: "Good character comes from living in communities—family, neighborhood, religious and civic institutions—where virtue is encouraged
and rewarded."[118] Unlike Cal Thomas's evangelical jeremiads, which
locate morality solely within the individual, Woodward has focused on the
connections between what Jean Bethke Elshtain calls "strong institutions"
and "strong virtues."[119] By emphasizing the importance of institutions,
such as the family, neighborhood, church, and school, to the health of
American society, Woodward has articulated a communal understanding
of moral virtue that bears little resemblance to the individualistic ethics
of evangelical culture warriors.

Don Wycliff, an African American Catholic, has brought a similar
focus to his work at the *Chicago Tribune* and the *New York Times*, blending
the insights of the black self-help tradition with Catholic social teaching.
In the interview, Wycliff said that Catholicism's focus on community has
shaped his writing "in almost every editorial" and noted that he has "a lot
more respect for the power of cultures and communities and small
groups and neighborhoods, and that kind of thing to affect change in
people's lives." Specifically, Wycliff cited the Catholic principle of subsidiarity as "fundamental to the kind of way I view the world," invoking a
doctrine that Greeley calls the "central theme of Catholic social theory."[120]

Subsidiarity, defined as the notion that "nothing should be done by a
larger organization that could be done by a smaller one," is implicit in
much of Wycliff's writing.[121] In a review of *Families in Peril*, he wrote that
Marian Wright Edelman's call for "more and stronger governmental
efforts [is] both right and wrong." Although government spending is
"indispensable," he said, "each child is first the responsibility of two specific adults." While praising Edelman's "tribute to . . . 'families, schools,
churches and mentors,'" he complained that "somewhere along the way,
the importance of that kind of self-confident assertion of values by the
black community was overshadowed by a concern with other things."[122]

In the interview, Wycliff said he felt a strong affinity for the "emphasis in a lot of Catholic social teaching on what Edmund Burke called 'little platoons': family, neighborhood, community, those sorts things." It is
by focusing on those "little platoons" that journalists such as Woodward,
Wycliff, and Dionne have brought the Catholic communitarian perspective into the pages of the *Washington Post, Newsweek,* and the *New York
Times*. Once on the margins of American public discourse, subsidiarity

and other terms in Catholic social thought are increasingly part of the public-policy lexicon.[123]

Communitarianism does not belong to Catholics alone. As noted earlier, Jewish thinkers such as Daniel Bell, Amitai Etzioni, Philip Selznick, and Alan Wolfe have been in the forefront of the communitarian movement. At the same time, there is something unmistakably Catholic about the way Catholic journalists have expressed their communitarian convictions. In *Bare Ruined Choirs,* Garry Wills observes that religious terminology "haunts a Catholic's speech in ways he is often unaware of."[124] The theme of subsidiarity, rarely found in the works of Jewish and Protestant intellectuals, can be found again and again in the writings of Catholic communitarians. The themes of sacramentality and the communion of saints also distinguish the works of Catholic journalists from that of their non-Catholic counterparts.

In his 1990 bestseller *Making Saints,* Woodward defended the Catholic idea of the communion of saints, articulating a sacramental vision of human connectedness that transcends even the grave:

> The cult of the saints presupposes that everyone who has existed, and everyone who will exist, is interconnected—that is, that there really is a basis in the structure of human existence for "the communion of saints." Otherwise, there would be no point in praying to the saints who have died or, for that matter, in praying for one another. But to assert that all human beings are radically connected over space, through time, and even beyond death is to counter the experience and assumptions of Western, free-enterprising societies which prize personal autonomy and the individuated self.[125]

By locating a critique of modern individualism within the context of the Catholic belief in saints, Woodward shows that the Catholic tradition contains resources for talking about community that are not found in other faiths.

Coming of age in the world of "ghetto Catholicism" was a powerful experience for both Woodward and Wycliff. Like Garry Wills, they "grew up different." In the interview, Woodward said that he grew up "in a parallel culture." Wycliff recalled growing up in the tight-knit world of eastern Texas African American Catholicism, saying that there is "far more of a fit" between Catholic social teaching and "what I've thought of my whole life as the way black people conducted their lives in communities." Significantly, both men spoke passionately about the influence of their common mentor, the late Frank O'Malley, who taught English at Notre Dame. "Coming out of Notre Dame with this powerful mentor," said Woodward, "you always thought of the big issues as central to human existence. Is there a God or isn't there? If there is, what is God like? What is my relationship to this God? All that sort of thing." An "electrifying lecturer," notes Arnold Sparr, O'Malley urged students to live an "integrated Christian life." He exposed them to the works of such European Catholic luminaries as Georges Bernanos, Etienne Gilson, Romano Guardini, and Jacques Maritain. He emphasized what Sparr calls a "uniquely Catholic way of looking at the world"; thus, it is not surprising to find Woodward and Wycliff sounding the themes of communitarianism and sacramentality.[126]

At the same time, it is surprising to find a Catholic communitarian perspective so forcefully articulated in the mainstream news media. Individualism is an enduring value in both American journalism and American society. "The good society of the news is populated by individuals who participate in it, but on their own terms," Gans writes, and individualism is portrayed as "a weapon against the dangers of both bigness and conformity."[127] Along the same lines, sociologists have long viewed individualism as a defining element of the American character, along with achievement, success, material comfort, and freedom.[128] By contrast, Catholic communitarianism historically has been depicted by both Protestant and secular intellectuals as a potential threat to the American values of individual freedom, civil liberties, and democracy.[129]

In light of individualism's seeming hegemony over American culture, what place remains for a communitarian—let alone, a communitarian Catholic—approach to journalism? First, it is important to realize that American culture has always been a complicated mixture of individualistic and communitarian impulses. As Bellah and colleagues remind us, a people's cultural tradition—"its symbols, ideals, and ways of feeling"—is composed of competing "strands" that together constitute "an argument about the meaning of the destiny its members share." In American society, the communal strands of the biblical and republican traditions have helped to balance the traditions of utilitarian and expressive individualism.[130]

Second, in recent decades the "quest for community" has found new vitality, as suggested by the sales figures for *Habits* and Robert Putnam's *Bowling Alone*. "[A] powerful strand of recent social criticism treats autonomy as a historical problem, not just as a goal," writes John McGreevy. The favorable reception of the Catholic communitarians Mary Ann Glendon, Charles Taylor, and Alasdair MacIntyre, McGreevy argues, indicates that the contemporary "fascination with intellectual and social 'community' [is changing] lingering apprehension about the threat posed to social cohesion by Catholic schools and churches into admiration."[131]

Paralleling the revival of the concept of community in American intellectual life, American journalism is experiencing a communitarian moment, as shown by the growing prominence of so-called civic and public journalism. "Civic journalism," writes Edward Fouhy, "is an attempt to reclaim the central role journalists must play in enriching the civic life of a community."[132] An overview in *Columbia Journalism Review* reports that the "public/civic journalism crowd draws on a number of sacred texts," including Dionne's *Why Americans Hate Politics* and Robert Putnam's *Bowling Alone.*[133] As one of the "most talked about innovations in journalism today," public and civic journalism have helped legitimate a new style of reporting that regards journalists as both citizens and observers.[134]

However, Catholic communitarianism has not become entirely mainstream. Individualism remains a core American value. Many journalists are critical of public and civic journalism, arguing that these approaches are not "real journalism."[135] And although the "civic" dimensions of community are well known to journalists and scholars, the Catholic imagination is still a minority voice in a culture strongly influenced by Anglo-American Protestantism. Though enamored with the Tocquevillian themes of citizenship, community, and civic republicanism, American journalists are not quite ready for the world of saints, sacraments, and subsidiarity.[136]

The Peace and Justice Story Line: Colman McCarthy and Wesley Pippert

The twenty Catholic and evangelical journalists interviewed for this project have gravitated toward the broad center of American politics. With the exception of Cal Thomas, they have staked out positions that mediate between the extremes of the left and the right. Two other notable exceptions to this middle-of-the-roadism are Colman McCarthy and Wesley Pippert. McCarthy wrote an opinion column at the *Washington Post* for more than thirty years; as a reporter for United Press International, Pippert covered President Jimmy Carter's White House, the Middle East, and the U.S. Congress.[137] Although they share communitarianism's misgivings about individualism, McCarthy (Catholic) and Pippert (evangelical) have articulated a far more penetrating critique of American society.

McCarthy is alone among nationally syndicated columnists in his outspoken pacifism, and he was an eloquent opponent of U.S military spending, the arms race, and American wars during his years at the *Post. The Progressive* has called McCarthy a "pacifist, a bit of an anarchist, a Catholic,
an animal-rights advocate, an ardent bicyclist, a stalwart opponent of
injustice, a teacher of nonviolence, a friend to the homeless, a foe of the
death penalty, a leftwing pro-lifer, and a fine writer."[138]

As noted in chapter 3, McCarthy's radicalism has deep roots in the lay
Catholic movement founded by Dorothy Day and Peter Maurin. Just as
Steinfels has brought the centrist style of *Commonweal* Catholicism to the
pages of the *New York Times,* McCarthy drew on the story forms of the
Catholic Worker during his years as a columnist. Reflecting the personalist
theology of its founders, a hallmark of *Catholic Worker* journalism is a
focus on everyday works of mercy and "instances which show God's work-
ings in everyday lives."[139] True to this legacy, many of McCarthy's *Washington Post* columns profiled a single character engaged in personal works
of charity and social justice. In one such column he told the story of
Bishop Edward O'Rourke, who had sold the "baronial 24-room Bishop's
mansion in the wealthy part of the town and moved into a bungalow in
the poorest slum in the city" to carry out Pope Paul VI's call for those who
have plenty to give to those who "lack necessities." He wrote, "Like the
Franciscans of the 13th century, O'Rourke announced that his door
would be open day and night to anyone, [and in] 24 years of the purest
kind of religious hospitality, thousands of Peoria's poor have been welcomed."[140] Like the Catholic Worker movement, McCarthy celebrated
the "hidden contributions of millions of solitary persons whose only activity is seeking truth and trying to ease the world's suffering."[141]

McCarthy's columns also told stories of reconciliation, peacemaking,
and forgiveness. In one such story, McCarthy wrote about "mothers,
fathers, and relatives who have lost loved ones to murderers but who
oppose the death penalty."[142] In another, he described how the former
hostage Terry Anderson forgave his Islamic fundamentalist captors, jux-
taposing Anderson's story with theological reflections on forgiveness
drawn from Martin Luther King, Jr.; Dostoevsky's *The Brothers Karamazov;*
and the Bible.[143]

National opinion columns usually report on the activities of senators,
cabinet secretaries, White House officials, and other government figures.[144] By bringing Bishop O'Rourke and the members of Murder Victim Families for Reconciliation into his columns, McCarthy extended

the journalistic news net to include people who would not ordinarily make the pages of the *Washington Post.* McCarthy also profiled activists, thinkers, and writers outside the world of Washington officialdom— and, in some cases, outside the twentieth century—such as Dorothy Day, Paul Hanly Furfey, Flannery O'Connor, St. Francis of Assisi, Mohandas Gandhi, E. F. Schumacher, Maria Montessori, A. J. Muste, I. F. Stone, and Woody Guthrie.[145] Like the *Catholic Worker,* he covered the poor and the downtrodden, draft resisters, men on death row, and Old Testament prophets. In a recent interview, McCarthy said that he "never went to a White House press conference" and that "you can learn more by going to soup kitchens, schools, prisons, and migrant camps."[146]

To be sure, McCarthy espoused a much more favorable view of the nation-state than his friends in the Catholic Worker movement. Dorothy Day's personalist "suspicion of politics in general and the large national state in particular" led the Catholic Worker movement to "disavow 'welfare' schemes, whether devised by church or state" in favor of "works of mercy."[147] By contrast, McCarthy praised federal-government programs in his columns as instruments of social justice. Yet, despite his strong support for the welfare state, he regularly criticized the use of state-sanctioned violence. In a column on the anti–death-penalty group Murder Victim Families for Reconciliation, McCarthy quoted a woman who challenged the legitimacy of capital punishment: "Killing Ronnie Dunkins [a death-row inmate] and telling these children that now the crime has been 'punished' and all is again right with the world sends a message that violence and vengeance are okay as long as they are state-sanctioned."[148] Condemnation of state violence can also be found in McCarthy's stories on the American military. In a 1993 column on defense conversion, McCarthy called the United States "the world's most violent and militaristic government" and argued that spending "defense conversion" funds on dual-use military technology meant that the "grand militaristic designs of the United States as global butt-kicker remain in place."[149] In another column, McCarthy criticized the "collective narcissism" of the Pledge of Allegiance. This "daily rite of obedience training," he wrote, "primes the young to accept unquestioningly the message of leaders that America is running the world's show but dispensing liberty and justice for all while doing it."[150]

Compared with the writings of Steinfels and Dionne, McCarthy's columns are downright countercultural. Instead of celebrating the compatibility of Catholicism and American values, they call attention to the stark contrast between the Christian Gospel and America's "culture of violence," articulating what Michael Baxter, a Catholic ethicist, calls a counter-American Catholic social ethic. By condemning the "mindless militarism," "flag-waving foolhardiness," and "grand militaristic designs" of the United State, McCarthy's columns question the over-identification of Christianity and American civil religion.[151]

Like that of the liberation theologians of Latin America, McCarthy's theological vision is best described as dialectical rather than analogical. In criticizing the United States for embracing a "war ethic," McCarthy has stressed the discontinuities between American culture and the Christian Gospel, rejecting what Tracy calls the "all too easy continuities and relaxed similarities between Christianity and culture, between God and the human, God and world."[152] Instead of looking for similarities in difference, McCarthy has shown that America falls short of Gospel values. Although the dialectical imagination is usually regarded as Protestant rather than Catholic, McCarthy's dialectical Catholicism is deeply rooted in the moral vision of the Catholic Worker movement.

Just as McCarthy's dialectical perspective sets him apart from Dionne and Steinfels, Wesley Pippert's peace and justice evangelicalism is a departure from the conservative political ideology of his co-religionists. Although a host of studies have documented the existence of an evangelical non-right, the public face of evangelicalism has long been identified with such groups as the Moral Majority and the Christian Coalition.[153] By bringing the perspectives of progressive evangelicals into American journalism, Pippert's news stories bear witness to a public evangelicalism outside the religious right.

As a reporter for United Press International from 1955 to 1988, Pippert worked in a genre that historically has deemphasized the reporter's personal voice. A close reading of his stories, however, reveals a consistent concern for social justice and peace despite such constraints. In the early 1980s, Pippert wrote a series of articles about the negative effect of the Reagan administration's cuts in welfare. In one article, he focused on religious opposition to cutbacks in food stamps, quoting a clergyman's remark that the "ancient prophets equated the provision of food with justice."[154] In another, he wrote that "millions of people—from infants to teen-agers, from young adults to the elderly—would be touched" by the budget reductions. In still another, he reported on liberal criticism of the proposed elimination of VISTA (often called the domestic Peace Corps), citing Sargent Shriver's comment that "you can't measure service on a yardstick of economics."[155] In *An Ethic of News: A Reporter's Search for Truth* (1989), Pippert explained that his news stories on the Reagan budget were part of his overall focus on justice and peace: "After being assigned to Congress at the start of the Reagan administration, I conceived and carried out a five-part series on how domestic budget cuts would affect the quality of life for Americans in the areas of health, education, welfare, and jobs. . . . Stories involving injustice do not lack newsworthiness, but members of the mass media often show insensitivity and lack of awareness toward them."[156]

Consistent with the conventions of wire-service reporting, Pippert rarely divulged his own views on the topic. On one occasion, however, he abandoned the stance of reportorial detachment. In a rare UPI commentary, Pippert wrote, "[T]he message of the Bible is that always it chooses life over death, always it comes down on the side of the poor and oppressed. From Genesis to Revelation it admonishes people to care for the widow, the orphan, and the stranger."[157] Pippert's emphasis on the biblical themes of justice and peace originated in a master's thesis he completed in Old Testament studies at an evangelical college (see chapter 3). A departure from the standard content of wire-service news stories, his use of the Bible in a UPI commentary reflects evangelicalism's emphasis on the authority of the scriptures.

By acknowledging the social implications of the biblical call for "justice and righteousness," Pippert parted company with mainstream evangelicalism's "one-individual-at-a-time" approach to transforming society.[158] In doing so, he reflected a new emphasis in evangelical political thought on the structural dimensions of social change. Pippert spoke for a new generation of evangelical political leaders who were fed up with the political conservatism of their co-religionists. Dubbed "reform-oriented" evangelicals by Robert Booth Fowler, these activists "insisted that many of the evils of the world were social and required social solutions."[159] Through organizations such as Evangelicals for Social Action, they challenged the image of evangelicalism as the Republican Party at prayer.

Just as McCarthy brought the voices of the Catholic left into his column at the *Washington Post*, Pippert extended the UPI news net to include the voices of progressive evangelicals such as Mark Hatfield and Paul Henry.[160] In one of his many pieces on the Reagan budget, Pippert cited Senator Hatfield's call for every government program to be "looked at with equal intensity—including the military."[161] In another story, he summarized a study of the religious views of U.S. congressmen that found that "the most extreme liberals of all were evangelicals with an integrated and people-concerned approach to religion."[162]

In *Memo for 1976: Some Political Options* (1976), Pippert wrote openly about his admiration for reformist evangelicals such as Henry and Hatfield: "The writing and ideas of Hatfield and [Congressman John B.] Anderson as well as those of young evangelical scholars Don Jones, Richard Pierard, Robert Linder, and Paul Henry, helped give me intellectual underpinnings. These men are redirecting the nation's forty million evangelicals to a new concern for the world around them."[163] By bringing these figures into his news stories for UPI, Pippert helped give voice to a segment of evangelicalism that exists outside the religious right.

What place does the justice-and-peace story line hold in American journalism? The American news business has become more open to this sort of journalism since the 1960s. The rise of advocacy journalism and the alternative press has made journalists more conscious of their role in fostering social change (see chapter 3). However, McCarthy's and Pippert's writings run counter to many of the enduring values of American journalism. While mainstream journalism has celebrated the value of individualism, they have stressed the importance of social justice. While mainstream journalism has emphasized the value of "responsible capitalism," they have questioned the legitimacy of corporate greed. While mainstream journalism has been consistently patriotic, they have challenged the pieties of American civil religion.[164]

McCarthy in particular has articulated positions that most American journalists do not support. His uncompromising pacifism and support for animal rights are unpopular among his colleagues and with the American public. McCarthy acknowledged in an interview that he tries to "keep a consistent ethic of non-violence" and that most liberal writers in mainstream dailies "rarely go near" some of the topics he addresses. Seventy-three newspapers bought his syndicated column in 1981; that number dropped to twenty-seven in 1996—a reflection of how far he diverges from American public opinion. In the wake of the Reagan revolution and the triumph of Clintonism, fewer and fewer Americans seemed interested in radical critiques of American society. In 1997, the Washington Post Writers Group canceled McCarthy's column.[165] The "lone voice at the *Post* in support of the poor, the homeless, and for peace," as Matthew Rothschild described McCarthy, was gone.[166] McCarthy now writes for the *Progressive*, reaching a smaller but much more sympathetic audience.

Like McCarthy, Pippert has left the news business. He worked for a year in the late 1980s as a special assistant to Congressman Paul Henry of

Michigan, who was one of his intellectual heroes. Pippert has traded the life of a wire-service reporter for a career as a journalism educator and now directs the Washington Program at the prestigious Missouri School of Journalism. Since his departure from the national press, no evangelical has been sounding the themes of social justice and peace at a major newspaper or magazine.

But progressive voices have not vanished from the world of elite journalism. Some, such as James Carroll of Boston's *Globe,* are even religious, combining the Social Gospel with analysis of public issues. At the same time, it is significant that McCarthy's voice has been excluded from mainstream journalism at a time that Thomas's columns appear in more than five hundred papers. As American journalism enters a new century, the religious right remains visible. The religious left is much harder to find.

The Testing-the-Scriptures Story Line: Jeffery Sheler

Religion journalism is enjoying something of a renaissance. One consequence of the media's greater attention to religion is that more Americans are being introduced to scholarship on the Bible. Although most people are unfamiliar with academic biblical criticism, readers of *Time, Newsweek,* and *U.S. News and World Report* regularly encounter stories about the quest for the historical Jesus, biblical archaeology, and other topics of scholarly inquiry. These stories serve an important cultural function by translating the often arcane jargon of biblical scholars into a form than a middlebrow U.S. magazine audience can understand. In addition to the books of the Jesus Seminar and various evangelical scholars, the weekly newsmagazines have exposed a large national audience to academic debates over the historical accuracy of the Bible. The issue of *U.S. News and World Report* with Jeffery Sheler's cover story, "Is the Bible True?" sold more than 101,000 copies.[167]

The journalists behind these stories have helped shape public discourse about the Bible in America. By focusing their readers' attention on certain books, scholars, and schools of thought—and not on others—they have played a gatekeeping role, determining the kinds of Bible scholarship that will reach the public. Because most of their readers will not review the academic literature themselves, the journalists are the filters through which serious scholarship must pass.

Reporters' religious beliefs play a role in news stories about the Bible. To be sure, most religion reporters bend over backward to include a wide range of perspectives, balancing the radical Jesus Seminar with the moderate Raymond Brown and the liberal Bishop Spong with the evangelical Billy Graham. Yet even the most balanced reporters make choices about the topics they write about, which scholars they profile, and how they will frame their questions. For much of the 1990s, the senior religion writers at *Time, Newsweek,* and *U.S. News and World Report* were practicing Catholics or evangelicals. I have already explored the influence of a Catholic, communitarian sensibility on the journalism of *Newsweek's* Kenneth Woodward. An equally strong case can be made for the influence of evangelicalism on the religion reporting of Jeffery Sheler of *U.S. News and World Report.*

"The most important conviction of evangelical scholars is that the Bible is true ... not just as religion but also as fact," Mark Noll writes in *Between Faith and Criticism: Evangelicals, Scholarship, and the Bible in America.*[168] More than any other American religious group, evangelicals have evinced a preoccupation with "truth."[169] Articulating what George Lindbeck calls a "cognitive–propositional" view of religion, evangelicals stress the ways in which the Bible makes "truth claims about objective realities."[170]

An evangelical preoccupation with truth is evident in Sheler's religion coverage. Whereas the Catholic Woodward has often bracketed the question, "Did it really happen?" in favor of the more subjective, "What does it mean?" Sheler has returned again and again to the accuracy of the Bible.[171] This cognitive–propositional concern for truth is best captured in the title of his recent book *Is the Bible True? How Modern Debates and Discoveries Affirm the Essence of the Scriptures.*[172] Words such as "veracity," "accuracy," "historicity," "real," "historical truth," and "history"[173] can be found throughout his coverage.

According to Noll, evangelical biblical scholars tend almost uniformly to be epistemological "realists."[174] For evangelicals, such realism is important because it suggests that the truth claims of the Bible can be evaluated through historical research. Sheler's confidence in the verifiability of scripture (within limits) reflects a longstanding belief among evangelicals that truth can be "reliably discovered by objective examination of the facts."[175] It also comports well with the fact-oriented epistemology of American journalism. In *Is the Bible True?* Sheler writes that "the questions that this study brings to the Bible and its historical claims are fundamentally journalistic ones: What really happened and why? What was really said? How reliable are the sources?"[176] They are also evangelical questions.[177]

It is one thing to frame questions in a distinctively evangelical way; it is quite another to answer those questions in a way that abides by the canons of journalistic professionalism. Given the constraints of objectivity, how have Sheler's stories reflected his religious background? The answer seems to lie in the journalistic ideal of "balance." Because American journalism has stressed the importance of giving balanced treatment to both sides of an issue, it is possible to include both liberal and conservative voices in a story without violating the rules of journalistic professionalism. This is exactly what Sheler has done. Although he has covered those who question traditional understandings of scripture (for example, Marcus Borg, John Dominic Crossan, and Robert Funk), he has given equal time to conservative biblical scholars. A careful look at the sources quoted in Sheler's stories reveals a substantial evangelical presence: Don Carson, James Hoffmeier, and Barry Beitzel of Trinity Evangelical Divinity School; Darrell Bock and Harold Hoehner of Dallas Theological Seminary; Donald Hagner of Fuller Theological Seminary; Edwin Yamauchi of Miami University; and Gregory Boyd[178] of Bethel College.

In his articles and his book, Sheler has opened the journalistic news net to evangelical scholars of scripture. Sheler acknowledges the importance of these scholars to his reporting in the introduction to *Is The Bible True?*

A new generation of biblical scholars, historians, and theologians emerged from the ranks of conservative evangelicalism who rejected the isolationism of their fundamentalist forebears and who increasingly became engaged in the scholarly discourse. Their renewed involvement in organizations such as the American Academy of Religion and the Society of Biblical Literature gave an important new voice to a high view of Scripture that had been sorely lacking in the academic mainstream during much the century.[179]

Evangelicals "now constitute a significant subgroup among biblical scholars at large," according to Noll, reflecting a "growing evangelical contribution to academic biblical study."[180] Because evangelical scripture scholars have joined the academic mainstream (holding doctorates from leading secular graduate programs), Sheler has been able to integrate them into his stories for *U.S. News and World Report.* Evangelical scholars are not the only conservatives who have appeared in his religion coverage. Sheler has regularly quoted moderately conservative scholars, including the Catholics Luke Timothy Johnson and Raymond Brown and the secular critic William Dever.[181]

Once again, Sheler has been careful to include a wide range of viewpoints. Following the familiar pro–con structure of the "balanced" news narrative, he has included the views of Jesus Seminar–style skeptics and conservative evangelicals in the same news stories. An example of this approach can be found in his 1992 Christmas cover story, in which he wrote: "[W]hile many have come to reject the historical veracity [of Jesus' birth], many others have found little reason to alter traditional understanding of a story that, at its heart, is a call to faith in a supernatural God." The "many others" cited in the story include both evangelical and non-evangelical scholars.[182] In cases such as this, readers come away with the impression that reputable scholars can be found on both sides of the question.

Yet Sheler has not really used his writing to advance an evangelical view of the Bible. Although he has certainly given greater visibility to evangelical scripture scholars, many of his stories question received understandings of scripture. In one story, Sheler wrote that "Jesus miraculously feeding the multitudes may be a metaphor for the Risen Christ feeding the faith of his followers."[183] In another, he wrote that "modern archaeology has found little tangible evidence from the Middle Bronze Age ... to corroborate the Biblical account" of the patriarchs.[184] By acknowledging that some passages of scripture may be more historically reliable than others, Sheler has engaged in what Noll calls "believing criticism," allowing that "historical, textual, literary, and other forms of research (if they are not predicated on the denial of the supernatural) may legitimately produce conclusions that overturn traditional evangelical beliefs about the Bible."[185]

Like most religion reporters, Sheler has been criticized from both the left and the right. The conservative *Christian Courier* called Sheler's *Is the Bible True?* "jaded with liberal bias," and the *Kirkus Reviews* wished for "a little more skepticism."[186] Along the same lines, a study by the liberal group Fairness and Accuracy in Media criticized all three newsweeklies for coverage of the Bible that is "so embarrassingly soft that it seems to be pandering to believers."[187] Despite such criticisms, Sheler's religion coverage has been well received by most observers. The *Review of Biblical Literature* has noted that Sheler "always presents other voices as fairly as possible," and *Publishers Weekly* has commended Sheler for "his ability to maintain a reasonably impartial perspective."[188] Ultimately, the perception of liberal or conservative bias depends on one's definition of the center. To a fundamentalist pastor or a radical skeptic, Sheler might seem biased. Because the journalistic notion of balance allows reporters to include the voices of people with whom they agree and disagree, Sheler has been able to integrate evangelical perspectives into the news while abiding by the conventions of professional journalism.

Conclusion

In *The Outrageous Idea of Christian Scholarship* George Marsden asks what difference Christian commitments could possibly make in academia. Answering his own question, he argues that the underlying commitments of Christian scholars have a real impact on their work.[189] This chapter poses a similar question, asking what difference religious commitments make in the world of journalism. Drawing on recent scholarship on the Catholic and Protestant imaginations, it argues that Catholic and evangelical journalists tell stories that embody the theological assumptions of their religious traditions.

These theological assumptions are evident in the five story lines identified earlier. While Thomas's columns dialectically highlight the conflicts dividing Christian conservatives from secular liberals, Steinfels's and Dionne's stories point to analogical similarities in difference that connect the right and the left. Consistent with the individualism of the "Protestant cultural code," Thomas's columns revolve around issues of personal morality.[190] Reflecting a communitarian Catholic sensibility, Woodward's and Wycliff's writings celebrate the sacramentality of human community and connectedness. McCarthy's peace-and-justice stories embody Catholicism's "preferential option for the poor"; Sheler's stories reflect an evangelical preoccupation with the truth claims of the Bible.

The reporters profiled in this chapter have not always reflected the theological perspectives usually attributed to their traditions. Pippert's peace-and-justice orientation differs from the individualistic, moral-reform agenda of evangelicalism, for example, and McCarthy's denunciation of American patriotism has little in common with the analogical imagination's emphasis on similarities in difference. The handful of stories Thomas has told about liberal–conservative common ground are a departure from evangelicalism's dialectical outlook. In *The Catholic Myth*, Greeley notes that the "analogical and dialectical imaginations exist side by side" in the minds of many individuals.[191] Such deviations from ideal typical accounts of the Catholic and Protestant imaginations call attention to the internal pluralism of the Catholic and evangelical traditions.

Figure 5. The Catholic and Protestant imaginations as reflected in five recurring story lines

Story Line	Sacramental vs. Biblicist	Analogical vs. Dialectical	Communitarian vs. Individualistic
Culture wars	Biblicist	Dialectical	Individualistic
Cultural consensus		Analogical	
Communitarian	Sacramental		Communitarian
Peace and justice		Dialectical	Communitarian
Testing the scriptures	Biblicist		

At the same time, it is striking how closely the stories by Catholic and evangelical journalists have reflected the outlook of their respective traditions. Figure 5 summarizes the elements of the Catholic and Protestant imaginations found in the five story lines. Consistent with the theories of Tracy and Greeley, the story lines favored by Catholics (cultural consensus and communitarian) have tended to be more sacramental, analogical, and communitarian. By contrast, the two evangelical Protestant story lines (culture wars and testing the scriptures) have been more biblicist, dialectical, individualistic, and focused on personal morality. The major exception is the peace-and-justice story line's combination of dialectical and communitarian themes, a Catholic–Protestant hybrid.

In taking the Catholic and Protestant imaginations into the mainstream, my respondents have combined the story forms of their religious communities with secular journalism. Thomas's columns for the Los Angeles Times Syndicate do not look much different from the ones he wrote for Jerry Falwell's *Fundamentalist Journal*. Some of McCarthy's pieces read as though they came out of the pages of the *Catholic Worker*. Although they represent a departure from his editorials for *Commonweal*, the religion stories by Steinfels betray his long association with the magazine. Indeed, columns by several of the respondents have appeared in the Catholic and evangelical press: *Commonweal* now features Dionne's *Washington Post* column, for example, and McCarthy's column ran for years in the *National Catholic Reporter*.

Along with new story forms, Catholics and evangelicals have brought a new cast of characters into American journalism, extending the news net to include voices from their religious communities. Journalists find it "easier to make contact with sources" who share "similar backgrounds and interests," Gans says in *Deciding What's News*.[192] It is easy to understand why Dorothy Day and Daniel Berrigan were regular visitors to McCarthy's column, given his longstanding ties to the Catholic Worker movement. Similarly, Woodward has brought Catholic thinkers such as MacIntyre and Taylor to *Newsweek*, and Sheler has integrated evangelical scripture scholars into his cover stories for *U.S. News and World Report*.

In bringing their religious commitments into the news, my respondents have had to translate their beliefs into a form that makes sense to those outside their religious traditions. Thomas, for example, has couched his critique of secular humanism in the language of American civil religion, and Steinfels and Dionne have appropriated the vocabulary of postwar American liberalism. Bridging evangelical biblicism and coverage of the Bible, Sheler has articulated a fit between the cognitive–propositional outlook of American evangelicalism and journalism's focus on empirical facts. In these and other ways, they have made connections between their religious commitments and the storytelling conventions of American journalism.

Admittedly, many of the stories that Catholic and evangelical journalists write look just like the stories by their secular colleagues. "Maybe in 5 percent of the stories or 10 percent of the stories we can bring our own lens, our own perspective," Pippert said. "I'm a wire-service reporter, and I don't think anybody would pick up my copy and say, 'This is really weird.' " Pippert worked in a genre that downplays the voice of the individual reporter; the impact of religion, however, is often difficult to detect in even the most opinionated writing. I once spoke with a *Washington Post* employee who read McCarthy's and Dionne's columns regularly and was quite surprised to learn that they were practicing Catholics. Had she missed the column in which McCarthy discussed his friendship with Dorothy Day? Had she overlooked Dionne's admission that he came to his "own basically liberal views largely because of, not in spite of, Christianity and the church"? Her reaction shows how elusive the influence of religion can be.

Although the theological footprints of the religious imagination are subtle, that does not mean they are not present.[193] Until recently, many film critics ignored Catholicism's influence on the films of Frank Capra, John Ford, and Alfred Hitchcock. Thanks to the scholarship of Richard Blake, Paul Giles, and Lee Lourdeaux, among others, it has become increasingly difficult to overlook the impact of religion on the works of these filmmakers.[194] This chapter has uncovered a similar Catholic sensibility in the world of American journalism. Many observers are unaware of the presence of religious themes in the *New York Times* and the *Washington Post*. It may be that they have not looked closely enough.

6   Religious Ways of Knowing

What role do personal *religious* commitments play in academic writing? Do the works of Christian scholars differ from those of their secular colleagues? Is there such a thing as "Christian sociology" or "Christian history"? An especially provocative answer to such questions comes from the pen of the evangelical historian Steven Keillor (who was not interviewed for this project). In *This Rebellious House: American History and the Truth of Christianity,* Keillor offers what he calls a "Christian interpretation of the American past."[1] A strange hybrid of left-wing historiography and evangelical theology, *This Rebellious House* self-consciously breaks many of the rules governing academic research in modern America. While his brother Garrison has delighted National Public Radio audiences for years with his tales of Lake Wobegon, Keillor has written a book which pushes the boundaries of evangelical scholarship. As one reviewer noted, "Keillor speaks forthrightly about God's providence and human rebellion against God's plan in a manner shunned by many prominent evangelical historians, let alone your typical thoroughly secularized academic, who would be likely to regard such pronouncements as if Keillor had suddenly started talking about UFOs in the middle of an exposition of the Monroe Doctrine."[2] Although Keillor has published widely in the field of Scandinavian studies and Minnesota history, his foray into Christian history was published by the evangelical InterVarsity Press. Mainstream academics do not get away with writing books that invoke divine providence.

This Rebellious House probably will never influence the academic mainstream, but it serves a valuable purpose by calling attention to the boundaries separating faith and scholarship, theology and history, and legitimate and illegitimate knowledge in American higher education. In *The*

Cultural Boundaries of Science (1999), Thomas Gieryn describes the mental maps scholars use to discriminate between science and non-science. These boundaries are used as a means of social control, Gieryn says, dictating where scholars "may not roam without transgressing the boundaries of legitimacy."[3] Although Gieryn writes mostly about the natural sciences, such boundaries have been equally ubiquitous in the social sciences. Judging by the nervousness with which evangelical scholars greeted it, *This Rebellious House* falls outside the boundaries of legitimate historical scholarship.

For the better part of a century, religious ways of knowing have remained outside the bounds of legitimate social-science knowledge.[4] In the social sciences, three barriers against religious viewpoints stand out. First, disciplines such as history and sociology have eliminated supernatural phenomena from consideration, rejecting accounts of divine intervention and spiritual experience as products of the human imagination. Employing what Kenneth Burke calls schemes of reduction, they have analyzed religion in terms of social conditions, psychological processes, material interests, and, in the case of some psychologists, brain chemistry.[5] A second barrier against religious viewpoints can be found in the empiricist heritage of the social disciplines. Attempts of theology and metaphysics to go "beyond the evidential world" are dismissed out of hand, and concepts such as original sin, grace, and redemption are barred from academic discourse.[6] A third difficulty for religious viewpoints lies in what Julie Reuben calls the marginalization of morality in American higher education.[7] The human sciences, including history, have long distanced themselves from substantive visions of the good society. Assuming that social problems are "primarily technical rather than moral or political," they have required scholars to separate moral judgments from empirical description and analysis.[8]

Given these barriers against religious points of view, it is not surprising to find Keillor's history of America relegated to the sidelines of academic discourse. Unlike Keillor, the Catholic and evangelical scholars interviewed for this project have avoided making claims about what Karl Giberson and Donald Yerxa call such "'wild cards' as private knowledge, divine interruptions, and Providence."[9] Although this has been a necessary condition for gaining admission to the mainstream, it raises questions about the degree to which religious historians have accommodated to secular academic culture.

With supernatural explanations excluded from their research, what makes the writings of Christian scholars different from those of their secular colleagues? Not much, says Bruce Kuklick. At "The Problem of Advocacy in Writing History," a conference sponsored by Wheaton College's Institute for the Study of American Evangelicals, Kuklick argued that Christian historians have failed to "show how God peeps through in history." In the quest for professional acceptance, they have adopted a "vision of history that they do not believe." In the absence of providential approaches to history, they have been unable to demonstrate how their "[religious] convictions lend some special insight into the study of the past."[10]

Have Catholic and evangelical scholars chosen professional credibility over faithfulness to their religious traditions? Does the abandonment of providential explanations mean that religiously committed historians have no special insights to bring to the table? In his talk, Kuklick implied that religious scholars must choose between providential historiography and acceptance by the secular academy—or, in his words, between "the secularism that the critical conception now entails [and being] laughed out of the profession."[11] Is the choice really so stark?

Faith-Based Scholarship in the Academy: Catholic and Evangelical Social Scientists

The careers of the twenty Catholic and evangelical social scientists interviewed for this project suggest that Kuklick has seriously underestimated the potential for credible, faith-based scholarship in mainstream academia. Scholars such as John DiIulio, Andrew Greeley, George Marsden, and Margaret Poloma have articulated a fit between their Christian commitments and the language of the contemporary academy (see chapter 4). They have rejected a rigid separation between facts and values and described their research in ways that blended religious and professional vocabularies. Appropriating the rhetorics of postmodernism, post-positivism, and multiculturalism, they have argued that Christian scholars deserve a place at the table.

It is one thing to talk about the inclusion of Christian perspectives in mainstream academic settings, as many of the respondents have done. It is quite another to show that such convictions actually make a difference in the writing of history or sociology. While Kuklick argues that Christian perspectives lend no "special insight into the study of the past," Leo Ribuffo doubts whether so-called Christian scholars "differ *in their schol-*

arship from other historians—or [from] sociologists, anthropologists, literary critics, and political scientists."[12] In recent decades, even religious scholars have questioned the possibility of doing "Christian history" or "Catholic sociology."

This chapter takes up the challenge posed by Kuklick and Ribuffo (as well as by Marsden), examining the difference that religious commitments actually make in the writings of Catholics and evangelicals in the disciplines of sociology, history, and political science. It analyzes the written work of the historians, sociologists, and political scientists interviewed for this study (see the Appendix). In the process, it shows how Catholics and evangelicals (together with scholars of other faiths) have blurred the boundaries between theology and history, morality and social science, and faith and knowledge. What does this religiously-committed scholarship look like? This chapter focuses on four ways in which Catholic and evangelical scholars have brought their religious commitments into academic research:

- Resisting reductionism.
- Using theological tropes in academic narratives.
- Uncovering "concealed affinities" between theology and social theory.
- Blending social ethics with social science.

Through these four modes of faith-based scholarship, Catholic and evangelical scholars have pushed the boundaries of legitimate academic knowledge in the social sciences. By engaging in the anti-reductionist study of religion, they have expanded the scope of social-scientific and historical inquiry to include phenomena, including the supernatural, that normally are off-limits to scholars. By plotting historical narratives using the tropes of Protestant irony and Catholic comedy, they have allowed theological assumptions to impinge on the writing of history. By calling attention to the connections between social theory and Christian theology, they have brought explicitly religious concepts into sociological discourse. And by blending social science and social ethics, they have combined empirical and normative ways of knowing.

At first glance, such religious border-crossing might look like a form of academic heresy. By blurring the boundaries between facts and values, the empirical and the normative, theology and social science, and faith and scholarship, they have challenged mainstream definitions of academic

knowledge. From another angle, however, such expressions of faith-based
scholarship are part of larger shift away from the value-free ideology of
social-science positivism. Critiques of reductionism can be found in every
social-science discipline. Historians are increasingly becoming aware of the
ideological assumptions implicit in narrative forms, including the tropes
of irony, comedy, tragedy, and romance. A host of sociological theorists
have called attention to the meta-assumptions, including the metaphysical
assumptions, that lie under all social theory. Finally, since the 1960s, communitarian, feminist, and neo-Marxist scholars have blurred the boundaries between social ethics and empirical research, participating in what
Alan Wolfe calls the "moral revival" of the social sciences.[13]

Because of these developments, the four faith-based approaches to
social science can be legitimated on secular academic grounds. Rather
than excommunicating themselves from mainstream academia, Catholic
and evangelical scholars have learned to justify religious ways of knowing
in the language of their professional colleagues. Instead of being laughed
out of the profession, they have gotten tenure at major universities, published scholarly books, and held positions of leadership in secular academic professional associations. Like their counterparts in American
journalism, they have positioned themselves at the intersection of professional and religious worlds.

Chapter 5 looked at the impact of the Protestant and Catholic traditions on the writings of Catholic and evangelical journalists. Drawing on
the same framework, this chapter will consider the extent to which these
differences between Catholics and Protestants have played out in the
works of social scientists.

The standard account of the Catholic and Protestant imaginations
contrasts Catholic sacramentalism with evangelical biblicism. Are evangelical scholars more likely to emphasize beliefs, doctrines, and texts
than their Catholic counterparts? Are Catholics more likely to emphasize
rituals, symbols, and stories? Do these differences shape the ways in
which Catholics and evangelicals study religion? According to David
Tracy and Andrew Greeley, the analogical imagination inclines Catholics
to regard society and culture in a more positive light than do Protestants.[14] Is the preference of evangelical Protestant historians for ironic
accounts of Christianity in America the product of a darker view of
human nature? Does the analogical imagination incline Catholics toward
more romantic or comedic understandings of American society and culture? Finally, a host of scholars argue that the Catholic tradition is more

communitarian than American Protestantism.[15] Are Protestants more likely to emphasize the agency of individuals over social-structural explanations? Are Catholics more likely than Protestants to connect social ethics with social science? By exploring these and other questions, this chapter analyzes the impact of religious commitments on the writings of the study's respondents.

Resisting Reductionism:
Catholic and Evangelical Studies of Religion

Many scholars in the social sciences now recognize that indiscriminate reductionism is a bad idea. Taking to heart Kenneth Burke's insight that "any selection of reality . . . must function also as a *deflection* of reality," they have criticized "over-socialized," "over-psychologized," "over-biologized," and "over-physicalized" accounts of human beings.[16] Among Catholic and evangelical scholars, anti-reductionism has taken the form of research that refuses to "treat religion as a product of deeper, more fundamental [forces]."[17] Through such scholarship, they have attempted show that religion makes a difference in ways that cannot be reduced to economic, social, or political factors.

In a 1995 address, Margaret O'Brien Steinfels, editor of *Commonweal*, described the anti-reductionist bent of the Catholic intellectual tradition: "It is characteristic of our tradition, at its best, to resist reductionism. . . . Findings in psychology, sociology, anthropology, history, neurobiology enrich our understanding of the human person and the human project, but they do not exhaust that meaning or determine that trajectory. We are neurons and neuroses but not only neurons and neuroses; neither DNA nor TGF [Transforming Growth Factor] fully determined who we are or what we will do this weekend."[18] Although Steinfels was talking about the Catholic intellectual tradition, her words could have been uttered by any number of prominent evangelical scholars.

In assessing Catholic and evangelical *anti*-reductionism it is helpful to consider exactly what the term means. Robert Bellah defines reductionism as the tendency "to explain the complex in terms of the simple and to find behind complex cultural forms biological, psychological, or sociological drives, needs, and interests."[19] In a similar vein, Donald MacKay called such complex-to-simple explanations "nothing buttery," arguing that by "reducing any phenomenon to its components you not only explain it, but explain it away." In the world of "nothing buttery," human qualities such as love, bravery, and sin are reduced to the "psychological or physiological mechanisms underlying the behavior in question."[20] An even richer understanding of reductionism can be found in the writings of Kenneth Burke. In "Money as a Substitute for God," Burke describes the shift from religious to economic accounts of human motivation, arguing that the "circumference" of reality in most disciplines has been narrowed to exclude the "'supernatural' as a motivating element."[21]

Obviously, reductionism comes in many forms. Some scholars reduce the supernatural to the natural; others reduce cultural phenomena (beliefs, ideas, meaning) to economic or material conditions. In their scholarship on religion, Catholics and evangelicals have challenged three types of reductionism: (1) reducing religious beliefs and symbols to material conditions; (2) reducing the supernatural to the natural; (3) reducing morality and values to economic and political self-interest. I will explore these challenges to reductionism in the new evangelical historiography (Mark Noll and George Marsden), the research of the "gang of four" (John Green, James Guth, Lyman Kellstedt, and Corwin Smidt), and the sociology of Andrew Greeley.[22]

Catholics and evangelicals certainly are not the only scholars who have challenged reductionism. Liberal Protestant, Jewish, and secular scholars have also articulated critiques of reductionist treatments of religion. Robert Bellah's "social science as public philosophy," Peter Berger's "rumor of angels," Alan Wolfe's "human difference," and Amitai Etzioni's "moral dimension," are all examples of non-reductionist approaches to sociology.[23] At the same, Catholics and evangelicals have pushed the critique of reductionism farther than most. Though many scholars argue that religious beliefs and practices cannot be reduced to material conditions, they have been reluctant to question the naturalistic underpinnings of their disciplines. Religion is still a this-worldly affair, albeit an irreducible one. By contrast, Catholics and evangelicals have displayed an openness to the supernatural that goes beyond the methodological atheism of most mainstream social science.[24]

"[T]he most important factor in creating a truly scientific study of religion was the growing participation in it of persons of faith," argue Rodney Stark and Roger Finke.[25] Many of those scholars were mainline Protestants or Jews, but Catholics and evangelicals have also played a central role in bringing the study of American religion back into the academic mainstream. As noted earlier, a 1993 survey of five hundred American religion scholars found that Catholics and evangelicals made up almost 50 percent of the field, signaling what Harry Stout and Robert Taylor call a shift from the "mainline Protestant orientation of the 1960s and 1970s to one more evangelical and Roman Catholic." During the same period, the study of American religion moved out of the American Society of Church History and its sponsoring divinity schools into the "mainstream of historical research." This, say Stout and Taylor, has been nothing short of a "historiographical mini-revolution."[26]

Evangelical Anti-Reductionism in American History

At the center of this mini-revolution are the evangelical historians Edith Blumhofer, Joel Carpenter, Nathan Hatch, George Marsden, Mark Noll, and Harry Stout (Hatch, Marsden, and Noll were interviewed for this study). Dubbed the "new evangelical historiography,"[27] the "Calvin College School of historiography,"[28] and the "evangelical historians,"[29] their scholarship has helped make the so-called evangelical paradigm the "single most powerful explanatory device adopted by academic historians to account for the distinctive features of American society, culture, and identity."[30] Through works such as *The Democratization of American Christianity* and organizations such as the Institute for the Study of American Evangelicals, they have helped put the study of conservative Protestantism back into American history.[31]

At its heart, the new evangelical historiography has been committed to an anti-reductionist vision of academic knowledge. According to the Catholic historian James Turner, evangelicals such as Marsden and Noll "take theological ideas seriously" and refuse to "reduce beliefs to an epiphenomenon of social forces or material circumstances."[32] When interviewed, Marsden talked about the importance of remaining open to many ways of viewing reality: "The goal of the historian is to get as many of those dimensions of human activity into the picture as possible, so that you want to take into account the social, the economic, the moral dimension, the political dimension, and the ideological–religious dimension. If I had to put any kind of label on it, it would be anti-reductionism—to resist reducing human behavior to any one of these dimensions."

Marsden attempts to do just that in *Fundamentalism and American Culture: The Shaping of Twentieth-Century Evangelicalism* (1980). Whereas Richard Hofstadter's *The Paranoid Style in American Politics* and books like it depict fundamentalism as the the "offshoot of a social adjustment [that] would die away when the cultural transformation was complete and the social causes removed," *Fundamentalism and American Culture* presents a nuanced portrait of the fundamentalist movement. Nowhere is this more evident than in the "Interpretations" section of the book, which is organized into four analytical chapters: "Fundamentalism as a Social Phenomenon," "Fundamentalism as a Political Phenomenon," "Fundamentalism as an Intellectual Phenomenon," and "Fundamentalism as an American Phenomenon."[33] This multidimensional structure reflects Marsden's conviction that it is "fruitless to attempt to explain historical development on the basis of any one of these factors." By including a chapter on fundamentalism as an intellectual phenomenon, Marsden resists the tendency of earlier historians to attribute fundamentalist beliefs to such factors as status anxiety, authoritarianism, or psychological strain. In response to Hofstadter's caricature of fundamentalists as anti-intellectual wahoos, Marsden shows that Protestant fundamentalism was rooted in an earlier intellectual tradition of Baconian science and the Scottish common-sense philosophy of Thomas Reid.

Fundamentalism in American Culture pays careful attention to intellectual and theological ideas, a hallmark of the new evangelical historiography. Like sociology, much of U.S. social and cultural history has tended to see the study of religion as a "tool to understand something other— something presumably more 'basic' and intrinsic to the discipline."[34] While acknowledging the value of social history, Marsden and Noll have stressed the relative autonomy of religious ideas in relation to social conditions. In preserving the autonomy of religious ideas, evangelical scholars have attempted to recover what Noll calls "a concern for truth in the study of religion." For most evangelical historians, religious ideas are more than just markers of group identity or cultural symbols. They are attempts to get at ultimate truth. In sharp contrast to postmodernism's rejection of authorial intention, note Stout and Taylor, evangelicals "celebrate the author and proceed to represent his or her ideas," and reject "hard social, economic, and psychological studies of writers and their audiences." For such scholars, "cultural history" is the "old intellectual history stripped of its apologetic patina, but nevertheless produced in the certainty that ideas can speak for themselves and that intellectual/cultural history carries transcendent 'meaning' in a way that structures and functions cannot."[35]

Beyond religious ideas, there are other, more explicit glimpses of the sacred in the works of evangelical historians. While rejecting providential accounts of history, scholars such as Marsden and Noll have made room for divine intervention in human affairs. In their books, God acts in history, albeit in ways that are difficult for historians to see. The boldest statement of this evangelical conviction can be found in the afterword of Marsden's *Fundamentalism and American Culture.* As does the "Concluding Unscientific Postscript" in Marsden's *The Soul of the American University,* the afterword drops a theological bombshell that is only implicit in the rest of the book: "The history of Christianity reveals a perplexing mixture of divine and human factors. [Although] the present work . . . is a study of things visible, [humans] live in the midst of contests between great and mysterious spiritual forces, which we understand only imperfectly and whose true dimensions we only occasionally glimpse." Although Marsden is careful to confine the historian's task to "observable cultural forces," he leaves open the possibility that God may be at work in the world of Protestant fundamentalism.[36]

Evangelical Anti-Reductionism in Political Science: The "Gang of Four"

By now most observers recognize that religion has made a comeback in American politics. Despite religion's strong showing in the public square, many political scientists have tended to ignore the connections between religion and politics. Ted Jelen attributes this blindspot to a "worldview difficulty," arguing that "many empirically oriented social scientists appear to hold perspectives so thoroughly secular that it is virtually inconceivable that religion could be politically consequential."[37]

   This has begun to change. Paralleling the heightened attention to religion in American history, political scientists have been busy rediscovering the religious factor in American politics.[38] No one has done more for the study of religion in political science than the research team of John Green, James Guth, Lyman Kellstedt, and Corwin Smidt (Green was interviewed for this project). Known informally as the "gang of four," they identify with some variety of evangelical Protestantism. A search of the Expanded Academic Index reveals ninety articles by or about the gang of four in such scholarly publications as the *American Political Science Review,* the *Journal of Politics, Social Forces, Polity, American Politics Quarterly,* the *Journal for the Scientific Study of Religion,* and *Sociology of Religion,* and in religious journals such as the *Christian Century, First Things,* and *Christianity Today.*[39] Since the 1980s, they have appeared in more than five hundred newspaper and magazine articles (including fifty appearances in the *New York Times* and the *Washington Post*), serving as the leading social-scientific interpreters of religion and voting in America.[40]

Unlike the new evangelical historians, Green, Guth, Kellstedt, and Smidt have written very little about Christian scholarship and the normative underpinnings of academic inquiry. There are no volumes comparable to Ronald Wells's *History and the Christian Historian* or Marsden's *The Outrageous Idea of Christian Scholarship*.[41] On the surface, their work appears to mirror the value-neutral approach of mainstream political science.

Yet a closer look reveals a subtle critique of reductionist approaches to politics. For decades, the dominant paradigm in the study of political behavior has paid "too little attention to the cultural forces" of religion and ethnicity, while assuming the "primacy of material interests."[42] In its crudest version, this paradigm reduces "human choice to a rational calculus of profit maximization" and economic self-interest.[43] By showing that religion shapes political behavior in ways that are not reducible to other social factors, Guth, Green, Kellstedt, and Smidt have challenged economistic accounts of political behavior. Together with political scientists such as David Leege and Kenneth Wald, they have favored "cultural theories of American political behavior."[44]

On rare occasions they have been explicit about the religious implications of what they are doing. The clearest statement of their normative presuppositions can be found in an essay published in the religious opinion magazine *First Things*. Titled, "It's the Culture, Stupid!" the essay articulates a cultural vision of politics that challenges Bill Clinton's 1992 campaign motto "It's the economy, stupid!" Along the way, it critiques the normative assumptions underlying economic approaches to political behavior:

> The notion that economics is the foundation of American partisan alignments has a rich pedigree, reaching back to the Federalist Papers, forward through Karl Marx and his followers, to modern, positivist social science. What is often forgotten is that assertions of economic primacy in public life often were—and still are—part of a distinctive political agenda. . . . Although these goals may well be meritorious, the almost credal commitment to the primacy of economics has been intellectually costly, obscuring key elements of American politics.

By criticizing their discipline's "almost credal commitment to the primacy of economics," the authors suggest that politics should be about

more than economic self-interest.[45] Green articulated a similar critique in
the interview, arguing, "[W]e have sociological and economic models that
don't take the content of people's cognition very seriously."

Consistent with this critique, the gang of four has paid close attention
to the content of religious beliefs and practices, developing survey questions that get at the religious commitments of ordinary Americans. Like
good anthropologists, they have tried to see evangelical religion from the
standpoint of the natives. Of course, the fact that Green, Guth, Kellstedt,
and Smidt *are* natives of American evangelicalism has made it much easier for them to reconstruct the religious belief systems of their respondents. "It is perhaps not coincidental," notes Jelen, "that much of the
empirical work in the study of religion and politics has been conducted
by scholars who are themselves affiliated with religious institutions. . . .
[O]ften, there is simply no substitute for a detailed, insiders' understanding of particular subcultures."[46]

Terms such as "dispensational pre-millenialism," "Biblical inerrancy,"
"born again," and "glossolalia" do not exactly roll off most academics'
tongues. To the extent that each religion has its own distinctive grammar
and vocabulary, social scientists "skilled in the language, the symbol system of a given religion" have a distinct advantage.[47] Before the 1980s,
most political scientists were blissfully unaware of the linkages between
evangelicalism and political behavior. Most did not have the foggiest idea
of how to measure religion, relying on antiquated denominational classification schemes and crude measures of religious beliefs. By developing
survey questions grounded in the "colloquial vocabulary" of American
evangelicalism (a vocabulary that they largely share), Green, Guth, Kellstedt, and Smidt have helped interpret the evangelical tradition to a wide
academic public.[48] In the process, they have provided strong empirical
evidence of the importance of religion in American politics.

Catholic Anti-Reductionism in Sociology: Andrew Greeley's Theory of Religion

Consistent with the biblicist heritage of the Protestant tradition, the evangelical scholars interviewed for this study have focused their attention on
religious beliefs, doctrines, ideas, and texts. Largely missing from evangelical approaches to history and political science is any sustained consideration of the symbolic, narrative, poetic, and ritual dimensions of
religion. A much more Catholic version of anti-reductionism can be

found in the sociological writings of Andrew Greeley. In books such as *Religion: A Secular Theory, The Religious Imagination,* and *Religion as Poetry,* Greeley has advanced a theory of the religious imagination that privileges experience, symbol, and story over the propositional side of religion.[49]

In *Confessions of a Parish Priest,* Greeley recounts the influence of Clifford Geertz, Mircea Eliade, David Tracy, John Navone, and John Shea on his theory of the religious imagination, calling it a synthesis of "theology and the social sciences."[50] Given these interdisciplinary influences, it is not surprising that much of his terminology is drawn from the world of theology. "Hope," "grace," and "sacrament" are just a few of the theological terms embedded in the theory.[51] Although Greeley distances himself from the "technical theological connotations" of such words, his use of theological terms in sociological theorizing has important consequences.[52] As Kenneth Burke points out, the cluster of terms academic scholars use—which he calls "terministic screens"—serve as filters that direct scholarly attention more toward some phenomena than others.[53] For most social scientists, words such as "hope" and "grace" are vague abstractions that do not belong in the lexicon of social theory.

By contrast, Greeley begins *Religion: A Secular Theory* with the proposition that human beings have a "propensity to hope."[54] Along with the category of "hope," Greeley draws on Tracy's notion of the limit experience, arguing that these "'disclosive' experiences reveal to us a world of meaning beyond the everyday."[55] According to Tracy, such experiences "may also disclose to us, however hesitantly, the character of that ultimate horizon of meaning which religious persons call 'gracious,' 'eventful,' 'faith-full,' 'revelatory.'"[56] In *The Religious Imagination* Greeley likens Tracy's limit experiences to Berger's "rumors of angels," Rudolph Otto's "encounters with the holy," and Shea's "experiences of mystery," locating his theory within a larger tradition of anti-reductionist approaches to religion.[57] By emphasizing humanity's orientation toward the transcendent, Greeley also reveals his indebtedness to the transcendental Thomism of Tracy and Bernard Lonergan, influences he acknowledges in his autobiography.[58]

Reflecting a Catholic understanding of the sacramentality of creation, Greeley's theory of the religious imagination looks for "experiences of grace" in the context of everyday life.[59] Based on survey research he conducted with William McCready, Greeley notes that ordinary events such as listening to music, moments of quiet reflection, watching little children, childbirth, sexual lovemaking, and reading a poem or a novel have

triggered intense religious experiences. Appropriating yet another theological term, Greeley argues that such "persons, places, times and behaviors [are] 'sacraments' in the sense that they represent situations and circumstances in which 'otherness' reveals itself."[60] Through the creative
and poetic faculties of the human personality (here Greeley draws on the
Catholic philosopher Jacques Maritain), these sacramental experiences
are encoded in stories and symbols (Passover, the Christmas creche, May
Crownings) that are transmitted by religious communities. "Religion
becomes a communal event," writes Greeley, when a person "becomes
aware that there is a correspondence or a correlation between the res-
onating picture or story in his imagination and the story passed on by his
religious heritage."[61]

Although he has been criticized in some quarters for being "too
empirical," Greeley argues that his theory "leaves more room for the
working of the Spirit . . . than almost any other social scientific model of
religion I know."[62] Given his openness to theological accounts of religious
experience, it is hard to dispute this claim. While making "no judgments"
as to whether the religious experiences he studies are "ultimately true or
false, revealing or deceptive, sacramental or wish-fulfilling," he acknowledges his personal belief in their revelatory power.[63] Following William
James, he argues that "we live in an open universe, filled with wonder and
surprise" and that "the wise person does not deny on a priori grounds any
possibility for surprise."[64]

In the past two decades, Greeley has published versions of the theory
in leading journals (the *American Sociological Review,* the *Journal of the
American Academy of Religion*) and with well-regarded presses (Macmillan,
Doubleday, Free Press, University of California Press, and Transaction
Publishers).[65] Although these works are less well known than his publications on ethnicity and American Catholics, they are still cited quite frequently. That they were published at all is an indication that the boundaries between theology and sociological theory are weakening. By bringing
"hope," "grace," and "sacrament" back into sociology, Greeley has helped
bridge the worlds of religion and social science.

Beyond "Nothing Buttery": Widening the Circumference of Reality

Together Catholic and evangelical scholars have resisted reductionism. In
U.S. history, they have made room for religious ideas and motivations. In
political science, they have rejected economistic accounts of political

behavior, rediscovering the religious factor in American politics.[66] In sociology, they have constructed theories of religion that leave open the possibility of supernatural experiences. In all three disciplines, they have made a case that religion cannot be reduced to deeper, more fundamental realities.[67]

By not reducing religious ideas to material conditions, politics to economic self-interest, and the supernatural to the natural, they have widened the Burkean circumference of reality to include religious beliefs, moral commitments, and supernatural experiences. In place of "nothing buttery," they have embraced a more-than-meets-the-eye approach. Like Berger in *A Rumor of Angels,* they have called for greater "openness in our perception of reality" and recognized that "all phenomena point toward that which transcends them."[68] Instead of reducing reality to a single dimension, they have expanded their conception of reality to include multiple levels (supernatural, cultural, material), none of which are reducible to the others. In doing so, they have made room for religion.

Theological Tropes in Academic Narratives: Protestant Irony and Catholic Comedy

Thanks to the work of narrative theorists, most historians now recognize that narrative is "not merely a neutral discursive form" and that scholars convey moral meanings by structuring their accounts around tropes such as irony, comedy, romance, and tragedy.[69] Kenneth Burke has called irony a "technical equivalent for the doctrine of original sin," and Hayden White calls romance "a drama of the triumph of good over evil, of virtue over vice, of light over darkness."[70] Catholics and evangelicals also have called attention to the theological meanings implicit in historical and social-scientific accounts of the world. Self-consciously and not so self-consciously, they have used the tropes of Protestant irony (in both its Niebuhrian and Lutheran forms) and Catholic comedy to structure their writings about Christianity and America.

The connections between faith and scholarship are apparent in books about religious experience and evangelical politics. When religion is the object of study, it is easy to see the relevance of personal religious beliefs. Much less obvious are the connections between religious commitments and the forms of academic storytelling. In recent decades, scholars have become much more self-conscious about the story lines, plot devices, and tropes that structure historical narratives. Recognizing that narrative is not neutral, they have focused on the ways historians make use of conventional story forms. Following White, they have paid special attention to the tropes of irony, comedy, romance, and tragedy, arguing that such tropes convey moral and political meanings.[71]

This is not an entirely new idea. In *The Irony of American History,* the neo-orthodox theologian Reinhold Niebuhr wrote that the Christian faith "tends to make the ironic view of human evil in history the normative one."[72] In the midst of the Cold War, Niebuhr questioned America's "illusions of innocence."[73] Under Niebuhr's influence, a generation of historians (figures such as Arthur Schlesinger, Jr., and Perry Miller) made the ironic mode central to their "interpretation of the American past."[74] Dubbed the "atheists for Niebuhr," they brought a biblical sense of human sinfulness to the writing of American history.[75]

Like Niebuhr's *The Irony of American History,* White's *Metahistory* calls attention to the connections between "Christian mythology" and the tropes used by academic historians. White sees the "emplotment" of historical events as an "essentially poetic act." Like novelists and poets, historians tell their stories using the tropes of comedy, tragedy, romance, and satire. By employing such "archetypal" story forms, they express certain truths about the human condition. While romance celebrates "the transcendence of man over the world in which he was imprisoned by the Fall," comedy and tragedy "suggest the possibility of at least partial liberation" from the power of sin and death.[76] Although historians are by no means theologians, White shows how the tropes they use incorporate theological assumptions about the world.

The theological implications of academic narration have not been lost on Catholic and evangelical scholars. In an interview with an Australian journal, Noll acknowledged the influence of Christian faith on what he called "strategies for narration."[77] Greeley displayed a similar awareness of narrative forms in *Confessions of a Parish Priest,* noting that "the story of these fifty years in my life and the life of American Catholicism is a strange mixture of comedy and tragedy."[78] Other Catholic and evangelical scholars have explored the implications of narrative theory in even greater depth.[79]

How do theological commitments influence the forms of academic storytelling? Contrasting Protestant irony with Catholic comedy, I argue in this section that evangelicals and Catholics have narrated the relationship between Christianity and American culture in fundamentally different ways. Echoing Niebuhr, the new evangelical historiography has articulated an ironic view of Christianity in American history, highlighting the mixture of good and evil in the Protestant past. By contrast, the "standard plot line" of American Catholic history is comedic, celebrating the integration of Catholics into the American mainstream.[80]

The contrast between Protestant irony and Catholic comedy reflects underlying differences between the Protestant and Catholic imaginations. The evangelical preference for an ironic reading of history is consistent with Protestantism's dialectical emphasis on the distance between God and humanity, church and world, and Christianity and U.S. culture. Its theological antecedents within Western Christianity can be found in Augustine, Luther, Niebuhr, and other champions of the doctrine of original sin.[81] Representing a very different theological sensibility, American Catholic historiography looks for analogical similarities in difference, emphasizing the reconciliation of Catholicism and American society.[82] In the comic worldview of American Catholicism, says Regis Duffy, "our particular cultural context is also the time and place for God's new creation in Christ."[83] These theological differences play themselves out in the stories evangelical and Catholic scholars tell about Christianity in America.

Evangelical Irony: The Ambiguous Legacies of "Christian America"

Like Niebuhr in *The Irony of American History*, the evangelical historians Nathan Hatch, George Marsden, and Mark Noll use the trope of irony to challenge America's illusions of innocence.[84] Marsden has written approvingly of Niebuhr's "deeply ironic" view of human nature, and Noll has called for a greater sense of "Lutheran irony" in American life:

> In religious terms, this irony is the sense that precisely when Christians mount their most valiant public efforts for God, they run the greatest risk of substituting *their* righteousness for the righteousness of Christ, and thereby subverting justification by faith. . . . In secular terms, "Lutheran irony" would be a bent of mind quick to perceive where the public crusade leads to unintended consequences: constitutional actions to free the slaves that result in vastly expanded power for the courts, or efforts to make the world safe for democracy (Wilson) that lead to the rise of a Hitler.[85]

Jean Bethke Elshtain argues that "Lutheran irony"[86] offers a useful corrective to the "optimism" and "triumphalism" of American political culture. "Lutherans," she writes, "do not look for salvation in the City of Man."[87]

This ironic reading of American history contrasts sharply with the religious right's romantic nostalgia for a lost golden age. While Jerry Falwell and Pat Robertson call for a return to America's Christian origins, the new evangelical historians question the myth of "Christian America." While the new Christian right blames "secular humanists" for the decline of American culture, Hatch, Marsden, and Noll argue that "evangelicals themselves were often partly to blame for the spread of secularism in contemporary American life."[88] In place of a Manichean story of good versus evil or Christians versus secularists, they point to the secularizing consequences of Protestant hegemony.

In *The Compass of Irony* (1969), D. C. Muecke writes, "[I]t is ironic when we meet what we set out to avoid . . . especially when the means we take to avoid something turn out to be the very means of bringing about what we sought to avoid."[89] By implicating evangelical Protestants in the secularization of American life, the new evangelical historians have brought an ironic interpretation to the study of American Christianity. This focus on unintended consequences is especially evident in Marsden's *The Soul of the American University: From Protestant Establishment to Established Non-Belief,* which rejects a quest for "many culprits" and analyzes the "unintended consequences of decisions that in their day seemed largely laudable." Instead of lamenting a "lost golden age when Christians ruled America," it offers a "critique of that old regime." Consistent with an ironic interpretation of American Christianity, Marsden argues that Protestant institutions served as their own grave diggers: "In higher education Protestants insisted on a universal academic ideal, underwritten by Enlightenment assumptions concerning . . . human nature's ability to progress toward a universal moral ideal. . . . Ironically . . . Protestant universalism . . . was one of the forces that eventually contributed to the virtual exclusion of religious perspectives from the most influential centers of American intellectual life."[90]

By constructing a white Protestant university that was closed to Catholics, Jews, and African Americans, American Protestants set in motion the forces of secularization. As Marsden's subtitle suggests, the exclusivism and intolerance of the "Protestant establishment" led, through a complicated chain of events, to the establishment of "non-belief."

A Niebuhrian view of history looks for the mixture of virtue and vice in the actions of historical agents. This focus on the ambiguities of

American history can be found throughout the new evangelical historiography, most notably in Marsden's *Fundamentalism and American Culture*
and Noll's *A History of Christianity in the United States and Canada*. Marsden
notes the "inevitable ambiguities in Christians' relationship to their culture" and argues that fundamentalists combined faithfulness to God with
the culturally defined "loves, allegiances, and understandings" of an
imperfect America.[91] Noll highlights both the glories and the "foibles" of
Christianity in America, arguing that the "legacies of 'Christian America'
are not unambiguous."[92]

In *The Irony of American History,* Niebuhr argues that an ironic sensibility can lead to contrition.[93] Through the self-critical examination of their
own religious tradition, the evangelical historians have called attention to
the sins of the Protestant past. For the new evangelical historiography, the
principal vice of "Christian America" was an uncritical marriage between
Protestantism and American culture, Christianity and the Enlightenment,
and religion and democracy. In *The Soul of the American University,* Marsden
notes that the synthesis of Christian learning and Enlightenment philosophy "put traditional Protestantism in a most vulnerable position."[94] Similarly, Noll's *Princeton and the Republic* argues that the late eighteenth century's "amalgam" of republican, Enlightenment, and Christian values
helped contribute to the secularization of public life.[95] In both books, well-
meaning Protestant churchmen work diligently to reconcile orthodox
Christian beliefs with Enlightenment thought, unintentionally setting the
stage for the secularization of American higher education. This ironic
focus on the "unintended results of people's actions" can also be found in
Hatch's *The Democratization of American Christianity* (1989). He calls the
rise of democratic Christianity in the early United States "riddled with
irony, unrealistic hope, and unfulfilled expectations" and portrays the
marriage of religion and democracy as an ambiguous development.[96]

Tragedy, as well as irony, can be found in the historical narratives of
the new evangelical historians. Although he acknowledges the "ironies of
the Princeton search for a republican Christian Enlightenment," Noll also
writes, "[M]erely to chronicle these ironies . . . is demeaning to a circle of
such great industry and accomplishment."[97] While commenting on the
Princeton book in the interview, Noll described his growing realization
that irony was not the right approach:

I've had a very interesting transition in working on the Princeton book.
Samuel Stanhope Smith was the central figure, and I got inside of him quite

well. The more I studied him, the less I liked what he said. The more I thought
he was wrong. He had just made several really bad mistakes that were in
themselves close to compromising basic Christian faith. But at the same time
I was also finding out more and more about the man's context and his life and
his connections and what he was trying to do, and my respect for the human
grew. So I was left at the end of the book trying to figure out, "How do I convey this?" It is the historical case that what he tried to do failed. And what
I probably wanted to say is, "And a good thing, too!" But I could also say that
irony is the wrong way of doing this. If anything, it's a tragedy, because the guy
was more honorable, more energetic, more faithful to his calling than I'll ever
be in my whole life.

No less sobering than Niebuhrian irony, Noll's tragic interpretation of
early Princeton calls attention to the ambiguous legacy of Protestant
America.

The new evangelical historians interpret the end of "Christian America" as both a blessing and a tragedy.[98] Never quite at ease with the marriage of Christianity and America, they see "no lost golden age to which
American Christians may return."[99] While lamenting the secularization of
American life, they view the decline of Protestant influence as an opportunity for Christians to "concentrate more on the Source of Life than on
the American Way of Life."[100] Refusing to equate the American city on a
hill with the city of God, they see American Christians as "pilgrims" who
owe only "limited allegiance to the regimes of their earthly sojourns."[101]

Catholic Comedy: Celebrating "American Catholicism"

A comparison of Catholic and evangelical historiography reveals very different assumptions about the relationship between Christianity and American society. Comedy, not irony, is the master trope of American Catholic
historiography. In sharp contrast to the evangelical critique of "Christian
America," Catholic historians celebrate "American Catholicism." While
evangelicals highlight the tensions between the Gospel and American
culture, the "standard plot line" of American Catholic historiography
assumes a "fundamental harmony between Catholicism and the political
institutions of the United States."[102] While evangelicals warn against
excessive cultural accommodation, Catholic scholars point approvingly to
the "inculturation" of Catholicism in the United States.[103] While evangelicals' treatments of "Christian America" draw on the Augustinian

themes of sin and human finitude, Catholics call attention to the incredible possibilities of American life.

In *God and Popular Culture,* Greeley calls Catholicism a "Comic Religion," contrasting Protestantism's suspicion of human cultural achievements with Catholicism's sacramental imagination. While the Protestant imagination tends to focus on the "idolatry of institutions," Catholicism finds God in all things, looking for grace in American culture.[104] This more benign reading of the relationship between Christianity and culture is reflected in the comic orientation of American Catholic historiography.

What does this comic orientation entail? In *Anatomy of Criticism* (1957), Northrop Frye writes, "[T]he theme of the comic is the integration of society, which usually takes the form of incorporating a central character into it." In most cases, the "obstacles to the hero's desires . . . form the action of the comedy, and the overcoming of them the comic resolution." Very often, the obstacles are "parental," with the action turning on the "clash between a son's and a father's will." Through a plot twist or two, these obstacles are overcome. The hero and heroine come together, and a "new society" forms around them. The appearance of this new society is celebrated by a "festive ritual," most often a wedding.[105]

It is striking how closely the standard plot line of American Catholic history, laid out in books such as Jay Dolan's *The American Catholic Experience* (1985) and Greeley's *The Catholic Experience* (1967), parallels Frye's description of the comic.[106] Like most comedies, this plot line concerns the integration of a main character (immigrant Catholics) into society (Protestant America). Initially, the prospects for romantic bliss appear bright, as Maryland Catholics identify the church with "American republicanism."[107] Yet, true to form, the romance between the star-crossed lovers (Catholics and American culture) is opposed by both sets of parents (Rome and Protestant nativists). While Protestant elites look down on poor Catholic immigrants, the Vatican condemns the liberal and democratic strains in American culture. Through the condemnation of modernism and the defeat of the Americanists, the papacy (a father figure if there ever was one) almost puts a stop to the courtship. In the end, parental opposition is not enough to stop the marriage from taking place. An unexpected twist in the plot—Vatican II—combined with the upward mobility of American Catholics assure Catholics' full integration into the American mainstream. In the wake of Vatican II, a "new Catholicism" comes into being—one that is "both Catholic and American."[108]

At least two American Catholic scholars use the metaphors of romantic comedy to describe the incorporation of Catholics into American society. In *The American Catholic Experience* and other works, Dolan describes
the Catholic "love affair with modernity,"[109] the "marriage between the
church and the age,"[110] the "American Catholic romance with modernity,"[111] and the "contemporary marriage between religion and culture,"[112] and notes that, "by the 1950s, the marriage between Catholicism
and the American liberal reform movement was consummated."[113]

Taking the metaphors of romance in a more radical direction, Dennis McCann adds a Freudian twist to the story:[114]

> It is as if once upon a time, among the youngest of the Brides of Christ,
> American Catholicism became frozen in some sort of Elektra complex, unable
> to mature in her infantile love for her American fatherland because of a re-
> pressed conflict with her fiercely protective mother, the church of Rome. . . .
> But adolescence came, as it inevitably does even to good little girls, when Vat-
> ican II disrupted the whole of Christ's rather diverse and far-flung family. . . .
> The young Bride began to assert herself, but herself she did not yet know. For
> she had yet to come to terms with her conflicting loves and loving conflicts
> with her parents.[115]

Although McCann writes about a "Bride of Christ" (American Catholicism), she is the product of the marriage between an "American father-
land" and "Holy Mother the Church."

Most American Catholic historians do not go as far as McCann's
Freudian interpretation. In an overview of Dolan's career, Martin Marty
notes that the historian "has no Oedipal case against the Church of the
past, as many liberated, late-twentieth-century Catholic writers . . . have
been developing."[116] At the same time, it is clear that most American
Catholic historians are pleased with the marriage of Catholicism and
American culture.

Such talk of "marriage," "romance," "brides," and "mother," brings to
mind Greeley's comparison of tragedy, comedy, and satire: "The Tragic
theory is that you must seek the Grail/girl forever and never be rewarded.
The Comic theory says you can find both and bring them home to
mother and live happily ever after. The Satire theory is that you marry the
Grail/girl and she makes you unhappy for the rest of your life, because
she turns out to be not worth the bother of pursuing."[117]

While the new evangelical historiography regards the marriage between Christianity and American culture as a source of considerable unhappiness, the comic plot line of American Catholic history wants to bring the girl (American culture) home to mother (the church) and live happily ever after.

Running through most of these accounts is the assumption of a "fundamental harmony" between Catholicism and American culture. In a highly suggestive work, Michael Baxter uncovers the theological underpinnings of American Catholic historiography, arguing that the historical works of John Tracy Ellis, Jay Dolan, David J. O'Brien, and (one might add) Andrew Greeley reflect an "Americanist" approach to Catholic social ethics.[118] Philip Gleason makes a similar point in "The New Americanism in Catholic Historiography," arguing that the post–Vatican II generation of American Catholic historians (Dolan, Patrick Carey, Gerald Fogarty) have been influenced by the presuppositions of liberal Catholic theology. Gleason has called Dolan's *The American Catholic Experience,* a work that "interprets Americanism and Modernism as successive phases of a progressive development that reached its belated culmination in the Second Vatican Council," the most influential embodiment of the new Americanist historiography.[119] Contrasting the hierarchical vision of the immigrant church with the "People of God" ecclesiology of the Second Vatican Council, Dolan celebrates the democratization of American Catholicism.[120]

But the champions of Americanization are not the only scholars being heard in American Catholic history. Gleason's more pessimistic reading of that history, articulated most recently in a history of American Catholic higher education, and Baxter's critique of the "Americanist tradition in Catholic social ethics" both question the compatibility of Catholicism and American culture.[121] Along the same lines, Mark Massa's *Catholics and American Culture: Fulton Sheen, Dorothy Day, and the Notre Dame Football Team* (1999) uses Niebuhrian irony to tell a "theological morality tale" about the loss of Catholic identity, acknowledging the "foreignness" of Niebuhr's Protestant hermeneutic.[122] Sounding a great deal like those writing the new evangelical historiography, these scholars articulate an Augustinian vision of the church as a "pilgrim city" and warn against the conflation of Catholicism and American culture.[123]

Yet such critics are a minority voice in a church dominated by what Scott Appleby calls the "Americanist center."[124] In place of an Augustinian vision of a pilgrim church, the scholars of the Americanist center embrace an analogical vision of Catholicism that is both American and Catholic. Rejecting irony as a mode of interpretation, they celebrate the comic reconciliation of Catholicism and American society.[125] Seeing "no dangers in dialogue with American democracy," as Greeley has written, they argue that "American institutions provide a situation in which Catholicism can grow and flourish as it has nowhere else in the world."[126] Embracing an indigenous Catholicism, they call attention to the presence of divine grace in American culture and argue that "some of the better characteristics of the American spirit certainly have their source in the Christian belief of new beginnings in Christ."[127]

Theological Commitments and Academic Storytelling

Catholics and evangelicals thus have narrated the relationship between Christianity and American culture in very different ways. While doing first-rate scholarship, they have employed story lines that bear the unmistakable imprint of the Protestant and Catholic imaginations. Although the historians and sociologists in this study are not theologians, they have brought theological assumptions into the writing of American history. In some cases, it is doubtful whether the author intended to communicate a theological message (see, for example, Dolan's use of the metaphors of romantic comedy). In other cases, however, such as Noll's "Lutheran irony" and Greeley's "comedy," the message is explicit, reflecting the scholar's self-conscious religious commitments. Whether implicit or explicit, unintentional or self-conscious, such theological tropes make a difference, incorporating assumptions about human nature, sin, and redemption into the very structure of academic narratives. In the process, they demonstrate the impact of religious beliefs on the writing of history.

Uncovering "Concealed Affinities" Between Theology and Social Theory

In his controversial critique of sociology, John Milbank points out that the great social theorists of the nineteenth century borrowed heavily from the theological and philosophical categories of the Christian tradition. One need not accept Milbank's claim that "'scientific' social theories are themselves theologies or anti-theologies in disguise" to recognize that theological presuppositions are often implicit in sociological theories, especially at the level of meta-theory.[128] Along the same lines, Catholic and evangelical social scientists have recognized such "concealed affinities" in their own research, uncovering the connections between contemporary debates over structure and agency and such theological categories as free will and predestination.[129]

Since the 1960s, it has become increasingly fashionable to focus on the "meta" dimensions of academic knowledge. Thanks to Hayden White's *Metahistory,* most historians now recognize the role of narrative forms (plot structure, tropes, metaphor) in the writing of history. Along the same lines, there has been a growing focus on "meta-theory" in American sociology.[130] Beginning with the publication of Alvin Gouldner's *The Coming Crisis of Western Sociology* (1970), this conversation has focused on the "background assumptions" inherent in sociological thought. In *The Coming Crisis,* Gouldner argued that "assumptions about man and society" shape the construction of theories. In some cases, these assumptions verge on metaphysics, involving "pervasive and primitive beliefs about what is real." Such beliefs "may involve an inclination to believe that the world and the things in it are 'really' *one* or 'truly' *many,* [or] a disposition to believe that the world is 'really' highly integrated and cohesive."[131]

Gouldner was not the first sociologist to highlight the metaphysical dimensions of social theory. Writing two decades before Gouldner, Father Paul Hanly Furfey wrote about the "metasociological value judgments" implicit in social research, calling for the creation of an explicitly Catholic sociology.[132] Although such arguments inspired a small network of Catholic sociologists, Furfey failed to gain a hearing in the sociological mainstream. By identifying the quasi-religious assumptions implicit in sociological thought, Gouldner's post-positivist sociology paved the way for a more open dialogue between theology and social science. Because most sociologists now recognize the existence of value judgments and background assumptions, it is no longer illegitimate to explore the religious dimensions of sociological theorizing.

The post-positivist climate of the social sciences in the past two decades has resulted in a host of articles and books discussing the possibilities of "Christian sociology."[133] The most radical of these explorations is Milbank's *Theology and Social Theory: Beyond Secular Reason* (1990), a work that articulates a scathing critique of mainstream sociology. Milbank makes the bold claim that "scientific 'social theories' are themselves theologies in disguise," adding that "contemporary theologies which forge alliances with such theories are often unwittingly rediscovering concealed affinities between positions that partake of the same historical origins."[134] Not surprisingly, Milbank's work has attracted criticism from theologians and sociologists. Whatever its limitations, *Theology and Social Theory* calls attention to at least one important truth: Sociological theories often have theological ancestors.

A vivid illustration of the theological roots of sociological theory can be found in sociologists' appropriation of a phrase from the New Testament. The biblical text can be found in Acts 17:28, when Paul argues that it is in God that "we live and move and have our being."[135] John Calvin used this passage in his *Institutes* to illustrate the sovereignty of God over human affairs, saying that "God by his power supports and maintains the world which he created."[136] What have social theorists done with this text? In a classic work of early American sociology, Albion Small wrote that "we live and move and have our being as parts of each other."[137] The French structuralist Louis Althusser used the same phrase to illustrate his deterministic theory of ideology, arguing that "it is in the 'Logos,' meaning in ideology, that we 'live, move and have our being.' "[138] Neither Small nor Althusser was writing as a theologian, of course. (Althusser was an outspoken atheist.) Moreover, by replacing God with social and cultural structures, both strayed far from orthodox Christian theology. At the same time, the presence of theological categories in their work is undeniable.[139]

Structure versus Agency, Predestination versus Free Will

Such submerged connections between theology and social theory were not lost on the respondents. Pointing to such connections, George Thomas argued that contemporary sociological debates about structure and agency "are simply reproducing the sixteenth-century debates over the sovereignty of God and free will."[140] The *Westminster Dictionary of Christian Theology* defines predestination as "the doctrine that God foreknows, and ordains, from all eternity, who will be saved."[141] Like the Protestant Reformer John Calvin, structurally oriented sociologists (such as Althusser and Thomas) emphasize constraints on human freedom, focusing on how social structures shape (one might say, "predestine") human action.[142] Like the theological opponents of predestination, agency-oriented sociologists celebrate human free will, making them the sociological heirs of Jacob Arminius, the seventeenth-century Dutch theologian who questioned Calvinist orthodoxy. Although most sociologists are unaware of these links, the links, as the quotes from Small and Althusser make clear, are embedded in the history of the discipline.

Acknowledging his own Calvinist leanings, Thomas said that he has "often thought that maybe that's why I'm a little more structural in my sociological theorizing." Reflecting a very different religious sensibility, rooted in the Arminian theology of charismatic evangelicalism, Margaret Poloma has advocated a more agent-centered approach to sociology. By uncovering the concealed affinities between theology and the structure–agency debate, Thomas and Poloma have practiced a form of meta-sociology, calling attention to the religious dimensions of social theory. This section of the chapter considers the religious background assumptions of both scholars. Contrasting what one might call the "Calvinist" and "Arminian" approaches to sociology, it documents the subtle influence of theological commitments on theoretical orientation.

Neo-Institutionalism and Calvinism: George Thomas

George Thomas is one of the leading voices of the "new institutionalist" approach to sociology.[143] Because of his close association with this school of thought, identifying the sociological influences on his intellectual development is relatively easy. Any theological analysis of Thomas's writings, however, is complicated by a kind of chicken-and-egg problem: Although he is well aware of the connections between his Calvinism and his structuralism, Thomas is far from certain which came first. "I said, maybe I'm drawn to the structural perspective because I'm Calvinist, but it could be the other way around," he said, "because actually I moved toward a Reformed faith at the time, in graduate school, when I was beginning to move more toward a structuralist perspective. So it's not like one clearly came before the other."

Difficulties of origin aside, there are clear conceptual parallels between Thomas's neo-institutionalist sociology and Calvinist theology.[144] Both downplay the freedom of social actors to shape their own destinies. Both emphasize the influence of larger forces on people's day-to-day decisions. Both reject methodological individualism. Both are pessimistic about human beings' capacity to change their situations. In Burke's terminology, both ground explanations of human action outside the "agency" of individual human beings, focusing on the "scene in which the agent acts" (the social structure), or, in the case of Calvinism, on a supernatural divine agent (God).[145]

In "Money as a Substitute for God," Burke argues that economics turns "monetary motives" into a "god-term" in terms of which everything else is explained.[146] Structural explanations function as something of a "god-term" in neo-institutionalist sociology. What the sovereign will of God is to Calvinist theology, social and cultural structures are to neo-institutionalists.[147] In the new institutionalism, social structure is "ontologically prior" to the individual, in effect predestining the lives of social actors.[148] Paralleling the transcendence of God in Calvinist theology, the "world level of social reality is culturally transcendent and causally important," structuring the activities of nation-states, organizations, and individuals.[149] Through the myths of "world culture" (what Thomas and his colleagues call the "salvation story" of the modern world), the message is conveyed that "salvation lies in rationalized structures grounded in scientific and technical knowledge."[150]

Like Calvinist theology, the new institutionalism leaves some room for human agency, rejecting a deterministic account of human social life. As John Boli and George Thomas have written, "[W]orld culture defines modern actors not as cultural dopes but as creative innovators who are the one and only source of change, adaptation, and restructuring." Along these lines, they argue that "global structures are maintained and transformed by the actors they constitute." At the same, they see human agency as heavily conditioned (or "structurally constituted," in the jargon of neo-institutionalism) by social and cultural structures.[151]

Thomas's Calvinist leanings are even more apparent in his book *Revivalism and Cultural Change: Christianity, Nation Building, and the Market in the Nineteenth-Century United States* (1989), which applies the neo-institutionalist perspective to the history of American religion. Although *Revivalism and Cultural Change* was written as a work of cultural sociology, it can also be read as an implicitly Calvinist critique of the doctrine of free will. In the book, Thomas traces the shift of American evangelicalism from a Calvinist to an Arminian understanding of the self, linking this transformation to larger political and economic changes. While the Calvinist churchmen of the eighteenth century preached the depravity of human beings and divine predestination, such views were abandoned by nineteenth-century revivalists. Because Calvinist theology "went against nineteenth century conceptions of liberty, rugged individualism, and the sovereignty of the people," it was forsaken in favor of an Arminian emphasis on "the autonomy of the individual." According to Thomas, there was a "structural isomorphism" between Arminian theology and the cultural order of the expanding market. The "revival-ist message was cognitively compelling," he writes, "because it corre-sponded to their everyday experience as shaped by the dominant cul-tural myth of individualism."[152] In other words, the shift from Calvinism to Arminianism was bound up with the cultural and economic transfor-mation of American society.

The Arminian evangelicals in *Revivalism and Cultural Change* thought they were free agents. Thomas's analysis suggests they were wrong. More myth than reality, the perceived "freedom" of evangelical converts was the consequence of a larger cultural shift toward the individualism of the free market. By demonstrating the impact of larger social forces on Arminian evangelicals, Thomas shows how their sense of free will was socially con-structed. Although it is couched in the language of neo-institutionalist sociology, *Revivalism and Cultural Change* effectively debunks the Armin-ian understanding of the free religious actor.

Making Room for Agency: Margaret Poloma

Like many sociologists of her generation, Margaret Poloma has accepted the post-positivist critique of value-free sociology. Recognizing that "back-ground assumptions are inescapably real and that reflexivity is a socio-logical virtue," she has written openly about the connections between her Christianity and her sociology. She has also used her religious experiences to understand the world of her research subjects (see chapter 4). In "Toward a Christian Sociological Perspective" (1982), she calls for an explicitly Christian approach to the discipline, arguing that sociology "rests on faith assumptions just as surely as theology does." In Poloma's case, these faith assumptions reflect her own theological commitments as a charismatic evangelical Christian.[153]

In *The Charismatic Movement: Is There a New Pentecost?* (1982), Poloma contrasts the Wesleyan theology of Pentecostalism with the "strict deter-ministic stance of Calvinism," showing that she is aware of the connections between Calvinist theology and determinism.[154] In her essay on Christian sociology, Poloma articulates an *anti*-deterministic vision of social theory that is consistent with the Arminian–Wesleyan roots of her own tradition. Noting that "a strictly deterministic image of person and society appears incompatible with the voluntaristic image inherent in orthodox Christian belief," she praises the dialectical model of Peter Berger and Thomas Luckmann for "allowing for a voluntary actor."[155]

To what extent have Poloma's religious commitments shaped her sociology? As it was with Thomas, the answer to this question is complicated. In her *Contemporary Theory* (1979), Poloma expresses strong support for a voluntaristic image of the human person, quoting Anthony Giddens's claim that "the social world ... has to be grasped as the skilled accomplishment of human subjects."[156] Because she wrote the textbook before she converted to charismatic evangelicalism, it is clear that Poloma's theoretical commitments preceded her encounter with Christian theology.

In spite of the continuities in her theoretical perspective, Poloma has thought a great deal about the connections between faith and sociology since her conversion. Like Thomas, she has exposed the concealed affinities between theology and the structure–agency debate. By articulating a fit between Christian thought and an agent-centered vision of sociology, she has called attention to the theological assumptions implicit in sociological theory.

"And Found No End, in Wandering Mazes Lost"

Most sociologists are probably unaware of Poloma's and Thomas's theological background assumptions. Poloma published her reflections on Christian sociology in *Sociological Analysis,* a journal that is seldom read by scholars outside the field of sociology of religion, and Thomas has not published his personal reflections on the connections between Christianity and social theory. In an e-mail follow-up to the interview, Thomas said that he did not think there was "such a thing as a Christian sociology in the sense of a social-scientific paradigm or scientific theory." At the same time, he said that "there could in fact be Christian critical theory" and that there "probably should be," adding that his own thinking on this "is part of a growing sense that the actual organized discipline of sociology is far from neutral." Such an approach would "have to be critical and plural: Christian critical theories."

Several other evangelical Protestant scholars interviewed for this study stressed the importance of human agency. Conspicuously absent from the structure–agency debate were the Catholic social scientists interviewed for this project.[157] Although this may be due partly to the small size of the sample (other Catholic intellectuals have addressed this issue[158]), it may also reflect enduring differences between the Catholic and Protestant imaginations. In *American Catholic Arts and Fictions: Culture, Ideology,*

Aesthetics (1992), Paul Giles writes that "Protestantism foregrounds the importance of free choice, individual conscience, and individual belief, while Catholicism places more emphasis upon a (religious or artistic) tradition which necessarily incorporates and objectifies the individual."[159] To the extent that the differences between "Calvinist" and "Arminian" approaches to sociology reflect intra-Protestant debates about the individual, the structure–agency debate may appeal more to Protestant than Catholic social scientists.

In Milton's *Paradise Lost,* the fallen angels argue interminably over "Providence, Foreknowledge, Will, and Fate—Fixed fate, free will, foreknowledge absolute," finding "no end, in wandering mazes lost."[160] In American sociology, an analogous debate rages over the relationship between structure and agency. As with its angelic counterpart, no end is in sight. Arguments about structure and agency cannot be resolved through appeals to the empirical world. If all theory is ultimately based on non-verifiable background assumptions, there is no longer a compelling reason to exclude religious assumptions from the conversation. The realization that such arguments cannot be settled through empirical research alone has helped create a space for the kind of meta-theoretical reflection practiced by Thomas and Poloma.

Blending Social Ethics with Social Science: Catholic Social Teaching and Public Policy

In a recent article, Alan Wolfe argues that the American social sciences are undergoing a "moral revival."[161] Robert Wuthnow notes that, although social scientists once emphasized a sharp separation between facts and values, "virtually every academic gathering is replete with discussions of normative issues."[162] Joining the moral revival, religious social scientists have found ways to blend Christian social ethics with the frameworks of their disciplines, joining the just-war tradition with international relations and theological critiques of racism with sociological analysis.

Like the relationship between theology and sociological theory, the relationship between morality and social science is long and complicated. At the beginning of the twentieth century, Julie Reuben writes, most social scientists were involved in contemporary social or political movements as "activists, advisors, or publicists." Crusading for the Social Gospel, for workers' rights, and for women's suffrage, scholars such as

Richard Ely and Herbert Baxter Adams did not draw a clear boundary between social ethics and social science. During this period, social-science departments routinely offered social-ethics courses.[163] With the ascendancy of positivism in the 1920s and 1930s, social scientists' moral engagement waned as scholars drew an increasingly firm boundary between empirical research and normative convictions.[164] By the postwar era, American sociology had embraced a value-neutral ideology that expressed itself in the "abstract empiricism" of quantitative research.[165] The "behavioral revolution" in political science had similar consequences for the study of politics, emphasizing the scientific pursuit of empirical data over normative commitments.[166]

Yet in the past thirty years, the boundary between social science and moral engagement has significantly weakened. The campus activism of the 1960s led many faculty to question the "association of objectivity with value neutrality," according to Reuben. Criticizing the "narrow, technical, and disconnected" character of academic knowledge, they called for a more politically engaged university.[167] In the social sciences, movements such as neo-Marxism, conflict sociology, feminism, and communitarianism helped reconnect morality and social research. The "revival of moral inquiry" in the social sciences, says Wolfe, has led to a "greater concern with questions of right and wrong, the nature of the good life, [and our] obligations to others."[168]

Religious concerns have played an important role in the moral reawakening of American social science. Many leading communitarian thinkers, including Robert Bellah, Jean Bethke Elshtain, and Ann Swidler, are people of faith (see chapter 5). In political science, the field of international relations has rediscovered religion as the "missing dimension of statecraft."[169] Once marginal to public-policy discussions, faith-based approaches are on the table at major think tanks such as the Brookings Institution and the American Enterprise Institute and at public-policy schools such as Harvard's John F. Kennedy School of Government.

Joining the moral revival, several of the Catholic social scientists interviewed for this project have articulated a fit between religious ethics and mainstream social science. They have rejected the value-free approach to their disciplines and emphasized the connections between normative reflection and empirical research (while taking care to distinguish between the two). The Catholic social scientists Bruce Russett and Gary Orfield, for example, have combined Christian social ethics and social research. Like John DiIulio, both have taught at Ivy League universities, and both have used the Catholic tradition to make sense of the ethical implications of public policy, bringing concepts and categories from their religious communities into mainstream social science.

Just-War Theory and "The Challenge of Peace": Bruce Russett

The author of twenty-two books and more than two hundred articles, Bruce Russett is a major figure in American political science. He is currently the editor of the *Journal of Conflict Resolution.* As the Dean Acheson Professor of International Relations at Yale University, he has pursued a research agenda that combines empirical sophistication with engagement in larger public issues. Although he is best known for his recent work on the "democratic peace" and the empirical finding that democracies are less likely to fight each other, he has also made major contributions to the study of nuclear deterrence and arms control.[170] Russett was trained as a quantitative social scientist during the height of the behavioral revolution and has spent much of his career addressing empirical questions. At the same time, a normative vision of world politics undergirds much of his research.

The field of international relations has long been divided between realist and communitarian approaches to world politics. As articulated by thinkers such as George Kennan, Hans Morganthau, and Reinhold Niebuhr, the realist tradition has tended to view "all human relations, including the relations between states, [as a] struggle for power."[171] By contrast, the communitarian perspective has shown hope about the prospects for what Russett calls "cooperative international relations." Rooted in a tradition stretching back to Grotius, Locke, and Kant, the communitarian approach looks for "stability within the chaos, probability within the randomness, [and] order within the anarchy" of international relations.[172] Given the presence of Protestant thinkers on both sides of the divide (Niebuhr, Grotius, Locke), it would be foolish to classify one approach as "Protestant" and the other "Catholic." At the same time, it is impossible to ignore the influence of Protestant neo-orthodoxy (and its sober view of human nature) on political realism.[173]

Never much of a "hard-nosed realist," Russett found himself attracted to the communitarian vision of Karl Deutsch while a graduate student at Yale in the early 1960s. At the time, Russett's embrace of communitarianism had little to do with his faith—raised Protestant, he had only recently become a Catholic. Yet in recent years he has pointed to the connections between the communitarian approach to international relations and Christian theology: "This alternative conception of international relations . . . speaks to me of a created order—a sinful order to be sure—that leaves us an opening for behavior that can be other-regarding while still self-regarding, imperfect but not condemning us to a choice between self-victimization and endless cycles of violence. Social science can help discern the music of the social spheres, and to comprehend some part of the social creation."[174] In books such as *Grasping the Democratic Peace* (1993) and *Triangulating Peace: Democracy, Interdependence, and International Organizations* (2001), Russett has discerned an "order of cooperation" that is consistent with the analogical and communitarian sensibility of the Catholic imagination.[175]

Russett has not always been so forthcoming about his normative commitments. As a junior faculty member at Yale, he began his career in a department that "expected us to be social scientists, not ideologues."[176] Yet, like many political scientists of his generation, Russett found himself drawn into the political debates of the 1960s. "If you're teaching an undergraduate international politics class in the late 1960s," he said, "you damn well have to address the question of Vietnam." In an effort to come to grips with the morality of the Vietnam war, he discovered just-war theory, immersing himself in the writings of Paul Ramsey, Robert Tucker, and Michael Walzer (all nonCatholics). Later, he discovered the work of Catholic theologians and ethicists such as J. Bryan Hehir, Monika Hellwig, and Joseph McKenna.[177] For the first time, Russett said, "I really made an explicit connection between the two parts of my life." During the 1974–75 academic year, he took part in the seminar, "Ethics and the U.S. Debate on Nuclear Weapons Strategy," co-sponsored by Georgetown University's Woodstock Theological Center and the Institute for the Study of Ethics and International Affairs.[178] Although he by and large remained an empirical social scientist, his interest in just-war theory soon led him into the borderlands between empirical research and normative theory.

Beginning with a 1972 article on nuclear deterrence, he began systematically to apply the principles of just-war theory to the world of public policy, bringing the most authoritative Catholic discourse on war and peace into the field of international relations. In "A Countercombatant Deterrent? Feasibility, Morality, and Arms Control," which was published in an edited volume of the seminar papers, he wrote that it was "immoral deliberately to kill civilians" and pointed out that counterpopulation warfare violated the just-war criteria of "proportionality," "discrimination," and "reasonable chance of success."[179] Although he acknowledged that his "search for an alternative deterrent strategy [was] rooted in a moral revulsion against plans deliberately to kill large numbers of civilians," Russett devoted a large section of the article to demonstrating the "feasibility" of having "military targets only"—which he called a "countercombatant" strategy.[180]

Along the same lines, Russett combined normative just-war arguments and an assessment of the feasibility of "no first use" in the article "No First Use of Nuclear Weapons" (1976).[181] Such careful distinctions between empirical and normative analysis can be found throughout Russett's writing on the morality of nuclear deterrence. "I know when I'm reasoning in a normative mode and when I'm doing empirical work," he said in the interview. "Nonetheless, [they] complement each other all the way through." He sees no point in "having a normative, prescriptive view of the world that has no empirical grounding in terms of what is possible."

It was Russett's skill in relating what is possible to the moral tradition of just-war theory that led Father Bryan Hehir to invite him to serve as principal consultant on "The Challenge of Peace," the U.S. Catholic Bishops' letter on war and peace.[182] Drawing on his work on nuclear deterrence—especially that on "countercombatant" strategy—Russett helped the bishops draft a document that applies "general principles to reasoning about local conditions."[183] Although it acknowledges the pacifist tradition in Christian social ethics, the pastoral's "analytical core" (whose first draft was written by Russett) relates the just-war theory to American nuclear strategy. Although it acknowledges the legitimacy of nuclear deterrence, "The Challenge of Peace" rejects the targeting of civilians, the first use of nuclear weapons, and limited nuclear war. Outlining a communitarian vision of international relations, it calls for greater cooperation in an "interdependent world."[184] The bishops' pastoral, which was criticized by Catholic pacifists for not going far enough and by Catholic hawks for going too far, maintains a tension between biblical and natural-law arguments, universal principles and local conditions, realism and idealism, and the just-war and pacifist traditions.[185]

In *Public Religions in the Modern World* (1994), José Casanova portrays the pastoral as an outstanding example of the "deprivatization" of religion in American society.[186] Coming in the wake of Ronald Reagan's military buildup, the bishops' letter generated enormous public debate. It was covered widely by the national media and became the most visible expression of Catholic social teaching ever directed at a mainstream U.S. audience. According to George Kennan, a leading postwar American foreign policy intellectual, "The Challenge of Peace" is "the most profound and searching inquiry yet conducted by any responsible collective body into the relations of nuclear weaponry, and indeed of modern war in general, to moral philosophy, to politics and the conscience of the national state."[187]

A "new literature on ethics and international relations [has] developed in the last ten years," notes the political scientist Stanley Hoffman.[188] Through his work as a political scientist and as principal consultant on "The Challenge of Peace," Russett has contributed to this burgeoning field of study. Although Russett's articles on just-war theory make up a relatively small proportion of his scholarly output (no more than a dozen out of two hundred articles), they are significant nevertheless. By blending "modern science and its theories" with "Christian morality and doctrine," he has lived out the vision articulated by the Second Vatican Council.[189] And by bringing the same kinds of arguments into mainstream social science, he has helped bridge the gap between Christian social ethics and social science.[190]

Religious Values and Race: Gary Orfield

Gary Orfield, a nationally recognized authority on school desegregation and civil-rights policy, has taught at Princeton University, the University of Virginia, and the University of Chicago. Since 1991 he has served as Professor of Education and Social Policy at Harvard University, teaching at both the Graduate School of Education and the John F. Kennedy School of Government. In books such as *Dismantling Desegregation: The Quiet Reversal of Brown v. Board of Education* (1997) and *The Closing Door: Conservative Policy and Black Opportunity* (1993), he has combined a passionate commitment to racial justice with solid empirical analysis, articulating a scholarly critique of America's retreat from the civil-rights agenda.[191]

Throughout his career, Orfield has kept one foot in the world of academia and the other in the world of the civil-rights community. As a University of Chicago graduate student in the 1960s, he followed Martin Luther King, Jr., around Mayor Daley's Chicago. He has served as a scholar in residence at the U.S. Commission on Civil Rights, a fellow at the Brookings Institution, a consultant for the U.S. Department of Education, and a court appointed expert in many school-desegregation cases. He frequently speaks to community groups and has done free research for civil-rights organizations. Most recently, he has served as co-director of the Civil Rights Project at Harvard University, a program that forges relationships among scholars, community organizations, and policymakers. By regarding the study of racial inequality as a "moral imperative," the Civil Rights Project seeks to "bridge the gap between theory and practice, and between academy and community."[192]

In 1997, Orfield helped organize a national conference on religion and civil rights that brought together theologians from a host of traditions, including Catholics, Protestants, Jews, Muslims, and Buddhists.[193] The conference papers have been published as *Religion, Race, and Justice in a Changing America* (1999), co-edited by Orfield and Holly Lebowitz. In a note to the book's introduction, Orfield acknowledges the place of religious values in his own research: "What we choose to study and whether or not we go beyond our research to try to apply it in the world are often matters of values, sometimes of religious values, but we rarely acknowledge that. . . . Since I am making what is probably my only appearance in the company of theologians, I decided to set aside my normal practice and say something about my own experience in print, since religious experience is the original source of this enterprise."[194]

Orfield follows this statement with an impassioned critique of racial injustice in America. Unlike Russett, Orfield does not draw explicitly from Catholic social teaching. Nevertheless, an implicitly Catholic sensibility undergirds much of his essay. Arguing that Christianity "contains rich traditions of theological thought on obligations that go beyond markets and individual satisfaction," he offers a communitarian Catholic critique of the individualism of American society.[195] And despite his strong convictions about racial justice, Orfield observes a careful distinction between moral values and empirical evidence. He portrays theological reflection and social-scientific research as distinct yet complementary approaches to public policy that should be interrelated. While theologians and ethicists need to be aware of the empirical facts of the situation, he writes, social scientists must recognize the larger ethical questions raised by their findings. For the future, Orfield advocates greater dialogue between theologians and social scientists about each other's premises. For "religion to make a difference," people of faith must understand both the theological principles of their traditions *and* the social realities of race in America.[196]

Putting Religious Ethics Back on the Public-Policy Agenda

Most social scientists do not think of religion when they hear Gary Orfield's name. Viewed against the backdrop of thirty years in political science, Orfield's involvement in the religion and civil-rights conference was a brief episode in a long career as a policy analyst. As a one-time event (his "only appearance in the company of theologians," he said) commemorated in an edited volume, its impact on the public-policy world was almost certainly modest.[197] Like Russett's articles on just-war theory, Orfield's volume on religion and civil rights, and the introductory essay that begins it, make up a relatively small proportion of his total scholarly output.

Yet from another angle, Orfield's and Russett's forays into the world of religious social ethics are of considerable importance. At various times in their careers, both men have assumed the role of Catholic public intellectual. Like DiIulio, they have used their Ivy League status to confer legitimacy on religious approaches to public policy. By organizing a conference on religion and civil rights under the auspices of Harvard University, Orfield heightened the visibility of theological perspectives on race. By lending his expertise as an international-relations scholar to "The Challenge of Peace," Russett helped enhance the academic respectability of Catholic social teaching.

Where are the evangelical social scientists in contemporary public-policy debates? In recent years, a host of evangelical scholars, including Don Eberly, Stephen Monsma, Richard Mouw, and James Skillin, have contributed to discussions of religious ethics and public policy. Despite heightened evangelical reflection on social ethics, none of the evangelical social scientists interviewed for this project has written widely on this topic.[198] Although this may simply be an artifact of the small sample, it may also reflect the relative weakness of evangelical social thought compared with its Catholic counterpart. As noted in chapter 5, evangelicals have tended to embrace an individualistic approach to politics. The fact that the evangelicals interviewed for this project have paid little attention to Christian social ethics is consistent with this individualistic tradition.

Conclusion

Three barriers stand against religious points of view in the academic social sciences: the boundary between the natural and the supernatural, that between the empirical and the non-empirical, and that between morality and social science. Yet Catholic and evangelical scholars have frequently transgressed those boundaries. Through anti-reductionist approaches to the study of religion, they have made room for religious phenomena in the social sciences. Through their reflections on the religious assumptions of the structure–agency debate, they have called attention to the concealed affinities between Protestant theology and social theory. Through their writings on just-war theory and racial justice, they have blurred the boundaries between morality and social science. Through the tropes of Catholic comedy and Protestant irony, they have used the story forms of the Catholic and Protestant imaginations to structure historical narratives.

In all of this, Catholics and evangelicals have resisted the modern tendency to "*think small:* to ask questions for which there were determinate and publicly verifiable answers."[199] By focusing on the meta dimensions of scholarly inquiry (metahistory, metatheory, metaphysics), they have called attention to the philosophical and religious assumptions that undergird all academic knowledge. By questioning the jurisdictional boundaries of the human sciences, they have challenged their disciplines' claims to reduce human social life to exclusively social-scientific explanations.[200] And by remaining open to religious ways of knowing, they have practiced a form of social science that points beyond itself to larger theological and ethical concerns.

As feminism, postmodernism, and multiculturalism have redefined the boundaries between legitimate and illegitimate knowledge, such border crossings have become increasingly common. Yet compared with the impact of these movements, the influence of religious scholars has been modest. David Hollinger, for example, has expressed doubt that Christianity is "generating a number of exciting new research programs, as feminism has proved able to do," and others have questioned whether Christian scholars are producing "anything uniquely or particularly Christian."[201] Even religious scholars are "not convinced—at least not yet—that Christian historians produce scholarship that is significantly different from [that of] their non-Christian colleagues."[202]

The faith-based scholarship profiled in this chapter suggests that these observers may be missing something. In many books and articles, Catholics and evangelicals have brought their religious commitments into their scholarship. Why have so few academics noticed? Part of the problem may have to do with the subtle influence of Christian faith.

As the case studies in this chapter make clear, Catholic and evangelical scholars have often favored the implicit rather than the explicit use of religious perspectives. The influence of Calvinism on Thomas's sociology is a case in point. Although Thomas privately acknowledges the parallels between sixteenth-century debates over the sovereignty of God and the structure–agency debate, he has not written publicly about these connections. The presence of theological irony in the works of evangelical historians is yet another example. Because it relies on ostensibly factual description, irony allows historians to make moral judgments without seeming to do so. As Robert Manoff points out, "the ironic account seems to enable the world to speak for itself"; in a secular culture, ironic narration "serves as a means to make the very judgments that once would have been referred to the highest authority," replacing "traditional God-language" with "modern irony-language."[203] Because of this shift, it is often difficult to tell whether a Christian historian is making a theological point or just being ironic. Despite the influence of Lutheran and Niebuhrian irony on the new evangelical historiography, few reviewers have picked up on these themes.

Another possible reason for the low profile of Catholic and evangelical perspectives in the academy is the respondents' tendency to translate the "thick" language of their religious traditions into more general or universal terms.[204] This is especially true of the Catholic respondents who draw on natural-law arguments. When Russett writes about just-war theory, he is drawing on a part of the Catholic intellectual tradition that is easily translated into secular terms. Although just-war theory is the most authoritative Catholic discourse on war and peace, it does not employ biblical or theological terminology. The U.S. Catholic Bishops' pastoral letters have been criticized for "watering down Christian norms to a 'least common denominator' sufficiently non-threatening to secular power."[205] A similar critique can be applied to Russett's work on nuclear ethics. Given the centrality of natural law and natural theology to the Catholic intellectual tradition, such a critique would hardly be fair.[206] Yet from the vantage point of the secular academy, just-war theory seems less obviously religious than biblical or theological ethics.

Any assessment of the visibility of faith-based scholarship must also pay attention to the physical location of religious discourse within a given book or article. Many of the respondents have confined explicitly religious discourse to the prefaces, notes, epilogues, and afterwords of their works. Marsden, for example, restricts his discussion of Christian scholarship to the preface and epilogue of *Fundamentalism and American Culture,* and Noll is most candid about his theological commitments in the opening and closing pages of *A History of Christianity in the United States and Canada.*[207] Along the same lines, Orfield discusses the relationship between his Catholic faith and his social science in a note to the introduction of *Religion, Race, and Justice in a Changing America.*[208] Similarly,

Russett confines his discussion of just-war theory to an explicitly normative section of his article on counter-combatant nuclear deterrence.[209]
These respondents have carried such religious themes into the rest of
their works to varying degrees. To the extent this is the case, the confes-
sional sections of their writings can be used to interpret what precedes
and follows them. At the same time, the segregation of religious language creates the impression that these scholars' Christian commitments
are less than integral to their scholarship.

Catholics and evangelicals engage in yet another form of religious segregation by publishing their most normative works with religious publishers and periodicals. Through works such as *The Search for Christian
America*, *The Scandal of the Evangelical Mind*, *A Christian View of History?*,
Religious Advocacy and American History, and *Christians and the American Revolution*, the new evangelical historians have brought an explicitly Christian framework to the study of American history. Yet with few exceptions,
these works have been published by evangelical publishers, in most cases
with the William B. Eerdmans Publishing Company of Grand Rapids,
Michigan.[210] A similar pattern can be found in the careers of Catholic and
evangelical political scientists. Russett has published his most normative
articles in *Commonweal*, *Worldview*, and the *Review of Politics*, and Guth,
Green, Kellstedt, and Smidt have confined their most evaluative writing
to *First Things*.[211] Although such religious venues have done much to
nurture Christian intellectual life, they have also isolated religious discourse from the academic mainstream.

To the extent they have focused their research on American religion,
Catholics and evangelicals have failed to gain the attention of the leading
scholars in their disciplines. According to Leo Ribuffo, the history of
Christianity remains "marginal to American historiography." Commenting
on the low visibility of evangelical scholars, Ribuffo notes that "political
and diplomatic historians, my own professional cohort for the past decade,
almost never know the work of such important scholars as George M.
Marsden and Mark Noll."[212] Leslie Woodcock Tentler makes a similar
point about the status of Catholic historiography in "On the Margins: The
State of American Catholic History."[213] Much the same can said be about
the political scientists and sociologists in the sample. In *Religion and the Culture Wars* (1996), Guth, Green, Kellstedt, and Smidt "complain some about
how they are ignored or disdained by fellow political scientists because of
their (at least originally evangelically inspired) interest in religion."[214]

All of this does not mean that Catholics and evangelicals have failed to make a difference. The growing influence of evangelical scholars, including several of the respondents, is impressively chronicled in Alan Wolfe's *Atlantic Monthly* cover story "The Opening of the Evangelical Mind." Accepting "with some qualifications" the claim that evangelicals "have finally made it in American academic life," Wolfe notes that "Conservative Christians have enlivened and enriched the humanities, political and social theory, and even some empirical social science."[215] Providing evidence of a similar trend, Catholics and evangelicals are prominently featured in several recent *Chronicle of Higher Education* stories about the revival of religion in the academy.[216]

Despite the understandable tendency to publish Christian scholarship with Christian publishers, Catholic and evangelical scholars have published at least some of their explicitly religious scholarship in secular venues. Marsden's *Outrageous Idea of Christian Scholarship* was published by Oxford University Press, and an account of Russett's work with the bishops appeared in the mainstream international-relations journal *International Security*.[217] As noted earlier, Greeley has published different versions of his theory of the religious imagination with Macmillan, Transaction, Doubleday, and the University of California Press, and in the *American Sociological Review* and the *Journal of the American Academy of Religion*.[218] Finally, DiIulio has written widely on religion and public policy for such publications as the *Brookings Review* and *City Journal*.[219]

Nor have Catholic and evangelical scholars eliminated explicitly Christian language from their writings. Considering the pressure to downplay the particularity of religious terminology, the extent to which theological language works its way into the respondents' books and articles is striking. "Grace," "sacrament," and "hope" appear frequently in Greeley's writings on the religious imagination.[220] Noll's history of North American Christianity evaluates the legacy of Christian America in light of the "incarnation" and the "theology of the cross."[221] Marsden invokes Niebuhr, Jonathan Edwards, and J. R. R. Tolkien in *Fundamentalism and American Culture*. Dolan's *The American Catholic Experience* draws openly on Vatican II's definition of church as the "people of God."[222] Although they are not as explicitly theological, Russett's articles on just-war theory and nuclear strategy draw on a vocabulary of "proportionality," "discrimination," and "reasonable chance of success," terms that are not ordinarily employed by international-relations specialists.[223] Although much of this language appears in these works' opening and closing pages, it can also be found in the intervening sections.

Thus, Catholics and evangelicals have been modestly successful at bringing their religious commitments into the academy. Blurring the boundaries between facts and values, theology and social science, and faith and knowledge, they have engaged in the deprivatization of religion. Implicitly and explicitly, intentionally and unintentionally, they have produced scholarship that differs in important ways from that of their secular colleagues. Could they have done more? In a recent essay, Jonathan Tucker Boyd urges Christian historians to experiment with "new possibilities for historical description, narrative, and argument, ones that promise to crack the door so long locked against the divine."[224] Similarly, Michael Baxter critiques Marsden's *Outrageous Idea of Christian Scholarship* for not being "outrageous enough" and calls for Christian scholarship that is "more comprehensive, integrated, unifying, totalizing."[225] In the future, some enterprising scholar may take up these calls for a more full-blown Christian scholarship. In the meantime, however, it is important to recognize the profound influence of religious commitments on the writings of today's Catholics and evangelicals. In light of the historic barriers against religious ways of knowing, it is remarkable how much religion matters in their work.

7   Openness and Obstacles

The scene was a well-appointed meeting room at Harvard University. The occasion was the October 2000 Conference on the Future of Religious Colleges.[1] Present were some of the most prominent Christian educators in America, including several of those interviewed for this project.[2] Most were veterans of the religion-and-higher-education-conference circuit. They were among the nation's leading experts on Christian higher education and well versed in the literature on faith in the academy.

Perhaps it was the Harvard location. Perhaps it was the critical mass of religious scholars. Perhaps it was the publication of Alan Wolfe's "The Opening of the Evangelical Mind" earlier that month.[3] Whatever the reason, Paul Dovre, the conference's organizer, noted that a "clearly distinguishable mood of hopefulness" hung over the proceedings and presenters.[4] In paper after paper, speakers painted an optimistic picture of the future of religion in the academy. George Marsden talked about the collapse of "progressive scientific humanism." Mark Noll pointed to the vitality of "Christian learning in a secularized academic environment" and argued that "the recent history of American higher education has witnessed a surprising recovery of learning informed by traditional religious convictions."[5] According to Beth McMurtrie of the *Chronicle of Higher Education,* "the educators portrayed the cultural climate as increasingly welcoming of religious scholars and hospitable to religious institutions."[6]

Such hopefulness was in sharp contrast to the "tales of doom and gloom" that had previously dominated the debate about religion and higher education.[7] In books such as James Burtchaell's *The Dying of the Light* (1998) and Marsden's *Soul of the American University* (1994), scholars had emphasized the themes of secularization and religious decline.[8] "Compared to conversations on this matter five years ago," said Dovre, president emeritus of Concordia College in Minnesota, the "mood is more optimistic."[9]

Despite the Harvard presenters' hopeful outlook, most of them qualified their optimism with a sober assessment of the barriers facing Christian educators. "Speaking only of the Christian parts of the fuller picture," Noll said, "I do not believe that we are experiencing a renaissance of Christian intellectual life." Although he acknowledged the growing participation of Christians in the academy, he noted that "momentum for institutions and for society as a whole is not the same as momentum for individual scholars."[10] Commenting on Noll's presentation, Robert Benne, a theologian, called the glass "half full."[11] While reflecting on the conference as a whole, Dovre wondered about the viability of religious scholarship "in an academy shaped by scientific determinism and/or postmodern fatalism."[12]

Half Full–Half Empty

Although it was originally applied to the arena of church-related colleges, Benne's "half-full" assessment of Christian higher education could easily be extended to the new-class professions as a whole. The respondents in this study, echoing the ambivalence of the conference participants (including Marsden and Noll), have alternated between optimistic and pessimistic accounts of the place of religion in professional life. While lamenting sociology's hostility toward religious perspectives, Andrew Greeley acknowledged that sociology conferences at which papers on religion are delivered are increasingly "jammed."[13] Peter Steinfels has observed both a "sympathetic entertainment of religious belief in intellectual circles" and an "anti-Catholic animus" in the media and higher education.[14]

My findings are consistent with such ambivalence. The preceding chapters documented both surprising openness and lingering obstacles to religious self-expression in journalism and the social sciences. The respondents appear to have gotten away with practices that seem—at least, on the surface—to violate the taboos of social-science positivism and journalistic empiricism: a charismatic sociologist reported being "slain in the spirit" in the course of her ethnographic research; a journalist reported blending the biblical concepts of justice and peace with the journalistic ideal of truth; a priest said he brought "grace," "hope," and "sacrament" into his sociological theory of religion; a Catholic journalist wrote about the communion of saints for *Newsweek* magazine; and a historian confessed his belief in divine providence in book published by Oxford University Press. Blurring the boundaries between faith and knowledge, facts and values, and church and profession, these respondents have engaged in the deprivatization of religion. In the interviews (chapters 3 and 4) and their writings (chapters 5 and 6), they have integrated faith and work.

However, many of the same respondents have expressed their beliefs in ways that are hidden, implicit, and difficult to detect. By translating explicitly religious terminology into the language of their professional colleagues they have downplayed the particularity of their theological commitments. By confining moral and religious truth claims to the opening and closing pages of their works—or, in some cases, to their private lives—they have segregated faith and knowledge. By qualifying displays of normative conviction with appeals to the rhetoric of objectivity, they have reaffirmed the boundary between religious and professional domains. And by expressing their religious beliefs in bits and pieces, they have often failed to articulate a coherent account of the relationship between faith and intellectual life.

Openness and obstacles, optimism and pessimism, half full and half empty. What accounts for the ambiguous situation of Catholic and evangelical professionals? Opportunities and constraints govern displays of religious identity in both fields. The burgeoning literature on the "revival of religion" in journalism and higher education shows a growing openness to religious viewpoints in professional life, an openness that has allowed my respondents to bring their beliefs into the content of their work. But at the same time, the limits to this openness call attention to persistent barriers against religious self-expression. Highlighting the protean character of religious faith in the new class, I will show how Catholics and evangelicals have merged elements of identity that are seemingly incompatible into what Robert Jay Lifton calls "odd combinations."[15] In doing so, I will avoid a one-sided emphasis on accommodation or resistance and argue that such religious proteanism contains both dangers and opportunities for people of faith.

Clothing the "Naked Public Square"

In a nation in which critics once lamented a "naked public square" devoid
of religious meanings, public religion has enjoyed a modest resurgence.[16]
In the 1980s, the new Christian right brought religious concerns back to
the center of American politics.[17] More recently, faith-based approaches
to public policy have been embraced by both Democrats and Republi-
cans, appearing in the national platforms of both parties.[18] For example,
Wendy Kaminer has observed a "striking re-moralization of public policy debates," and the evangelical Ronald Sider has noted that "religion
and its contribution to public life . . . [have] been all over the front pages
of our most prestigious newspapers."[19] Although such public expressions
of faith are a recurring theme in American history, the heightened prominence of religious discourse is hard to overlook.

Along with the rise of a faith-based politics, a more general resurgence
of spirituality has occurred in U.S. culture. Dubbed the "spiritual marketplace" and the "quest culture" by Wade Clark Roof, this renewed interest in all things spiritual has been fueled in part by a massive expansion
in religious publishing. "The printing and sale of books on spirituality and
the sacred in the nineties is nothing less than phenomenal," writes Roof.
Christian publishing has grown into a $4 billion industry, and books on
new-age, Eastern, and alternative spirituality regularly "top the sales
charts."[20] More recently, the world of literary publishing has displayed
what *Publisher's Weekly* calls a "new openness" to religious themes.[21]

This spiritual marketplace has extended to the boardrooms of U.S.
business. *Business Week* devoted its seventieth-anniversary cover story to
"the growing presence of spirituality in corporate America," and *Fortune*
has profiled efforts to "bridge the traditional divide between spirituality
and work." Both articles cite Gallup data showing that almost half of
Americans had "had occasion to talk about their faith in the workplace in
the past 24 hours." From office Bible studies to *Fortune*-500 vision quests,
"spirituality in the workplace is exploding," *Business Week* reports.[22]

Religious Resurgence in Journalism and Academia

Paralleling the religious resurgence in American public life, the news
media and higher education have evinced a growing interest in matters
of faith. Although they are traditionally more secular than the worlds of

politics, publishing, and business, these quintessential enlightenment professions are in the midst of what Wolfe has called a "welcome revival of religion."[23] In both journalism and academia, this revival has taken the form of heightened attention to religious and moral concerns, greater openness to religious perspectives, and the growing participation of people of faith.

Religion Reporting Is "Hot"

Spurred by reader demand and the increasing visibility of religion in American politics, religion reporting has become a hot area in U.S. journalism.[24] As noted earlier, national media coverage of religion has doubled in the past decade, rising from 488 stories in the 1980s to 1,044 in the 1990s.[25] During roughly the same period (1980–95), the membership of the Religion Newswriters Association (RNA) also doubled. According to the association's president, Richard Dujardin, about four hundred reporters are covering religion nationwide, 265 of whom belong to the RNA.[26] Several major metropolitan newspapers, including the *Dallas Morning News*, the Twin Cities' *Star Tribune*, and the *Arizona Republic*, have added religion sections, and most Public Broadcasting Service (PBS) affiliates air the program *Religion and Ethics Newsweekly*, funded by Lilly Endowment.[27] Likewise, in a 1996 survey of 227 religion news specialists, 64 percent said that religion coverage had increased over the past five years at their news organizations.[28] The 1990s also saw major stories about the religion beat in the *American Journalism Review, Nieman Reports*, and the *Columbia Journalism Review.*[29]

Reflecting this trend, religion has become an increasingly important part of the curriculum at America's leading journalism schools. Partnering with religion and theology faculty at their respective institutions, both Northwestern's Medill School of Journalism and Columbia's Graduate School of Journalism offer joint master's programs in religion and journalism.[30] The catalogue for the Missouri School of Journalism now includes a course titled, "Religion Writing and Reporting," and the university recently sponsored a lecture series on religion in the practice of law, medicine, and journalism.[31] In the past ten years, several foundation-supported programs for working journalists have also been created, including the Pew Program on Religion and the News Media and the Lilly Project on Religion in the News, both of which are coordinated by Mark Silk of Trinity College's Center for the Study of Religion in Public Life.[32]

Journalism educators, says Allan Andrews, have demonstrated "heightened interest" in ethics, religion, and the media.[33]

With greater media attention to religion has come the growing participation in journalism of people of faith. According to a survey conducted in 1992, 72 percent of print and broadcast journalists across the country considered religion "somewhat" or "very" important to their lives; a more recent survey, for the RNA, suggests that "well over three-fourths of religion reporters are themselves highly religious."[34] Moreover, there is evidence that even journalists in New York and Washington, D.C., are becoming more religious. According to a recent study, the share of national journalists attending religious services monthly increased from 14 percent in 1980 to 30 percent in 1995 (53 percent of Americans attend services monthly). During the same period, the proportion that claimed no religion dropped from 50 percent to 22 percent.[35] In 1999, Gegrapha held its first international conference, with more than 140 Christian journalists in attendance.[36] Around the same time, students at Missouri's School of Journalism formed the Fellowship of Christian Journalists.[37] According to Laurie Goodstein, religion correspondent for the *New York Times,* there are "many more people of faith . . . in our newsrooms than is commonly believed." Although many believers remain "closeted," more and more are speaking and writing openly about matters of faith.[38]

A "Welcome Revival" of Religion in the Academy

For most of the twentieth century, the dominant story line in American higher education has emphasized the triumph of secularization and the exclusion of religion from academic discourse. In books such as *The Soul of the American University, The Dying of the Light, Exiles from Eden,* and *Faith and Knowledge,* scholars have mourned the "disengagement of colleges and universities from their Christian churches" and the "establishment of non-belief."[39] Though many remain pessimistic, a growing number of observers argue that religion is "making a dramatic comeback on America's campuses."[40] Wolfe, for example, has written about a "welcome revival of religion in the academy," and James Turner has noted that "among the most striking of recent developments on the American academic scene is a sharply rising interest in the relationship of religion and higher education."[41] A word search of the *Chronicle of Higher Education* found that the annual number of stories that contained the word "religion" increased dramatically between 1990 and 1999.[42]

The academic study of religion is on the rise across the disciplines. Between 1990 and 1999, the membership of the American Academy of Religion surged from 5,543 to 9,189, a 60 percent increase.[43] From religion and voting studies to research on faith-based social-service providers, social scientists are paying more attention to the role of faith in American life. As the *Los Angeles Times* has reported, "Once a largely forgotten factor in social research . . . religion is now a hot a field of inquiry."[44] In the 1990s, both the American Political Science Association and the American Sociological Association established religion sections (the former has more than 450 members), and the Society for the Scientific Study of Religion and the Association for the Sociology of Religion have enjoyed a period of intellectual vitality.[45] In the 1980s and 1990s, the study of American religion moved from the margins to the "mainstream of historical research," according to Harry Stout and Robert Taylor.[46] In professional education, the number of medical schools offering "spiritual or belief-based healing courses" increased from three in 1992 to seventy-two in 2000.[47] "[T]he intersection of religion and science is a topic gaining increased currency among at least some academics," notes the *Chronicle of Higher Education*.[48]

Even more so than the religious resurgence in American journalism, the revival of religion in the academy has been aided by the support of philanthropy. Over the past few decades, the Pew Charitable Trusts, Lilly Endowment, the John Templeton Foundation, and, most recently, the Ford Foundation have awarded millions of dollars in grants for the study or practice of religion in higher education.[49] Thanks to the support of foundations and other donors, more than one hundred fifty academic centers and institutes dedicated to religion have been established since the mid-1980s.[50] These include the Center for the Study of Religion at Princeton, the Institute for Religion and World Affairs at Boston University, and the Institute for the Advanced Study of Religion at Yale University. Foundation money has also been instrumental in promoting the academic study of religion in the disciplines of history, sociology, political science, medicine, and law, and the natural sciences.

Not only has religion grown as a topic of study; the past fifteen years have witnessed an increasing openness to religious perspectives in higher education. Across the disciplines, scholars have criticized the exclusion of religious viewpoints from academic debates. Through more than forty religious professional associations, including Christians in Political Science, the Society for Values in Higher Education, and the Association for

Religion and Intellectual Life, scholars have searched for ways to integrate faith and scholarship. The Society of Christian Philosophers, founded in 1978, is now the largest single-interest group in American philosophy. Its one thousand members make up about 12 percent of the membership of the American Philosophical Association.[51] Reflecting a more interreligious focus, eight hundred faculty, staff, and administrators (including twenty-eight college presidents) gathered at Wellesley College in 1998 for a conference on religious pluralism and spirituality in higher education. According to Diana Chapman Walsh, Wellesley's president, "a broader, deeper, and more daring form of intellectual discourse is taking shape in these academic circles" as spirituality and scholarship converge.[52] Similarly, 1,200 faculty and staff took part in programs funded under Lilly Endowment's $15.6 million Religion and Higher Education Initiative. In a 1999 survey of program participants, 60 percent perceived a "growing openness towards religious perspectives in American higher education."[53]

The increased prominence of religion in journalism and academia has not gone unnoticed by secular observers. In *Sleeping with Extra-Terrestrials: The Rise of Irrationalism and the Perils of Piety* (1999), Kaminer says that, "what is striking about journalists and intellectuals today, liberal and conservative alike, is not their mythic Voltairian skepticism, but their deference to belief and utter failure to criticize, much less satirize, America's romance with God." Waxing nostalgic for the days of H. L. Mencken and Walter Lippmann, Kaminer laments what she calls the "pious biases" of American journalists.[54] Likewise, in an article titled, "Where Are the Secularists?" Paul Kurtz argues that most "leaders in business, industry, the media, and academia" will not "admit to being an unbeliever."[55] Although they are couched in polemical language (and no doubt are exaggerated), such statements reveal just how far the religious resurgence in the knowledge professions has progressed.

Resources for Religious Self-Expression

Religion is thus enjoying a modest comeback in journalism and academia. What has this meant for the Catholic and evangelical professionals interviewed for this project? Although some of my respondents—notably, Andrew Greeley, Colman McCarthy, Wesley Pippert, and Kenneth Woodward—began their careers well before the contemporary religious resurgence, they have been professionally active long enough to benefit from the heightened attention to religion. For many others, including Fred Barnes, John DiIulio, E. J. Dionne, George Marsden, and Mark Noll, the "welcome revival" of religion in journalism and academia took place precisely as they were reaching the peak of their careers.[56]

My respondents have accrued some dividends from the increasing openness to religion. At the very least, the growing interest in religion and spirituality has removed much of the stigma attached to personal religious faith. In professions in which religion reporting is "hot,"[57] the so-called faith factor is taken seriously,[58] religion conferences are "jammed,"[59] and growing numbers of colleagues attend public worship, the public display of religious identity is not quite so deviant as it once was. Beyond lessening the stigma of religious faith, the revival of religion has given my respondents resources for religious self-expression in their professions. These resources are organizational, financial, and cultural.[60] Together, they have made it easier for Catholics and evangelicals to bring their beliefs into the content of their work.

Organizational Resources

From new religious professional associations and academic centers for religion to informal networks of scholars, the contemporary religious resurgence has furnished Catholics and evangelicals with many of the "focused centers, sustained conversations, and loose networks of relationships" necessary for maintaining a religious presence in their occupations.[61] For those respondents who study religion—Jay Dolan, Philip Gleason, Nathan Hatch, George Marsden, Mark Noll, and John Van Engen—centers such as the Institute for the Study of American Evangelicals (Wheaton College), the Cushwa Center for the Study of American Catholicism (Notre Dame), the Erasmus Institute (Notre Dame), the Boisi Center for Religion and American Public Life (Boston College), the Institute for the Advanced Study of Religion (Yale), and the Center for the Study of Religion (Princeton) have provided much needed organizational support. These centers have also put them in contact with one another. A single event at Washington's Ethics and Public Policy Center, where David Aikman is a senior fellow, included Fred Barnes, John DiIulio, John Green, and Richard Ostling.[62] Over the years, many of the religion scholars interviewed for this study have attended conferences at the Cushwa Center and the Institute for the Study of American Evangelicals.

In the public-policy arena, new programs at the Brookings Institution and the Manhattan Institute have created a space for both journalists, such as E. J. Dionne, and scholars, such as John DiIulio, to write about religion and public life.[63] Along the same lines, the Religion and Politics section of the American Political Science Association has served as a forum for John Green and the gang of four. In the news business, the Religion Newswriters Association, which is not new but is much larger than it once was; Gegrapha; the Lilly Project on Religion and the News; and a flurry of conferences on religion and the media have provided a space for many of my respondents—including David Aikman, Fred Barnes, Richard Ostling, Peter Steinfels, and Kenneth Woodward—to talk about the intersection of faith and their profession. Together with the religious colleges and universities, scholarly associations, publishing houses, and periodicals created by the Catholic and evangelical subcultures (as described in chapter 2), these organizations have provided an intellectual home for my respondents.

Financial Resources

The growing support of private philanthropy has also played a central role in the contemporary resurgence of religion. Since the 1970s, Lilly, Pew, Templeton, and Ford have poured hundreds of millions of dollars into religion-related projects.[64] Just as much of the institutional infrastructure described earlier was created through gifts from such foundations (the Erasmus Institute, the Center for the Study of Religion at Princeton, and the Lilly Project on Religion and the News), many of the individuals interviewed for this project have been the beneficiaries of philanthropic largesse.[65] As the founding director of the Cushwa Center, Jay Dolan has received at least a half-dozen Lilly grants over his long career. Similarly, the architects of the new evangelical historiography— Nathan Hatch, George Marsden, and Mark Noll—have long been supported by the generosity of Pew and Lilly, as have John Green and the gang of four. Programs funded by Pew have played a critical role in increasing the visibility of evangelical scholarship; the renewal of American Catholic historiography owes much to the support of Lilly.[66] It is not an overstatement to say that the contemporary field of American religion was created largely thanks to the support of Pew and Lilly. By making it possible for scholars to hold the conferences, publish the books, and build the networks, philanthropy has helped confer legitimacy on the religion-centered research agendas of Catholic and evangelical academics.

Even the journalists in the sample have been the beneficiaries of religious philanthropy. E. J. Dionne is currently co-director of the Pew Forum on Religion and Public Life, and Peter Steinfels co-directs the Pew-funded American Catholics in the Public Square project.[67] Likewise, Steinfels, Dionne, Woodward, and Ostling have spoken at foundation-supported gatherings on religion and journalism. All told, at least sixteen of the forty respondents, or nearly 40 percent of the sample, have participated in projects, programs, or conferences on religion funded by Pew or Lilly.

Cultural Resources

Finally, my respondents have benefited from the increasing availability of cultural resources, such as stories, symbols, rhetorics, and scripts, that legitimate the presence of religion and morality in public life.[68] As Silk points out, the story forms in the news usually "mirror public attitudes," and journalists operate with "ideas of what religion is and is not, of what it ought and ought not be—with topoi—that derive, to varying degrees, from religious sources."[69] In an era in which public religious discourse is on the rise, journalists are even more likely to gravitate toward religious themes. Capitalizing on the heightened visibility of religion in American politics, Catholic and evangelical journalists have brought their insights as religious insiders into the news. Fred Barnes and Pippert have written about the use of "born-again" language by presidents and presidential candidates such as Jimmy Carter, Ronald Reagan, and George W. Bush, and Cal Thomas has drawn on his experiences as a staff member in the Moral Majority.[70]

As secular intellectuals have struggled to understand the religious right, Catholic and evangelical scholars have carved out new roles for themselves as public interpreters of American religion. Marsden's *Fundamentalism and American Culture* (1981) appeared at a moment in American history in which the Moral Majority was becoming a major political force. The careers of the gang of four were undoubtedly aided by the political resurgence of religion.[71] John DiIulio's career as a social scientist and public official cannot be understood apart from the growing influence of faith-based approaches to public policy. And the increased volume of religious discourse in American higher education (in the *Chronicle of Higher Education*, for instance) has helped legitimate the religious scholarship of my respondents.

Besides capitalizing on the return of religious discourse in public life, the men and women interviewed for this project have been assisted by dual epistemological shifts in journalism and the social sciences. As Michael Schudson has observed, there is a "simmering disaffection with objective reporting" among American journalists. At the same time, an "epistemological revolution occurring in the academy today" has led social scientists to question the notion that there is one universal, "commitment-neutral" body of knowledge that is accessible to everyone.[72] Although these shifts have been rooted in wider—and, for the most part, secular—intellectual movements such as postmodernism, post-positivism, communitarianism, multiculturalism, feminism, and the social activism of the 1960s, they have made it easier for Catholics and evangelicals to bring their convictions into professional discourse. The journalists in the study have drawn on advocacy journalism, civic journalism, and feminism, approaches that, according to Schudson, run counter to the dominant "ideal of objectivity and its conventions."[73] In the social sciences, they have used the turn to postpositivism, postmodernism, feminism, and multiculturalism to justify the use of Christian perspectives in mainstream academic discourse.

Obstacles to Religious Self-Expression

My respondents have clearly benefited from the growing openness to religion in American public life. Empowered by the organizational, financial, and cultural resources available for bridging faith and profession, Catholics and evangelicals have brought their religious commitments into the workplace. At the same time, they have encountered persistent obstacles to religious self-expression in journalism and social science. These obstacles are rooted in the structural and cultural features of the modern professions and have limited their ability to integrate faith and work, speak in explicitly Christian terms, and articulate systematic connections between religion and professional life.

Professional–Religious Boundaries

Foremost among these obstacles is the continuing existence of firm institutional boundaries between religious and professional worlds. Although individual acts of religious self-expression (or "individual-level deprivatization," in Mark Regnerus and Christian Smith's terms) have helped to raise the public profile of faith, they have done little to change the basic structure of the social-scientific and journalistic professions.[74] Because most social-scientific knowledge continues to be produced in disciplines—and, in many cases, in subdisciplines—that have "lost their connections with any larger reality," it is increasingly difficult to integrate faith and scholarship.[75] It is, says Noll, "much easier to create informal networks . . . than to re-direct large institutions."[76] Thus, although religion has been deprivatized, there has been no re-integration or de-differentation of religious and professional spheres.[77]

Nor do most of my respondents want to collapse the boundaries between church and profession, religion and journalism, and faith and the academy (although many would like to relax them). Like their co-religionists in American politics, they have viewed the differentation of social institutions as a precondition for religious freedom and intellectual progress. Drawing on theological arguments from inside the Catholic and Protestant traditions, they have defended the notion that "different spheres of activity enjoy a relative autonomy."[78] Following Saint Thomas on the distinction between the disciplines—as well as Abraham Kuyper, Herman Dooyewerd, and John Henry Newman—they have recognized the legitimacy of different areas of professional competence.[79]

Such disciplinary and professional boundaries do not lack religious justification. When they are rigidly drawn, however, they have made it difficult for my respondents to integrate religion and work. Even in an era of blurred genres and interdisciplinary approaches such as women's studies, African American studies, and area studies, loyalty to the disciplinary guild trumps other loyalties. "We usually envision disciplines, fields, and areas of scholarship as being surrounded by mental 'walls' or 'moats' that help accentuate their mutual separateness in our minds," says Eviatar Zerubavel. Because disciplinary criteria continue to govern graduate training, hiring, tenure, and promotion, efforts to bring theology into dialogue with other fields continue to be viewed as a form of intellectual trespassing—or what Zerubavel calls "mental promiscuity."[80] Support for objectivity is weakening, but U.S. journalists have persisted in distancing themselves from religious and political ideologies. In a profession in which the confusion of fact and opinion was once likened to the mixing of church and state in government, discussions of "Christian," "Marxist," or "feminist" approaches to journalism continue to make most reporters nervous.[81]

The Problem of Translation

Closely related to the persistence of professional–religious boundaries are the pressures that Catholics and evangelicals face to translate explicitly religious language into secular terminology. Commenting on the demands of a pluralistic intellectual milieu, Steinfels argued that "even when you are explicitly religious you have to ... translate those beliefs or views or experiences into something analogous, in general terms, that people from non-religious as well as other religious traditions might be able to connect with." While Pippert has struggled to articulate his commitment to peace and justice "in a news way," others have translated their theological commitments into generic appeals for morality and values (Cal Thomas), natural law arguments (Bruce Russett), or ironic narration (Nathan Hatch).

These pressures are not unique to journalists and social scientists. According to Jean Bethke Elshtain, the dominant tradition of liberal political philosophy holds that "when religious persons enter the public sphere they are obliged to do so in a secular civic idiom shorn of any explicit reference to religious commitment and belief."[82] Similarly, George Lindbeck argues that, for those people who "share in the intellectual high culture of our day," religious traditions have "become foreign texts that are much easier to translate into currently popular categories than to be read in terms of their intrinsic sense."[83] Finally, Stephen Hart notes the tendency of some religious social movements to translate "expansive" theological or ethical claims into the more "constrained" language of interests and technique. (In an earlier essay, Hart used the terms "thick" and "thin".[84])

To be sure, there is much to be said for being "bilingual and bicultural."[85] Through translation my respondents have helped bridge the worlds of faith and the professions. Rather than acting as conversation stoppers, they have contributed to the ongoing dialogue between Christianity and public life.[86] Yet it is possible that something may have been lost in the translation. By filtering out overt references to the transcendent, the supernatural, and the explicitly Christian, Catholics and evangelicals may inadvertently have contributed to the secularization of public discourse. By speaking in secular terms, they may have concealed the influence of religious faith on their work.

Fragmentation and the Loss of Coherence

The respondents in this study have not always spoken in secular terms. As Garry Wills has pointed out, religious terminology "haunts a Catholic's speech in ways he is often unaware of"; as an example, he cites Senator Eugene McCarthy's use of the phrases "occasion of sin," "having scruples," and "particular friendship."[87] Like McCarthy, the Catholics and evangelicals interviewed for this project have laced their writings with religious terminology such as "subsidiarity," "sacrament," "communion of saints," "justice," "predestination," "righteousness," and "examination of conscience." Through religious language, they have infused their work with religious significance.

At the same time, one senses that my respondents could have done more to unpack the meaning of such theological terms. Their speech may be haunted by Christian terminology, but they have often used these terms in isolation from their larger theological and intellectual contexts. While dropping terms such as "examination of conscience" and "subsidiarity" into journal articles and newspaper editorials, they have failed to articulate the larger frameworks within which such words make sense. Many of my respondents have explained the theological terms that appear in their writings (for example, Andrew Greeley, Mark Noll, George Marsden, and Kenneth Woodward), but many others have not. In such cases, religious language has functioned like a secret code, rich in theological meaning for insiders yet unintelligible for those outside the tradition.

In the book *After Virtue,* Alasdair MacIntyre chronicles the breakdown of coherent moral traditions in modern societies. According to MacIntyre, we are often left with only the "fragments of a conceptual scheme, parts which now lack those contexts from which their significance derived." Although we continue to use many of the key expressions, he argues, we have lost our comprehension of their larger meanings.[88] In some ways, the same analysis could be applied to the place of religious language in the professions of journalism and social science. Although a host of religious terms continue to find their way into professional discourse, their larger meanings have often been lost on readers and listeners.

Beyond Accommodation and Resistance: Protean Religious Selves

What is the place of personal religious faith in the new class? Must Catholics and evangelicals accommodate to the "secular" ethos of their professions, or is there room for religious self-expression? Is the glass half empty or half full? In pursuit of answers to these questions, this chapter has analyzed both the opportunities and the constraints governing the display of religious identities in journalism and social science.

From one angle, Catholics and evangelicals have succeeded admirably in integrating religion and profession. Capitalizing on the growing openness of their colleagues to matters of faith and the growing availability of organizational, financial, and cultural resources, they have articulated strong connections between religion and work. Resisting the pressures of assimilation and accommodation (at least partially), they have brought their convictions into professional life. By importing overtly Christian perspectives into journalism and social science, they have rejected the compartmentalization of faith and knowledge.

Yet from another angle, the picture is not nearly so bright. Constrained by professional and disciplinary boundaries, they have distanced themselves from the roles of "theologian" and "advocate," resisting the full integration of religious perspectives into their work. By translating their beliefs into secular categories, they have downplayed the particularity of the Catholic and evangelical traditions. And by expressing their convictions in bits and pieces of Christian terminology, they have failed to articulate a systematic connection between religion and work.

Previous scholarship on religion in the new class is characterized by a one-sided emphasis on accommodation or resistance—that is, either Catholics and evangelicals are selling their souls to the secular new class, or they are transforming the workplace. Following David O'Brien, Christian Smith, and Eviatar Zerubavel, I have found it helpful to avoid such either—or logic and have focused instead on the "ongoing process of interaction" between professional and religious identities, faith and knowledge, and Christianity and American culture.[89] This approach, according to Zerubavel, "allows for the possibility, and even promotes the idea, of maintaining multiple identities simultaneously (such as being a jogger, a schoolteacher, a Catholic, a dog-owner, a vegetarian, a Latino, a Democrat, a father, as well as a jazz fan) without having to give up any one of them in order to claim another."[90] From this both–and perspective, it is possible to see my respondents as accommodating and resisting, "engaged" and "distinctive," religious and professional.[91]

"We are becoming fluid and many-sided," Robert Jay Lifton noted in In *The Protean Self*. The modern American tendency is to combine "mutually irreconcilable realities" into protean selves, Lifton argues, and these "odd combinations" are a source of creativity and cultural innovation. This proteanism is especially common among immigrants and racial minorities. Living in the tensions between Old World and New World, black culture and white culture, Europe and America, they have expressed themselves through "double meanings" and cultural hybridity.[92]

As religious "immigrants" to the professional worlds of journalism and social science, my respondents have experienced such proteanism firsthand.[93] In combining the mutually irreconcilable realities of faith and profession, they have become fluid and many-sided. By synthesizing sociology and personal religious experience, theology and historical narration, and objective journalism and religious commitment, they have expressed themselves in odd combinations that do not always hang together.[94]

For some Catholic and evangelical thinkers, this proteanism is evidence of the weakening of religious identity. James Hunter has warned of a "cognitive contamination" of religious worldviews, and Eugene McCarraher has lamented the triumph of "Starbucks Catholicism" among young Catholic urban professionals. The Catholic professional–managerial class prefers "inclusiveness," "diversity," "empowerment," and "choice," McCarraher notes—words that "have arisen from the corporate culture of fin-de-siecle America."[95]

There is much to be said for these critiques. Yet another side of Catholic and evangelical proteanism deserves equal attention: the "unexpected combinations" in the works of Catholic artists noted by Paul Giles in *American Catholic Arts and Fictions*. "[Jack] Kerouac or Mary McCarthy or indeed Flannery O'Connor," he says, "can reveal more about the Catholic experience in the United States than many wearisome issues of the *Catholic Digest*." Although they were influenced by secular intellectual movements and ideologies, these writers brought a Catholic sensibility to their works. By showing where religious sensibility "lingers and manifests itself in less obvious, even strange and unpredictable ways," Giles says, they have had a powerful impact on American culture.[96]

Like their counterparts in the arts, the journalists and scholars interviewed for this project have manifested their religious beliefs in "less obvious"—even strange and unpredictable—ways. What could be less obvious than the presence of theological irony in the works of Hatch, Marsden, and Noll? What could be stranger than the intermingling of romance fiction, theology, and academic sociology in the career of Andrew Greeley? What could be more unpredictable than the punchline to Dionne's story of the pope and the rain doctors?

Such religious proteanism contains both dangers and opportunities. As they did in the past, hybridity and syncretism have the potential to undermine the coherence of religious traditions. In an era which we are all "syncretists," Catholic and evangelical professionals must work harder to hold on to their core beliefs.[97] At the same time, "odd combinations" are a recurring theme in the history of Christianity. From Saint Paul's dialogue with the Stoics on Mars Hill to medieval Catholicism's encounter with Aristotle, Christians have critically appropriated the insights of those outside the faith.[98] As Christian journalists and scholars struggle to make sense of the challenges of postmodernism, pluralism, and globalization, they will inevitably draw on the wisdom of Athens and the faith of Jerusalem. With God's help and a lot of practice, they may yet learn to sing the songs of Zion in a foreign land.

Appendix

The Sample

This study is based on interviews with a sample of forty prominent Catholics and evangelicals who work in the professions of journalism and the academic social sciences (see Figure 1). All of the evangelicals in the sample self-identify as evangelicals or as members of evangelical denominations, and the Catholic half of the sample is restricted to practicing Catholics.[1] The sample of twenty journalists and twenty social scientists (in history, sociology, and political science) was obtained through snowball sampling.[2] Previously identified Catholics and evangelicals in both professions were contacted and asked to provide the names of high-profile co-religionists in the same fields.

The task of identifying evangelical journalists and social scientists was made somewhat easier by the continuing existence of formal evangelical professional and academic associations, such as the Conference on Faith and History and Christians in Political Science; special programs and centers for evangelicals, such as the Institute for the Study of American Evangelicals and the Pew Evangelical Scholars Program; and evangelical periodicals and journals, such as *Christianity Today* and *Christian Scholar's Review.* Social-science faculty at evangelical colleges and prominent evangelical journalists were also a source of names. Identifying Catholics in both professions was more difficult because of the lack of active Catholic professional and academic associations in most fields. The staff of *Commonweal,* the Catholic Historical Association and its journal, Thomas Landy of Collegium, the Ethics and Public Policy Center, the Cushwa Center for the Study of American Catholicism, faculty at Catholic colleges and universities, members of the Association for the Sociology of Religion, publications such as *America* and *CrossCurrents,* and previously identified journalists and scholars were helpful in generating a list of practicing Catholics in both professions.

The sample of Catholic and evangelical journalists is restricted to those who work, or who have worked, at large metropolitan newspapers and national news or opinion magazines, with a preference given to those in Washington, D.C., and New York.[3] All of the journalists interviewed for this project have worked in Washington or New York at some point in their careers. Given these criteria, the master list of thirty evangelical and forty Catholic journalists was easily winnowed to ten evangelicals and ten Catholics at the upper levels of New York and Washington journalism. Three-fourths of the sample consists of news reporters; the remainder is made up of editorial and opinion writers.[4]

The sample of Catholic and evangelical social scientists is restricted to the most published and cited individuals from both religious groups.[5] Once a list of historians, sociologists, and political scientists had been generated (130 Catholics and 90 evangelicals), CD-ROM versions of the Social Science Citation Index, the ABC Pol Sci index, Sociofile, the Humanities Index, the Humanities Citation Index, the America: History and Life index, and the Religion Index were used to determine the most published and cited Catholics and evangelicals in each discipline. Five political scientists, eight historians, and seven sociologists were interviewed for this study.

Notes

Preface

1. Hector Becerra, "Atheists Decry Post-Attack Focus on God," *Los Angeles Times,* 6 October 2001, pt. 2, 18. According to the Pew Center for the People and Press, the proportion of Americans who said that the influence of religion was increasing "jumped dramatically from 37 percent in March to 78 percent in November": see Jane Lampman, "Americans See Religion as Gaining Clout in Public Life," *Christian Science Monitor,* 7 December 2001.

2. E. J. Dionne, "Unshakable Rockaway," *Washington Post,* 13 November 2001, A31. Dionne weighed in on the morality of the war in Afghanistan in "A Just Struggle," *Washington Post,* 26 September 2001, A25.

3. Cal Thomas, "Will They Fool Us Twice," 3 October 2001, Tribune Media Services, available from <http://www.townhall.com/columnists/calthomas/ct20011003.shtml>; idem, "Getting Ready for Another Battle," 20 September 2001, Tribune Media Services, available from <http://www.townhall.com/columnists/calthomas/ct20010920.shtml>

4. Colman McCarthy, "Violence Breeds More Violence," *Los Angeles Times,* 17 September 2001, pt. 2, 9. Andrew Greeley expressed a similar low opinion of the war in "An Eye for an Eye?" available on-line at <http://www.beliefnet.com>.

5. The quotation is from Bruce Russett, "What Kind of War?" *Commonweal,* 28 September 2001, 9; see also Dionne, "Just Struggle," A25. In his column, Peter Steinfels questioned the pacifist claim that violence begets violence, noting that "violence can breed justice as well as injustice": see Peter Steinfels, "Beliefs," *New York Times,* 27 October 2001, D6.

6. Alan Wolfe, "The Opening of the Evangelical Mind," *Atlantic Monthly,* October 2000, 55–76.

Chapter 1. Secular Callings

1. E. J. Dionne, "Religion and the Media: Keynote Address," *Commonweal,* 24 February 1995, 26–30.

2. Mark Pedelty, *War Stories: The Culture of Foreign Correspondents* (London: Routledge, 1995).

3. Erving Goffman, *The Presentation of Self in Everyday Life* (New York: Anchor Books, 1959).

4. Peter L. Berger, *Redeeming Laughter: The Comic Dimension of Human Experience* (New York: Walter De Gruyter, 1997), 14.

5. There are many scholarly definitions of evangelicalism. James Davison Hunter defines evangelicalism as a theologically conservative Protestant movement committed to "(1) the belief that the Bible is the inerrant word of God, (2) the belief in the divinity of Christ, and (3) the belief in the efficacy of Christ's life, death, and physical resurrection for the salvation of the human soul": James Davison Hunter, *American Evangelicalism: Conservative Religion and the Quandary of Modernity* (New Brunswick, N.J.: Rutgers University Press, 1983), 7. David Bebbington identifies four hallmarks of evangelicalism: "*conversionism,* the belief that lives need to be changed; *activism,* the expression of the gospel in effort; *biblicism,* a particular regard for the Bible; and *crucicentrism,* a stress on the sacrifice of Christ on the cross": Wheaton College Institute for the Study of American Evangelicals, Web site, <http://www.wheaton.edu/isae/ defining_evangelicalism.html>. In *American Evangelicalism: Embattled and Thriving* (Chicago: University of Chicago Press, 1998), Christian Smith narrows the definition to those who self-identify as evangelicals. The political scientists John Green, James Guth, Lyman Kellstedt, and Corwin Smidt have defined evangelicalism denominationally, as those affiliated with conservative Protestant denominations, and doctrinally, as those who assent to certain core evangelical doctrines: see David Leege and Lyman Kellstedt, ed., *Rediscovering the Religious Factor in American Politics* (Armonk, N.Y.: M. E. Sharpe, 1993). In general, evangelicals are more conservative than mainline Protestants.

6. Although the discipline of history spans the social sciences and humanities, it is described as a social science in this study.

7. Peter L. Berger, *The Sacred Canopy: Elements of a Sociological Theory of Religion* (New York: Anchor Books, 1967), 100. George Marsden uses the concept of methodological secularization in *The Soul of the American University: From Protestant Establishment to Established Nonbelief* (New York: Oxford University Press, 1994), 156.

8. Not all journalists and academics are so irreligious. In 1992, David H. Weaver and G. Cleveland Wilhoit surveyed journalists across the country rather than just in New York and Washington, finding that reporters are almost as religious as the American public. This survey was reported in John Dart and Jimmy Allen, *Bridging the Gap: Religion and the News Media* (Nashville, Tenn.: Freedom Forum First Amendment Center, 1993). Dart and Allen reported similar results from a survey of their own. And in *The Struggle for America's Soul: Evangelicals, Liberals, and Secularism* (Grand Rapids, Mich.: Eerdmans, 1989), Robert Wuthnow noted that natural scientists and faculty in applied fields were considerably more devout than their colleagues in the humanities and social sciences.

9. Karlyn H. Keene et al., "Politics of the Professoriate," *Public Perspective,* July–August 1991, 86, LEXIS-NEXIS Academic Universe.

10. George Gallup, Jr., "Americans More Religious Now Than Ten Years Ago, but Less So Than in 1950s and 1960s," *Poll Analyses;* available on-line at <http:// www.gallup.com/poll/releases/pr010329.asp>.

11. S. Robert Lichter, Stanley Rothman, and Linda Lichter, *The Media Elite: America's New Power Brokers* (Bethesda, Md.: Adler and Adler, 1986); S. Robert Lichter and Linda Lichter, "The Media Get Religion: National Media Coverage of Religion in America 1969–1998," *Media Monitor,* May–June 2000, 8, available on-line at <http:// www.cmpa.com/mediamon/mm050600.htm>

For a critique of Lichter et al.'s survey, see Dart and Allen, *Bridging the Gap.* Despite its flaws, *The Media Elite* remains the only major study to ask about the religious views of New York and Washington journalists. Other surveys examine the religious beliefs of journalists across the country.

12. See B. Bruce-Briggs, ed., *The New Class?* (New Brunswick, N.J.: Transaction Publishers, 1979), for an overview of the concept; Steven Brint, *In an Age of Experts: The Changing Role of Professionals in Politics and Public Life* (Princeton, N.J.: Princeton University Press, 1994); Alvin Gouldner, "The New Class Project I," *Theory and Society* 6,. no. 4 (1978): 153–204.

13. Brint, *Age of Experts*, 15.

14. Ibid., 13.

15. Louis Bolce and Gerald DeMaio, "Religious Outlook, Culture War Politics, and Antipathy toward Christian Fundamentalists," *Public Opinion Quarterly* 63, no. 1 (1999): 508, Infotrac, Expanded Academic ASAP.

16. Peter L. Berger, "The Desecularization of the World: A Global Overview," in *The Desecularization of the World: Resurgent Religion and World Politics*, ed. Peter L. Berger (Grand Rapids, Mich.: Eerdmans, 1999), 10.

17. Max Weber, "Science as a Vocation," in *From Max Weber: Essays in Sociology*, ed. H. H. Gerth and C. Wright Mills (New York: Oxford University Press, 1946), 154.

18. Edward Shils, *The Intellectuals and the Powers* (Chicago: University of Chicago Press, 1972), 71.

19. The first two quotes are from Alvin Gouldner, "The New Class Project, Part I," 177. The second is from Robert Merton, "The Normative Structure of Science," in *Culture and Society: Contemporary Debates*, ed. Jeffrey Alexander and Steven Seidman (New York: Cambridge University Press, 1990), 67–74.

20. Charles Derber, William Schwartz, and Yale Magrass, *Power in the Highest Degree: Professionals and the Rise of a New Mandarin Order* (New York: Oxford University Press, 1990), 61, 65. For a theoretical account of professional jurisdictions, see Andrew Abbott, *The System of Professions: An Essay on the Division of Expert Labor* (Chicago: University of Chicago Press, 1988).

21. The phrase "epistemological divide" comes from Terry Eastland's remarks at a *Commonweal* magazine forum on religion and the media. He is quoted in "Good News," *Commonweal*, vol. 24 (February 1995), 3–4.

22. Richard Flory, "Promoting a Secular Standard: Secularization and Modern Journalism" (paper presented at the conference on "The Secular Revolution," Chapel Hill, N.C., June 2001), 630. On professional boundaries see Thomas Gieryn, "Boundary-Work and the Demarcation of Science from Non-Science," *American Sociological Review* 48, no. 6 (1983): 781–95. For an authoritative treatment of boundaries, see Michele Lamont and Virag Molnar, "The Study of Boundaries Across the Social Sciences," *Annual Review of Sociology*, forthcoming.

23. Gaye Tuchman, "Objectivity as Strategic Ritual," *American Sociological Review* 77. no. 1 (1972): 660–70; Michael Schudson, *Discovering the News: A Social History of the American Newspaper* (New York: Basic Books, 1978); David Mindich, *Just the Facts: How "Objectivity" Came to Define American Journalism* (New York: New York University Press, 1998).

24. Paul Baumann, "Epistemological Muddles: Religion and the Media," *Commonweal*, 7 October 1994, 4–5.

25. Wuthnow, *Struggle for America's Soul;* Peter Novick, *That Noble Dream: The "Objectivity Question" and the American Historical Profession* (New York: Cambridge University Press, 1988); Jon H. Roberts and James Turner, *The Sacred and the Secular University* (Princeton, N.J.: Princeton University Press, 2000); Dorothy Ross, *The Origins of American Social Science* (New York: Cambridge University Press, 1991); Mary O. Furner, *Advocacy and Objectivity: A Crisis in the Professionalization of American Social Science, 1865–1905* (Lexington: University of Kentucky Press, 1973).

26. Julie Reuben, *The Making of the Modern University: Intellectual Transformation and the Marginalization of Morality* (Chicago: University of Chicago Press, 1996).

27. Roberts and Turner, *The Sacred and the Secular University*, 36.

28. Berger, *Sacred Canopy*, 100; Marsden, *Soul of the American University*, 156. The quote comes from Roberts and Turner, *The Sacred and the Secular University*, 51.

29. James Gilbert, *Redeeming Culture: American Religion in an Age of Science* (Chicago: University of Chicago Press, 1997), 14.

30. Douglas Porpora, *Landscapes of the Soul: The Loss of Moral Meaning in American Life* (New York: Oxford University Press, 2001), 8. On reductionism and professional jurisdictions see Abbott, *System of Professions*.

31. Mark Silk, *Unsecular Media: Making News of Religion in America* (Chicago: University of Illinois Press, 1995), 16.

32. Schudson, *Discovering the News*, 72.

33. Flory, "Promoting a Secular Standard," 609; Richard Hofstadter, *The Age of Reform* (New York: Vintage, 1955); Bruce Evensen, "The Evangelical Origins of the Muckrakers," *American Journalism* 6 (1989): 5–29.

34. Myer Reed, "An Alliance for Progress: The Early Years of the Sociology of Religion in the United States," *Sociological Analysis* 42. no. 1 (1981): 27–46; Christian Smith, "Secularizing American Higher Education: The Case of Early American Sociology," paper presented at The Secular Revolution: Power, Interests, and Conflict in the Secularization of American Public Life, conference, Chapel Hill, N.C., June 2001, 219.

35. Reed, "Alliance for Progress," 39.

36. Reuben, *Making of the Modern University;* Roberts and Turner, *The Sacred and the Secular University.*

37. William Sullivan, "What Is Left of Professionalism after Managed Care?" *Hastings Center Report* 29, no. 2 (1999): 9. Sullivan gives an overview of three approaches to the history of professionalism in America.

38. Harold Perkin, *The Third Revolution: Professional Elites in the Modern World* (London: Routledge, 1996), 331. Perkin is quoted in Sullivan, "What Is Left of Professionalism," 10.

39. Brint, *Age of Experts*, 36, 40. Brint argues that during the twentieth century, the American professions underwent a shift from a morally engaged "social trustee professionalism" to a technical "expert professionalism" that is less concerned with the common good.

40. David Hollinger, "The 'Secularization' Question and the United States in the Twentieth Century," *Church History* 70, no. 1 (2001): 137. For an account of the collapse of the Protestant establishment in a number of areas, including journalism and higher education, see William Hutchison, ed., *Between the Times: The Travail of the Protestant Establishment in America, 1900–1960* (New York: Cambridge University Press, 1989).

41. The most extensive account of the secularization of the university can be found in Marsden, *Soul of the American University.*

42. Reuben, *Making of the Modern University*, 188.

43. Novick, *That Noble Dream*, 1.

44. Myer Reed, "After the Alliance: The Sociology of Religion in the United States from 1925 to 1949," *Sociological Analysis* 43, no. 3 (1982): 191; Smith, "Secularizing American Higher Education."

45. Reed, "After the Alliance," 193.

46. Wuthnow, *Struggle for America's Soul*, 160.

47. Flory, "Promoting a Secular Standard," 607–608. For a discussion of *Time*'s role in the Protestant establishment, see Dennis Voskuil, "Reaching Out: Mainline Protes-

tantism and the Media," in *Between the Times: The Travail of the Protestant Establishment, 1900–1960,* ed. William Hutchison (New York: Cambridge University Press, 1989), 72–92.

48. Christian Smith presents a much more historicized version of the secular revolution in "Introduction: Re-Thinking the Secularization of American Public Life," paper presented at The Secular Revolution: Power, Interests, and Conflict in the Secularization of American Public Life, conference, Chapel Hill, N.C., June 2001.

49. José Casanova provides an excellent overview of the processes of privatization and differentiation in *Public Religions in the Modern World* (Chicago: University of Chicago Press, 1994). See also Olivier Tschannen, "The Secularization Paradigm: A Systematization," *Journal for the Scientific Study of Religion* 30, no. 4 (1991): 395–415.

50. See Berger, "Desecularization of the World"; Rodney Stark, "Secularization, R.I.P." *Sociology of Religion* 60, no. 3 (1999): 249–73.

51. Casanova, *Public Religions,* 5–6, 215.

52. Alan Wolfe, "A Welcome Revival of Religion," *Chronicle of Higher Education,* 19 September 1997, B4; Alicia Shepherd, "The Media Get Religion," *American Journalism Review,* December 1995, 18–26; Lichter and Lichter, "The Media Get Religion," 8.

53. On resistance to "individual-level privatization," see Mark Regnerus and Christian Smith, "Selective Deprivatization among American Religious Traditions: The Reversal of the Great Reversal," *Social Forces* 76, no. 4 (1998): 1347–73.

54. Mainline Protestantism maintains an important presence in American public life: Wuthnow argues that it is "quietly influential": see Robert Wuthnow and John Evans, eds., *The Quiet Hand of God: Faith-Based Activism and the Public Role of Mainline Protestantism* (Berkeley: University of California Press, 2002).

55. Robert Bellah, Richard Madsen, William M. Sullivan, Ann Swidler, and Steven M. Tipton, *Habits of the Heart: Individualism and Commitment in American Life* (Berkeley: University of California Press, 1996), 238; Casanova, *Public Religions,* 135–207; Regnerus and Smith, "Selective Deprivatization," 1.

56. The Protestant mainline continues to play an important role in American higher education in the fields of academic theology, religious history, and religious studies. Likewise, mainline denominations continue to sponsor an extensive network of church-related colleges. At the same time, mainline Protestantism's influence has greatly diminished compared with its hegemony a century ago. For an assessment of the mainline's role in higher education, see Douglas Sloan, *Faith and Knowledge: Mainline Protestantism and American Higher Education* (Louisville, Ken.: Westminster John Knox Press, 1994); Dorothy Bass, "Church-Related Colleges: Transmitters of Denominational Cultures?" in *Beyond Establishment: Protestant Identity in a Post-Protestant Age,* ed. Jackson Carroll and Wade Clark Roof (Louisville, Ken.: Westminster John Knox Press, 1993), 157–72. See also Hutchison, *Between the Times.*

57. Andrew Greeley, "Is There an American Catholic Elite?" *America,* 6 May 1989, 428. See also James Davidson et al., "Persistence and Change in the Protestant Establishment, 1930–1992," *Social Forces* 74, no. 1 (1995): 157. Although Catholics remain underrepresented in the cultural elite, they have made impressive gains since the 1930s.

58. Sloan, *Faith and Knowledge,* 228, 226.

59. Powers, "The Roman Legion," *National Journal,* 15 August 1998, 1930; S. Robert Lichter, Linda S. Lichter, and Daniel R. Amundson, "Media Coverage of Religion in America," Center for Media and Public Affairs, Washington, D.C., April 2000, available on-line at <http://www.cmpa.com/archive/relig2000.htm>.

60. David Astor, "Cal Thomas in Select 500 Club for Columnists," *Editor and Publisher,* 8 May 1999, 44.

61. For an account of evangelicalism's tension with secular modernity, see Hunter, *American Evangelicalism*. For a similar treatment of Catholicism, see Philip Gleason, *Contending with Modernity: Catholic Higher Education in the Twentieth Century* (New York: Oxford University Press, 1995). For an evangelical critique of value-free objectivity, see George Marsden, *The Outrageous Idea of Christian Scholarship* (New York: Oxford University Press, 1997). On the inability of intellectual elites to understand Catholicism's belief in the transcendent, see James Martin, "Anti-Catholicism in the United States: The Last Acceptable Prejudice," *America*, 25 March 2000, 10. On Catholic resistance to reductionism, see Margaret O'Brien Steinfels, "The Catholic Intellectual Tradition," in *Occasional Papers* (Washington, D.C.: Association of Catholic Colleges and Universities, 1995), available on-line from <http://www.fordham.edu/thirdagectr/mstein.htm>. For a discussion of the conflict between religious tradition and journalistic skepticism, see "Good News," *Commonweal*, 24 February 1995, 3–4.

62. Gleason is the most persuasive advocate of this interpretation: see Philip Gleason, *Keeping the Faith: American Catholicism Past and Present* (Notre Dame, Ind.: University of Notre Dame Press, 1989). Eugene McCarraher also emphasizes the negative consequences of professionalization in "The Saint in the Gray Flannel Suit: The Professional–Managerial Class, the Figure of 'The Layman,' and American-Catholic-Religious Culture, 1945–1965," *U.S. Catholic Historian*, summer–fall 1997, 99–118.

63. Michael Novak, *The Rise of the Unmeltable Ethnics* (New York: Macmillan, 1973), 41, 43.

64. Hunter, *American Evangelicalism*, 112, 15. See also James Davison Hunter, "The New Class and the Young Evangelicals," *Review of Religious Research* 22, no. 2 (1980): 155–69.

65. The phrase "Americanization–secularization hypothesis" is taken from David O'Brien, *From the Heart of the American Church: Catholic Higher Education and American Culture* (Maryknoll, N.Y.: Orbis Books, 1994), 25. O'Brien is a critic of this model.

66. Gleason, *Keeping the Faith*, 79, 77.

67. D. G. Hart, "History in Search of Meaning: The Conference on Faith and History," in *History and the Christian Historian*, ed. Ronald Wells (Grand Rapids, Mich.: Eerdmans, 1998), 68. Hart is skeptical about the possibility of developing a distinctively Christian approach to history.

68. The quote is from Stephen Warner, "Religion, Boundaries, and Bridges," *Sociology of Religion* 58, no. 3 (1997): 233. See also Wade Clark Roof, "Religious Borderlands: Challenges for Future Study," *Journal for the Scientific Study of Religion* 37, no. 1 (1998): 1–14.

69. O'Brien, *Heart of the American Church*, 25, 33, 161. Andrew Greeley, *The American Catholic: A Social Portrait* (New York: Basic Books, 1977), makes a similar argument about the capacity of American Catholics to hold their American and Catholic identities together.

70. Smith, *American Evangelicalism*, 120.

71. Paul Bramadat, *The Church on the World's Turf: An Evangelical Christian Group at a Secular University* (New York: Oxford University Press, 2000), 22–23.

72. John Schmalzbauer, "Evangelicals in the New Class: Class versus Subcultural Predictors of Ideology," *Journal for the Scientific Study of Religion* 32, no. 4 (1993): 330–42. In this article, I draw on British scholarship on subcultures of resistance. See Dick Hebdige, *Subculture: The Meaning of Style* (London: Methuen, 1979). See also David Harrington Watt's work on the evangelical subculture and resistance in *A Transforming Faith: Explorations of Twentieth-Century American Evangelicalism* (New Brunswick, N.J.: Rutgers University Press, 1991).

73. Robert Wuthnow, *God and Mammon in America* (New York: Macmillan, 1994); Stephen Hart, *What Does the Lord Require? How American Christians Think about Economic Justice* (New York: Oxford University Press, 1992); Bellah et al., *Habits of the Heart.*

74. Brint, *Age of Experts;* Michele Lamont, *Money, Morals, and Manners: The Culture of the French and the American Upper-Middle Class* (Chicago: University of Chicago Press, 1992).

75. Gieryn, "Boundary-Work"; Bruce-Briggs, *New Class?;* Hunter, "Young Evangelicals and the New Class"; Schmalzbauer, "Evangelicals in the New Class."

76. Wuthnow, *God and Mammon.*

77. The term "submerged" is borrowed from Michael Schudson's discussion of submerged normative traditions in American journalism: see Schudson, *Discovering the News.*

78. The phrase "odd combinations" comes from Robert Lifton, *The Protean Self: Human Resilience in an Age of Fragmentation* (New York: Basic Books, 1993).

79. Richard Rorty, "Religion as Conversation-Stopper," *Common Knowledge* 3, no. 1 (1994): 1–6.

Chapter 2. From the Margins to the Mainstream

1. Daniel Callahan, review of *Science, Jews, and Secular Culture: Studies in Mid-Twentieth Century American Intellectual History,* by David Hollinger, *Commonweal,* 10 October 1997, 25.

2. Joel Carpenter, *Revive Us Again: The Reawakening of American Fundamentalism* (New York: Oxford University Press, 1997), 192.

3. Michael Paulson, "Spiritual Life," *Boston Globe,* 2 December 2000, B2.

4. Michael Paulson, "Evangelicals Find Place at 'Mainstream Colleges,'" *Boston Globe,* 20 February 2000, A1, LEXIS-NEXIS Academic Universe.

5. Mark Noll, "The Future of Religious Colleges: Looking Ahead by Looking Back," paper presented at the Conference on the Future of Religious Colleges, Harvard University, Cambridge, Mass., 6–7 October 2000, 9.

6. James T. Fisher, "Alternative Sources of Catholic Intellectual Vitality," *U.S. Catholic Historian* 13 (1997): 83.

7. Gay Talese, *The Kingdom and the Power* (New York: Bantam Books, 1970), 68, 70.

8. H. L. Mencken, as quoted in George Marsden, *Fundamentalism and American Culture: The Shaping of Twentieth-Century Evangelicalism, 1870–1925* (New York: Oxford University Press, 1980), 187. "More about Catholicism and the Presidency," *New Republic,* 11 May 1927, 113, as quoted in John T. McGreevy, "Thinking on One's Own: Catholicism in the American Intellectual Imagination, 1928–1960," *Journal of American History* 84, no. 1 (1997); Richard Hofstadter, *Anti-Intellectualism in American Life* (New York: Vintage, 1963); Paul Blanshard, *American Freedom and Catholic Power* (Boston: Beacon Press, 1949). For more on anti-Catholicism in American intellectual life, see McGreevy, "Thinking on One's Own": 97–131.

9. Alan Wolfe, "The Opening of the Evangelical Mind," *Atlantic Monthly,* October 2000, 55–76.

10. Ethan Bronner, "Notre Dame Combining Research and Religion," *New York Times,* 10 December 1997, B10, LEXIS-NEXIS Academic Universe.

11. The three stages should be seen as overlapping rather than as separate. The first stage of upward mobility, for example, can be said to overlap the second and third stages in the sense that upward mobility among Catholics and evangelicals was more or less continuous throughout the twentieth century.

The Catholic and evangelical communities did not go through these three stages at precisely the same times in American history. Although there is an "amazing similarity between phases in the history of American Catholic universities and similar phases in the history of Protestant higher education," Noll points out, it is "set off by a generation or two": see Mark Noll, "Football, Neo-Thomism, and the Silver Age of Catholic Higher Education," *Books and Culture,* October 1996, 31. My account of the three stages of Catholic and evangelical engagement in academic and professional life (upward mobility, subcultural institution building, and de-ghettoization) is indebted to the standard secondary works on both groups. See Philip Gleason, *Contending with Modernity: Catholic Higher Education in the Twentieth Century* (New York: Oxford University Press, 1995), and idem, *Keeping the Faith: American Catholicism Past and Present* (Notre Dame, Ind.: University of Notre Dame Press, 1987); David J. O'Brien, *From the Heart of the American Church: Catholic Higher Education and American Culture* (Maryknoll, N.Y.: Orbis Books, 1994); David Salvaterra, *American Catholicism and the Intellectual Life* (New York: Garland, 1988); William Halsey, *The Survival of American Innocence: Catholicism in an Era of Disillusionment, 1920–1940* (Notre Dame, Ind.: University of Notre Dame Press, 1980); Robert Wuthnow, *The Restructuring of American Religion* (Princeton, N.J.: Princeton University Press, 1988); Carpenter, *Revive Us Again;* George Marsden, *Reforming Fundamentalism: Fuller Seminary and the New Evangelicalism* (Grand Rapids, Mich.: Eerdmans, 1987); Mark Noll, *The Scandal of the Evangelical Mind* (Grand Rapids, Mich.: Eerdmans, 1994). For a comparison of Catholics and evangelicals, see William Shea, *The Lion and the Lamb: Evangelicals and Catholics at the Millennium* (New York: Oxford University Press, forthcoming). For an interesting stage theory of ethnicity, see Andrew Greeley, *Why Can't They Be Like Us? America's White Ethnic Groups* (New York: E. P. Dutton, 1971), 53–59. Greeley's six steps are: (1) cultural shock; (2) organization and emergent self-consciousness; (3) assimilation of the elite; (4) militancy; (5) self-hatred and anti-militancy; and (6) emerging adjustment. Greeley's first, second, and fourth phases are analogous to my subcultural institution building stage, and his steps three, five, and six parallel my de-ghettoization stage.

12. See Christian Smith, *American Evangelicalism: Embattled and Thriving* (Chicago: University of Chicago Press, 1998).

13. Evangelicals were the dominant religious group among all Americans, including the upper-middle class, in the nineteenth century but found themselves disproportionately concentrated in the working class after the mainstream denominations embraced liberal Protestantism.

14. John Tracy Ellis, "American Catholics and the Intellectual Life," in *Catholicism in America,* ed. Philip Gleason (New York: Harper and Row, 1970), 117–18; Robert Wuthnow, "Living the Question: Evangelical Christianity and Critical Thought," paper presented at Faith That Works, conference, Wheaton, Ill., spring 1990, 6.

15. Andrew Greeley, *The American Catholic: A Social Portrait* (New York: Basic Books, 1977), 65.

16. These cohorts group respondents from the General Social Surveys (1972–96) who reached college age during the following periods: 1920–29, 1930–39, 1940–49, 1950–59, 1960–69, 1970–79, and 1980–89. (The 1980–89 cohort is not used in Figure 3 because of a change in the General Social surveys' occupation codes.) Respondents age twenty-five and younger are excluded from Figure 2 based on the assumption that some people do not earn a college degree until age twenty-five. Respondents age thirty and younger are excluded from Figure 3 based on the assumption that many people do not become employed in the professional and managerial occupations (or finish graduate school) until their late twenties or early thirties. African Americans are not included in the evangelical category because of the tremendous differences between white and black evangelicals. (Although they are conservative in theology, many African American Protestants eschew the term "evangelical.") Latinos who identify as white rather than black are included in the evangelical category.

17. Wuthnow, *Restructuring of American Religion;* idem, "Living the Question," 6.

18. Evangelical religious affiliation is measured using a denominational classification scheme developed by Lyman Kellstedt and John Green in "Knowing God's Many People: Denominational Preference and Political Behavior," in *Rediscovering the Religious Factor in American Politics,* ed. David C. Leege and Lyman A. Kellstedt (Armonk, N.Y.: M. E. Sharpe, 1993), 53–69.

19. Smith, *American Evangelicalism,* 76–77.

20. Peter L. Berger, "Ethics and the Present Class Struggle," *Worldview* 21, no. 4 (1978): 6–11; idem, "The Worldview of the New Class: Secularity and Its Discontents," in *The New Class?* ed. B. Bruce-Briggs (New Brunswick, N.J.: Transaction Publishers, 1979), 49–56; Alvin Gouldner, "The New Class Project I," *Theory and Society* 6, no. 2 (1978): 153–204; James Davison Hunter, *American Evangelicalism: Conservative Religion and the Quandary of Modernity* (New Brunswick, N.J.: Rutgers University Press, 1983).

21. Upward mobility provided Catholics and evangelicals with the economic resources needed to build intellectual and religious movements. On the resource-mobilization approach to social movements, see Mayer N. Zald and John D. McCarthy, "Resource Mobilization and Social Movements: A Partial Theory," in *Social Movements in an Organizational Society,* ed. Mayer N. Zald and John D. McCarthy (New Brunswick, N.J.: Transaction Publishers, 1987), 15–48. Likewise, in *Political Process and the Black Insurgency, 1930–1970* (Chicago: University of Chicago Press, 1982), 94–105, the social-movements scholar Doug McAdam argues that the emergence of a black middle class led to a period of African American institution building, including the strengthening of colleges and churches, paving the way for the Civil Rights Movement. The move of Catholics and evangelicals into the professional middle class helped facilitate a similar era of organizational expansion.

22. Christian Smith argues that religious subcultures with well-defined boundaries foster religious strength: see Smith, *American Evangelicalism,* 119.

23. Garry Wills, "Memories of a Catholic Boyhood," in idem, *Bare Ruined Choirs: Doubt, Prophecy, and Radical Religion* (New York: Doubleday, 1972), 15, 18, 19.

24. Margaret Mary Reher, *Catholic Intellectual Life in America: A Historical Study of Persons and Movements* (New York: Macmillan 1989), 95, 97. Reher is quoted in George Marsden, *The Soul of the American University: From Protestant Establishment to Established Nonbelief* (New York: Oxford University Press, 1994), 273. See Marsden on academic freedom's growing sacredness. Gleason, *Contending with Modernity,* 104–84.

25. Marsden, *Soul of the American University,* 273.

26. Salvaterra, *American Catholicism,* 234.

27. Gleason, *Contending with Modernity,* 82, 85, 168.

28. Sparr, *To Promote, Defend, and Redeem: The Catholic Literary Revival and the Cultural Transformation of American Catholicism, 1920–1960* (Westport, Conn.: Greenwood, 1990), 11.

29. O'Brien, *Heart of the American Church,* 41.

30. Salvaterra, *American Catholicism;* Gleason, *Contending with Modernity;* Halsey, *American Innocence.*

31. Joseph Schrembs, "The Catholic Philosophy of History," *Catholic Historical Review* 20, no. 1 (1934): 2; Ross J. S. Hoffman, "Catholicism and Historismus," *Catholic Historical Review* 24, no. 4 (1939): 401–402.

32. Salvaterra, *American Catholicism.*

33. Will Herberg, *Protestant–Catholic–Jew: An Essay in American Religious Sociology* (New York: Doubleday, 1955), 154. On Catholic subcultural institutions, see Gleason, *Keeping the Faith,* 66–71, and Greeley, *Why Can't They Be Like Us?* 55.

34. David J. O'Brien, *Public Catholicism* (New York: Macmillan, 1989).

35. Thomas J. Harte, "Catholics as Sociologists," *American Catholic Sociological Review* 13, no. 1 (1952): 5.

36. Robert Maynard Hutchins, as quoted in Gleason, *Contending with Modernity*, 246–47.

37. Christopher Lynch, *Selling Catholicism: Bishop Sheen and the Power of Television* (Lexington: University Press of Kentucky, 1998); Lee Lourdeaux, *Italian and Irish Filmmakers in America* (Philadelphia: Temple University Press, 1990); Richard A. Blake, *After Image: The Indelible Catholic Imagination of Six American Filmmakers* (Chicago: Loyola Press, 2000); Anthony B. Smith, "Sinners, Judges, and Calvarymen: John Ford and Popular American Catholicism," in *American Catholic Traditions: Resources for Renewal*, ed. Sandra Yocum Mize and William Portier (Maryknoll, N.Y.: Orbis Books, 1997), 115–29.

38. For an account of Catholic influence on American popular culture in the 1950s, see Fisher, "Alternative Sources," 81–94. On a more intellectual level, Catholics were beginning to have an influence on the nascent American conservative movement: see Patrick Allitt, *Catholic Intellectuals and Conservative Politics in America, 1950–1985* (Ithaca, N.Y.: Cornell University Press, 1993).

39. Blanshard, *American Freedom and Catholic Power.* For examples of anti-Catholicism from *The Nation* and *New Republic,* see McGreevy, "Thinking on One's Own."

40. Susan Harding, *The Book of Jerry Falwell: Fundamentalist Language and Politics* (Princeton, N.J.: Princeton University Press, 2000), 74. In *Tennessee v. John Scopes* (1925), a high-school teacher (Scopes) was found guilty of violating that state's anti-evolution statute. The case was used by journalists to poke fun at fundamentalist Protestants. For the authoritative history of the Scopes trial, see Edward J. Larson, *Summer for the Gods: The Scopes Trial and America's Continuing Debate over Science and Religion* (Cambridge, Mass. Harvard University Press, 1998).

41. Noll, *Scandal of the Evangelical Mind,* 109. See also Marsden, *Reforming Fundamentalism,* and Carpenter, *Revive Us Again.*

42. Carpenter provides a superb account of this period in *Revive Us Again.* On the transdenominational nature of evangelicalism, see Marsden's introduction in George Marsden, ed., *Evangelicalism and Modern America* (Grand Rapids, Mich.: Eerdmans, 1984), vii–xix. My treatment of this period is also indebted to Wuthnow's *Restructuring of American Religion,* Smith's *American Evangelicalism,* and Marsden's *Reforming Fundamentalism.* See also Joel Carpenter, "Fundamentalist Institutions and the Rise of Evangelical Protestantism, 1929–1942," *Church History* 49 (March 1980): 62–75.

43. National Association of Evangelicals, "Excerpts from the First Meeting of NAE in St. Louis, Missouri April 7–9, 1942," *United Evangelical Action,* March–April 1992, 9.

44. Harold J. Ockenga, "Christ for America," in *United We Stand: A Report of the Constitutional Convention of the National Association of Evangelicals,* LaSalle Hotel, Chicago, 3–6 May 1943, 5–6, as quoted in Carpenter, *Revive Us Again,* 149.

45. See Marsden, *Reforming Fundamentalism,* 6–7, for a discussion of anti-separatism among evangelicals. American Council on Education, *American Universities and Colleges* (Washington, D.C.: American Council on Education, 1936, 1948, 1960).

46. Fred Beuttler, "American Evangelicalism 1880–1980: A Primer for the Third Generation," *The Crucible* 1, no. 2 (1991): 3–13.

47. Ibid.

48. *Directory of Religious Organizations in the United States* (Falls Church, Va.: McGrath Publishing, 1982); Paula Simon, "Christian Legal Society Fall Conference," *The Crucible* 1, no. 2 (1991): 46–47; Robert Snyder, "The Conference on Christianity and Literature," *The Crucible* 1, no. 4 (1991): 41.

49. Thomas Askew, "Retirement Reflections," *Conference on Faith and History Newsletter,* spring 2000, 1.

50. Michael Hamilton, "We're in the Money! How Did Evangelicals Get So Wealthy, and What Has It Done to Us?" *Christianity Today,* 12 June 2000, 41.

51. On the emergence of the postwar evangelical intellectual network, see Noll, *Scandal of the Evangelical Mind,* and Marsden, *Reforming Fundamentalism.*

52. Hunter, *American Evangelicalism,* 15–17.

53. Carl F. H. Henry, "Do We Need a Christian University?" *Christianity Today,* 9 May 1960, 4; idem, "Christian Education and Culture," *Christianity Today,* 10 November 1958, 5. The phrase "world-life view" was widely used by evangelicals during this period.

54. Stephen Board, "Moving the World with Magazines: A Survey of Evangelical Periodicals," in *American Evangelicals and the Mass Media,* ed. Quentin J. Schultze (Grand Rapids, Mich.: Zondervan, 1990), 119–42.

55. John Ferre, "Searching for the Great Commission: Evangelical Book Publishing since the 1970s," in Schultze, *American Evangelicals,* 99–118.

56. Quentin J. Schultze, "The Invisible Medium: Evangelical Radio," in Schultze, *American Evangelicals,* 171–95. The reference to symbol production can be found in Donald Heinz, "The Struggle to Define America," in *The New Christian Right,* ed. Robert C. Liebman and Robert Wuthnow (Hawthorne, N.Y.: Aldine, 1983), 137.

57. Gay Talese, *The Kingdom and the Power* (New York: Bantam Books, 1970); George Cornell, "Religion's New Entree to the City Room," *Christianity Today,* 14 October 1996, 10; Grant Wacker, as quoted in "Historian Smith, 72, Dies," *Christianity Today,* 7 April 1997, 57; Alvin Plantinga, "A Christian Life Partly Led," in *Philosophers Who Believe: The Spiritual Journeys of 11 Leading Thinkers,* ed. Kelly James Clark (Downers Grove, Ill.: InterVarsity Press, 1993), 81.

58. The marketing and audience-research data reported in Schultze, *American Evangelicals,* show that evangelical publishing and broadcasting reach an overwhelmingly evangelical audience.

59. In *American Evangelicalism,* Smith argues that the boundaries separating religious subcultures from the larger society are continually redefined.

60. On the identity crisis of American Catholic institutions and individuals, see Philip Gleason, "Immigrant Assimilation and the Crisis of Americanization," in idem, *Keeping the Faith,* 58–81.

61. For an account of anti-Catholicism among American intellectuals, see McGreevy, "Thinking on One's Own."

62. Ibid.; Ellis, "American Catholics and the Intellectual Life," 116; John Kane, "Catholic Separatism," in *Catholicism in America,* ed. William Clancy (New York: Harcourt, Brace, and Company, 1954), 47, 56. For an account of Catholic self-criticism and "anti-ghettoism," see Gleason, *Contending with Modernity,* 287–96, and Greeley, *Why Can't They Be Like Us?* 56–58.

63. Langdon Gilkey, *Catholicism Confronts Modernity* (New York: Seabury Press, 1975), 32. The Gilkey quote appears in Jay Dolan, *The American Catholic Experience: A History from Colonial Times to the Present* (New York: Doubleday, 1985), 428. See Dolan for an account of this period.

64. Salvaterra, *American Catholicism;* Gleason, "Immigrant Assimilation," 58–81.

65. Gleason, *Contending with Modernity;* James T. Burtchaell, *The Dying of the Light: The Disengagement of Colleges and Universities from their Christian Churches* (Grand Rapids, Mich.: Eerdmans, 1998); For a much more positive assessment of Catholic higher education, see O'Brien, *Heart of the American Church.*

66. Eugene McCarraher, "Smile When You Say 'Laity' (an Analysis of the Lay Revolution in the Catholic Church)," *Commonweal,* 12 September 1997, 12.

67. Interview with Russett; Andrew Greeley, "Is There an American Catholic Elite?" *America,* 6 May 1989, 426–29. In an analysis of *Who's Who in America* (1930 and 1992),

James Davidson, Ralph Pyle, and David Reyes report a dramatic increase in the representation of Catholics in the cultural elite: see James Davidson, Ralph Pyle, and David Reyes, "Persistence and Change in the Protestant Establishment, 1930–1992," *Social Forces,* 74, no. 1 (1995): 157.

68. "569 College and University Endowments," 13 April 2001, and "College and University Endowments, 1999–2000," *Chronicle of Higher Education,* available on-line at <http://chronicle.com/stats/endowments/endowment_results.php3>; "America's Best Colleges; Best Colleges 2000," *U.S. News and World Report,* 30 April 1999, LEXIS-NEXIS Academic Universe.

69. Charles Taylor, "A Catholic Modernity?" in James L. Heft, ed., *A Catholic Modernity? Charles Taylor's Marianist Award Lecture* (New York: Oxford University Press, 1999), 13–37.

70. William Shea compares the founding of the National Association of Evangelicals to Vatican II in "Evangelicals, Catholics, and Modernity: Growing Up in a Brave New World," public lecture, College of the Holy Cross, 1 February 2002, Worcester, Mass. Marsden, *Reforming Fundamentalism,* 7–11.

71. Edward J. Carnell, *The Case for Orthodox Theology* (Philadelphia: Westminster, 1959), 11; Carl F. H. Henry, *Remaking the Modern Mind* (Grand Rapids, Mich.: Eerdmans, 1946).

72. See Noll, *Scandal of the Evangelical Mind,* for an account of the influence of British and Dutch Reformed Protestants on American evangelical intellectual life.

73. Robert Booth Fowler, *A New Engagement: Evangelical Political Thought, 1966–1976* (Grand Rapids, Mich.: Eerdmans, 1982).

74. The best account of the political reawakening of evangelicals is in Wuthnow, *Restructuring of American Religion.* See also Kenneth Woodward', "Born Again! The Evangelicals," *Newsweek,* 25 October 1976, 68–78; and Harding, *Book of Jerry Falwell,* 19–20.

75. See James D. Hunter, *Evangelicalism: The Coming Generation* (Chicago: University of Chicago Press, 1987), for an application of Mary Douglas's notion of symbolic boundaries to evangelicalism.

76. Wolfe, "Opening of the Evangelical Mind," 61. See also Richard Quebedeaux, *The Young Evangelicals* (New York: Harper and Row, 1974); Noll, *Scandal of the Evangelical Mind.*

77. Hunter, *American Evangelicalism,* 112; Richard Quebedeaux, *The Worldly Evangelicals* (New York: Harper and Row, 1978).

78. Smith, *American Evangelicalism,* 14, 15.

79. Michael Paulson, "Evangelicals Find Place at Mainstream Colleges," *Boston Globe,* 20 February 2000, A1; James Turner, "Something to Be Reckoned With: The Evangelical Mind Reawakens," *Commonweal,* 15 January, 1999, 11–14, LEXIS-NEXIS Academic Universe.

80. "569 College and University Endowments."

81. "1999 Freshman Merit Scholars," *Chronicle of Higher Education,* 3 March 2000, available on-line at <http://chronicle.com/weekly/v46/i26/stats/4626merit.htm>. For the 2001 college rankings, see "America's Best Colleges." Leo Reisberg, "Enrollments Surge at Christian Colleges," *Chronicle of Higher Education,* 5 March 1999, A42. The fall 2000 data are from the Council of Christian Colleges and Universities Web site at <http://www.cccu.org>.

82. Smith, *American Evangelicalism,* 89–112.

83. James Turner, "Something to Be Reckoned With," 12.

84. William Shea, "A Vote of Thanks to Voltaire," in Heft, *A Catholic Modernity?* 61. Shea argues that Noll and Marsden are among the American evangelical Protestants

who serve as "models of the basic stance of the church toward culture to which Vatican II subscribed."

85. Smith, *American Evangelicalism*, 144; John Schmalzbauer, "Evangelicals in the New Class: Class versus Subcultural Predictors of Ideology," *Journal for the Scientific Study of Religion* 32, no. 4 (1993): 230–42.

86. For more on Catholicism's analogical tradition, see David Tracy, *The Analogical Imagination: Christian Theology and the Culture of Pluralism* (New York: Crossroad, 1981).

87. Salvaterra, *American Catholicism;* Gleason, "Immigrant Assimilation," 77.

88. Dean Hoge, "What Is Most Central to Being a Catholic?" *National Catholic Reporter,* 29 October 1999, 13; Andrew Greeley, *The Catholic Imagination* (Berkeley: University of California Press, 2000).

89. Nathan Hatch, as quoted in Robert Wuthnow, *Christianity and Civil Society* (Valley Forge, Penn.: Trinity Press International, 1996), 65; Alan Wolfe, "Catholic Universities Can Be the Salvation of Pluralism on American Campuses," *Chronicle of Higher Education,* 26 February 1999, B6.

90. Three hundred of the 11,000 economists in academia (2.7 percent) belong to the Association of Christian Economists, and 500 (approximately) of 15,000 American historians (3.3 percent) belong to the Conference on Faith and History. The 1,000 members of the Society of Christian Philosophers make up 12 percent of the 8,300 or so philosophy Ph.D.s in the United States. The membership of the Association of Christian Economists is from <http://www.gordon.edu/ace/aboutace.html>. Academic economists make up 50 percent of the 22,000 members of the American Economic Association, according to the association's Web page at <http://www.vanderbilt.edu/aea/org.htm>. The membership figure for the Conference on Faith and History is from Elesha Coffman, "Christian History Corner: Soul Crisis at the Conference on Faith and History," 27 October 2000 posting to *Christianity Today,* on-line ed., at <http://www.christianitytoday.com/ct/2000/143/55.0.html>. The data on the American Historical Association is from the association's Web page at <http://www.theaha.org/info>. The membership of the Society of Christian Philosophers is from Thomas V. Morris, "Introduction," in *God and the Philosophers: The Reconciliation of Faith and Reason,* ed. Thomas V. Morris (New York: Oxford University Press, 1994), 5. The number of philosophy Ph.D.s in the United States (a rough indicator of the number of philosophers) is from "Philosophy as a Profession: Data on the Profession, Selected Demographic Information on Philosophy Ph.D's, 1995" on the American Philosophical Association's Web page at <http://www.apa.udel.edu/apa/profession/selected.html>.

91. The circulation of *Christianity Today* is about 180,000. *Books and Culture* (an attempt at an evangelical version of the *New York Review of Books*) has 16,000 subscribers. The circulation of *National Catholic Reporter* is 47,000, and *America*'s circulation stands at 42,368. *Commonweal* currently has a paid circulation of 18,367. Finally, the neoconservative, but largely Catholic and evangelical, *First Things* has a circulation of about 30,000. Since *Christianity and Crisis* folded, *Christian Century* is the only major general-interest mainline Protestant magazine; it has a circulation of 33,000. The circulation figures for *Christianity Today, Christian Century,* and *Books and Culture* are from William Placher, "Helping Theology Matter: A Challenge for the Mainline" *Christian Century,* 28 October 1998, 994–99. The figures for *Commonweal, America,* and *National Catholic Report* are from the Catholic Press Association Web site at <http://www.catholicpress.org>. The circulation of *First Things* is from Michael Novak et al., "Neocon v. Theocon: An Exchange," *New Republic,* 3 February 1997, 28–30.

92. George Marsden, *The Outrageous Idea of Christian Scholarship* (New York: Oxford University Press, 1997), 101.

93. For an account of the rise and fall of mainline Protestant engagement with academic culture, see Douglas Sloan, *Faith and Knowledge: Mainline Protestantism and American Higher Education* (Louisville, Ken.: Westminster John Knox Press, 1994). Grant Wacker argues that evangelicals often see themselves as the religious custodians of American society: see Grant Wacker, "Uneasy in Zion: Evangelicals in Postmodern Society," in *Evangelicalism and Modern America*, ed. George Marsden (Grand Rapids, Mich.: Eerdmans, 1984), 17–28.

94. *Time* profile of religion and philosophy, as summarized in Kelly James Clark, "Introduction: The Literature of Confession," in *Philosophers Who Believe: The Spiritual Journeys of 11 Leading Thinkers*, ed. Kelly James Clark (Downers Grove, Ill.: InterVarsity Press, 1993), 7.

95. Clark, "Introduction," 9. The statistic is from Thomas Morris, ed., *God and the Philosophers: The Reconciliation of Faith and Reason* (New York: Oxford University Press, 1994), 5.

96. Harry S. Stout and Robert M. Taylor, Jr., "Studies of Religion in American Society: The State of the Art," in *New Directions in American Religious History*, ed. Harry S. Stout and D. G. Hart (New York: Oxford University Press, 1997), 21, 31.

97. George W. Hunt, "American Catholic Intellectual Life," *America*, 6 May 1989, 416.

98. Ted G. Jelen, "Research in Religion and Mass Political Behavior in the United States: Looking Both Ways after Two Decades of Scholarship," *American Politics Quarterly* 26, no. 1 (1998): 110–35 (the quote is on 118). See also James L. Guth, "Secular Scholars and the Religious Right," *Chronicle of Higher Education*, 7 April 1993.

99. See the special issue "What's God Got to Do with the American Experiment?" *Brookings Review*, spring 1999; Robert N. Bellah, "Religion and the Shape of National Culture," *America*, 31 July–7 August 1999, 9; Thomas Landy, "A Sociology of Communitarianism" (unpublished paper, Center for Religion, Ethics, and Culture, College of the Holy Cross, Worcester, Mass., 1996). Catholics and evangelicals have also been a prominent part of Robert Putnam's Saguaro Seminar on Civic Engagement in America (see <http://www.ksg.harvard.edu/saguaro>), Amitai Eztioni's Communitarian Network, and Jean Elshtain's Council on Civil Society.

100. Pointing to the writings of Bryan Hehir, Lisa Cahill, Charles Curran, Margaret Farley, David Hollenbach, and others, George Hunt called the 1980s a golden age of Catholic social ethics: George Hunt, "American Catholic Intellectual Life," *America*, 6 May 1989, 417.

101. William J. Weston, "Restructuring and Changing Market Share among Elite American Christian Intellectuals," paper presented to the Religious Research Association, Boston, November 1999.

102. James T. Burtchaell, "The Decline and Fall of the Christian College," *First Things*, April and May 1991, 22–29, 30–32. Among the books in the area of religion and higher education written by Catholics and evangelicals are Marsden, *Soul of the American University* and *The Outrageous Idea*; Burtchaell, *Dying of the Light*; O'Brien, *Heart of the American Church*; D. G. Hart, *The University Gets Religion: Religious Studies in American Higher Education* (Baltimore: Johns Hopkins University Press, 1999); and Gleason, *Contending with Modernity*.

103. Alan Wolfe, "Religion and American Higher Education: Rethinking a National Dilemma," *Current*, July 1996, 33, LEXIS-NEXIS Academic Universe. See also idem, "A Welcome Revival of Religion in the Academy," *Chronicle of Higher Education*, 19 September 1997, B4.

104. Michael Paulson, "Evangelicals Find Place at Mainstream Colleges," *Boston Globe*, 20 February 2000, A1, LEXIS-NEXIS Academic Universe.

105. Lippmann, as quoted in McGreevy, "Thinking On One's Own,"102; Mencken, as quoted in Harding, *Book of Jerry Falwell,* 68.

106. "Here's the Media Elite," *Washingtonian,* August 1997, 63; Barbara Matusow, "Powers of the Press," *Washingtonian,* August 1997, 60, Infotrac, Expanded Academic ASAP; S. Robert Lichter, Linda S. Lichter, and Daniel R. Amundson, "Media Coverage of Religion in America: 1969–1998," Center for Media and Public Affairs, Washington, D.C., April 2000, available on-line at <http://www.cmpa.com/archive/relig2000.htm>

107. A group of evangelical reporters recently formed an international fellowship of Christian journalists called Gegrapha. This emerging network of Washington-based evangelical journalists, which grew out of two conferences of Christian journalists held in Washington in 1992 and 1997, includes David Aikman, formerly of *Time;* Fred Barnes of the *Weekly Standard;* and Julia Duin of the *Washington Times.* See Gegrapha's Web site at <http://www.gegrapha.org>.

108. Many of these journalists (Barnes, Dionne, McCarthy, Thomas) have also published in the Catholic and evangelical press, in publications such as *Commonweal, Christianity Today, World,* and the *National Catholic Reporter,* showing the links between religious and journalistic communities of discourse.

109. David Astor, "Cal Thomas in Select 500 Club for Columnists," *Editor and Publisher,* 8 May 1999, 44.

110. Kenneth Woodward, "Has the Church Lost Its Soul?" *Newsweek,* 4 October 1971, 80–89; Jeff Cohen, "Media Coverage of Religion: An Overview," Fairness and Accuracy in Media (FAIR), New York, December 1999, available on-line at <http://www.fair.org/articles/media-religion.html>.

Chapter 3. Faith in Journalism

1. See M. S. Larson, *The Rise of Professionalism: A Sociological Analysis* (Berkeley: University of California Press, 1977); Talcott Parsons, "The Professions and Social Structure," in *Essays in Sociological Theory, Pure and Applied* (Glencoe, Ill.: Free Press, 1949), 185–99; Andrew Abbott, *The System of Professions* (Chicago: University of Chicago Press, 1988); Harold Wilensky, "The Professionalization of Everybody," *American Journal of Sociology* 70, no. 2 (1964): 137–58; Charles Derber, Yale Magrass, and William A. Schwartz, *Power in the Highest Degree: Professionals and the Rise of a New Mandarin Order* (New York: Oxford University Press, 1990).

2. Gaye Tuchman, "Objectivity as Strategic Ritual," *American Sociological Review* 77, no. 1 (1972): 660–79; Michael Schudson, *Discovering the News: A Social History of the American Newspaper* (New York: Basic Books, 1978); Herbert Gans, *Deciding What's News* (New York: Random House, 1979), 182–83.

3. See Mark Fitzgerald, "From 'Objectivity' to the 'Gay Agenda': Gay Journalists Feeling Extra Pressure, Criticism on the Job," *Editor and Publisher,* 25 September 1999, 10; A. Kent MacDougall, "Confessions of a Closet Leftist: A Veteran Reporter Reveals His 24-Year Undercover Career (A. Kent MacDougall, former reporter for the *Wall Street Journal*)," *Time,* 6 February 1989, 58.

4. Gans, *Deciding What's News,* 183.

5. Barnes, Dionne, and Thomas, as quoted in Sally Quinn, "The G-Word and the A-List," *Washington Post,* 12 July 1999, C1, LEXIS-NEXIS Academic Universe.

6. S. Robert Lichter and Linda Lichter, "The Media Get Religion," *Media Monitor,* May–June 2000, available on-line at <http://www.cmpa.com/mediamon/mm050600.htm>.

7. Nicholas Mills, *The New Journalism* (New York: McGraw-Hill, 1974); James Aultschull, *From Milton to McLuhan: The Ideas behind American Journalism* (Baltimore, Md.: Johns Hopkins University Press, 1990); Schudson, *Discovering the News.*

8. David G. Weaver and G. Cleveland Wilhoit, *The American Journalist* (Bloomington: Indiana University Press, 1991).

9. Society of Professional Journalists, "Code of Ethics," 1996, available on-line at <http://www.spj.org>.

10. Schudson, *Discovering the News,* 186. For a conservative evangelical professor's discussion of the decline of objectivity, see Marvin Olasky, *Prodigal Press: The Anti-Christian Bias of the American News Media* (Wheaton, Ill.: Crossway Books, 1988). Olasky calls for a new vision of objectivity that makes room for the spiritual.

11. Erving Goffman, *Stigma: Notes on the Management of Spoiled Identity* (New York: Simon and Schuster, 1963); Peter L. Berger, *The Sacred Canopy* (New York: Doubleday, 1967); James Davison Hunter, *American Evangelicalism: Conservative Religion and the Quandary of Modernity* (New Brunswick, N.J.: Rutgers University Press, 1983).

12. See Gaye Tuchman, *Making News: A Study in the Construction of Reality* (New York: Free Press, 1978); Kay Mills, *A Place in the News: From the Women's Page to the Front Page* (New York: Dodd and Mead, 1988).

13. S. Robert Lichter, Stanley Rothman, and Linda Lichter, *The Media Elite: America's New Power Brokers* (Bethesda, Md.: Adler and Adler, 1986).

14. Martin Luther, as quoted in "Our Daily Bread," Gospel Communications Network, Web site, 5 September 1994, available on-line at <http://www.gospelcom.net/rbc/odb/odb-09-05-94.shtml>.

15. After leaving *Fortune,* Holt was the editor of the *Journal of Commerce.* Most recently, he has served as a guest instructor at Wheaton College.

16. See Steven Brint, *In an Age of Experts: The Changing Role of Professionals in Politics and Public Life* (Princeton, N.J.: Princeton University Press, 1994).

17. Don Holt, "A Record Start to a Global Career," *Wheaton Alumni,* April–May 1991, 7.

18. David J. O'Brien, *Public Catholicism* (New York: Macmillan, 1989).

19. Stephen Hart, *What Does the Lord Require? How Americans Think about Economic Justice* (New York: Oxford University Press, 1992).

20. Wendy Griswold, "The Fabrication of Meaning: Literary Interpretation in the United States, Great Britain, and the West Indies," *American Journal of Sociology* 92, no. 5 (1986): 1077–117.

21. Schudson, *Discovering the News,* 186.

22. For an astute analysis of the role of the social critic, see Alan Wolfe, *Marginalized in the Middle* (Chicago: University of Chicago Press, 1996).

23. Schudson, *Discovering the News,* 176–94. On the use of objectivity to hide political convictions, see Jack Newfield, "Journalism: Old, New and Corporate," in *The Reporter as Artist: A Look at the New Journalism,* ed. Ronald Weber (New York: Hastings House, 1974), 56. Newfield is quoted in Schudson, *Discovering the News,* 184. On this era of journalism's history, see also Aultschull, *From Milton to McLuhan.*

24. O'Brien, *Public Catholicism;* James T. Fisher, *The Catholic Counterculture in America: 1933–1962* (Chapel Hill: University of North Carolina Press, 1989).

25. Robert Booth Fowler, *A New Engagement: Evangelical Political Thought, 1966–1976* (Grand Rapids, Mich.: Eerdmans, 1982); Richard Quebedeaux, *The Young Evangelicals* (New York: Harper and Row, 1974).

26. Hunter, *American Evangelicalism.*

27. Wesley Pippert, *An Ethic of News: A Reporter's Search for Truth* (Washington, D.C.: Georgetown University Press, 1989), 43.

28. Richard Hofstadter, *The Age of Reform* (New York: Vintage, 1955); Bruce Evensen, "The Evangelical Origins of the Muckrakers," *American Journalism* 6 (1989): 5–29.

29. Schudson, *Discovering the News;* Aultschull, *From Milton to McLuhan.*

30. Pippert, *An Ethic of News,* 13.

31. McCarthy still writes frequently for the *Washington Post,* as well for the *Progressive* and other opinion magazines.

32. O'Brien, *Public Catholicism;* Fisher, *Catholic Counterculture.* For a discussion of progressive evangelicalism, see Quebedeaux, *The Young Evangelicals.* See also Fowler, *A New Engagement,* and Hunter, *American Evangelicalism.*

33. O'Brien, *Public Catholicism,* 246.

34. On the decline of the public intellectual, see Russell Jacoby, *The Last Intellectuals: American Culture in the Age of Academe* (New York: Farrar, Straus, and Giroux, 1987); Richard A. Posner, *Public Intellectuals: A Study of Decline, A Critical Analysis* (Cambridge, Mass.: Harvard University Press, 2001). In an important essay, Robert Boynton argues that African Americans are reviving the tradition of the public intellectual: see Robert Boynton, "The New Intellectuals," *Atlantic Monthly,* March 1995, 53–70. Religious public intellectuals are playing a similar role.

35. Brint, *Age of Experts.*

36. Garry Wills, *Bare Ruined Choirs: Doubt, Prophecy, and Radical Religion* (New York: Doubleday, 1972); Rodger Van Allen, *Being Catholic: Commonweal from the Seventies to the Nineties* (Chicago: Loyola University Press, 1994); Rodger Van Allen, *The Commonweal and American Catholicism* (Philadelphia: Fortress, 1974); Willliam Clancy, "Catholicism in America," in *Catholicism in America,* ed. William Clancy (New York: Harcourt, Brace, and Company, 1954), 9–24; John Murray Cuddihy, *No Offense: Civil Religion and Protestant Taste* (New York: Seabury, 1978).

37. The magazine has since relocated to Manhattan's upper west side.

38. Peter Steinfels, "Religion and the Media: Keynote Address," *Commonweal,* 24 February 1995, 5.

39. Idem, "Constraints of the Religion Reporter," *Nieman Reports* 47, no. 2 (1993): 4.

40. Ibid., 5.

41. Steinfels, as quoted in Van Allen, *Being Catholic,* 114.

42. John Kane, "Catholic Separatism," in Clancy, *Catholicism in America,* 56.

43. Van Allen, *Being Catholic.*

44. Steinfels, "Constraints," 5.

45. E. J. Dionne, "Response: An Agenda for the Church," *Woodstock Report,* March 1994, 8.

46. Peter Steinfels, "Prophet and Politician," in *Generation of the Third Eye,* ed. Daniel Callahan (New York: Sheed and Ward, 1965), 216.

47. Charles Kadushin, *The American Intellectual Elite* (Boston: Little, Brown, 1974); Russell Jacoby, *The Last Intellectuals: American Culture in the Age of Academe* (New York: Farrar, Straus, and Giroux, 1987).

48. Steinfels, as quoted in Kenneth L. Woodward, "The U.S. Church: 'Unify Us,'" *Newsweek,* 8 October 1979, 40.

49. Kadushin, *American Intellectual Elite.*

50. David J. O'Brien, "Contemporary Reflections: 1985, 1995," *U.S. Catholic Historian* 13, no. 1 (1995): 54. For an analysis of Catholic "anti-ghettoism," see Philip Gleason, *Keeping the Faith: American Catholicism Past and Present* (Notre Dame, Ind.: University of Notre Dame Press, 1987), 184–87.

51. Pam Janis, "Classic Cokie: A Beltway Insider since Infancy," *Detroit News,* 22 January 1997, E1, LEXIS-NEXIS Academic Universe.

52. See the paperback edition of E. J. Dionne, *Why Americans Hate Politics* (New York: Simon and Schuster, 1991).

53. Cokie Roberts, *We Are Our Mothers' Daughters* (New York: William Morrow, 1998), 5.

54. Kay Mills, *A Place in the News.*

55. Roberts, *Our Mothers' Daughters,* 100.

56. Ibid., 124.

57. *This Week with David Brinkley,* ABC Television, 21 April 1996, transcript, LEXIS-NEXIS Academic Universe.

58. Ibid.

59. Ibid.

60. Jeff Cohen, as quoted in Paul Hendrickson, "Roberts Rules," *Washington Post Magazine,* 20 June 1993, W8, LEXIS-NEXIS Academic Universe.

61. Cokie Roberts and Steven V. Roberts, "Heed the Voices of Moderation in Abortion Debate," *Daily News,* 22 May 1997, 57.

62. Cokie Roberts and Steven V. Roberts, "The President Needs to Pray, Then Come Clean," *Daily News,* 12 August, 1998, 29.

63. Miriam Therese Winter, Adair Lummis, and Allison Stokes, *Defecting in Place: Women Claiming Responsibility for Their Own Spiritual Lives* (New York: Crossroad Publishing, 1995), 32.

64. According to a profile of Barnes in the *Wheaton Record,* an evangelical college newspaper, the born-again question created a "hissing in the audience and produced hundreds of negative letters": see Anthony Trendl, "Barnes Speaks on Clinton, Farrakhan," *Wheaton Record,* 25 March 1994, 1.

65. Chuck Conconi, "Personalities," *Washington Post,* 11 October 1984, B3, LEXIS-NEXIS Academic Universe.

66. Chancellor, as quoted in John Dart and Jimmy Allen, *Bridging the Gap: Religion and the News Media* (Nashville, Tenn.: Freedom Forum First Amendment Center, 1993), 47.

67. Lichter et al., *Media Elite,* 21–22.

68. For the neoconservative critique of the new class, see B. Bruce-Briggs, *The New Class?* (New Brunswick, N.J.: Transaction Publishers, 1979). For an analysis of populism in American culture, see Michael Kazin, *The Populist Persuasion: An American History* (New York: Basic Books, 1995). See also "Antielitism and the New Class Warfare," in Alan Crawford, *Thunder on the Right: The "New Right" and the Politics of Resentment* (New York: Pantheon Books, 1980), 165–80. For a negative assessment of populist anti-elitism, see Richard Hofstadter, *Anti-Intellectualism in American Life* (New York: Vintage, 1963).

69. *Forbes MediaCritic* 1, no. 2 (1994): 10.

70. Fred Barnes, "The Moviegoer," *Weekly Standard,* 9 August 1999, 4.

71. Idem, "The Harassment of Gary Bauer," *Weekly Standard,* 11 October 1999, 12.

72. "Here's the Media Elite," *Washingtonian,* August 1997, 63, LEXIS-NEXIS Academic Universe; Barbara Matusow, "Powers of the Press," *Washingtonian,* August 1997, 60, LEXIS-NEXIS Academic Universe.

73. See James Bennet, "Iconoclastic Weekly Grabs Attention on Right," *New York Times,* 23 May 1996, B12.

74. Irving Kristol, "The Adversary Culture," in *The Third Century,* ed. Seymour Martin Lipset (Chicago: University of Chicago Press, 1979), 327–44.

75. Hunter, *American Evangelicalism,* 111. On the appropriation of neo-conservative new-class theory by the Christian right, see Crawford, *Thunder on the Right,* 165–80.

76. Seth Ackerman, "The Most Biased Name in News: Fox News Channel's Extraordinary Right-Wing Tilt," *A Special FAIR Report,* August 2000, 1; Marshall Sella, "The Red-State Network," *New York Times Magazine,* 24 June 2001, 26. LEXIS-NEXIS Academic Universe. Fox has actually used FAIR's Jeff Cohen as a commentator.

77. For an analysis of the cultural populism of Bill O'Reilly and Chris Matthews, see Noam Scheiber, "Chris Matthews and Bill O'Reilly v. the Working Man," *New Republic,* 25 June 2001, 22–25.

78. Barnes, as paraphrased in "Christian Collegiate Journalists Encouraged to Go into Mainstream Media," press release, Association of Christian Collegiate Media, 16 March 1996, 1.

79. Ibid.

80. Fred Barnes, "The Misfits," *Weekly Standard,* 24 August 1998, 6.

81. Chris Lehmann, "It's Class; Stupid: How the Culture Wars Sank Populism," Institute for Public Affairs, 18 October 1998, 24, LEXIS-NEXIS Academic Universe.

82. Richard Harwood, "Are Journalists Elitist?" *American Journalism Review,* June 1995, 30.

83. Tuchman, "Objectivity as Strategic Ritual"; Thomas Gieryn, "Boundary-Work and the Demarcation of Science from Non-Science: Strains and Interests in Professional Ideologies of Scientists," *American Sociological Review* 48, no. 6 (1983): 781–95. See Michele Lamont, *Money, Morals, and Manners* (Chicago: University of Chicago Press, 1992). In *The World of Goods: Towards an Anthropology of Consumption* (London: Routledge, 1996), 12, Mary Douglas and Baron Isherwood argue that consumer goods serve as fences and bridges, both uniting and dividing social groups. In my analysis of journalism and social science I use the metaphors of fence and bridge to describe how objectivity rhetoric connects and separates professional and religious worlds.

84. Steinfels is no longer a senior religion correspondent at the *New York Times.* He continues to write the biweekly "Beliefs" column, however, a role that he said allows more room for perspective and interpretation, though not outright advocacy.

85. Tuchman, "Objectivity as Strategic Ritual."

86. George Marsden, "The State of Evangelical Christian Scholarship," *Reformed Journal* 37, no. 9 (1987): 12–16; Mark Noll, *The Scandal of the Evangelical Mind* (Grand Rapids, Mich.: Eerdmans, 1994); Gleason, *Keeping the Faith;* David Salvaterra, *American Catholicism and the Intellectual Life* (New York: Garland Publishing, 1988).

87. Aultschull, *From Milton to McLuhan.*

88. Peter Steinfels, speech given at the University of Notre Dame, Notre Dame, Ind., 30 November 1994.

89. Pippert, *An Ethic of News,* 8.

90. Robert Wuthnow, *Christianity and Civil Society* (Valley Forge, Penn.: Trinity Press International, 1996).

Chapter 4. Faith in the Academy

1. Stephen Carter, *The Culture of Disbelief: How Law and Politics Trivialize Religious Devotion* (New York: Basic Books, 1993), 23, 25.

2. For a review of the survey literature on the religiosity of college professors, see Martin J. Finkelstein, *The American Academic Profession: A Synthesis of Social Science Inquiry since World War II* (Columbus: Ohio State University Press, 1984), and Robert Wuthnow, *The Struggle for America's Soul: Evangelicals, Liberals, and Secularism* (Grand Rapids, Mich.: Eerdmans, 1989).

3. Max Weber, "Science as a Vocation," in *From Max Weber: Essays in Sociology,* ed. Hans Gerth and C. Wright Mills (New York: Oxford University Press, 1946), 129–56. On the specific influence of Weber on American social-scientific notions of value-neutrality, see Fred R. Dallmayer and Thomas A. McCarthy, eds., *Understanding and Social Inquiry* (Notre Dame, Ind.: University of Notre Dame Press, 1977. On the role of positivism, value-neutrality, and the ideology of objectivity in the social sciences, see Richard Bernstein, *The Restructuring of Social and Political Theory* (Philadelphia: University of Pennsylvania Press, 1976).

4. Alvin W. Gouldner, "Anti-Minotaur: The Myth of a Value-Free Sociology," in *The New Sociology: Essays in Social Science and Social Theory in Honor of C. Wright Mills,* ed. Irving Louis Horowitz (New York: Oxford University Press, 1965), 196, 204.

5. Peter Novick, *That Noble Dream: The "Objectivity Question" and the American Historical Profession* (Cambridge: Cambridge University Press, 1988), 11, 2.

6. James Farr, "Remembering the Revolution: Behavioralism in American Political Science," in *Political Science in History: Research Programs and Political Traditions,* ed. James F. Farr, John S. Dryzek, and Stephen T. Leonard (Cambridge: Cambridge University Press, 1995), 203–204.

7. Ibid., 204.

8. See M. S. Larson, *The Rise of Professionalism: A Sociological Analysis* (Berkeley: University of California Press, 1977); Alvin Gouldner, "The New Class Project I," *Theory and Society* 6, no. 2 (1980): 153–204; Eliot Freidson, *Profession of Medicine: A Study in the Sociology of Applied Knowledge* (Chicago: University of Chicago Press, 1988); Robert K. Merton, "The Normative Structure of Science," in idem, *The Sociology of Science* (Chicago: University of Chicago Press, 1973), chap. 13; Talcott Parsons, "The Professions and Social Structure," in idem, *Essays in Sociological Theory, Pure and Applied* (Glencoe, Ill.: Free Press, 1949), 185–99; Michael Mulkay, "The Norms and Ideology of Science," *Social Science Information* 15, no. 4–5 (1976): 637–56; Andrew Abbott, *The System of Professions* (Chicago: University of Chicago Press, 1988); Harold Wilensky, "The Professionalization of Everybody," *American Journal of Sociology* 70, no. 2 (1964): 137–58; Thomas Gieryn, "Boundary-Work and the Demarcation of Science from Non-Science," *American Sociological Review* 48, no. 6 (1983): 781–95; Charles Derber, Yale Magrass, and William A. Schwartz, *Power in the Highest Degree: Professionals and the Rise of a New Mandarin Order* (New York: Oxford University Press, 1990).

9. Bernstein, *Restructuring of Social and Political Theory,* 5.

10. George Marsden, *The Soul of the American University: From Protestant Establishment to Established Nonbelief* (New York: Oxford University Press, 1994), 430.

11. Idem, *The Outrageous Idea of Christian Scholarship* (New York: Oxford University Press, 1997), 7.

12. Andrew M. Greeley, *An Ugly Little Secret: Anti-Catholicism in North America* (Kansas City, Mo.: Sheed Andrews and McMeel, 1977), 2.

13. Erving Goffman, *The Presentation of Self in Everyday Life* (New York: Doubleday, 1959), 112. For an earlier application of Goffman's concept of "backstage" to academic careers, see Phillip Hammond, ed., *Sociologists at Work* (New York: Basic Books, 1964), as cited in Albert Hunter, "Introduction: Rhetoric in Research, Networks of Knowledge," in *The Rhetoric of Social Research: Understood and Believed,* ed. Albert Hunter (New Brunswick, N.J.: Rutgers University Press, 1990), 1–22.

14. James Turner, "Catholic Intellectual Traditions and Contemporary Scholarship," lecture, Cushwa Center for the Study of American Catholicism, University of Notre Dame, Notre Dame, Ind., 8 April 1997, 2. Reprints are available from the Cushwa Center.

15. Joel Carpenter and Kenneth W. Shipps, "Preface," *Making Higher Education Christian: The History and Mission of Evangelical Colleges in America,* ed. Joel Carpenter and Kenneth W. Shipps (Grand Rapids, Mich.: Eerdmans: 1987), xiii.

16. Goffman, *Presentation of Self.*

17. These figures are from the Sociofile CD-ROM index (January 1974–June 1996), the Social Science Citation Index (1981–90), and Hallinan.

18. James Jasper, "The Politics of Abstractions: Instrumental and Moralist Rhetoric in Public Debate," *Social Research* 59, no. 2 (1992): 322.

19. Ibid., 328.

20. David J. O'Brien, *From the Heart of the American Church: Catholic Higher Education and American Culture* (Maryknoll, N.Y.: Orbis Books, 1994); Philip Gleason, *Contending*

with Modernity: Catholic Higher Education in the Twentieth Century (New York: Oxford University Press, 1995).

21. Barbara Schneider, "ASA President Maureen Hallinan: She's in a Class by Herself," *Footnotes* newsletter, vol. 23, no. 7 (1995), 1.

22. Ibid., 10.

23. The Jesuit paleontologist and theologian Teilhard de Chardin used the term "omega point" to refer simultaneously to the end of evolution, the kingdom of God, and Jesus Christ: see Teilhard de Chardin, *The Phenomenon of Man* (New York: Harper Perennial, 1976).

24. See William V. D'Antonio, James D. Davidson, Dean R. Hoge and Ruth A. Wallace, *Laity: American and Catholic* (Kansas City, Mo.: Sheed and Ward, 1996). See also Miriam Therese Winter, Adair Lummis, and Allison Stokes, *Defecting in Place: Women Claiming Responsibility for Their Own Spiritual Lives* (New York: Crossroad Publishing, 1995).

25. Wendy Griswold, "The Fabrication of Meaning: Literary Interpretation in the United States, Great Britain, and the West Indies," *American Journal of Sociology* 92 (1986): 1077–117.

26. For more on the social scientist as social critic, see Alan Wolfe, *Marginalized in the Middle* (Chicago: University of Chicago Press, 1996). For an account of the pragmatic, normative origins of the American social sciences, see Dorothy Ross, *The Origins of American Social Science* (New York: Cambridge University Press, 1991).

27. John DiIulio, Michael Hout, Gary Orfield, and Bruce Russett, all Catholic social scientists, combined rhetorics drawn from the public-policy–oriented branch of social science with a Catholic concern for peace and justice.

28. Eight of the twenty Catholic and evangelical social scientists interviewed used epistemological rhetorics to critique the ideology of objectivity.

29. The quotation is from Todd Gitlin, *The Twilight of Common Dreams* (New York: Henry Holt, 1995), 200–201. See also Pauline Marie Rosenau, *Post-Modernism and the Social Sciences* (Princeton, N.J.: Princeton University Press, 1992), and Novick, *That Noble Dream.*

30. Nina J. Easton, "The Crime Doctor Is In: But Not Everyone Likes Prof. John DiIulio's Message," *Los Angeles Times,* 2 May 1995, E1, LEXIS-NEXIS Academic Universe.

31. For more on DiIulio as a White House official, see Adelle Banks, "DiIulio Walks a Fine Line between Faith and Policy," Religious News Service, 14 March 2001, 1; Sebastian Mallaby, "DiIulio's Good-Faith Effort," *Washington Post,* 20 August 2001, A15, LEXIS-NEXIS Academic Universe; Elizabeth Becker, "Head of Religion-Based Initiative Resigns," *New York Times,* 18 August 2001, LEXIS-NEXIS Academic Universe. DiIulio, as quoted in Banks, "DiIulio Walks a Fine Line," 1.

32. Richard Bernstein, "A Thinker Attuned to Doing," *New York Times,* 22 August 1998, A17, LEXIS-NEXIS Academic Universe.

33. John DiIulio, "Jeremiah's Call," *Prism,* March–April 1998, 33.

34. Idem, "Having Faith in Church Aiding State," interview by Mary Leonard, *Boston Globe,* 4 January 1988, E1, LEXIS-NEXIS Academic Universe.

35. Jerome H. Skolnick, "Tough Guys," *American Prospect,* January–February 1997, 86, Infotrac, Expanded Academic ASAP.

36. Wolfe, *Marginalized in the Middle; * Ross, *Origins of American Social Science.*

37. Robert Orsi, *The Madonna of 115th Street: Faith and Community in Italian Harlem, 1880–1950* (New Haven, Conn.: Yale University Press, 1988).

38. John DiIulio, "My Black Crime Problem, and Ours," *City Journal* 6, no. 2 (spring 1996): 14–28, from <www.city-journal.org>.

39. John Leland. "Savior of the Streets," *Newsweek,* 1 June 1998, 20–25.

40. Joe Klein, "In God They Trust," *New Yorker,* 16 June 1997, 44.

41. The first quote is from Klein, "In God They Trust," 44; the second, on Moyers and Bennett, is from the interview.

42. DiIulio, "Jeremiah's Call," 23.

43. John DiIulio, "Kids Who Kill," interview by Michael Cromartie, *Books and Culture,* January–February 1997, 10.

44. Andrew M. Greeley, *The American Catholic: A Social Portrait* (New York: Basic Books, 1977), 256.

45. Although DiIulio's mentor James Q. Wilson no longer identifies himself as a practicing Catholic, he has written widely on the topics of morality and the common good. William Bennett, the conservative gadfly and DiIulio's co-author on the book *Body Count: Moral Poverty and How to Win America's War against Crime and Drugs* (New York: Simon and Schuster, 1996), grew up in an Irish Catholic neighborhood in Brooklyn and has continued to emphasize religious themes in his writings on virtue and community.

46. DiIulio, "Having Faith," E1.

47. Richard Morin, "Onward Christian Soldier: John DiIulio Ready to Go to the Mat with a Faith-Based Approach to Crime," *Washington Post,* 26 February 2001, C1.

48. John J. DiIulio, "The Political Theory of Compassionate Conservatism," *Weekly Standard,* 23 August 1999. This article was obtained from the magazine's Web page at <http://www.weeklystandard.com>. It is now available on-line only to subscribers.

49. Greeley published more than eighty articles in academic sociology journals between January 1974 and June 1996: Sociofile CD-ROM index. He was cited more than four hundred times by other social scientists between 1981 and 1990: Social Science Citation Index (1981–90). The Religion Index (1949–96) contained more than two hundred references to Greeley.

50. Andrew M. Greeley, *Confessions of a Parish Priest* (New York: Pocket Books, 1987), 33.

51. Ibid., 220.

52. Peter Kivisto, "The Brief Career of Catholic Sociology," *Sociological Analysis* 50, no. 4 (1989): 351–61.

53. See John T. McGreevy, "Thinking on One's Own: Catholicism in the American Intellectual Imagination, 1928–1960," *Journal of American History* 84, no. 1 (1997): 97–131, for an account of anti-intellectual images of Catholicism. See Philip Gleason, *Keeping the Faith in America: American Catholicism Past and Present* (Notre Dame, Ind.: University of Notre Dame Press, 1987), for an account of Catholic responses to postwar liberal charges of intolerance and antidemocratic values.

54. Andrew M. Greeley, "The Crooked Lines of God," in *Authors of Their Own Lives: Intellectual Biographies by Twenty American Sociologists,* ed. Bennett Berger (Berkeley: University of California Press, 1990), 138.

55. Loretta Morris, "Secular Transcendence: From ACSS to ASR," *Sociological Analysis* 50, no. 4 (1989): 329–49; Joseph Varacalli, "Catholic Sociology in America: A Comment on the Fiftieth Anniversary Issue of *Sociological Analysis,*" *International Journal of Politics, Culture, and Society* 4, no. 2 (1990): 249–62; Gleason, *Keeping the Faith.*

56. Greeley, *Confessions,* 232.

57. John Kotre, *The Best of Times, the Worst of Times: Andrew Greeley and American Catholicism: 1950–1975* (Chicago: Nelson-Hall, 1978), 50.

58. Andrew M. Greeley, *Religion as Poetry* (New Brunswick, N.J.: Transaction Publishers, 1995), 7.

59. On the boundary rhetoric of science, see Gieryn, "Boundary-Work."

60. Andrew M. Greeley, *The Catholic Myth* (New York: Doubleday, 1990), 70.

61. Idem, "Crooked Lines of God,"137.

62. Idem, *Confessions*, 235.

63. Ibid., 246, 248.

64. Ibid., 395.

65. Kotre, *Best of Times*.

66. Greeley, *Confessions*, 245–46.

67. Ibid., 411.

68. Ibid., 246.

69. Ibid., 409.

70. Andrew M. Greeley, *The Cardinal Sins* (New York: Warner Books, 1981). Greeley's *Death in April* (New York: McGraw-Hill, 1980) and *The Magic Cup: An Irish Legend* (New York: McGraw-Hill, 1979) preceded *The Cardinal Sins*, but they were not as controversial or successful.

71. Greeley, "Crooked Lines of God," 145–46.

72. Andrew M. Greeley, "Bricolage among the Trash Cans: The Process of Creativity," *Society*, January 1993, 70–76, Expanded Academic ASAP.

73. Andrew M. Greeley, "Anything but Marginal," in *Generation of the Third Eye*, ed. Daniel Callahan (New York: Sheed and Ward, 1965).

74. George Marsden, *Fundamentalism and American Culture: The Shaping of Twentieth-Century Evangelicalism, 1870–1925* (New York: Oxford University Press, 1980).

75. Leonard Sweet, "Wise as Serpents, Innocent as Doves: The New Evangelical Historiography," *Journal of the American Academy of Religion* 56 (fall 19988): 398, 400.

76. Harry Stout and Robert Taylor, "Studies of Religion in American Society: The State of the Art," in *New Directions in American Religious History*, ed. Harry Stout and D. G. Hart (New York: Oxford University Press, 1997), 24.

77. Marsden, *Soul of the American University*. John Patrick Diggins wrote a positive review of *Soul of the American University* for the *New York Times Book Review*, 17 April 1994.

78. George Marsden, "What Has Athens to Do with Jerusalem? Religious Commitment in the Academy," plenary address, annual meeting of the American Academy of Religion, Washington, D.C., 21 November 1993); idem, "Church, State and Campus," *New York Times*, 26 April 1994, A23. LEXIS-NEXIS Academic Universe; idem, "Religious Professors Are the Last Taboo," *Wall Street Journal*, 22 December 1993, LEXIS-NEXIS Academic Universe.

79. Alan Wolfe, "Religion and American Higher Education: Rethinking a National Dilemma," *Current*, July 1996, 33, LEXIS-NEXIS Academic Universe.

80. For an account of evangelicals' tendency to portray themselves as victims, see Os Guiness, "More Victimized Than Thou," in *No God but God: Breaking with the Idols of Our Age*, ed. Os Guiness and John Seel (Chicago: Moody Press, 1992), 81–93. For a critique of this tendency in the wider culture, see Todd Gitlin, "The Rise of 'Identity Politics,'" in *Legacy of Dissent: Forty Years of Writing from* Dissent *Magazine*, ed. Nicolaus Mills (New York: Touchstone Books, 1994), 141–49.

81. Wolfe, "Religion and American Higher Education," 33; Robert Wuthnow, "Living the Question: Evangelical Christianity and Critical Thought," *CrossCurrents* 90, no. 40 (1990): 160–76, from <www.crosscurrents.org>.

82. Marsden began *Soul of the American University* while on the faculty of Duke University and finished after he had taken a position at the University of Notre Dame.

83. Marsden, *Soul of the American University*, 429, 440.

84. The other evangelical historians interviewed for this project shared Marsden's critique of Enlightenment objectivity.

85. Marsden, "What Has Athens to Do with Jerusalem?" 1.

86. George Marsden, *The Outrageous Idea of Christian Scholarship* (New York: Oxford University Press, 1997), 27.

87. Marsden, *Soul of the American University,* 430.

88. Wolfe, "Religion and American Higher Education," 33.

89. Stanley Fish, "Why We Can't All Just Get Along," *First Things,* February 1996, 26.

90. Stout and Taylor, "Studies of Religion in American Society," 46.

91. George Marsden, "Common Sense and the Spiritual Vision of History," in *History and Historical Understanding,* ed. C. T. McIntire and Ronald Wells (Grand Rapids, Mich.: Eerdmans, 1984), 57.

92. See idem, "The State of Evangelical Christian Scholarship," *Reformed Journal* 37, no. 9 (1987): 12–16.

93. Nicholas Wolterstorff, a philosopher at Yale and once a colleague of Marsden's at Calvin College, has commented on the similarities between Kuyper and Kuhn: see Nicholas Wolterstorff, "The Grace That Shaped My Life," in *Philosophers Who Believe: The Spiritual Journeys of 11 Leading Thinkers,* ed. Kelly James Clark (Downers Grove, Ill.: InterVarsity Press, 1993), 259–75.

94. Poloma has published more than thirty articles in sociological journals: Sociofile CD-ROM index (January 1974–June 1996). She is the author or co-author of eight books and was completing a book on the Pentecostal and charismatic revival of the 1990s as the study was being conducted. The Religion Index (1949–96) contains more than forty articles and book reviews by or about Poloma.

95. Margaret Poloma, *The Charismatic Movement: Is There a New Pentecost?* (Boston: Twayne Publishers, 1982); idem, *The Assemblies of God at the Crossroads: Charisma and Institutional Dilemmas* (Knoxville: University of Tennessee Press, 1986).

96. Being "slain in the spirit," "resting in the spirit," "going under the power," and the "sacred swoon" are a few of the terms used to designate a phenomenon in which "the person falls (usually) backwards when being prayed over"; it is "believed to be caused by an overwhelming presence of God": see Poloma, *Assemblies of God,* 84.

97. Poloma has written two books and several articles on the effects of prayer and prayer experiences, including Margaret Poloma and B. F. Pendleton, *Exploring Neglected Dimensions of Religion in Quality of Life Research* (Lewiston, N.Y.: Edwin Mellen Press, 1991), and Margaret Poloma and George H. Gallup, Jr., *Varieties of Prayer: A Survey Report* (Philadelphia: Trinity Press International, 1991).

98. Margaret Poloma, "'Toronto Blessing': Charisma, Institutionalization, Revival," *Journal for the Scientific Study of Religion* 36, no. 2 (1997): 257–71. See also Patricia Adler and Peter Adler, *Membership Roles in Field Research: Qualitative Methods,* vol. 6 (Beverly Hills, Calif.: Sage Publications, 1987).

99. Gaye Tuchman, "Objectivity as Strategic Ritual," *American Journal of Sociology* 77, no. 1 (1972): 660–79.

100. Greeley, *Confessions,* 246.

101. Ibid., 363.

102. Marsden, *Outrageous Idea,* 45, 47.

103. Idem, "Common Sense and the Spiritual Vision of History," 59.

104. Elizabeth Fox-Genovese, "Advocacy and the Writing of American Women's History," in *Religious Advocacy and American History,* ed. Bruce Kuklick and D. G. Hart (Grand Rapids, Mich.: Eerdmans, 1997), 97.

105. Ibid," 103–104.

106. "A Rebellion against History's Fuzzy Future," *New York Times,* 2 May 1998, A15.

107. Marsden, "Common Sense and the Spiritual Vision of History," 59.

108. DiIulio, "Jeremiah's Call."

109. Andrew M. Greeley, "Sociology and the Catholic Church: Four Decades of Bitter Memories," *Sociological Analysis* 50, no. 4 (1989): 394–95.

110. David Tracy, "Catholic Classics in American Liberal Culture," in *Catholicism and Liberalism,* ed. David Hollenbach (Cambridge: Cambridge University Press, 1994), 196, 201–202. Tracy contrasts "public" epistemology with the more "sectarian" approach of narrative theologians.

111. According to Marsden, common-sense realism was the dominant epistemology of nineteenth-century evangelicalism: see George Marsdem, *Fundamentalism and American Culture* (New York: Oxford University Press, 1980).

112. Similarly, Bruce Russett did not examine the implications of Catholic just-war theory for the study of international relations until well into his career, and Margaret Poloma was well established as a professional sociologist before she wrote about a "Christian sociological perspective" for *Sociological Analysis* (1982). See Margaret M. Poloma, "Toward a Christian Sociological Perspective: Religious Values, Theory, and Methodology," *Sociological Analysis* 43, no. 2 (1982): 95–108.

113. Wolfe, *Marginalized in the Middle,* 14.

114. Mark Noll, "Scientific History in America: A Centennial Observation from a Christian Point of View," *Fides et Historia* 14 (fall–winter 1981): 27.

115. Novick, *That Noble Dream,* 628.

116. Thomas Haskell, "Objectivity Is Not Neutrality: Rhetoric vs. Practice in Peter Novick's *That Noble Dream,*" *History and Theory* (May 1990): 131.

117. See Robert Bellah, *Beyond Belief: Essays on Religion in a Post-Traditionalist World* (Berkeley: University of California Press, 1970); Bernstein, *Restructuring of Social and Political Theory;* Alan Wolfe, "Social Science and the Moral Revival: Dilemmas and Difficulties," unpublished paper presented at The Revival of Moral Inquiry, conference, Woodrow Wilson Center, Smithsonian Institution, Washington, D.C., 15–16 May 1995.

Chapter 5. Journalism and the Religious Imagination

1. William Powers, "The Roman Legion," *National Journal,* 15 August 1980, 1930, Infotrac, Expanded Academic ASAP.

2. Gaye Tuchman, "Objectivity as Strategic Ritual," *American Sociological Review* 77, no. 1 (1972): 660–79; Michael Schudson, *Discovering the News: A Social History of the American Newspaper* (New York: Basic Books, 1978); Herbert Gans, *Deciding What's News* (New York: Random House, 1979). See Jay Rosen, *What Are Journalists For?* (New Haven, Conn.: Yale University Press, 1999) for a critique of mainstream journalism's detachment from political and moral engagement.

3. Hayden White, *The Content of the Form* (Baltimore: Johns Hopkins University Press, 1987), ix.

4. Michael Schudson, *The Power of News* (Cambridge, Mass.: Harvard University Press, 1995), 55.

5. James S. Ettema and Theodore L. Glasser, "Narrative Form and Moral Force: The Realization of Innocence and Guilt through Investigative Journalism," *Journal of Communications* 38, no. 3 (1988): 11.

6. Gans, *Deciding What's News,* 205.

7. On cultural resources, see Rhys Williams, "Visions of the Good Society and the Religious Roots of American Political Culture," *Sociology of Religion* 60, no. 1 (1999): 1. On narrative, see Robert Wuthnow, *Christianity in the Twenty-First Century: Reflections on the Challenges Ahead* (New York: Oxford University Press, 1995); Robert Bellah, *The Broken Covenant: American Civil Religion in a Time of Trial* (Chicago: University of Chicago Press, 1992): Andrew M. Greeley, *The Catholic Myth* (New York: Doubleday, 1997);

Stanley Hauerwas and L. Gregory Jones, eds., *Why Narrative? Readings in Narrative Theology* (Grand Rapids, Mich.: Eerdmans, 1989).

8. On "culture as toolkit," see Ann Swidler, "Culture in Action: Symbols and Strategies," *American Sociological Review* 51, no. 2 (1986): 273–87. For the cultural "building-blocks" concept, see Stephen Hart, *What Does the Lord Require? How American Christians Think about Economic Justice* (New Brunswick, N.J.: Rutgers University Press, 1996).

9. Greeley, *Catholic Myth*, 44, 46.

10. Robert Bellah, "Religion and the Shape of National Culture," *America*, 31 July 1999, 10.

11. Paul Giles, *American Catholic Arts and Fictions* (London: Cambridge University Press, 1992); Lee Lourdeaux, *Italian and Irish Filmmakers in America: Ford, Capra, Coppola, and Scorsese* (Philadelphia: Temple University Press, 1990); Richard Blake, *Afterimage: The Indelible Catholic Imagination of Six American Filmmakers* (Chicago: Loyola Press, 2000).

12. Andrew M. Greeley, *The Catholic Imagination* (Berkeley: University of California Press, 2000), 1.

13. Peter Thuesen, "The Leather-Bound Shrine in Every Home," *Books and Culture*, March–April 2000, 20.

14. For an account of evangelicalism's high view of the authority of scripture, see James D. Hunter, *American Evangelicalism: Conservative Protestantism and the Quandary of Modernity* (New Brunswick, N.J.: Rutgers University Press, 1983).

15. Colleen McDannell convincingly argues that Protestants value material culture (religious pictures, objects, and so on) as much as Roman Catholics. At the same time, McDannell points out that much of Protestant material culture consists of words (usually biblical quotations or words) made into things: see Colleen McDannell, *Material Christianity* (New Haven, Conn.: Yale University Press, 1995).

16. Gerard Manley Hopkins, "God's Grandeur," in *The Later Poetic Manuscripts of Gerard Manley Hopkins in Facsimile*, ed. Norman H. MacKenzie (New York: Garland Publishing, 1991), 96. See Greeley's summary of Tracy's theory in *Catholic Myth*, 45.

17. David Tracy, *The Analogical Imagination: Christian Theology and the Culture of Pluralism* (New York: Crossroad, 1981), 408, 415.

18. On the evangelical penchant for boundaries, see Christian Smith, *American Evangelicalism: Embattled and Thriving* (Chicago: University of Chicago Press, 1998).

19. Greeley, *Catholic Imagination*, 111.

20. Bellah, "Religion and the Shape of National Culture," 10.

21. The quote is from Smith, *American Evangelicalism*, 189. On evangelical individualism, see Dennis Hollinger, *Individualism and Social Ethics: An Evangelical Syncretism* (Lanham, Md.: University Press of America, 1983); James L. Guth et al., *The Bully Pulpit: The Politics of Protestant Clergy* (Kansas City: University Press of Kansas, 1997); Harold Bloom, *The American Religion* (New York: Simon and Schuster, 1992). On the communalism of the Catholic social ethic, see Greeley, *Catholic Myth*, 289–309.

22. William Dinges et al., "A Faith Loosely Held: The Institutional Allegiance of Young Catholics," *Commonweal*, 17 July 1998, 13–19. William J. Byron argues that social justice is an integral component of Catholic social thought in "Ten Building Blocks of Catholic Social Teaching," *America*, 31 October 1998, 10–11.

23. Guth et al., *Bully Pulpit*, 14.

24. Christian Smith, *Christian America? What Evangelicals Really Want* (Berkeley: University of California Press, 2000), 13, 7.

25. David J. O'Brien, *Public Catholicism* (Maryknoll, N.Y.: Orbis, 1996), 7.

26. Peter Steinfels, "Constraints of the Religion Reporter," *Nieman Reports* 47, no. 3 (1993): 5.

27. Mark Silk, *Unsecular Media: Making News of Religion in America* (Chicago: University of Illinois Press, 1995).

28. Tracy, *Analogical Imagination,* 415.

29. Gans, *Deciding What's News,* 42–69.

30. Tuchman, *Making News,* 23.

31. For a discussion of evangelicals as bricoleurs in the secular world, see Paul A. Bramadat, *The Church on the World's Turf: An Evangelical Christian Group at a Secular University* (New York: Oxford University Press, 2000), 147.

32. Smith, *American Evangelicalism,* 124.

33. James D. Hunter, *Culture Wars: The Struggle to Define America* (New York: Basic Books, 1992).

34. David Astor, "Cal Thomas in Select 500 Club for Columnists," *Editor and Publisher,* 8 May 1999, 44.

35. Cal Thomas, *Occupied Territory* (Brentwood, Tenn.: Wolgemuth and Hyatt, 1987).

36. Dean Ridings, review of *Occupied Territory,* by Cal Thomas, *Fundamentalist Journal,* 7 April 1988, 58.

37. Cal Thomas, "W. as Reagan III, not Bush II," *Times-Picayune,* 27 November 1999, B7; idem, "Our Lost Virtue," *Times-Picayune,* 13 May 1995, B7; idem, "Christians Suffer Discrimination Too," *Times-Picayune,* 3 May 1999, B5; idem, "The Religious Right vs. the Pagan Left," *Times-Picayune,* 16 June 1994, B7; idem, "Confronting Our Moral Decay," *Times-Picayune,* 13 December 1993, B7.

38. Idem, "Guns, Human Hands, Human Hearts," *Times-Picayune,* 27 May 1999, B7; idem, "Making Sense of the Prayer Debate," *Times-Picayune,* 25 November 1994, B7; idem, "Religious Right"; idem, "The Final Insult," *Times-Picayune,* 2 August 1995, B7; idem, "Fair Is Fair," *Times-Picayune,* 26 March 1994, B7; idem, "GOP Should Focus on Policy Issues," *Times-Picayune,* 17 May 1994, B5; idem, "Newt's Boycott," *Times-Picayune,* 13 January 1995, B7l; idem, "Apathy and Ignorance Are in Abundance in Nation Today," *Times-Picayune,* 27 November 1998, B7; idem, "Surveying the Students," *Times-Picayune,* 3 January 1995, B5; idem, "Religious Right."

39. Hunter, *Culture Wars,* 144.

40. Cal Thomas, "Clinton's Biggest Mistake So Far," *Times-Picayune,* 29 January 1993, B7. See also Hunter, *Culture Wars,* and Michael Lienesch, *Redeeming America: Piety and Politics in the New Christian Right* (Chapel Hill: University of North Carolina Press, 1993).

41. Thomas, "Religious Right."

42. Idem, "Prayer Debate."

43. Idem, "Hugh Grant, *Newsweek,* and Life," *Times-Picayune,* 17 July 1995, B7.

44. Idem, "Prayer Debate."

45. Idem, "Final Insult."

46. Idem, "Prayer Debate."

47. Idem, "Spiritual Wall?" *Times-Picayune,* 5 April 1995, B7.

48. Lienesch, *Redeeming America,* 193.

49. James D. Hunter, "Before the Shooting Begins," *Columbia Journalism Review,* July–August 1993, 29–33, Expanded Academic ASAP.

50. Gans, *Deciding What's News,* 56–60.

51. Cal Thomas, "The Moral Issues," *Times-Picayune,* 2 May 1994, B5; idem, "Crime: Still Avoiding the Cause," *Times-Picayune,* 4 August 1994, B7; idem, "Lost Virtue."

52. Thomas, "Newt's Boycott," *Times-Picayune,* 13 January 1995, B7.

53. Guth et al., *Bully Pulpit,* 14.

54. Cal Thomas, "Mr. Theologian," *Times-Picayune,* 7 October 1994, B7.

55. Gans, *Deciding What's News,* 20, 62–68.

56. Cal Thomas, "RU-486 and Soulless Technology," *Times-Picayune*, 23 May 1994, B7; idem, "Lost Virtue"; idem, "The Moral Issues," B5.

57. Ridings, review of *Occupied Territory*, 58.

58. Gans, *Deciding What's News*, 56–60.

59. Cal Thomas, "Adopted Cause," *Times-Picayune*, 26 June 1995, B5.

60. Idem, "Lost Virtue."

61. Idem, "Falwell, White, Forge a 'Redemption,'" *Times-Picayune*, 29 October 1999, B7.

62. Cal Thomas and Ed Dobson, *Blinded by Might: Can the Religious Right Save America?* (Grand Rapids, Mich.: Zondervan, 1999), 97.

63. Ibid., 181–82.

64. Ibid., 8.

65. "Limits of Politics," *Christian Century*, 17 March 1999, 299. Richard Mouw is quoted on the dust jacket of Thomas and Dobson, *Blinded by Might*.

66. James Dobson, "The New Cost of Discipleship," *Christianity Today*, 6 September 1999, 56.

67. Thomas and Dobson, *Blinded by Might*, 10.

68. Ibid., 57.

69. Ibid., 36, 88, 143.

70. Ibid., 10, 57, 191.

71. Ibid., 117.

72. Thomas, *Occupied Territory;* Cal Thomas, "In Culture Wars It's God vs. Guns," *Times-Picayune*, 23 June 1999, B7

73. E. J. Dionne, "A Shift Looms: The President Sees Consensus while Religious Leaders Disagree about the Church–State Divide," *Washington Post*, 3 October 1999, B1, LEXIS-NEXIS Academic Universe; Peter Steinfels, "Beliefs," *New York Times*, 25 June 1994, A12.

74. Peter Steinfels, "Beliefs," *New York Times*, 31 December 1993, A8; E. J. Dionne, "A Political Classic," *Washington Post*, 1 August 1997, A21; Peter Steinfels, "Beliefs," *New York Times*, 30 October 1999, A13; E. J. Dionne, "The Minnesota Compact," *Washington Post*, 11 July 1995, A17, LEXIS-NEXIS Academic Universe; Peter Steinfels, "Beliefs," *New York Times*, 6 June 1992, sec. 1, 10; E. J. Dionne, "Radical Realist," *Washington Post*, 19 January 1997, W8.

75. Steinfels, "Constraints," 5.

76. E. J. Dionne, *Why Americans Hate Politics* (New York: Simon and Schuster, 1992), 32–33.

77. Tracy, *Analogical Imagination*, 408.

78. Greeley, *Catholic Imagination*, 6.

79. Peter Steinfels, "Beliefs," *New York Times*, 18 March 1995, sec. 1, 9.

80. Peter Steinfels, "Methodists Vote to Retain Policy Condemning Homosexual Behavior," *New York Times*, 3 May 1988, A22, LEXIS-NEXIS Academic Universe.

81. Peter Steinfels, "Orthodox Priest Leads Protestant Group," *New York Times*, 19 November 1989, A30, LEXIS-NEXIS Academic Universe.

82. E. J. Dionne, "After the Brawl Was Over: Let's Stop Our Self-Righteous Infighting," *Washington Post*, 20 October 1991, C1, LEXIS-NEXIS Academic Universe.

83. Idem, "Survey of Electorate Finds Weak Political Parties and Conflicts over Change," *New York Times*, 22 August 1992, D27, LEXIS-NEXIS Academic Universe.

84. Dionne, *Why Americans Hate Politics*, 11.

85. Ibid., 14.

86. Ibid., 19.

87. Ibid., 14.

88. Idem, "After the Brawl Was Over."

89. Peter Steinfels, "Beliefs," *New York Times,*17 February 1995, A9.

90. E. J. Dionne, "America and the Catholic Church: Conflicts with Rome and within," *New York Times,* 24 December 1986, A1, LEXIS-NEXIS Academic Universe.

91. Philip Gleason, "The New Americanism in Catholic Historiography," *U.S. Catholic Historian* 11, no. 3 (1993): 16.

92. E. J. Dionne, "As Pope Confronts the Dissenters, Whose Catholicism Will Prevail?" *New York Times,* 23 December 1986, A1, LEXIS-NEXIS Academic Universe.

93. Steinfels, "Constraints," 5.

94. Peter Steinfels, "Prophet and Politician," *Generation of the Third Eye,* ed. Daniel Callahan (New York: Sheed and Ward, 1965), 220. See Mel Piehl, *Breaking Bread: The Catholic Worker and the Origin of Catholic Radicalism in America* (Philadelphia: Temple University Press, 1982), for an account of Cogley's break with the Catholic Worker movement.

95. E. J. Dionne, "A Church Misrepresented," *Washington Post,* 17 August 1993, A21.

96. On the relationship between Catholicism and American liberalism, see Philip Gleason, "American Catholics and Liberalism, 1789–1960," in *Catholicism and Liberalism: Contributions to American Public Philosophy,* ed. R. Bruce Douglass and David Hollenbach (New York: Cambridge University Press, 1994), 45–75. In *Why Americans Hate Politics,* Dionne favorably cites Daniel Bell, *The End of Ideology* (Glencoe, Ill.: Free Press, 1965); Arthur Schlesinger, Jr., *The Vital Center: The Politics of Freedom* (New Brunswick, N.J.: Transaction Publishers, 1997); and Reinhold Niebuhr, *Children of Light and the Children of Darkness* (New York: Prentice-Hall, 1974).

97. Godfrey Hodgson, *America in Our Time: From World War II to Nixon* (New York: Random House, 1976), 93. On the affinities between ideological traditions and tropes, see Hayden White, *Metahistory: The Historical Imagination in Nineteenth-Century Europe* (Baltimore: Johns Hopkins University Press, 1975); Robert Nisbet, *Social Change and History: Aspects of the Western Theory of Development* (New York: Oxford University Press, 1969).

98. Gans, *Deciding What's News,* 51; Tuchman, "Objectivity as Strategic Ritual."

99. John McGreevy, "Thinking on One's Own: Catholicism in the American Intellectual Imagination, 1928–1960," *Journal of American History* 84, no. 1 (1997): 97–132.

100. Jeffrey Alexander, "Citizen and Enemy as Symbolic Classification: On the Polarizing Discourse of Civil Society," in *Cultivating Differences: Symbolic Boundaries and the Making of Inequality,* ed. Michele Lamont and Marcel Fournier (Chicago: University of Chicago Press, 1992), 289–308.

101. Paul Blanshard, *American Freedom and Catholic Power* (Boston: Beacon Press, 1949). On liberal Catholic reactions to Blanshard, see Gleason, "American Catholics and Liberalism," 45–75.

102. An example of *Commonweal*'s emphasis on the "neutral grays" can be found in John Kane, "Catholic Separatism," in *Catholicism in America,* ed. William Clancy (New York: Harcourt, Brace, and Company, 1954), 47–57.

103. E. J. Dionne, "Response," in *Disciples and Democracy,* ed. Michael Cromartie (Grand Rapids, Mich.: Eerdmans, 1994), 19.

104. Melissa Healy, "New Movement Plots More Civil Way of Living," *Los Angeles Times,* 15 December 1996, A1, LEXIS-NEXIS Academic Universe. See also Bellah et al., *Habits of the Heart;* Amitai Etzioni, *The Spirit of Community: The Reinvention of American Society* (New York: Simon and Schuster, 1994).

105. Alan Wolfe, *Whose Keeper? Social Science and Moral Obligation* (Berkeley: University of California Press, 1991).

106. Thomas Landy, "A Sociology of Communitarianism" (unpublished paper, Center for Religion, Ethics, and Culture, College of the Holy Cross, Worcester, Mass., 1996).

107. Landy points out that the leading Protestant communitarian (Bellah) is in the most Catholic of Protestant denominations, the Episcopal church.

108. Landy, "Sociology of Communitarianism," 8, 23; Bellah, "Religion and the Shape of National Culture," 9.

109. Kenneth Woodward, "The American Self," review of *Habits of the Heart*, by Robert Bellah et al., *Newsweek*, 29 April 1985, 70.

110. E. J. Dionne, "The Labeling Game," *Washington Post*, 11 August 1996, W13, LEXIS-NEXIS Academic Universe.

111. Brookings Institution, "Sacred Places, Civic Purposes," Web page, available at <http://www.brookings.org/gs/projects/sacredplaces.htm>. Dionne was also co-director of the Pew Forum on Religion and Public Life: see <http://www.pewforum.org>.

112. E. J. Dionne, "Can Government Nurture Civic Life?" *Brookings Review*, fall 1996, 3; E. J. Dionne, ed., *Community Works: The Revival of Civil Society in America* (Washington, D.C.: Brookings Institution, 1998); E. J. Dionne and John DiIulio, eds., *What's God Got to Do with the American Experiment? Essays on Religion and Politics* (Washington, D.C.: Brookings Institution, 2000).

113. E. J. Dionne, "Why Americans Hate Politics: A Reprise," *Brookings Review*, winter 2000, 8–11.

114. Idem, "Can Government Nurture Civic Life?" 3.

115. Kenneth Woodward, "What Is Virtue?" *Newsweek*, 13 June 1994, 38–39; idem, "Should the President Be Forgiven?" *Newsweek*, 23 November 1998, 70.

116. Idem, "The New Narcissism," *Newsweek*, 30 January 1978, 72.

117. Idem, "American Self," 70.

118. Idem, "What Is Virtue?" 39.

119. Ibid.

120. Andrew M. Greeley, *The American Catholic: A Social Portrait* (New York: Basic Books, 1977), 263.

121. Ibid.

122. Don Wycliff, "Going Under, Getting Ahead," review of *Families in Peril: An Agenda for Social Change*, by Marian Wright Edelman, *New York Times Book Review*, 7 June 1987, 12.

123. For an account of the influence of the Catholic principle of subsidiarity on George W. Bush's campaign themes, see Alison Mitchell, "Bush Draws Campaign Theme from More Than Heart," *New York Times*, 12 June, 2000, A1, LEXIS-NEXIS Academic Universe. Although subsidiarity is not mentioned by name, the article describes Bush adviser John DiIulio's conviction that the federal government should step in "only when problems become too big for other institutions." See chap. 4 for more on DiIulio's appropriation of the Catholic social ethic.

124. Garry Wills, *Bare Ruined Choirs: Doubt, Prophecy, and Radical Religion* (New York: Doubleday, 1972), 17.

125. Kenneth Woodward, *Making Saints: How the Catholic Church Determines Who Becomes a Saint, Who Doesn't, and Why* (New York: Simon and Schuster, 1990), 404.

126. Arnold Sparr, *To Promote, Defend, and Redeem: The Catholic Literary Revival and the Cultural Transformation of American Catholicism, 1920–1960* (New York: Greenwood Press, 1990), 124, 125, 131.

127. Gans, *Deciding What's News*, 50–51.

128. Rupert Wilkinson, *The Pursuit of American Character* (New York: Harper and Row, 1988). The classic list of core American values (including individualism, achievement, success, material comfort, and freedom) can be found in Robin Williams, *American Society: A Sociological Interpretation* (New York: Knopf, 1965).

129. McGreevy, "Thinking on One's Own," 130–31.

130. Bellah et al., *Habits of the Heart,* 27.

131. McGreevy, "Thinking on One's Own," 130–31. Robert Putnam, *Bowling Alone: The Collapse and Revival of American Community* (New York: Touchstone, 2001). On 11 June 2002, the sales rank on Amazon.com for *Bowling Alone* was very high, at 1,069. By 1995, *Habits of the Heart* had sold more than 400,000 copies, according to Herbert Gans, "Sociology's Best-sellers," *Contemporary Sociology* 26, no. 2 (1997): 134. This is more than all but a few sociology titles in the postwar era.

132. Fouhy, as quoted in Mike Hoyt, "Are You Now or Will You Ever Be, a Civic Journalist?" *Columbia Journalism Review,* September–October 1995, 29.

133. "Movement Manifestos," *Columbia Journalism Review,* September–October 1995, 32.

134. Art Charity, "Reluctant Sea Change: Resources Abound for Journalists Seeking Information about Public Journalism's Role," *The Quill,* January–February 1996, 23.

135. Hoyt, "Are You Now," 27–33.

136. In an insightful essay, Mark Massa argues that the "analogical language of mediation, community, and sacrament really does represent a different set of cultural emphases than the dialectical language of direct experience, individualism, and communal restraint." He argues that the United States "was, and to some extent still is, a culture powerfully shaped by the 'dialectical imagination' ": see Mark Massa, "The New and Old Anti-Catholicism and the Analogical Imagination," *Theological Studies* 62, no. 3 (2001): 567–68. See Rosen, *What Are Journalists For?* for a discussion of the influence of civic republicanism on public journalism.

137. McCarthy writes occasionally for the *Post,* the *Progressive,* and other publications. Pippert directs the Washington program at the University of Missouri School of Journalism.

138. Matthew Rothschild, "Parish of Heretics," *Progressive,* March 1997, 4.

139. Nancy L. Roberts, *Dorothy Day and the Catholic Worker* (Albany: State University of New York Press, 1984), 39. See also Piehl, *Breaking Bread.*

140. Colman McCarthy, "The Bishop of Peoria," *Washington Post,* 25 February 1995, A17.

141. Idem, *Inner Companions* (New York: Acropolis Books, 1975), 167.

142. Idem, "Victims against Violence," *Washington Post,* 25 April 1992, A27.

143. Idem, "Perspective; Forgiveness: Human and Practical," *Washington Post,* 20 January 1992, B5.

144. Tuchman, *Making News,* 23; Gans, *Deciding What's News,* 42–69.

145. Colman McCarthy, "The Catholic Worker's Long Mission," *Washington Post,* 17 April 1993, A23; idem, *Inner Companions,* 184–90, 88–91, 211–16; idem, "A Universal Sort of Holiday," *Washington Post,* 25 December 1992, A19; idem, "Third World Bank That Lends a Hand," *Washington Post,* 2 November 1986, G2; idem, "The Mediator Is the Message," *Washington Post,* 2 September 1990, F6; idem, "On Peace Education," *Washington Post,* 19 June 1983, H2; idem, "Facing the Facts of Contra Funds Abuse," *Washington Post,* 6 July 1986, G2; idem, "We Need a People's Anthem," *Washington Post,* 16 December 1989, A31.

146. David Astor, "Less Op-Ed Variety as McCarthy Let Go," *Editor and Publisher,* 8 February 1997, 30.

147. Piehl, *Breaking Bread,* 119; Roberts, *Dorothy Day,* 8.

148. McCarthy, "Victims against Violence," A27.

149. Colman McCarthy, "The Defense Conversion That Isn't," *Washington Post,* 9 March 1993, C10.

150. Idem, "Nationalism, Narcissism, and the Pledge," *Washington Post,* 18 September 1988, F2.

151. Idem, "Everyday Violence as Deadly as Killeen's," *Washington Post,* 5 November 1991, C9. Michael Baxter, "Reintroducing Virgil Michel: Towards a Counter-Tradition of Catholic Social Ethics in the United States," *Communio* 24 (1997): 499–528. Colman McCarthy, "Praying or Braying: Pro-War Means Anti-Life," *Washington Post,* 3 March 1991, F6; idem, "Flag-Waving And Foolhardiness," *Washington Post,* 7 April 1991, F2; idem, "Defense Conversion."

152. Colman McCarthy, "Countering Violence at Home," *Washington Post,* 23 July 1991, D13; Tracy, *Analogical Imagination,* 417.

153. See Hart, *What Does the Lord Require?* for evidence of evangelical support for economic justice.

154. Wesley G. Pippert, "Furor over Food Stamps," United Press International, 17 March 1981, evening cycle, LEXIS-NEXIS Academic Universe.

155. Idem, "Former Officials Protest End of VISTA," United Press International, 23 March 1982, morning cycle, LEXIS-NEXIS Academic Universe.

156. Idem, *An Ethic of News: A Reporter's Search for Truth* (Washington, D.C.: Georgetown University Press, 1989), 48.

157. Idem, "Washington Window: Reagan and the Clergy Disagree," United Press International, 28 March 1983, evening cycle, LEXIS-NEXIS Academic Universe.

158. Ibid.; Smith, *American Evangelicalism,* 187.

159. Robert Booth Fowler, *A New Engagement: Evangelical Political Thought, 1966–1976* (Grand Rapids, Mich.: Eerdmans, 1982), 96.

160. Senator Hatfield's name is mentioned in seventy of Pippert's UPI stories (5 percent of those available on LEXIS-NEXIS Academic Universe in the mid-1990s).

161. Wesley G. Pippert, "Social Programs on Fiscal Tightrope," United Press International, 14 February 1981, morning cycle, LEXIS-NEXIS Academic Universe.

162. Idem, United Press International, 19 December 1991, morning cycle, LEXIS-NEXIS Academic Universe.

163. Idem, *Memo for 1976: Some Political Options* (Downers Grove, Ill.: InterVarsity Press, 1974), 13.

164. Gans, *Deciding What's News,* 42–69.

165. Astor, "Less Op-Ed Variety."

166. Matthew Rothschild, "Parish of Heretics: *Washington Post* Fires Pacifist Columnist Colman McCarthy, *Progressive,* March 1997, 4.

167. Lisa Granatstein, "News Still Sells on Newsstands," *Mediaweek,* 21 February 2000, 59, Infotrac, Expanded Academic ASAP.

168. Mark Noll, *Between Faith and Criticism: Evangelicals, Scholarship and the Bible in America* (San Francisco: Harper and Row, 1986), 143

169. Kathleen C. Boone, *The Bible Tells Them So: The Discourse of Protestant Fundamentalism* (Albany: State University of New York Press, 1989), 12.

170. George A. Lindbeck, *The Nature of Doctrine: Religion and Theology in a Postliberal Age* (Philadelphia: Westminster, 1984), 16.

171. Kenneth Woodward, *The Book of Miracles* (New York: Simon and Schuster, 2000), 26.

172. Jeffery L. Sheler, *Is the Bible True? How Modern Debates and Discoveries Affirm the Essence of the Scriptures* (San Francisco: Harper San Francisco, 1999).

173. Idem, "Mysteries of the Bible," *U.S. News and World Report,* 17 April 1995, 60, LEXIS-NEXIS Academic Universe; idem, "Who Was Jesus?" *U.S. News and World Report,* 20 December 1993, 58–66; idem, "The Bible's Last Secrets," *U.S. News and World Report,*

7 October 1991, 64–69; idem, "In Search of Jesus," *U.S. News and World Report,* 8 April 1996, 46–53; idem, "A Gift to the Magi, Explained," *U.S. News and World Report,* 20 December 1999, 58, LEXIS-NEXIS Academic Universe; idem, "King David: Not the Man He Used to Be?" *U.S. News and World Report,* 19 March 2001, 45.

174. Noll, *Between Faith and Criticism,* 146.

175. George Marsden, *Fundamentalism and American Culture: The Shaping of Twentieth-Century Evangelicalism, 1870–1925* (New York: Oxford University Press, 1980), 20.

176. Sheler, *Is the Bible True?* 2.

177. Noll argues that evangelical epistemology is closer to "nineteenth-century positivism" than to postmodernism: see Noll, *Between Faith and Criticism,* 146–47.

178. Sheler, "Who Was Jesus?"; idem, *Is the Bible True?;* idem, "Mysteries of the Bible"; idem, "Why Did He Die?" *U.S. News and World Report,* 24 April 2000, 50–55; idem, "The Arrest and Trial," *U.S. News and World Report,* 16 April 1990, 49; idem, "Cutting Loose the Holy Canon," *U.S. News and World Report,* 8 November 1993, 75; idem, "Who Was Jesus?"; idem, "Bob Funk's Radical Reformation Roadshow," *U.S. News and World Report,* 4 August 1997, 55–56.

179. Idem, *Is The Bible True?* 13.

180. Noll, *Between Faith and Criticism,* 142.

181. Sheler, "In Search of Jesus"; idem, "The First Noel," *U.S. News and World Report,* 21 December 1992, 78–89; idem, "Mysteries of the Bible." Dever is a former fundamentalist who now describes himself as a "secular humanist historian." See Gustav Niebuhr's interview with Dever in "Q&A: Balancing Biblical Faith and Archaeological Facts," *New York Times,* 4 August 2001, B9.

182. Sheler, "The First Noel," 80.

183. Idem, "Who Was Jesus?" 65.

184. Idem, "Mysteries of the Bible."

185. Noll, *Between Faith and Criticism,* 158.

186. Wayne Jackson, "Is the Bible True?" review of *Is the Bible True? How Modern Debates and Discoveries Affirm the Essence of the Scriptures,* by Jeffery L. Sheler, *Christian Courier Online,* 13 December 1999, available on-line at <http://www.christiancourier.com/penpoints/bibletruth.htm>; "Is the Bible True? How Modern Debates and Discoveries Affirm the Essence of the Scripture," review of *Is the Bible True?* by Jeffery L. Sheler, *Kirkus Reviews,* 15 October 1999, Infotrac, Expanded Academic ASAP.

187. Jeff Cohen, "Media Coverage of Religion: An Overview," FAIR, December 1999, available on-line at <http://www.fair.org/articles/media-religion.html>.

188. The *Review of Biblical Literature* is an official publication of the Society of Biblical Literature, the leading professional association for scripture scholars in the United States. See Bob Becking, review of *Is the Bible True? How Modern Debates and Discoveries Affirm the Essence of the Scriptures,* by Jeffery L. Sheler, *Review of Biblical Literature,* 5 June 2000, available on-line at <http://www.bookreviews.org/reviews/0060675411.html>. See also Review of *Is the Bible True? How Modern Debates and Discoveries Affirm the Essence of the Scriptures,* by Jeffery L. Sheler, *Publisher's Weekly,* 25 October 1999, 71.

189. George Marsden, *The Outrageous Idea of Christian Scholarship* (New York: Oxford University Press, 1997), 59.

190. Robert Bellah, "Religion and the Shape of National Culture," 10.

191. Greeley, *Catholic Myth,* 45.

192. Gans, *Deciding What's News,* 125.

193. I am indebted to Richard Blake's *AfterImage* for the term "theological footprints."

194. Blake, *AfterImage;* Giles, *American Catholic Arts and Fictions;* Lourdeaux, *Italian and Irish Filmmakers.*

Chapter 6. Religious Ways of Knowing

1. Steven J. Keillor, *This Rebellious House: American History and the Truth of Christianity* (Downers Grove, Ill.: InterVarsity Press, 1996), 11.

2. John Wilson, "Against the American Grain: A Provocative Christian Reading of American History, from Columbus to Clinton," review of *This Rebellious House: American History and the Truth of Christianity,* by Steven J. Keillor, *Christianity Today,* 11 November 1996, 59.

3. Thomas F. Gieryn, *The Cultural Boundaries of Science: Credibility on the Line* (Chicago: University of Chicago Press, 1999), 16.

4. Douglas Sloan, *Faith and Knowledge: Mainline Protestantism and American Higher Education* (Louisville, Ken.: Westminster John Knox, 1994), viii.

5. Burke, as quoted in Joseph R. Gusfield, "Introduction," in Kenneth Burke, *On Symbols and Society,* ed. Joseph R. Gusfield (Chicago: University of Chicago Press, 1989), 16.

6. Huston Smith, *Why Religion Matters: The Fate of the Human Spirit in an Age of Disbelief* (New York: HarperCollins, 2001), 97. See also George Marsden, "Christianity and the Rules of the Academic Game," in *Religious Advocacy and American History,* ed. Bruce Kuklick and D. G. Hart (Grand Rapids, Mich.: Eerdmans, 1997), 3–27.

7. Julie Reuben, *The Making of the Modern University: Intellectual Transformation and the Marginalization of Morality* (Chicago: University of Chicago Press, 1996).

8. Robert Bellah, Richard Madsen, William Sullivan, Ann Swidler, and Steven Tipton, *The Good Society* (New York: Random House, 1991), 163. See also Alan Wolfe, "Moral Inquiry in Social Science," in *The Nature of Moral Inquiry in the Social Sciences: Occasional Papers of the Erasmus Institute* (Notre Dame, Ind.: Erasmus Institute, 1999), 1–20.

9. Karl W. Giberson and Donald A. Yerxa, "Providence and the Christian Scholar," *Journal of Interdisciplinary History* (September 1999): 123, Infotrac, Expanded Academic ASAP.

10. Bruce Kuklick, "On Critical History," in Kuklick and Hart, *Religious Advocacy,* 58–59. For an insightful analysis of Kuklick's critique of evangelical historiography, see Jonathan Tucker Boyd, "If We Ever Needed the Lord Before," *Books and Culture,* May/June 1998, available on-line at <http://www.christianitytoday.com/bc/9b3/9b3040.html>.

11. Kuklick, "On Critical History," 58.

12. Ibid., 59. Leo Ribuffo, "Afterword: Cultural Shouting Matches and the Academic Study of American Religious History," in Kuklick and Hart, *Religious Advocacy,* 227.

13. Alan Wolfe, "The Revival of Moral Inquiry in the Social Sciences," *Chronicle of Higher Education,* 3 September 1999, B4.

14. David Tracy, *The Analogical Imagination: Christian Theology and the Culture of Pluralism* (New York: Crossroad, 1981); Andrew M. Greeley, *The Catholic Imagination* (Berkeley: University of California Press, 2000).

15. See Robert Bellah, "Religion and the Shape of National Culture," *America,* 31 July 1999, 9.

16. Kenneth Burke, "Language as Action: Terministic Screens," in *On Symbols and Society,* 115, 122.

17. Mark Noll, "The Potential of Missiology for the Crises of History," in Bruce Kuklick and D. G. Hart, *History and the Christian Historian* (Grand Rapids, Mich.: Eerdmans, 1998), 111.

18. Margaret O'Brien Steinfels, "The Catholic Intellectual Tradition," in *Occasional Papers* (Washington, D.C.: Association of Catholic Colleges and Universities, 1995), available on-line at <http://www.fordham.edu/thirdagectr/mstein.htm>.

19. Bellah et al., *The Good Society,* 162.

20. Donald MacKay, *The Clockwork Image: A Christian Perspective on Science* (Leicester, U.K.: InterVarsity Press, 1974).

21. Kenneth Burke, "Money as a Substitute for God," in *On Symbols and Society,* 161.

22. Leonard Sweet, "Wise as Serpents, Innocent as Doves: The New Evangelical Historiography," *Journal of the American Academy of Religion* 56, no. 3 (1988): 397–416.

23. Robert Bellah, Richard Madsen, William M. Sullivan, Ann Swidler, and Steven M. Tipton, *Habits of the Heart: Individualism and Commitment in American Life* (Berkeley: University of California Press, 1985); Peter L. Berger, *A Rumor of Angels: Modern Society and the Rediscovery of the Supernatural* (New York: Anchor, 1990); Amitai Etzioni, *The Moral Dimension: Towards a New Economics* (New York: Free Press, 1990); Alan Wolfe, *The Human Difference: Animals, Computers, and the Necessity of Social Science* (Berkeley: University of California Press, 1993).

24. The term "methodological atheism" was popularized by Peter L. Berger in *The Sacred Canopy: Elements of a Sociological Theory of Religion* (New York: Anchor Books, 1969), 180. For an example of non-reductionist evangelical sociology, see the description of Christian Smith's project "Morality, Culture, and the Power of Religious Faith: Explaining the Effect of Religion in Social Life," funded by Pew Charitable Trusts, at <http://www.nd.edu/~csp/sociology.html>. My thinking on religion and reductionism was shaped by my participation in a January 2001 meeting of this project in Fort Lauderdale, Florida.

25. Rodney Stark and Roger Finke, *Acts of Faith: Explaining the Human Side of Religion* (Berkeley: University of California Press, 2000), 15.

26. The same survey found that Catholicism and evangelicalism were by far the most popular topics of research, pursued by almost 40 percent of respondents, while evangelical and Catholic authors (scholars such as Jay Dolan, Nathan Hatch, George Marsden, Mark Noll, and Harry Stout) dominated the list of most influential books and articles. See Harry S. Stout and Robert M. Taylor, Jr., "Studies of Religion in American Society: The State of the Art," in *New Directions in American Religious History,* ed. Harry S. Stout and D. G. Hart (New York: Oxford University Press, 1997), 15, 21.

27. Sweet, "Wise as Serpents," 397.

28. Douglas Sweeney, "Taking a Shot at Redemption: A Lutheran Considers the Calvin College School of Historiography," *Books and Culture,* May–June 1998, 43.

29. Sweeney, "Taking a Shot," 43.

30. Jon Butler, "Born-Again America? A Critique of the New 'Evangelical Thesis' in Recent American Historiography," unpublished paper given at the Organization of American Historians meetings, spring 1991. Butler's paper is quoted in Stout and Taylor, "Studies of Religion," 19.

31. Nathan Hatch, *The Democratization of American Christianity* (New Haven, Conn.: Yale University Press, 1989).

32. James Turner, "Something to Be Reckoned with: The Evangelical Mind Reawakens," *Commonweal,* 15 January 1999, 12.

33. George Marsden, *Fundamentalism and American Culture: The Shaping of Twentieth-Century Evangelicalism, 1870–1925* (New York: Oxford University Press, 1980), 199–228.

34. Stout and Taylor, "Studies of Religion," 21.

35. Ibid., 46.

36. George Marsden, *The Soul of the American University: From Protestant Establishment to Established Nonbelief* (New York: Oxford University Press, 1994), 429–444; idem, *Fundamentalism and American Culture,* 229–30.

37. Ted Jelen, "Research in Religion and Mass Political Behavior in the United States: Looking Both Ways after Two Decades of Scholarship," *American Politics Quarterly* 26, no. 1 (1998): 110–35, Infotrac, Expanded Academic ASAP.

38. David C. Leege and Lyman A. Kellstedt, eds., *Rediscovering the Religious Factor in American Politics* (Armonk, N.Y.: M. E. Sharpe, 1993).

39. Expanded Academic Index, 1980–2001.

40. LEXIS-NEXIS Academic Universe.

41. Ronald Wells, ed., *History and the Christian Historian* (Grand Rapids, Mich.: Eerdmans, 1998); George Marsden, *The Outrageous Idea of Christian Scholarship* (New York: Oxford University Press, 1997).

42. David C. Leege, Joel A. Lieske, and Kenneth D. Wald, "Toward Cultural Theories of American Political Behavior: Religion, Ethnicity and Race, and Class Outlook," in *Political Science: Looking to the Future*, ed. William Crotty (Evanston, Ill.: Northwestern University Press, 1991), 195; Jelen, "Research in Religion," 110–35.

43. Meredith Ramsey, "Redeeming the City: Exploring the Relationship between Church and Metropolis," *Urban Affairs Review* 33, no. 5 (1998): 596.

44. Leege et al., "Toward Cultural Theories," 193–238. Although such cultural theories are becoming widespread throughout the social sciences, they have been especially attractive to people of faith. Leege is a practicing Lutheran, and Wald has been involved in Reconstructionist Judaism.

45. Lyman A. Kellstedt, John C. Green, James L. Guth, and Corwin E. Smidt, "It's the Culture, Stupid! 1992 and Our Political Future," *First Things*, April 1994, 29.

46. Jelen, "Research in Religion," 110–35.

47. The quote is from George Lindbeck, *The Nature of Doctrine: Religion and Theology in a Postliberal Age* (Philadelphia: Westminster Press, 1984), 34; it is Lindbeck's definition of what is means to "become religious." Kellstedt, Guth, Green, and Smidt are skilled in the "cultural-linguistic" system of evangelical Protestantism.

48. Jelen, "Research in Religion," 110–35.

49. Andrew M. Greeley, *Religion: A Secular Theory* (New York: Free Press, 1982); idem, *The Religious Imagination* (Los Angeles: Sadlier, 1981); idem, *Religion as Poetry* (New Brunswick, N.J.: Transaction Publishers, 1995), 50.

50. Idem, *Confessions of a Parish Priest: An Autobiography* (New York: Pocket Books, 1987), 246.

51. Idem, *Religion*, 15, 79.

52. Ibid., 50.

53. Burke, "Language as Action," 114–25.

54. Greeley, *Religion*, 15.

55. Ibid., 23.

56. Tracy, as quoted in ibid., 24.

57. Ibid., 8.

58. Idem, *Confessions*, 248.

59. Idem, *Religious Imagination*, 8.

60. Idem, *Religion*, 78–80.

61. Idem, *Religious Imagination*, 17.

62. Ibid., 6.

63. Ibid.

64. Idem, "The Paranormal Is Normal: A Sociologist Looks at Parapsychology," in *The Sociology of Andrew M. Greeley* (Atlanta: Scholars Press, 1994), 599.

65. Idem, "Theology and Sociology: On Validating David Tracy," *Journal of the American Academy of Religion* 59, no. 4 (1991): 643–53; idem, "Protestant and Catholic: Is the Analogical Imagination Extinct?" *American Sociological Review* 54, no. 4 (1989):

485–503; idem, *Religion;* idem, *The Catholic Myth: The Beliefs and Behaviors of American Catholics* (New York: Doubleday, 1990); idem, *Catholic Imagination;* idem, *Religion as Poetry.*

66. Leege and Kellstedt, *Rediscovering the Religious Factor.*

67. Noll, "The Potential of Missiology," 111.

68. Berger, *Rumor of Angels,* 179–80.

69. Hayden White, *The Content of the Form* (Baltimore: Johns Hopkins University Press, 1987), ix.

70. Burke, as quoted in Richard Reinitz, *Irony and Consciousness: American Historiography and Reinhold Niebuhr's Vision* (Lewisburg, Penn.: Bucknell University Press, 1980), 19; Hayden White, *Metahistory: The Historical Imagination in Nineteenth-Century Europe* (Baltimore: Johns Hopkins University Press, 1975), 9.

71. For a sophisticated exploration of the use of irony in American historiography, see Reinitz, *Irony and Consciousness,* 19. See also Martin Marty, "Irony (Fig.) and (Lit.) in Modern American Religion," *Journal of the American Academy of Religion* 53, no. 2 (1985): 187–99. For the classic analysis of tropes and historical writing, see White, *Metahistory.* On the use of tropes and narrative forms in science and social science, see Joseph Gusfield, "The Literary Rhetoric of Science: Comedy and Pathos in Drunk Driver Research," *American Sociological Review* 41, no. 1 (1976): 16–34; Albert Hunter, ed., *The Rhetoric of Social Research: Understood and Believed,* ed. Albert Hunter (New Brunswick, N.J.: Rutgers University Press, 1990); John S. Nelson, Allan Megill, and Donald M. McCloskey, eds., *The Rhetoric of the Human Sciences* (Madison: University of Wisconsin Press, 1987).

72. Reinhold Niebuhr, *The Irony of American History* (New York: Charles Scribner's Sons, 1952), 155.

73. Reinitz, *Irony and Consciousness,* 94.

74. Ibid., 13.

75. For more on the infatuation of secular scholars with Niebuhr, see Arthur Schlesinger, Jr., "The Thirteen Books You Must Read to Understand America: Schlesinger's Syllabus," *American Heritage,* February–March 1998, 30–36; Sean Wilentz, "The Vital Centrist," *New Republic,* 25 December 2000, 23; James Nuechterlein, "Sin, Theodicy, and Politics," *First Things,* November 1998, 7–8.

76. White, *Metahistory,* x, 7–9.

77. Mark Noll, "Professing History, Interview with Professor Mark Noll," *Lucas: An Evangelical History Review* 13 (June 1992): 96.

78. Andrew M. Greeley, *Confessions of a Parish Priest* (New York: Pocket Books, 1987), 21.

79. C. Marcille Frederick, "Doing Justice in History: Using Narrative Frames Responsibly," in *History and the Christian Historian,* ed. Ronald Wells (Grand Rapids, Mich.: Eerdmans, 1998), 220–34. On the evangelical discovery of postmodern narrative theory, see Charlotte Allen, "Is Deconstruction the Last Best Hope of Evangelical Christianity?" *Lingua Franca,* December–January 2000, 47–59; Michael Baxter, "Writing History in a World without Ends: A Critique of Three Histories of Catholicism in the United States," unpublished paper presented at the Religion and Culture Workshop of the Center for the Study of American Religion, Princeton University, Princeton, N.J., spring 1996. Baxter's paper was subsequently published as "Writing History in a World without Ends: An Evangelical Catholic Critique of United States Catholic History," *Pro Ecclesia* 5 (fall 1996): 440–69.

80. For a critical analysis of the "standard plot line" of American Catholicism, see Baxter, "Writing History." In his dissertation, "In Service to the Nation: A Critical Analysis of the Formation of the Americanist Tradition in Catholic Social Ethics"

(Ph.D. diss., Duke University, Durham, N.C., 1996), Baxter differentiates between the comic drama of the Gospel narrative (which he affirms) and the comic drama of Catholic Americanists (which he rejects). In this chapter, I discuss the presence of the latter story line in the works of Dolan and Greeley.

81. Nuechterlein links Niebuhr's sober view of human nature to the Augustinian tradition in "Sin, Theodicy, and Politics," 7–8. For a discussion of "Lutheran irony," see Mark Noll, "The Lutheran Difference," *First Things,* February 1992, 31–40. See also Jean Bethke Elshtain, "God and Man in the Oval Office; From the Eye of the Storm: A Pastor to the President Speaks Out," *New Republic,* 22 March 1999, 37. For an assessment of the contemporary relevance of Augustine, see idem, *Augustine and the Limits of Politics* (Notre Dame, Ind.: University of Notre Dame Press, 1995).

82. For an overview of the analogical and dialectical imaginations, see Tracy, *Analogical Imagination.*

83. Regis Duffy, *An American Emmaus: Faith and Sacrament in the American Culture* (New York: Crossroad, 1995), 31.

84. Reinitz, *Irony and Consciousness,* 94.

85. Marsden, *Outrageous Idea,* 97; Noll, "Lutheran Difference," 31–40.

86. The Lutheran ethicist Jean Bethke Elshtain's discussion of Lutheran irony reminds us that the evangelical historians are not alone in their appreciation of theological irony. The first volume of the history of twentieth-century American religion by Martin Marty, also a Lutheran, is *Modern American Religion: The Irony of It All, 1893–1919* (Chicago: University of Chicago Press, 1986). Marty reflects on the role of irony in historical interpretation in "Irony (Fig.) and (Lit.)," 187–99.

87. Elshtain, "God and Man," 37.

88. Mark A. Noll, Nathan O. Hatch, and George M. Marsden, *The Search for Christian America* (Westchester, Ill.: Crossway Books), 1983, 17.

89. D. C. Muecke, *The Compass of Irony* (London: Methuen, 1969), 102.

90. Marsden, *Soul of the American University,* 8, 5.

91. Reinitz, *Irony and Consciousness;* Niebuhr, *Irony of American History;* Marsden, *Fundamentalism and American Culture,* v, 230.

92. Mark Noll, *A History of Christianity in the United States and Canada* (Grand Rapids, Mich.: Eerdmans, 1992), 420, 553.

93. Niebuhr, *Irony of American History,* 155.

94. Marsden, *Soul of the American University,* 93.

95. Mark Noll, *Princeton and the Republic, 1768–1822: The Search for a Christian Enlightenment in the Era of Samuel Stanhope Smith* (Princeton, N.J.: Princeton University Press, 1989), 10.

96. Nathan Hatch, *The Democratization of American Christianity* (New Haven, Conn.: Yale University Press, 1989), 16.

97. Noll, *Princeton and the Republic,* 298.

98. Idem, *History of Christianity,* 552.

99. Noll et al., *Search for Christian America,* 17.

100. Noll, *History of Christianity,* 552.

101. Marsden, *Outrageous Idea,* 98.

102. Baxter, "Writing History," 2.

103. William Portier "Americanism and Inculturation, 1899–1999," *Communio* 27 (spring 2000): 141.

104. Andrew M. Greeley, *God in Popular Culture* (Chicago: Thomas More Press, 1988), 95, 113.

105. Northrop Frye, *Anatomy of Criticism: Four Essays* (Princeton, N.J.: Princeton University Press, 1957), 43, 163–64.

106. Jay Dolan, *The American Catholic Experience: A History from Colonial Times to the Present* (New York: Doubleday, 1985); Andrew M. Greeley, *The Catholic Experience: An Interpretation of the History of American Catholicism* (New York: Doubleday, 1967).

107. Dolan, *American Catholic Experience*, 110.

108. Ibid., 453–454.

109. Idem, "American Catholicism and Modernity," *CrossCurrents*, summer 1981, 151.

110. Ibid., 157–58.

111. Idem, *American Catholic Experience*, 319.

112. Idem, "American Catholicism and Modernity," 161.

113. Idem, *American Catholic Experience*, 407.

114. Although he writes as a theologian, McCann has been strongly influenced by American Catholic historiography.

115. Dennis McCann, *New Experiment in Democracy: The Challenge for American Catholicism* (Kansas City, Kans.: Sheed and Ward, 1987), 5.

116. Martin Marty, "Locating Jay Dolan," *U.S. Catholic Historian* 19, no. 1 (2001): 102.

117. Greeley, *God and Popular Culture*, 112.

118. Baxter, "Writing History," 2–3.

119. Philip Gleason, "The New Americanism in Catholic Historiography," *U.S. Catholic Historian* 11, no. 3 (1993): 16.

120. Dolan, *American Catholic Experience*, 9.

121. Philip Gleason, *Contending with Modernity: Catholic Higher Education in the Twentieth Century* (New York: Oxford University Press, 1995); Michael Baxter, "In Service to the Nation: A Critical Analysis of the Formation of the Americanist Tradition in Catholic Social Ethics" (Ph.D. diss., Duke University, Durham, N.C., 1996).

122. William Portier, "Catholics in the Mainstream," review of *American Catholicism*, by Mark Massa, *CrossCurrents*, winter 1999, 568; Mark Massa, *Catholics and American Culture: Fulton Sheen, Dorothy Day, and the Notre Dame Football Team* (New York: Crossroad, 1999), 14.

123. Baxter, "Writing History," 22.

124. R. Scott Appleby, "The Triumph of Americanism: Common Ground for Catholics in the Twentieth Century," in *Being Right: Conservative Catholics in America*, ed. Mary Jo Weaver and R. Scott Appleby (Bloomington: Indiana University Press, 1995), 37–62.

125. Peter Steinfels writes persuasively of a "crisis of irony" in American liberal Catholicism, arguing that "somewhere in the passage from 1968 to 1978, in the years of Pope Paul VI after Humanae Vitae and of Richard Nixon before and after Watergate, and somewhere in the passage from liberal Catholicism to the Catholic left, irony seemed to disappear": see Peter Steinfels, "Reinventing Liberal Catholicism: Between Powerful Enemies and Dubious Allies," *Commonweal*, 19 November 1999, 30.

126. Greeley, *Catholic Experience*, 19.

127. Duffy, *American Emmaus*, 31–32.

128. John Milbank, *Theology and Social Theory: Beyond Secular Reason* (Oxford: Blackwell, 1990), 3. On "meta-theory," see George Ritzer, "The Current Status of Sociological Theory: The New Syntheses," in *Frontiers of Social Theory: The New Syntheses*, ed. George Ritzer (New York: Columbia University Press, 1990), 1–30.

129. The expression "concealed affinities" is from Milbank, *Theology and Social Theory*, 3.

130. Ritzer, "Current Status of Sociological Theory."

131. Alvin Gouldner, *The Coming Crisis of Western Sociology* (New York: Basic Books, 1970), 28, 31.

132. Paul Hanly Furfey, *The Scope and Method of Sociology: A Metasociological Treatise* (New York: Harper and Brothers, 1953), 14. Furfey outlined his vision of Catholic

sociology in "Why a Supernatural Sociology?" *American Catholic Sociological Review* 1, no. 4 (1940): 167–71. For a discussion of the parallels between Furfey and Gouldner, see Joseph Fitzpatrick, "Catholic Sociology Revisited: The Challenge of Alvin Gouldner," *Thought* 53, no. 209 (1978): 123–32. On the similarities between Furfey's work and contemporary meta-theory, see Peter Kivisto, "The Brief Career of Catholic Sociology," *Sociological Analysis* 50, no. 4 (1989): 351–61.

133. Benton Johnson, "Sociological Theory and Religious Truth," *Sociological Analysis* 38, no. 4 (1977): 368–88; David Lyon, "The Idea of a Christian Sociology: Some Historical Precedents and Current Concerns," *Sociological Analysis* 44, no. 3 (1983): 227–42; Margaret M. Poloma, "Toward a Christian Sociological Perspective: Religious Values, Theory, and Methodology," *Sociological Analysis* 43, no. 2 (1982): 95–108; David Lyon, *Sociology and the Human Image* (Leicester, U.K.: InterVarsity Press, 1985); Charles P. de Santo, Calvin Redekop, and William L Smith-Hinds, eds., *A Reader in Sociology: Christian Perspectives* (Scottdale, Penn.: Herald Press, 1980); Paul A. Marshall, Sander Griffioen, and Richard J. Mouw, eds., *Stained Glass: Worldviews and Social Science* (Lanham, Md.: University Press of America, 1989); Richard Perkins, *Looking Both Ways: Exploring the Interface between Christianity and Sociology* (Grand Rapids, Mich.: Zondervan, 1987); Kieran Flanagan, *The Enchantment of Sociology* (New York: St. Martin's Press, 1996); Milbank, *Theology and Social Theory*.

134. Milbank, *Theology and Social Theory*, 3.

135. Acts 17.28 RSV.

136. John Calvin, *The Institutes of Christian Religion,* ed. Tony Lane and Hilary Osborne (Grand Rapids, Mich.: Baker Book House, 1987), 69–70.

137. Small, as quoted in Robert Friedrichs, *A Sociology of Sociology* (New York: Free Press, 1970), 105.

138. Louis Althusser, *Lenin and Philosophy and Other Essays,* trans. Ben Brewster (New York: Monthly Review Press, 1971), 171.

139. For a Christian critique of Althusser, see Lyon, *Sociology and the Human Image.* For an analysis of Small's place in early American sociology, see Arthur J. Vidich and Stanford M. Lyman, *American Sociology: Worldly Rejections of Religion and their Directions* (New Haven, Conn.: Yale University Press, 1985). Vidich and Lyman argue that sociologists such as Small replaced God with the social system.

140. For an account of the structure–agency debate, see Kieran Healy, "Conceptualising Constraint: Mouzelis, Archer and the Concept of Social Structure," *Sociology* 32, no. 3 (1998): 509–23; Margaret Archer, *Culture and Agency: The Place of Culture in Social Theory* (Cambridge: Cambridge University Press, 1996); Anthony Giddens, *The Constitution of Society* (Cambridge: Polity, 1984); Mustafa Emirbayer and Ann Mische, "What Is Agency?" *American Journal of Sociology* 103, no. 4 (1998): 962; William H. Sewell, Jr., "A Theory of Structure: Duality, Agency, and Transformation," *American Journal of Sociology* 98, no. 1 (1992): 29.

141. Alan Richardson and John Bowden, *The Westminster Dictionary of Theology* (Philadelphia: Westminster Press, 1983), 460–62, s.v. "Predestination" (M. J. Langford).

142. For an account of the theology and development of Calvinism. see John T. McNeill, *The History and Character of Calvinism* (New York: Oxford University Press, 1954).

143. For an overview of the new institutionalism, see Walter Powell and Paul DiMaggio, eds., *The New Institutionalism in Organizational Analysis* (Chicago: University of Chicago Press, 1991).

144. There is no evidence that any of the other neo-institutionalists share Thomas's theological commitments. In a follow-up e-mail, he noted that the "leading institutionalists" come from a wide range of religious backgrounds, including Mennonite,

Roman Catholic, and Christian Science: "Of the colleagues I have collaborated with, none have any leanings toward Calvinism."

145. Burke, *On Symbols and Society,* 135.

146. Idem, "Money as a Substitute for God," 168–76.

147. Although they are central to neo-institutionalist analysis, social and cultural structural explanations do not preclude the possibility of divine intervention in human affairs. A full-blown Calvinist sociology would specify more clearly the relationship between divine "first" causes and structural "secondary" causes.

148. Martha Finnemore, "Institutional Environments and Organizations: Structural Complexity and Individualism," *International Organization* 50, no. 2 (1996): 325–47, Expanded Academic ASAP.

149. John W. Meyer, John Boli, George M. Thomas, and Francisco O. Ramirez, "World Society and the Nation-State," *American Journal of Sociology* 103, no. 1 (1997): 148.

150. Ibid., 174.

151. John Boli and George M. Thomas, "Introduction," in *Constructing World Culture: International Nongovernmental Organizations since 1875,* ed. John Boli and George M. Thomas (Stanford, Calif.: Stanford University Press, 1999), 4.

152. George Thomas, *Revivalism and Cultural Change: Christianity, Nation Building, and the Market in the Nineteenth-Century United States* (Chicago: University of Chicago Press, 1989), 82–83.

153. Poloma, "Toward a Christian Sociological Perspective," 95.

154. Margaret Poloma, *The Charismatic Movement: Is There a New Pentecost?* (Boston: Twayne Publishers, 1982), 126.

155. Idem, "Toward a Christian Sociological Perspective," 98.

156. Idem, *Contemporary Sociological Theory* (New York: Macmillan, 1979), 7.

157. Although she grew up Catholic, Poloma was attending a charismatic Episcopal congregation at the time of the interview.

158. Steinfels has argued that the "human person is neither radically individualistic nor socially determined" and that the Catholic intellectual tradition makes room "for grace and free will, thought, conscience, choice": see Steinfels, " Catholic Intellectual Tradition," <http://www.fordham.edu/thirdagectr/mstein.htm>.

159. Paul Giles, *American Catholic Arts and Fictions: Culture, Ideology, Aesthetics* (New York: Cambridge University Press, 1992), 15.

160. John Milton, as quoted in Richardson and Bowden, *Westminster Dictionary of Theology,* 43, s.v. "Arminianism" (J. C. O'Neill).

161. Alan Wolfe, "The Revival of Moral Inquiry in the Social Sciences," *Chronicle of Higher Education,* 3 September 1999, B4.

162. Robert Wuthnow, "The Fine Art of Being Fashionably Moral: Normativity and Scholarship in the Social Sciences," in *The Nature of Moral Inquiry in the Social Sciences,* 63.

163. Julie Reuben, "The University and Its Discontents," *Hedgehog Review* 2, no. 3 (2000): 76.

164. Idem, *The Making of the Modern University: Intellectual Transformation and the Marginalization of Morality* (Chicago: University of Chicago Press, 1996).

165. For a description and critique of "abstract empiricism," see C. Wright Mills, *The Sociological Imagination* (New York: Oxford University Press, 1959).

166. James Farr, "Remembering the Revolution: Behavioralism in American Political Science," in *Political Science in History: Research Programs and Political Traditions,* ed. James Farr, John S. Dryzek, and Stephen T. Leonard (Cambridge: Cambridge University Press, 1995), 198–224.

167. Reuben, "The University and Its Discontents," 84, 86.

168. Wolfe, "Revival of Moral Inquiry." See also idem, "Moral Inquiry."

169. Douglas Johnston and Cynthia Sampson, eds., *Religion: The Missing Dimension of Statecraft* (New York: Oxford University Press, 1994).

170. Bruce Russett, *Grasping the Democratic Peace: Principles for a Post–Cold War World* (Princeton, N.J.: Princeton University Press, 1993).

171. Joel H. Rosenthal, *Righteous Realists: Political Realism, Responsible Power, and American Culture in the Nuclear Age* (Baton Rouge: Louisiana State University Press, 1991), 2.

172. Bruce Russett, "Science, Faith, and World Politics," in *As Leaven for the World: Catholic Reflections on Faith, Vocation, and the Intellectual Life,* ed. Thomas Landy (Franklin, Wisc.: Sheed and Ward, 2001), 389.

173. For a discussion of Protestant neo-orthodox influences on the realist approach to international relations, see Leo Ribuffo, "Religion and American Foreign Policy: The Story of a Complex Relationship," *National Interest,* summer 1998, 36–49.

174. Russett, "Science, Faith, and World Politics," 389. Russett also articulates this view in "Not All the Nations Furiously Rage Together," in *Higher Learning and the Catholic Traditions,* ed. Robert E. Sullivan (Notre Dame, Ind.: Notre Dame Press, 2001), 83.

175. Russett, "Science, Faith, and World Politics," 389; idem, *Grasping the Democratic Peace;* Bruce Russett and John R. Oneal, *Triangulating Peace: Democracy, Interdependence, and International Organizations* (New York: Norton, 2001).

176. Russett, "Science, Faith and World Politics," 382.

177. Russett cites the Catholic ethicists Joseph McKenna and William V. O'Brien in "A Countercombatant Deterrent? Feasibility, Morality, and Arms Control," in *The Military–Industrial Complex: A Reassessment,* ed. Sam C. Sarkesian (Beverly Hills, Calif.: Sage Publications, 1972), 201–242. Russett thanks Paul Ramsey in the essay.

178. Russett published a chapter in the edited volume resulting from the Georgetown seminars. See Bruce Russett, "A Countercombatant Alternative to Nuclear MADness," in *Ethics and Nuclear Strategy?* ed. Harold P. Ford and Francis X. Winters (Maryknoll, N.Y.: Orbis Books, 1977), 124–43.

179. Idem, "A Countercombatant Deterrent?" 229–35.

180. Ibid., 203, 218.

181. Idem, "No First Use of Nuclear Weapons: To Stay the Fateful Lightning," *Worldview* 19, no. 11 (1976): 9–11.

182. U.S. Catholic Bishops, "The Challenge of Peace. God's Promise and Our Response: A Pastoral Letter on War and Peace," in *Catholic Social Thought: The Documentary Heritage,* ed. David O'Brien and Thomas Shannon (Maryknoll, N.Y.: Orbis Books, 1992), 492–571.

183. Bruce Russett, "Are the Bishops' Pastoral Letters Passe?" *Commonweal,* 20 November 1998, 14–18, Expanded Academic ASAP.

184. U.S. Catholic Bishops, "The Challenge of Peace," 549.

185. For an excellent collection of responses to "The Challenge of Peace," see Philip Murnion, ed., *Catholics and Nuclear War: A Commentary on "The Challenge of Peace," the U.S. Catholic Bishops' Pastoral Letter on War and Peace* (New York: Crossroad, 1983).

186. José Casanova, *Public Religions in the Modern World* (Chicago: University of Chicago Press, 1994).

187. George F. Kennan, "The Bishops' Letter," *New York Times,* 1 May 1983, 21.

188. Stanley Hoffman, "The Political Ethics of International Relations," in *Ethics and International Relations: A Reader,* ed. Joel Rosenthal (Washington, D.C.: Georgetown University Press, 1995), 24.

189. Russett is quoting from the Second Vatican Council's "Pastoral Constitution of the Church in the Modern World": see Russett, "Science, Faith, and World Politics," 390.

190. For an example of Catholic social teaching in a mainstream journal, see idem, "Ethical Dilemmas of Nuclear Deterrence," *International Security* 8, no. 4 (1984): 36–54.

191. Gary Orfield, Susan Eaton, and Elaine Jones, *Dismantling Desegregation: The Quiet Reversal of Brown v. Board of Education* (New York: New Press, 1997); Gary Orfield and Carol Ashkinaze, *The Closing Door: Conservative Policy and Black Opportunity* (Chicago: University of Chicago Press, 1993).

192. The mission statement for Harvard University's Civil Rights Project is available on-line at <http://www.law.harvard.edu/groups/civilrights/mission.html>.

193. A press release for the Religion and Civil Rights Conference calls it the "first major national conference on religion and civil rights in over twenty years." The release is available on-line at <http://www.law.harvard.edu/groups/civilrights/conferences/religion/pressrelease.html>.

194. Gary Orfield, "Introduction: Religion and Racial Justice," in *Religion, Race, and Justice in a Changing America*, ed. Gary Orfield and Holly Lebowitz (New York: Century Foundation Press, 1999), 182.

195. Ibid., 10–11.

196. Ibid., 14, 17.

197. Orfield has also been involved with Collegium, an organization that works with faculty at Catholic colleges and universities, and the University of Notre Dame's Erasmus Institute.

198. Mark Noll notes the growing sophistication of evangelical social ethics in *The Scandal of the Evangelical Mind* (Grand Rapids, Mich.: Eerdmans, 1994). Noll comes the closest to touching on this area in works such as *Adding Cross to Crown: The Political Significance of Christ's Passion* (Grand Rapids, Mich.: Baker Books, 1996). Marsden addressed this topic in *Outrageous Idea*. Finally, the "gang of four"—Guth, Green, Kellstedt, and Smidt—have occasionally touched on normative themes in their political-science scholarship.

199. Jon H. Roberts and James Turner, *The Sacred and the Secular University* (Princeton, N.J.: Princeton University Press, 2000), 36.

200. In *The System of Professions: An Essay on the Division of Labor* (Chicago: University of Chicago Press, 1988), Andrew Abbott argues that professions enlarge their jurisdictions by reducing another profession's understanding of a problem to their own. In challenging social-scientific reductionism, Catholic and evangelical scholars have resisted the expansion of the social sciences into the jurisdictions of theology and philosophy.

201. The first quote is from David Hollinger, "Jewish Intellectuals and the De-Christianization of American Public Culture in the Twentieth Century," in Stout and Hart, *New Directions in American Religious History*, 476. The second quote is from Ronald Wells, who was paraphrasing the views of "several well-known historians," in Tim Stafford, "Whatever Happened to *Christian* History?" *Christianity Today*, 2 April 2001, 42.

202. John Fea, "Confessions of a 'Pile-man': Work and the Scholarly Task of the Christian Historian," *Network Communique*, spring 2001, 6.

203. Robert Karl Manoff, "Writing the News (by Telling the 'Story')," in *Reading the News*, ed. Robert Karl Manoff and Michael Schudson (New York: Pantheon Books, 1987), 227–28. Manoff is summarizing the argument in Wayne Booth's "The Empire of Irony," *Georgia Review* 37, no. 4 (1983): 719–37. The phrases "traditional God-language" and "modern irony-language" are from Booth's essay.

204. On the tendency of religious social movements to downplay the particularity of biblical and theological language in favor of "thinner" discourses, see Stephen

Hart, "Cultural Sociology and Social Criticism," *Newsletter of the Sociology of Culture Section of the American Sociological Association*, vol. 9, no. 3, 1995, 3–6. Hart uses the term "thick" to refer to discourses that include terminology and language from specific moral and religious traditions. "Thin" discourses, by contrast, are framed in more universal, lowest-common-denominator terms.

205. Michael Budde, "The Changing Face of American Catholic Nationalism," *Sociological Analysis* 53, no. 3 (1992): 252.

206. Tracy notes that American Catholic social ethicists have increasingly stressed "an appeal to public, shareable reasons rather than 'private' beliefs," so a "responsible Catholic social ethic in a pluralist and democratic society will be obliged to make its case on grounds acceptable, in principle, to both the Catholic and wider Christian community, on the one hand, and to the larger secular pluralistic, democratic, and in that basic sense, 'liberal' society on the other": see David Tracy, "Catholic Classics in American Liberal Culture," in *Catholicism and Liberalism*, ed. David Hollenbach (Cambridge: Cambridge University Press, 1994), 212, 196.

207. Marsden, *Fundamentalism and American Culture*, v–viii, 229–30; Noll, *History of Christianity*, 1–6, 550–53. On the tendency of all scholars to confine autobiographical material to the prefaces, epilogues, afterwords, and endnotes of their books, see Phillip Hammond, ed., *Sociologists at Work* (New York: Basic Books, 1964), as cited in Albert Hunter, "Introduction: Rhetoric in Research, Networks of Knowledge," in *The Rhetoric of Social Research: Understood and Believed*, ed. Albert Hunter (New Brunswick, N.J.: Rutgers University Press, 1990), 1–22.

208. Orfield, "Introduction," 182. Orfield discusses the connections between theology and social policy in the body of the article.

209. Russett, "A Countercombatant Deterrent?" 229–35.

210. Noll et al., *Search for Christian America;* Noll, *Scandal of the Evangelical Mind;* George Marsden and Frank Roberts, eds., *A Christian View of History?* (Grand Rapids, Mich.: Eerdmans, 1975); Kuklick and Hart, *Religious Advocacy;* Mark Noll, *Christians and the American Revolution* (Grand Rapids, Mich.: Eerdmans, 1977).

211. Bruce Russett, "Is NATO's War Just? Questions about Kosovo," *Commonweal*, 21 May 1999, 13; idem, "Pastoral Letters Passe?"; idem, "Star Wars: A Moral Mirage? In the Wake of the Bishops' 'Challenge,'" *Commonweal*, 11 April 1986, 209–13; idem, "Proportionality in War: The Hard Scales of Prudence and Justice," *Worldview* 16, no. 3 (1973): 42–44; idem, "No First Use"; idem, "Extended Deterrence with Nuclear Weapons: How Necessary, How Acceptable?" *Review of Politics* 50, no. 2 (1988): 182–203; Kellstedt et al., "It's the Culture," 28–33.

212. Leo Ribuffo, "Afterword," 222.

213. Leslie Woodcock Tentler, "On the Margins: The Study of American Catholic History," *American Quarterly* 45, no. 1 (1993): 104–28.

214. Martin Marty, "The Public Shelf (Books on the Debate over Religion in Public Life)," *Christian Century*, 20 November 1996, 1134–36; John C. Green, James L. Guth, Corwin E. Smidt, and Lyman A. Kellstedt, *Religion and the Culture Wars: Dispatches from the Front* (Lanham, Md.: Rowman and Littlefield, 1996).

215. Alan Wolfe, "The Opening of the Evangelical Mind," *Atlantic Monthly*, October 2000, 55–76.

216. Idem, "A Welcome Revival of Religion in the Academy," *Chronicle of Higher Education*, 19 September 1997, B4; Carolyn J. Mooney, "Devout Professors on the Offensive," *Chronicle of Higher Education*, 4 May 1994; D. W. Miller, "Measuring the Role of the 'Faith Factor' in Social Change," *Chronicle of Higher Education*, 26 November 1999, A21.

217. Marsden, *Outrageous Idea;* Russett, "Ethical Dilemmas," 36–54.

218. Greeley, *Religion;* idem, *Religious Imagination;* idem, *Religion as Poetry;* idem, "Theology and Sociology; idem, "Protestant and Catholic; idem, *Catholic Myth;* idem, *Catholic Imagination.*

219. John DiIulio, "Supporting Black Churches: Faith, Outreach, and the Inner-City Poor," *Brookings Review,* spring 1999, 42–45; idem, "My Black Crime Problem, and Ours," *City Journal,* spring 1996.

220. Greeley, *Religion,* 15, 79.

221. Noll, *History of Christianity,* 550–53.

222. Dolan, *American Catholic Experience,* 9.

223. Russett, "A Countercombatant Deterrence?" 229–35.

224. Boyd, "If We Ever Needed the Lord Before," 40.

225. Baxter, "Not Outrageous Enough," 14.

Chapter 7. Openness and Obstacles

1. See Beth McMurtrie, "Future of Religious Colleges Is Bright, Say Scholars and Officials," *Chronicle of Higher Education,* 20 October 2000, A41.

2. Philip Gleason, George Marsden, Mark Noll, and Peter Steinfels participated in the conference.

3. Alan Wolfe, "The Opening of the Evangelical Mind," *Atlantic Monthly,* October 2000, 55–76. The issue with Wolfe's cover story was included in the packet of conference materials.

4. Paul Dovre, "Through a Glass Darkly," paper presented at the Conference on the Future of Religious Colleges, Cambridge, Mass., October 2000, 9.

5. George Marsden, "Religious Scholars in the Academy: Anachronism or Leaven?" paper presented at the Conference on the Future of Religious Colleges, Cambridge, Mass., October 2000), 4; Mark Noll, "The Future of Religious Colleges: Looking Ahead by Looking Back," paper presented at the Conference on the Future of Religious Colleges, Cambridge, Mass., October 2000, 9.

6. McMurtrie, "Future of Religious Colleges."

7. Robert Benne, "The Glass Is Half Full, Say the President and the Professor" paper presented at the Conference on the Future of Religious Colleges, Cambridge, Mass., October 2000, 1.

8. James Burtchaell, *The Dying of the Light: The Disengagement of Colleges and Universities from Their Christian Churches* (Grand Rapids, Mich.: Eerdmans, 1998); George Marsden, *The Soul of the American University: From Protestant Establishment to Established Non-Belief* (New York: Oxford University Press, 1994).

9. Dovre, "Through a Glass Darkly," 2.

10. Noll, "Future of Religious Colleges," 9–10.

11. Benne, "Glass Is Half Full," 1.

12. Dovre, "Through a Glass Darkly," 10.

13. Greeley, as quoted in Fran Schumer, "A Return to Religion," *New York Times Magazine,* 15 April 1984, 90, LEXIS-NEXIS Academic Universe.

14. Peter Steinfels, as quoted in ibid.," 90; Peter Steinfels, "Beliefs," *New York Times,* 4 March 2000, A13.

15. Robert Jay Lifton, *The Protean Self: Human Resilience in an Age of Fragmentation* (New York: Basic Books, 1993), 5.

16. Richard John Neuhaus, *The Naked Public Square: Religion and Democracy in America* (Grand Rapids, Mich.: Eerdmans, 1984). In *Public Religions in the Modern World* (Chicago: University of Chicago Press, 1994), José Casanova convincingly documents the global "deprivatization" of religion.

17. See Robert Wuthnow, *The Restructuring of American Religion: Society and Faith since World War II* (Princeton, N.J.: Princeton University Press, 1988); see also Robert C. Liebman and Robert Wuthnow, eds., *The New Christian Right* (New York: Aldine Publishing, 1983).

18. For the Republican Party's position on faith-based social services, see "Republican Platform 2000: Renewing America's Purpose Together," Republican Party Web site, available online at <http://www.rnc.org/gopinfo/platform>. For the Democratic Party's position, see "2000 National Democratic Platform," Democratic Party Web site, available on-line at <http://www.democrats.org/issues/platform/platform.html>.

19. Wendy Kaminer, *Sleeping with Extra-Terrestrials: The Rise of Irrationalism and Perils of Piety* (New York: Pantheon Books, 1999), 31; Ronald Sider, "Where Are We Now on the Faith-Based Initiatives?" *Prism E-Pistle*, 15 August 2001, 1.

20. Wade Clark Roof, *Spiritual Marketplace: Baby Boomers and the Remaking of American Religion* (Princeton, N.J.: Princeton University Press, 1999), 46, 98–99. The $4 billion figure is from Lynn Garrett et al., "Smooth Selling for CBA in Atlanta," *Publisher's Weekly*, 23 July 2001, 16.

21. Kimberly Winston, "Literary Lions Dare to Roar About Religion," *Publisher's Weekly*, 21 August 2000, S12.

22. Laura Nash, as quoted in Michelle Conlin, "Religion in the Workplace: The Growing Presence of Spirituality in Corporate America," *Business Week*, 1 November 1999, 150; see also Marc Gunther, "Spirituality: God and Business," *Fortune*, 9 July 2001, 58.

23. The phrase "quintessential enlightenment profession" comes from E. J. Dionne's interview for this project; Alan Wolfe, "A Welcome Revival of Religion in the Academy," *Chronicle of Higher Education*, 19 September 1997, B4.

24. Alicia C. Shepard, "The Media Get Religion," *American Journalism Review*, December 1995, 19.

25. S. Robert Lichter and Linda Lichter, "The Media Get Religion: National Media Coverage of Religion in America 1969–1998," *Media Monitor*, May–June 2000, 1, 8, available on-line at <http://www.cmpa.com/Mediamon/mm050600.htm>.

26. Dujardin, as quoted in Shepard, "The Media Get Religion," 20.

27. Mark F. Baldwin, "Religion: Read All About It," *The Lutheran*, February 1997, 22; M. S. Mason, "Newsman Sees Growing Interest in Religion," *Christian Science Monitor*, 22 September 1997, 13, LEXIS-NEXIS Academic Universe.

28. This study was reported in John Dart and Jimmy Allen, *Bridging the Gap: Religion and the News Media* (Nashville, Tenn.: First Amendment Center, 2000).

29. Shepard, "The Media Get Religion"; John Dart, "The Pull of Faith: Noxious, Negligible, or Negotiable?" *Nieman Reports*, fall 1997, 5; David Baird, "Pressing Candidates on Their Faith: The Religion Thing," *Columbia Journalism Review*, September–October 1992.

30. The Garrett-Medill Center, a joint venture of Northwestern's Medill School of Journalism and the Garrett-Evangelical Theological Seminary, has received substantial funding from both Pew and Lilly.

31. Abigail Beshkin, "A Joint Master's Program in Religion and Journalism Announced," *Columbia University News*, 19 October 2000; Michelle Poblete, "Religion Quarter Opens New Worlds," *Inside Medill News*, 3 August 2001.

32. For more information on these programs, see the Leonard E. Greenberg Center for the Study of Religion in Public Life Web page at <http://www.trincoll.edu/depts/csrpl>.

33. Allan Andrews, "Journalism Educators Signal Heightened Interest in Ethics, Religion," *Free!*, 19 October 1998, available on-line at <http://www.freedomforum.org/templates/document.asp?documentID=4338>.

34. David H. Weaver and G. Cleveland Wilhoit's 1992 survey was reported in Dart and Allen, *Bridging the Gap*, 43; Mark F. Baldwin, "Most Religion Reporters Are Religious," *The Lutheran*, February 1997, 24. See also Dart and Allen, *Bridging the Gap*.

35. Lichter and Lichter, "The Media Get Religion."

36. This group was an outgrowth of two conferences of Christian journalists held in 1992 and 1997. This emerging network of Washington-based evangelical journalists includes David Aikman (formerly of *Time*), Fred Barnes of the *Weekly Standard*, and Julia Duin of the *Washington Times*. For more on Gegrapha, see the Web page at <http://www.gegrapha.org>.

37. The Fellowship of Christian Journalists' Web page is available at <http://digmo.com/~fcj/index.html>.

38. Laurie Goodstein, "Diversity and the News," panel discussion at the University of Michigan, Ann Arbor, 2 February 1998), available on-line at <http://www.journalism.org/ccj/resources/aasum4.html>.

39. Marsden, *Soul of the American University;* Burtchaell, *Dying of the Light;* Mark Schwehn, *Exiles from Eden: Religion and the Academic Vocation in America* (New York: Oxford University Press, 1993).

40. Diego Ribaneneira, "A Campus Revival: National Conference's Popularity Symbolizes New Focus on Spirituality," *Boston Globe*, 26 September 1998, A1, LEXIS-NEXIS Academic Universe.

41. Wolfe, "A Welcome Revival of Religion in the Academy," B4; James Turner, "Catholic Intellectual Traditions and Contemporary Scholarship," lecture delivered at the University of Notre Dame, Notre Dame, Ind., 8 April 1997. See also Teresa Watanabe, "The New Gospel of Academia," *Los Angeles Times*, 18 October 2000, A1, LEXIS-NEXIS Academic Universe; Carolyn Mooney, "Devout Professors on the Offensive," *Chronicle of Higher Education*, 4 May 1994; Diane Winston, "Campuses Are a Bellwether for Society's Religious Revival," *Chronicle of Higher Education*, 16 January 1998, A60; Eric Goldscheider, "Spiritual Rebirth: Chancellor Foresees Return of Religion," *Boston Globe*, 3 October 1999, 11, LEXIS-NEXIS Academic Universe; D. W. Miller, "Measuring the Role of 'the Faith Factor' in Social Change," *Chronicle of Higher Education*, 26 November 1999, A21; Conrad Cherry et al., *Religion on Campus* (Chapel Hill: University of North Carolina Press, 2001).

42. In the early 1990s, there were about eighty stories each year that contained the word "religion." By the late 1990s, the *Chronicle* was averaging 130 to 140 "religion" stories per year: unpublished research by Kathleen Mahoney, John Schmalzbauer, and James Youniss, with the assistance of Mandy Savitz.

43. American Academy of Religion, *2000 Annual Report* (Atlanta: American Academy of Religion, 2000), 4.

44. Watanabe, "New Gospel of Academia," A1.

45. See the American Political Science Association, Religion and Politics Section, Web page at <http://www.gac.edu/oncampus/academics/poli-sci/relpol/r&p.html>.

46. Harry S. Stout and Robert M. Taylor, Jr., "Studies of Religion in American Society: The State of the Art," in *New Directions in American Religious History*, ed. Harry S. Stout and D. G. Hart (New York: Oxford University Press, 1997), 15.

47. Daniel Barbarisi, "More Physicians Explore Legitimacy of Spiritual Healing," *Boston Globe*, 12 December 2000, B3, LEXIS-NEXIS Academic Universe.

48. Vincent Kiernan, "Can Science and Theology Find Common Ground?" *Chronicle of Higher Education*, 30 April 1999, A17.

49. Gerald Reiner, "Charitable Groups Directing Big Money to Studies of Religions' Social Impact," *Hartford Courant*, 31 October 1998, A1, LEXIS-NEXIS Academic Universe; "Foundations Boost Funding for Study of Religion," *Philanthropy News Digest*, 24 October 2000; "Major Foundations Fund Religious Initiatives," *Philanthropy News Digest*, 3 January 2001; David L. Wheeler, "Foundation Seeks to Create Field Melding Science and Theology," *Chronicle of Higher Education*, 11 April 1997. For an overview of Lilly Endowment funding in this area, see <http://www.resourcingchristianity.org>. For Pew's contribution, see <http://www.pewtrusts.org>.

50. Kathleen Mahoney, John Schmalzbauer, and James Youniss, *Revitalizing Religion in the Academy: Summary of Lilly Endowment's Initiative on Religion and Higher Education* (Chestnut Hill, Mass.: Boston College, 2000), 5; idem, "Religion: A Comeback on Campus," *Liberal Education*, November 2001.

51. The membership of the Society of Christian Philosophers is from Thomas V. Morris, "Introduction," in *God and the Philosophers: The Reconciliation of Faith and Reason*, ed. Thomas V. Morris (New York: Oxford University Press, 1994), 5. According to the report "Philosophy as a Profession: Data on the Profession, Selected Demographic Information on Philosophy Ph.D's, 1995," there are about 8,500 philosophy Ph.D.s in the United States. This report is available on the American Philosophical Association Web site, at <http://www.apa.udel.edu/apa/profession/selected.html>

52. The figures are from the Education as Transformation Project (Wellesley College) Web page at <http://www.wellesley.edu/RelLife/transformation>; Diana Chapman Walsh, "Introduction Transforming Education: An Overview," in *Education as Transformation: Religious Pluralism, Spirituality and a New Vision for Higher Education in America*, ed. Victor H. Kazanjian, Jr., and Peter L. Laurence (New York: Peter Lang, 2000), 1.

53. Mahoney et al., *Revitalizing Religion*, 3, 7.

54. Kaminer, *Sleeping with Extra-Terrestrials*, 27.

55. Paul Kurtz, "Where Are the Secularists?" *Free Inquiry*, winter 1997–98, available on-line at <http://www.secularhumanism.org/library/fi/kurtz_18_1.html>.

56. Wolfe, "Welcome Revival," B4.

57. Shephard, "The Media Get Religion," 19.

58. Miller, "Measuring the Role," A21.

59. Greeley, as quoted in Schumer, "Return to Religion," 90.

60. In a suggestive essay, Christian Smith describes the role of cultural, material, and organizational resources in the secularization of American higher education. Although Smith was writing about large institutions and I am writing about individuals, his approach sheds light on the resources used to sacralize the careers of Catholic and evangelical journalists and scholars: see Christian Smith, "Introduction: Re-Thinking the Secularization of American Life," paper presented at The Secular Revolution: Power, Interests, and Conflict in the Secularization of American Life, conference, University of North Carolina, Chapel Hill, N.C., June 2001, 30–31.

61. The quote is from Bryan Hehir, keynote address, Catholic Commission on Intellectual and Cultural Affairs meeting, College of the Holy Cross, Worcester, Mass., November 1999.

62. See "How the Faithful Voted: A Conversation with John C. Green and John DiIulio," *Center Conversations*, March 2001, 1–12.

63. See the Sacred Places, Civic Purposes (Brookings Institution) Web page at <http://www.brookings.org/gs/projects/sacredplaces.htm>.

64. In 1992, Gayle White reported that Lilly "has handed out religion grants at the rate of about $30 million a year": see Gayle White, "Consider the Lilly's Impact on Religion," *Atlanta Constitution,* 19 September 1992, E6, LEXIS-NEXIS Academic Universe. This number has undoubtedly gone up. Between 1989 and 2000, Lilly's Religion and Higher Education initiative funded $15.6 million in grants. In 1999 and 2001, Lilly Endowment awarded "theological exploration of vocation" grants of approximately $2 million each to forty-eight church-related colleges. These figures do not include the grants Lilly awarded for religion research outside the religion-and-higher-education field. Meanwhile, between 1995 and 2000, the Pew Charitable Trusts gave out approximately $94 million in religion grants: see <http://www.pewtrusts.org>. During the 1990s, Pew spent $14 million on programs for evangelical scholars: see Michael Paulson, "Evangelicals Find Place at Mainstream Colleges," *Boston Globe,* 20 February 2000, A1, LEXIS-NEXIS Academic Universe. Templeton and Ford have also awarded millions of dollars in religion grants.

65. The term "institutional infrastructures" comes from George Marsden, *The Outrageous Idea of Christian Scholarship* (New York: Oxford University Press, 1997), 101.

66. Turner, as quoted in Marshall Ledger, "Stopping By," *Trust Magazine,* January 2000.

67. See the Pew Forum on Religion and Public Life Web page at <http://pewforum.org>. The American Catholics in the Public Square Web page is at <http://www.catholicsinpublicsquare.org>.

68. For a discussion of the role of cultural resources in social movements, see Rhys Williams, "Constructing the Public Good: Social Movements and Cultural Resources," *Social Problems* 42, no. 1 (1995): 124–45.

69. Mark Silk, *Unsecular Media: Making News of Religion in America* (Chicago: University of Illinois Press, 1995), 53, 55.

70. See Fred Barnes, "Washington Diarist: Born Again," *New Republic,* 20 May 1985, 42.

71. George Marsden, *Fundamentalism in American Culture* (New York: Oxford University Press, 1981).

72. Michael Schudson, *Discovering the News: A Social History of the American Newspaper* (New York: Basic Books, 1978), 193; Charles T. Mathewes, "The Academic Life as a Christian Vocation," *Journal of Religion* 79, no. 1 (1999): 110.

73. Schudson, *Discovering the News,* 186.

74. See Mark Regnerus and Christian Smith, "Selective Deprivatization among American Religious Traditions: The Reversal of the Great Reversal," *Social Forces* 76, no. 4 (1998): 1347–73, Infotrac, Expanded Academic ASAP.

75. Turner, "Catholic Intellectual Traditions," 7.

76. Noll, "Future of Religious Colleges," 10.

77. In *Public Religions in the Modern World* (Chicago: University of Chicago Press, 1994), José Casanova distinguishes between deprivatization and de-differentiation, arguing that the latter is not as possible (or desirable) in modern societies.

78. Peter Steinfels, speech, University of Notre Dame, Notre Dame, Ind., 30 November 1994.

79. Andrew Greeley, "Sociology and the Catholic Church: Four Decades of Bitter Memories," *Sociological Analysis* 50, no. 4 (1989): 394–95.

80. Eviatar Zerubavel, "The Rigid, the Fuzzy, and the Flexible: Notes on the Mental Sculpting of Academic Identity," *Social Research* 62, no. 4 (1995): 1093–1107, Infotrac, Expanded Academic ASAP.

81. Edwin L. Shuman, as quoted in Schudson, *Discovering the News,* 80. Stephen D. Reese describes the *Wall Street Journal*'s response to a socialist reporter in "The News Paradigm and the Ideology of Objectivity: A Socialist at *The Wall Street Journal,*" *Critical Studies in Mass Communication* 7 (1990): 390–409.

82. Jean Bethke Elshtain, "The Bright Line: Liberalism and Religion," *New Criterion* 17, no. 7 (1999): 4, Infotrac, Expanded Academic ASAP.

83. George Lindbeck, *The Nature of Doctrine: Religion and Theology in a Postliberal Age* (London: Society for Promoting Christian Knowledge, 1984), 124.

84. Stephen Hart, *Cultural Dilemmas of Progressive Politics: Styles of Engagement among Grassroots Activists* (Chicago: University of Chicago Press, 2001); idem, "Cultural Sociology and Social Criticism," *Newsletter of the Sociology of Culture Section of the American Sociological Association,* vol. 9, no. 3 (1995), 1, 3–6.

85. David O'Brien, *From the Heart of the American Church: Catholic Higher Education and American Culture* (Maryknoll, N.Y.: Orbis Books, 1994), 25, 33.

86. The metaphor of "conversation stoppers" is taken from Richard Rorty, "Religion as Conversation-Stopper," *Common Knowledge* 3, no. 1 (1994): 1–6.

87. Garry Wills, *Bare Ruined Choirs: Doubt, Prophecy, and Radical Religion* (New York: Doubleday, 1972), 17.

88. Alasdair MacIntyre, *After Virtue* (Notre Dame, Ind.: University of Notre Dame Press, 1984), 2.

89. O'Brien, *Heart of the American Church,* 25, 33, 161; Christian Smith, *American Evangelicalism: Embattled and Thriving* (Chicago: University of Chicago Press, 1998); Zerubavel, "The Rigid," 1093–1107.

90. Zerubavel, "The Rigid," 1093–1107.

91. This dual emphasis on engagement and distinction is from Smith, *American Evangelicalism,* 118–19.

92. Robert Jay Lifton, *The Protean Self: Human Resilience in an Age of Fragmentation* (New York: Basic Books, 1993), 1, 39–41, 50.

93. The phrase religious "'immigrants' to these professional worlds" is taken from Philip Gleason, *Keeping the Faith: American Catholicism Past and Present* (Notre Dame, Ind.: University of Notre Dame Press, 1989), 67.

94. Lifton, *Protean Self,* 5.

95. James Davison Hunter, *American Evangelicalism: Conservative Religion and the Quandary of Modernity* (New Brunswick, N.J.: Rutgers University Press, 1983), 15, 112. See also idem, "The New Class and the Young Evangelicals," *Review of Religious Research* 22, no. 2 (1980): 155–69; Eugene McCarraher, "Smile When You Say 'Laity' (an Analysis of the Lay Revolution in the Catholic Church)," *Commonweal,* 12 September 1997, 12.

96. Paul Giles, *American Catholic Arts and Fictions: Culture, Ideology, Aesthetics* (New York: Cambridge University Press, 1992), 23, 25.

97. Mark Buchanan, "We're All Syncretists Now: Not Just Religious, Spiritual," *Books and Culture,* January–February 2000, 2.

98. The long history of Christian engagement with pluralism has been noted by many Catholic and evangelical scholars. For an evangelical perspective, see Smith, *American Evangelicalism,* 100–101. For a Catholic view, see Scott Holland, "This Side of God: A Conversation with David Tracy," *CrossCurrents* 52, no. 1 (2002), available on-line at <http://www.crosscurrents.org/tracyspring2002.htm>. According to Tracy (as paraphrased by Holland), "Christian theology began when Greek questions were asked about a Hebrew narrative."

Appendix. The Sample

1. The denominational classification scheme is taken from Lyman Kellstedt and John Green, "Knowing God's Many People: Denominational Preference and Political Behavior," in *Rediscovering the Religious Factor in American Politics,* ed. David Leege and Lyman Kellstedt (Armonk, N.Y.: M. E. Sharpe, 1993), 53–69.

2. Twenty Catholic and evangelical journalists were interviewed for the project. One journalist later chose not to take part in the study. My conclusions, however, were shaped by all twenty interviews.

3. Four of the twenty journalists, or 20 percent, in the sample are women. One is African American. Because this is a study of elites—and of Catholic and evangelical elites, in particular—women and minorities tend to be underrepresented.

4. All of the editorial and opinion writers in the sample have worked as reporters.

5. Only three of the twenty Catholic and evangelical social scientists in the sample are women, and none is African American or Latino. This may reflect the underrepresentation of women and minorities at the upper levels of each discipline, as well as the underrepresentation of women and minorities among Catholic and evangelical academics.

Index

Accommodation to secular culture, 11–13, 16, 43, 203–206; of Catholics, 32; of evangelicals, 35, 36

Aikman, David, 197, 198

American Catholic Experience, 166–167, 168

"Americanization/secularization" hypothesis, 12–13, 214n

"Analogical imagination," 112–113, 239n; in academic narratives, 162, 169; in cultural consensus story line, 122–127; in journalism, 143–144

Anti-Catholicism, 19, 27, 31, 41, 190; in higher education, 74–75, 89, 90; liberalism and, 126

Anti-modernism, 20, 23; Catholic, 25–26; of evangelicals, 27

Anti-reductionism, 149, 150, 151–160; of evangelical historians, 153–155; of evangelical political scientists, 155–157; of Greeley, 157–159

Appleby, R. Scott, 168

"Arminian" sociology, 171–172, 174–176

Assimilation, 11–13, 31, 74–75; of Catholics, 32; of evangelicals, 35, 36; resistance to, 204

"Backstage" region, 75, 79

Barnes, Fred, 64–68; list of top journalists, 41; populist anti-elitism, language of, 64–68; and religious resurgence, 197, 199; and secular press, 45, 66–67

Baxter, Michael, 136, 168, 188, 245n–246n

Baylor University, 20, 35–36

Bellah, Robert, 111, 113

Benne, Robert, 190

Bennett, William, 82, 85, 129–130

Berger, Peter, 2, 5, 78

Bible: in culture wars story line, 119–120; evangelical biblical scholarship, 140–142; and justice and peace, language of, 52–53; in peace and justice story line, 137; in testing the scriptures story line, 139–143

Blinded by Might, 120–122

Boston College, 20, 33, 37

Bracketing of religious language: in journalism, 47, 48–50, 71; in social science, 76, 77–81

Bridging languages. *See* Multivocal bridging languages

Brint, Steven, 5, 55, 212n

Brookings Institution, 39, 82, 128, 198

Burke, Kenneth, 151, 152, 160

Calvin College, 28, 37, 96–97, 153

"Calvinist" sociology, 171–174, 184–185

Carter, Stephen, 73, 107

Casanova, Jose, 9–10

Catholic colleges and universities: distinctiveness of, 37; endowment, 33; enrollment, 25–26, 33; mission of, 78–79; prestige, 19, 33; secularization of, 32, 43

Catholic comedy. *See* Comedy, trope of

Catholic feminism, language of, 61–64

Catholic historians: American Catholic Historical Association, 24; and American religious history, 38–39, 152–153, 165–169, 243n; marginality of, 186; "New Americanism," 125, 168; and philanthropy, 198. *See also* Appleby, R. Scott; Dolan, Jay; Gleason, Philip; Massa, Mark

"Catholic imagination," 16, 37, 111–113; in journalism, 114–116, 143–145; in social science, 150–151, 158–159, 162, 169

Catholic philosophers, 27, 37, 38. *See also* Neo-Thomism

Catholic political scientists, 39. *See also* Orfield, Gary; Russett, Bruce

Catholics: influence on academy, 32–33, 37–40, 184–188; intellectual prestige, 19, 42, 43; magazines and journals, 24, 37, 55–60, 125–126, 186; professional associations, 24, 26, 37; publishing, 24; resistance to secularization, 13, 16, 25; self-criticism, 31, 90; upward mobility, 19–22, 43, 87–90

"Catholic social ethic": and DiIulio, 86–87, 238n; and Wycliff, 130–131

Catholic sociologists, 24, 26, 32, 89. *See also* Greeley, Andrew; Hallinan, Maureen

Catholic Worker, 26; and Dionne, 59; and McCarthy, Colman, 52, 54–55, 134, 135, 144–145; and Steinfels, Peter, 125–126

Centers and institutes, 195, 198

Challenge of Peace, 180–181

Chardin, Pierre Teillhard de, 80

Charismatic movement. *See* Pentecostal/ Charismatic movement

Chicago, University of, 89–92

"Christian America" myth, 163–164

Christianity Today, 24, 29, 37

Civic journalism, 16, 133, 200

Civil religion, 118, 120, 136

Civil society, 127, 128

Cogley, John, 56, 125–126

"Cognitive-propositional" model of religion, 140

Comedy, trope of, 150, 162, 165–169

Commonweal, 24, 26, 37; and 11 September 2001, 57; and cultural consensus story line, 125–126; and Dionne, 1, 60, 126; and Steinfels, Margaret, 56; and Steinfels, Peter, 55–60, 69, 125–126, 144

Communitarianism: and African Americans, 130, 131; of Catholic imagination, 113; Catholic intellectuals and, 39, 127–128; communitarian story line, 115, 127–133; and Dionne, xiii–xiv, 128; in international relations, 179, 180; religious intellectuals and, 127–128; story line, 127–133; and Woodward, 128–133; and Wycliff, 130–132

"Concealed affinities," 149, 169–176

Conference on the Future of Religious Colleges, 189–190

Cultural consensus story line, 114, 122–127

Cultural resources, 111, 199–200

Culture wars story line, 114, 116–122

Cushwa Center for the Study of American Catholicism, 197, 198

Day, Dorothy, 54–55, 134, 135

De-ghettoization, 20, 30–36, 36, 43; of Catholics, 31–33, 36–37, 60–61; of evangelicals, 33–36

Deprivatization, 9–10, 16, 191, 200

"Dialectical imagination," 112–113; in culture wars story line, 117, 121–122; in journalism, 143–144; in peace and justice story line, 136

Differentiation, 9, 10, 201

DiIulio, John, 82–87; "Catholic social ethic" and, 86–87, 238n; and objectivity, 106, 108; religion and public policy, 39, 82–87; and religious resurgence, 197, 198, 199; social science pragmatism, language of, 82–85

Dionne, E. J., 55–56, 58–61, 122–127; communitarian story line, xiii–xiv, 115, 128; cultural consensus story line, 114, 122–127; intellectual refinement, language of, 55–56, 58–61; and journalistic empiricism, 1–3, 2–3, 5; list of top journalists, 41; and "odd combinations," 205; religion and public policy, 39; and religious resurgence, 197, 198, 199; and secular press, 45; and 11 September 2001, xiii–xiv; and supernatural, 1–3; and *Washington Post,* 41–42

Distinctiveness, 20; of Catholics, 37, 38, 43; of evangelicals, 36, 38, 43

Dolan, Jay, 166–168, 197, 198

Dovre, Paul, 189, 190

Dowd, Maureen, 11, 18

Education. *See* Higher education

Ellis, Monsignor John Tracy, 21, 31, 62

Elshtain, Jean Bethke, 162–163, 202

Empiricism, 2–3, 6, 8; in journalism, 2–3, 6, 8, 45; language of, 87–90; in social science, 6, 8, 73–74, 147

"Enduring values," 115–116; individualism, 115, 132, 138; moderatism, 115, 120, 126; responsible capitalism, 115, 138; and "social disorder news," 119

Epistemological rhetorics, 87–103
Evangelical colleges and universities: distinctiveness of, 37; endowment, 35; enrollment, 28, 36; prestige, 35–36; secularization of, 35, 43
Evangelical historians: and American religious history, 38–39, 152–155, 243n; Conference on Faith and History, 24, 29, 37; "new evangelical historiography," 93–94, 153; and philanthropy, 198; and providentialism, 146, 147, 148. *See also* Hatch, Nathan; Keillor, Steven; Marsden, George; Noll, Mark; Stout, Harry
Evangelical left, 34, 52, 54, 83, 136–138
Evangelical philosophers, 24, 37, 38, 196
Evangelical political scientists, 39, 155–157. *See also* "Gang of four"; Green, John; Guth, James; Kellstedt, Lyman; Smidt, Corwin
Evangelicals: definition of, 210n; influence on academy, 30, 35, 37–40, 184–188; intellectual prestige, 19, 35, 42, 43; magazines and journals, 24, 29, 37, 186; negative images of, 5, 19, 27, 41, 64–65; in politics, 9, 34, 52, 120–122, 136–138; professional associations, 24, 28–29, 37–39, 195–196; publishing, 24, 29, 186; radio and television ministries, 29; upward mobility, 20–23
Evangelical sociologists, 24, 102–103. *See also* Poloma, Margaret; Thomas, George

Fact/value distinction, 77–78, 79, 104–105; in journalism, 3, 6, 8, 44–45; in professions, 6; and secularization, 8; in social science, 8, 73–74, 77–78, 180, 182; value-commitment, 79–80
Feminism: and Catholicism, 33, 64, 81; and evangelicalism, 34; in journalism, 61–64
Financial resources, 40–41, 193, 195–196
Fox-Genovese, Elizabeth, 105–106
Fox News, 67, 68
Fragmentation of traditions, 191, 202–203, 204
Frye, Northrop, 166
Fundamentalism, 19, 27, 33–35
Fundamentalism and American Culture, 93, 97, 153–155, 164, 185
Fundamentalist Journal, 117, 120
Furfey, Paul Hanly, 135, 170

"Gang of four," 39, 155–157, 186, 198, 199
Gans, Herbert, 45, 111, 115–116
Geertz, Clifford, 91–92
Gegrapha, 37, 68, 194, 198
Genovese, Eugene, 106
Gieryn, Thomas, 146–147, 211n, 227n
Giles, Paul, 205
Gleason, Philip: and Catholic assimilation, 12, 32, 36–37; on Catholic higher education, 32; on "new Americanism," 168; and religious resurgence, 197
Goffman, Erving, 2, 47, 75
Gouldner, Alvin, 6, 73, 170
Greeley, Andrew, 87–93, 157–159; on anti-Catholicism, 74–75; and Catholic cultural elite, 11, 32–33; on Catholic imagination, 37, 111–113; "Catholic social ethic," 86; and Catholic upward mobility, 21; comedy and, 161; on 11 September 2001, xiv; empiricism, language of, 87–90; fiction of, 92–93; interpretive social science, language of, 90–93; and objectivity, 91, 104, 107–108; and "odd combinations," 205; and religious resurgence, 190, 196–197; religious terminology and, 203; theory of ethnicity, 216n; theory of religion, 91–92, 157–159
Green, John, 39, 155–157, 186, 197, 198
Guth, James, 39, 155–157, 186

Habits of the Heart, 127, 128–129, 132
Hallinan, Maureen, 77–81
Hart, Stephen, 50, 202
Harvard University: Catholics at, 18; Conference on the Future of Religious Colleges, 189–190; and DiIulio, 83, 85; and Dionne, 60; evangelicals at, 18
Hatch, Nathan, 37, 153, 162–164, 197, 198
Hatfield, Mark, 137, 138
Hehir, J. Bryan, 18, 179, 180
Henry, Carl F. H., 29, 33
Henry, Paul, 137, 138, 139
Higher education: presence of Catholics in, 11; presence of evangelicals in, 11; Protestants and early history, 7–8; religious affiliation of professoriate, 5; religious resurgence in, 40, 189–190, 194–200; secularization of, 5–9, 73–75, 94–97, 147, 189–190. *See also* Catholic colleges and universities; Evangelical colleges and universities

History: American religious history, 38–39,
152–155, 160–169, 195, 243n; anti-
reductionism in, 153–155; objectivity
in, 73–74, 105–107. *See also* Catholic
historians; Evangelical historians
Holt, Don, 48–49
Hout, Michael, 229n
Hunter, James, 12, 116, 205

Individualism, 113, 119, 132, 138, 173–174
Institute for the Study of American Evan-
gelicals, 197
"Instrumental rhetoric," 78
Intellectual refinement, language of,
55–61
Interpretive social science, language of,
90–93
Interviewing procedures, 15
Irish Catholics: Greeley on, 87–88, 92; and
Hallinan, 79, 80; in journalism, 11, 18,
27, 42; and McGrory, 50; upward
mobility of, 21
Irony, trope of, 150, 160–165, 247n
Italian Catholics, 84

Jasper, James, 78
Jelen, Ted, 39, 155, 157
John Paul II, Pope, 1–3, 32, 63–64
John Templeton Foundation, 40–41
Journalism: presence of Catholics in, 11;
presence of evangelicals in, 11; Protestant history of, 7–8, 53; religion coverage, 8–9, 139, 193–194; religious affiliation of journalists, 5, 46, 65, 194, 210n;
religious resurgence in, 46, 193–194,
196–200; secularization of, 5–9, 45,
66–67
Justice and peace, language of, 51–55
Justice and peace story line. *See* Peace and
justice story line
Just war theory, xiv, 177–181, 185

Keillor, Steven, 146–147
Kellstedt, Lyman, 39, 155–157, 186
Kristol, Irving, 67
Kuhn, Thomas, 97, 99
Kuklick, Bruce, 148, 149
Kuyper, Abraham, 98–99

Lamont, Michele, 211n, 215n, 227n
Landy, Thomas, 127
Law, Cardinal Bernard, 63
Liberal Catholicism, 56–61, 70–71, 125–
127, 247n

Lifton, Robert Jay, 191, 204–205
Lilly Endowment, 40–41, 193, 196, 198–
199, 257n
Lindbeck, George, 140, 202
"Lutheran irony," 162–163

McAdam, Doug, 217n
McCann, Dennis, 167
McCarraher, Eugene, 32, 205
McCarthy, Colman, 54–55, 133–136,
138–139; cancellation of column, 138
and 11 September 2001, xiv; justice and
peace, language of, 54–55; peace and
justice story line, 115, 133–136, 138–
139; and religious resurgence, 196–197;
and *Washington Post*, 41–42
McCarthy, John D., 217n
McGrory, Mary, 41, 50, 110
MacIntyre, Alasdair, 203
Mainline Protestants: and early social science, 7–8; in higher education, 7–8,
38–40, 213n; in journalism, 8; and
secularization, 8, 20
Marginality: of Catholics, 11, 18–27, 93,
186; of evangelicals, 11, 18–23, 27–30,
94–96
Marsden, George, 82, 93–99, 153–155;
anti-reductionism of, 153–155; on
Catholic higher education, 25; on
Christian scholarship, 37–38; irony
and, 162–165; and objectivity, 96–99,
105, 106, 107, 108; and "odd combina-
tions," 205; particularity of religious
language, 187; post-modernism and,
93–99; on religion and higher education, 17, 74, 94–98; and religious resurgence, 189, 197, 198, 199; segregation
of religious language, 185
Massa, Mark, 168, 239n
Matthews, Chris, 11, 110
Media. *See* Journalism
Meta-theory, 150, 170
"Methodological atheism," 3
Methodology of study, 14–15, 114, 207–208
Milbank, John, 169–170, 171
Moderatism, 115, 120, 126
Modernity, engagement with, 32–33, 36,
38, 43
"Moralist rhetoric," 78
Morality: in culture wars story line, 117–
119; exclusion from journalism, 6;
exclusion from social science, 6, 8, 147,
177; "moral revival" in social science,
176–178; Pippert on, 44

Moral Majority, 119, 120
"Moral revival," 150, 176–178
Multiculturalism, 13, 16, 75, 105–106
Multivocal bridging languages, 15–16;
    Catholic feminism, 61–64; "Catholic
    social ethic," 86–87; charismatic reli-
    gious experience, 82, 99–103; episte-
    mological rhetorics, 81–82, 87–103;
    intellectual refinement, 55–61; inter-
    pretive social science, 90–93; in jour-
    nalism, 46, 47, 50–68, 71–72; justice
    and peace, 51–55; populist anti-elitism,
    64–68; post-modernism, language of,
    93–99; public policy rhetorics, 81, 82–
    87; in social science, 81–103; social
    science pragmatism, 82–85

Narrative: in academy, 160–169; and
    Catholic scholars, 161, 165–169; and
    evangelical scholars, 161–165; and
    Greeley, 91–93; journalistic, 58, 110–
    111; religious, 111; religious and pro-
    fessional, 16
National Association of Evangelicals, 28, 33
Neo-conservatives, 66, 67
Neo-institutionalism, 172–174
Neo-Thomism, 26, 32, 89
New class, xv, 5, 12–13, 14, 66–67
New Republic, 19, 27, 41, 42
"News net," 116, 123
Newsweek, 34, 41, 42, 45
New York Times: and Catholics, 11, 18–19,
    27, 41–42; and Dionne, 1; and Dowd,
    11; and evangelicals, 11, 30; historic
    Protestant bias at, 7; and Steinfels,
    55–56
Niebuhr, Reinhold, 59, 126, 161, 164, 178
Noll, Mark, 153–155; anti-reductionism of,
    153–155; on evangelical biblical schol-
    arship, 140, 141, 142; on Harvard Uni-
    versity, 18; irony and, 162–165; and
    obstacles to religion, 201; and "odd
    combinations," 205; on evangelical
    intellectual life, 35; on positivism, 109;
    particularity of religious language, 187;
    and religious resurgence, 189, 190,
    197, 198; religious terminology and,
    203; segregation of religious language,
    185
Notre Dame, University of, 19, 20, 25, 33,
    37, 40; Cushwa Center for the Study of
    American Catholicism, 197, 198; and
    Hallinan, Maureen, 78; and Woodward,
    131–132; and Wycliff, 131–132

Objectivity, 16; conflict with post-modern-
    ism, 105; in journalism, 6–8, 44–47,
    51–52, 68–72, 201; journalistic balance,
    141–143; and secularization, 8; in social
    science, 6, 8, 73–76, 103–109
Objectivity, critique of, 16, 200; in journal-
    ism, 46, 51–52, 71; in social science,
    75, 82, 96–99, 177
O'Brien, David, 13, 61, 204
"Odd combinations," 16, 191, 204–206
O'Reilly, Bill, 67
Orfield, Gary, 177–178, 181–183
Organizational resources, 195–196,
    197–198
Ostling, Richard, 42, 197, 198, 199

Pacifism, xiv, 54, 134–136, 138, 180–181
"Particularizing refinement." See Intellec-
    tual refinement
Peace and justice, language of. See Justice
    and peace, language of
Peace and justice story line, 115, 133–139
Pentecostal/charismatic movement,
    99–103, 174
Pepperdine University, 20, 35
Pew, J. Howard, 29
Pew Charitable Trusts, 40–41, 193,
    198–199, 257n
Philanthropy, 40–41, 198–199, 257n. See
    also John Templeton Foundation; Lilly
    Endowment; Pew Charitable Trusts
Philosophy. See Catholic philosophers;
    Evangelical philosophers
Pippert, Wesley, 44–45, 51–55, 133, 136–
    139; justice and peace, language of, 51–
    55; and objectivity, 71; peace and justice
    story line, 115, 133, 136–139; and reli-
    gious resurgence, 196–197, 199; trans-
    lation of religious language, 53, 202
Political science: anti-reductionism in,
    155–157; ethics and international rela-
    tions, 181; objectivity in, 74; religion
    and politics subfield, 39, 155, 195, 198.
    See also Catholic political scientists;
    Evangelical political scientists
Poloma, Margaret, 82, 99–103, 172,
    174–176
Pope John Paul II. See John Paul II, Pope
Populist anti-elitism, language of, 64–68
Positivism, 74
Post-modernism, 43, 200; and evangelicals,
    35; in higher education, 75–76, 81–82,
    93–99; language of, 93–99; and objec-
    tivity, 105

Post-positivism, 81–82, 108–109, 200; and
Greeley, 87, 90–91, 93; and Poloma,
103
Privatization, 9, 45–46, 47–48, 71, 76. *See
also* Deprivatization
Professional boundaries, 6, 200–201, 204;
in journalism, 44–45, 68–69, 72, 211n;
in social science, 74, 76, 104–105, 146–
147, 184
Professions: civic conception of, 8; "expert
professionalism," 49, 212n; presence of
Catholics in, 11; presence of evangeli-
cals in, 11; religious deprivatization in,
9–10; religious identity in, 13, 191, 204–
205; religious resurgence in, xiii, 10,
16; secularization of, 5–9
Proteanism, 203–206
"Protestant cultural code," 113, 143
"Protestant imagination," 16, 111–113,
143–144, 150–151
Protestant irony. *See* Irony, trope of
Protestants. *See* Evangelicals; Mainline
Protestants
Providentialism, 146–148, 155
Public journalism. *See* Civic journalism
Public policy and religion, 39, 82–87, 177–
183, 195, 198
Public policy rhetorics, 81, 82–87

Race and religion, 181–182
Realism, 7, 70, 106
Reductionism, 6, 147. *See also* Anti-reductionism
Religion, revival of. *See* Religious resurgence
Religious conservatives, 34, 83, 117–122,
163
Religious resurgence: in business, 192; critique of, 196; in higher education, 40,
189–190, 194–200; in journalism, 46,
193–194, 196–200; "moral revival," 150;
obstacles to, 190, 191, 200–203; in politics, 192; in professions, xiii, 10, 16;
public opinion data, 209n; in publishing, 192; religious self-expression and,
190–191; resources for, 196–200
Religious studies, 39–40, 195
Religious ways of knowing, 146–188; anti-
reductionism, 149, 150, 151–160; exclusion of, 6, 8, 147; social ethics and
social science, 149, 150, 176–183; tension with professionalism, 3, 6; theological tropes, 149, 150, 160–169;

theology and social theory, 149, 150,
169–176
Resistance to secularization, 9–10, 13–14,
16, 20, 203–206; among Catholics, 25;
among evangelicals, 29; in social sci-
ence, 184
Resources for religious self-expression. *See*
Cultural resources; Financial resources;
Organizational resources
Responsible capitalism, 115, 138
Reuben, Julie, 147, 176–177
Revivalism and Cultural Change, 173–174
Revival of religion. *See* Religious resurgence
Ribuffo, Leo, 148–149, 186
Rivers, Eugene, 82, 84–85, 86, 87
Roberts, Cokie, 11, 41, 61–64, 110
Roberts, Jon, 6
Russert, Timothy, 1–2, 41, 110
Russett, Bruce, 177–181, 183; on Catholic
intellectuals, 32; and 11 September
2001, xiv; and just war theory, xiv, 177–
181, 185; segregation of religious lan-
guage, 186; translation of religious
language, 202

Sacramentality, 112, 131–132, 158–159
Sample, 14–15, 207–208
Schudson, Michael, 51–52, 111, 200
Secularization: of Catholic colleges and
universities, 32, 43; and differentiation,
9, 10; of evangelical colleges and uni-
versities, 35, 43; of higher education,
5–9, 73–75, 94–97, 189–190; and irony,
185; of journalism, 5–9, 45, 66–67; and
mainline Protestants, 7–8, 20; and new
class, 5; and objectivity, 8; and privatiza-
tion, 9, 10; theory of, xv, 9. *See also*
Resistance to secularization
Segregation of religious language, 185–
186, 191
Separatism, 20, 24, 27–28, 31, 33–34
Shea, John, 91, 92
Sheler, Jeffery, 139–143
Silk, Mark, 114, 199
Sixties, 51–52, 117–118, 122, 124, 177
Smidt, Corwin, 39, 155–157, 186
Smith, Christian, 13, 20, 35, 36, 204
"Social disorder news," 119
Social ethics and social science, 149, 150,
176–183, 251n
Social movements, 23, 217n
Social science pragmatism, language of,
82–85

Sociology, 73, 74, 170, 195. *See also* Catholic sociologists; Evangelical sociologists
Soul of the American University, 40, 94, 97, 163, 164
"Starbucks Catholicism," 32
Steinfels, Margaret, 56, 126
Steinfels, Peter, 19, 55–61, 122–127; cultural consensus story line, 114, 122–127; and 11 September 2001, xiv, 57, 209n; intellectual refinement, language of, 55–61; and irony, 247n; and objectivity, 69, 70–71; and religious resurgence, 190, 198, 199; and translation of religious language, 61, 202
Story lines, 16; of Catholic and evangelical journalists, 114–116; and Catholic imagination, 115; communitarian, 115, 127–133; cultural consensus, 114, 122–127; culture wars, 114, 116–122; peace and justice, 115, 133–139; testing the scriptures, 115, 139–143. *See also* Narrative
Stout, Harry, 39, 153, 154, 195, 243n
Structure/agency debate, 171–176
subcultural boundaries, 20, 23, 34–35, 36, 43
Subcultural institution building, 19–20, 23–30, 37–38; Catholic, 24–27, 131, 132; evangelical, 27–30; and resources, 23; as social movement, 23, 217n
Subsidiarity, 87, 130–131, 203, 238n
Sullivan, Andrew, 124
Supernatural: in journalism, 1–3, 6; in social science, 6, 99–103, 146–147, 155

Taylor, Robert, 39, 154, 195, 243n
Tentler, Leslie Woodcock, 186
Testing the scriptures story line, 115, 139–143
Theological tropes, 149, 150, 160–169
Theology and race, 181–182
Theology and social theory, 91–92, 149, 150, 157–159, 169–176
This Rebellious House, 146–147
Thomas, Cal, 116–122; critique of religious conservatives, 120–122; culture wars story line, 114, 116–122; and 11 September 2001, xiv; and Fox News, 67; and religious resurgence, 199; and secular press, 45; syndication of column, 11, 42; translation of religious language, 202
Thomas, George, 171–174, 175, 184–185

Thomism. *See* Neo-Thomism
Tillich, Paul, 38
Time, 34, 41, 42, 45
Toner, Robin, 19
Topoi in news, 114, 199
Tracy, David: on analogical imagination, 112–113; on dialectical imagination, 136; and epistemology, 106–107, 252n; and Greeley, 87, 92; on limit experiences, 158; and pluralism, 258n
Translation of religious language, 191, 201–202, 204; in journalism, 61, 71–72, 145, 202; and particularity, 187–188; in social science, 81, 185, 202
Tuchman, Gaye, 69, 104, 116
Turner, James, 6, 35, 36, 40, 75

Upward mobility, 20–23, 43; of Catholics, 19–22, 87–90; of evangelicals, 20–23
U.S. News and World Report, 139–143

Value-neutrality. *See* Fact/value separation
Values. *See* "Enduring values"
Van Engen, John, 197
Vatican II, 31–32, 36, 107

Washington Post, 41–42, 66
Weber, Max, 6, 73, 78, 113
Weekly Standard, 42, 67, 68
Wheaton College, 20, 28, 35–36, 37; and Holt, 49; Institute for the Study of American Evangelicals, 197; and Pippert, 54
White, Hayden, 110–111, 160, 161
Why Americans Hate Politics, 124, 133
Wills, Garry, 24, 131, 202–203
Wilson, James Q, 83
Wolfe, Alan: on Catholic higher education, 37; on evangelical intellectual life, 19, 35, 187; morality and social science, 109, 176; on religious resurgence in higher education, 194; and social criticism, 108
Woodward, Kenneth, 128–133; communitarian story line, 115, 128–133; and religion reporting, 42; and religious resurgence, 196–197, 198, 199; religious terminology and, 203
Wuthnow, Robert, 14, 21, 22, 72, 96
Wycliff, Don, 130–132

Zald, Mayer, 217n
Zerubavel, Eviatar, 201, 204